Building a Dream

Building a Dream

The Co-operative Retailing System in Western Canada, 1928–1988

Brett Fairbairn

Western Producer Prairie Books
Saskatoon, Saskatchewan

Copyright © 1989 by Federated Co-operatives Limited
Western Producer Prairie Books
Saskatoon, Saskatchewan

The CO-OP word and logo are registered trademarks of Interprovincial Cooperative Limited (IPCO). They are proudly displayed by FCL and those other co-operatives across Canada that are IPCO members, with that organization's consent and on condition that its regulations to ensure proper use of these trademarks are vigilantly observed.

Cover design by Warren Clark/GDL
Cover photographs courtesy Federated Co-operatives Limited. From top: lumber workers at Canoe, British Columbia; retail outlet in Saskatoon; the Co-op Refinery at Regina; and overseas students touring the refinery, 1965. All uncredited photographs are from the files of the *Co-operative Consumer* newspaper.

Printed and bound in Canada

Western Producer Prairie Books is a unique publishing venture located in the middle of western Canada and owned by a group of prairie farmers who are members of Saskatchewan Wheat Pool. From the first book in 1954, a reprint of a serial originally carried in the weekly newspaper *The Western Producer*, to the book before you now, the tradition of providing enjoyable and informative reading for all Canadians is continued.

Canadian Cataloguing in Publication Data

Fairbairn, Brett, 1959–

   Building a dream: the co-operative retailing system in western Canada, 1928–1988

   Includes bibliographical references and index.
   ISBN: 0–88833–285–8 (bound); 0–88833–286–6 (bound, corporate ed.); 0–88833–287–4 (pbk, corporate ed.)
1. Consumer cooperatives — Prairie Provinces — History.
2. Cooperation — Prairie Provinces — History.   3. Cooperative societies — Prairie Provinces — History.   Retail trade — Prairie Provinces — History.   I. Title.

HD3290.A3P637 1989   334'.5'09712   C89–098006–3

To Elena

CONTENTS

PART NINE: CONCLUSION

Author's Preface

This book is a history of western Canada's Co-operative Retailing System, or in other words, of the way in which retail co-operatives in the West have worked together, of the wholesales they have founded, and of Federated Co-operatives Limited, the product of the mergers over the years of the various provincial co-op wholesales.

Retail co-operatives began working together by forming their own wholesale societies in 1927–28 — 1928 was the first year of operations for the first of these wholesales. In particular, Saskatchewan Co-op Wholesale, whose charter was continued through following amalgamations, was organized in 1928 and had its first annual meeting in 1929. In commemoration of the sixtieth anniversary of these events, the Board of Directors of Federated Co-operatives Limited commissioned this book. Their terms of reference were to produce a comprehensive history of the system which was also in a readable and popular style. It is not always easy to do both these things at once, but the author has made a serious attempt to do so.

For those not familiar with the Co-operative Retailing System, this book is intended to be informative and educational. For those within the system, it is intended to have an additional function: to be discussed and thought about. It does not present only names, numbers, or anecdotes, nor is it an "official" history in the usual sense of that word. This book tries to interpret the past, hoping to enable readers not only to know what happened, but to *understand* what happened, to appreciate different ideas and different views of events. It also tries to tackle controversial subjects head-on. The Co-operative Retailing System is a vast, decentralized, and democratic grouping. With three-quarters of a million active individual members, several thousand elected officials and many more staff, and over 330 autonomous local units in four provinces, the system contains a multitude of ideas and a great diversity of experience. Some — but, by reasons of space, not by any means all — of this diversity is reflected in the present book.

The chapters in this book are numerous, short, and thematic. As much as possible, each is self-contained, and concludes with questions or points for thought and discussion. They are grouped into nine parts (an introduction, a conclusion, and seven others related to specific periods in the system's history). These divisions are for convenience only, and various chapters range more broadly as they follow specific themes.

The chapters are supported by the appendices at the back of the book, which contain important explanatory and background material. Appendix One provides a glossary of terms, and incorporates explanations of the abbreviations used in the text. Appendix Two lists top officers and managers of the wholesales described in the book. Appendix Three provides a general chronology of events, and the remaining appendices summarize sales, savings, and other statistics of growth and performance.

This book is based on extensive research and interviews. Between the fall of 1987 and the fall of 1988 the author conducted archival research and talked to individuals in every western province, and at the national archives of Canada in Ottawa. In many respects, one year of research cannot do justice to the magnitude of the subject. There are many individuals in the system who have contributed to its history and have important things to say about it, but of those many the author has talked to only a selected group, selected not always in terms of importance, but also by availability and pertinence to specific questions. To those not consulted, the author extends apologies — and an eagerness to talk and gain more and improved material for future editions.

The remarks quoted in this book are here because of their significance, because they are especially good expressions of a viewpoint, or for colour. The same applies to examples taken from the histories of individual retail co-ops. No attempt has been made systematically to cover or name all co-ops, all important individuals, or even all people interviewed. Those named are named as examples, and not as a sign that others are unimportant. Where people quoted are not named, this is done to avoid encumbering the text with names that will have no significance for the average reader, or out of respect for the position or sensitivities of the person involved. In all cases the author has detailed records and can give assurance that the quotations are genuine. It would have been fairer in many ways not to name *any* individuals, nor *any* retail co-operatives. The author hopes he may be forgiven for naming some and not others, for the sake of producing a more readable and interesting book.

In the text, remarks quoted in the present tense ("a retail manager *says* . . .") are drawn from interviews with the author, unless otherwise noted. Spelling and punctuation in quotations have been modified to suit the style used for the book. Financial statistics and information on events and dates are drawn from annual reports and financial statements consulted by the author at FCL home office, unless otherwise noted. The author hopes the use of abbreviations and short forms in the text will not cause confusion; it is important for the purposes of saving space and avoiding repetition. Federated Co-operatives Limited is "FCL" at almost every occurrence. The word "co-op" has been used as an alternative to "co-operative," even if not strictly approved in formal writing. The farmers' grain marketing co-ops of the prairie provinces are referred to as the "wheat pools," even though this was only their popular name, not their legal one, for most of their existence. Readers are referred to Appendix One for further examples.

No book, least of all this one, is the product of a single person. Special thanks go to Harold Baker, Harold Chapman, Jim Conly, Ed Klassen, Bryan Tastad, and Jack Trevena, who spent countless hours reading drafts and going through them in meetings, advising the author as to content, emphasis, and style. No writer could hope for a committee with any broader or deeper knowledge of the subject, nor could any committee be expected to have greater dedication or care in its work. Harold Empey conveyed the comments of the FCL board and senior management, who devoted careful attention to the manuscript and lent their considerable knowledge and expertise. The directors of FCL, and president Vern Leland in particular, should be commended for the courage and wisdom involved in undertaking a project of this kind, and trusting an outside person to do it. The staff of FCL and of the archives named below should be thanked for invaluable technical assistance; a list also follows of those who contributed their time and energy to talk to the author or send materials for use in the book. Greatest and most heartfelt thanks go to Norma, who put up with the clacking of computer keys on many occasions until five in the morning, and Elena, born in 1988 as the Co-operative Retailing System celebrated its 60th anniversary, whose contented and happy disposition was her own contribution to this book.

*   *   *

Archives

Federated Co-operatives Limited, Saskatoon
Glenbow-Alberta Institute, Calgary
Provincial Archives of Alberta, Edmonton
Provincial Archives of British Columbia, Victoria
Provincial Archives of Manitoba, Winnipeg
Public Archives of Canada, Ottawa
Saskatchewan Archives Board, Regina and Saskatoon

Libraries

Co-operative College of Canada, Saskatoon
Co-operative Resource Centre, Centre for the Study of Co-operatives,
    University of Saskatchewan
Dept. of Archives and Special Collections, Elizabeth Dafoe Library,
    University of Manitoba
Legislative Library, Province of Alberta
Legislative Library, Province of Manitoba
Legislative Library, Province of Saskatchewan
Murray Memorial Library, University of Saskatchewan
National Library, Ottawa

Individuals

B. N. Arnason	Bruce Arnott
Harold Baker	Gordon Barker
Bill Baumgartner	Pat Bell
Harold Benson	Bill Bergen
Les Brown	Ken Casey
Harold Chapman	Hume Compton
Jim Conly	Allan Dickson
Tony Dummer	Harold Empey
George Felstead	Art Ford
Bun Fraser	Bruno Friesen
Dorothy Fowler	Grant Howard
Morris Jevne	Norm Krivoshen
Ray Labossiere	Norma Lee
Vern Leland	Red McAndrews
Art Matley	Bob Matthewson
Fr. J. Megret	Leif Osback
Clare and Vi Pyett	Smokey Robson
Gordon Sinclair	Don Slimmon
Glenora Slimmon (Donna Rochdale)	Dave Stewart
Wayne Thompson	Don Tullis
Elmer Wiebe	Gordon Wright

PART ONE: INTRODUCTION

1

The Co-operative
Retailing System in 1988

Many people are familiar with their local "co-op," but they may not be familiar with what lies behind it.

In communities from the Lakehead to the Pacific coast, through farming and lumbering areas, in mining and fishing centres, and in the midst of large cities, people know their co-op as a business or as a community institution. But in one case, the co-op is a food store; in another case, a service station. Or it may be a bulk petroleum plant, a feed mill, a hardware store, a lumber yard, an agro centre. Frequently it is more than one of these. There are just about as many kinds and mixes of co-ops as there are communities that they serve.

What do all these different co-ops, in very different regions, have in common? All are owned by the people they serve. Investors, business people, or parent corporations don't call the shots in these co-ops—local people do, ordinary local people. Local people who shop there. There are no profits to be taken away to far-off cities. All earnings are returned to the customers, or reinvested in the co-op, and kept right in the local community. All of these co-ops operate according to certain internationally recognized principles—principles that make them true co-operatives and ensure they remain under the control and at the service of local people (see Chapter 2). And all these co-ops are members of the Co-operative Retailing System.

Co-ops work with each other to purchase and manufacture goods jointly. In this way they obtain higher volumes and greater savings, and these savings are passed on to their members. "The Co-operative Retailing System" is a phrase used to describe how all the co-ops work together. The system consists of the local co-ops, plus Federated Co-operatives Limited (FCL), a co-operative that they own together. Federated Co-operatives Limited, its subsidiaries, and

1

other co-operatives of which FCL is a member, purchase and manufacture products that the local co-ops jointly distribute.

Members of the Co-operative Retailing System are also linked to co-operators throughout Canada and the world. Through Interprovincial Cooperative Limited (IPCO), of which FCL is manager and part owner, the Co-operative Retailing System is part of a nation-wide CO-OP distribution network that includes regional co-operative wholesales in every part of Canada, as well as the prairie wheat pools. And through the Canadian Co-operative Association, a national educational and representative body, the Co-operative Retailing System is linked to other kinds of co-operatives and to a world-wide co-operative movement encompassing some five hundred million people.

In 1987, the last year for which full statistics are available, there were about 750,000 individuals in western Canada who were members of the Co-operative Retailing System, and they and their families purchased nearly two *billion* dollars worth of merchandise through their co-operatives. On this amount the system made savings of nearly $90 million, money that in a profit-making enterprise would no longer have belonged to the customers. Federated Co-operatives Limited, as wholesaler and manufacturer for this system, supplied $1.4 *billion* in goods for the retail co-operatives to sell to their members. This put FCL seventy-third in the *Financial Post* listing of the top 500 industrial corporations.[1]

The system controls extensive assets throughout western Canada, including a lumber mill and plywood plant at Canoe, British Columbia; feed mills and distribution centres in most provinces; and, most significantly, an oil refinery at Regina—Consumers' Co-operative Refineries Limited—which is the site of construction of the Co-op Upgrader, at $700 million the largest project in Saskatchewan's history. The upgrader is the first facility of its kind in Canada, capable of converting heavy crude oil into a lighter product that can be fed directly into the refinery on the same site to produce finished gasoline and other products.

The savings distributed by the system and the assets it owns represent wealth and services put back into the communities from which consumers' dollars came. Especially in small towns, where many other services have disappeared, the local Co-op remains as a pivot of the local economy. Wealth, power, and profits tend to accumulate in larger centres; one of the purposes of the Co-operative Retailing System is to distribute them more fairly, to ensure that it is local people, not far-off investors, who control and derive the benefits from local commerce. From time to time many people have talked about "Canadian ownership": co-operatives are not only Canadian-owned, they are *locally* owned and directed by the people they serve. No other form of business can make this claim.

Sales, savings, and material assets are not the most important part of the Co-operative Retailing System. One of the principles of co-operatives has been to develop not only services and financial strength, but also to develop people—to give consumers experience of ownership and participation, of influence over decisions about quality, prices, and sales policy; to educate and inform members and the public; to develop the leadership skills of elected co-operative officials, and the technical skills of employees. Thousands of ordinary people in western Canada have gained experience through leadership roles in their co-operatives, and many have also applied the understanding and skills they gained to other areas of community and public life. Many other people, especially in western Canada's rural communities, were introduced to the retailing and wholesaling business when they became employees of their co-operatives, and have developed professional expertise through their involvement.

The Co-operative Retailing System of western Canada, from the smallest co-op gas bar up to the giant Co-op Upgrader, has been built with nothing but the volunteer labour, capital, and spending volume contributed by western Canadian consumers, and the efforts of the staff they hired to run their co-operatives, plus an idea: the idea of consumer co-operation, brought from Europe with the settlers, which had to be learned and taught over the decades by co-operative leaders and educators.

The following chapters describe the origins and development of the Co-operative Retailing System, from the formation of the earliest retail co-operatives, through the creation of the system itself when retail co-operatives banded together in 1927–28 to form their own wholesales, through to 1988. The path followed by consumer co-operatives over these years was neither smooth nor easy. There was nearly continuous expansion, but alongside it came serious challenges, rapid change, and some setbacks that proved to be the learning experiences of the system. Like all businesses, co-operatives sometimes fell short of their goals; like all democracies, they talked about their shortcomings openly and bluntly; like all popular movements, they developed, learned (including from their mistakes), and grew to the stature necessary to meet the problems of the day. Many of these challenges were unique, but a few seem to have been perennial: the ongoing need to become more market-oriented and centralized in order to compete, or the constant need to renew member relations and co-operative education. Because of such perennial concerns, the history of the system is not only a record of past events: it is also an opportunity to learn.

2

The Principles and Philosophy of Co-operation

Before the first co-operative was founded in the Canadian West, co-operation was already an international philosophy, well established in many European countries. Immigrants who came to the four western provinces brought with them knowledge of co-operatives and played an important role in the development of consumer co-operation in the new territories and provinces, British and Nordic immigrants, in particular, being most prominent among the founders and leaders of early co-ops. It is important to understand the fundamental ideas of co-operation that these immigrants gave to Canada.

The Co-operative Idea

The idea of the co-operative form of business developed in England in the first decades of the nineteenth century. Robert Owen, an industrialist, and other reformers, saw co-operative colonies as a means by which poor working people could escape the misery that they were experiencing within the competitive economic system. Inspired by Owen and by the political and trade-union movements of the British working class, later co-operative organizers developed means by which the workers could help themselves.

The most famous of the early British co-operatives was the Rochdale Society of Equitable Pioneers founded in 1844. Instead of creating a whole co-operative community, something they could only do with the help of a wealthy patron, the workers in Rochdale decided to start with a small store in their own neighbourhood. They still maintained that the store was only the means to an end, a way to accumulate working-class capital which they could eventually use to found an all-encompassing co-operative colony. But when the working class began to keep stores for itself, these stores gradually became so successful that the older idea of a co-operative community was forgotten.[1]

The Rochdale society set such an example that to this day the principles of co-operation, as defined by the International Co-operative Alliance (ICA), an association of co-operatives from many countries including Canada, are referred to as the "Rochdale Principles." As re-formulated in 1966, these principles are as follows:[2]

4

1. Open and Voluntary Membership

Membership of a co-operative society should be voluntary and available without artificial restriction or any social, political, religious or racial discrimination to all persons who can make use of its services and are willing to accept the responsibilities of membership.

2. Democratic Control

Co-operative societies are democratic organizations. Their affairs should be administered by persons elected or appointed in a manner agreed by the members and accountable to them. Members of primary societies should enjoy equal rights of voting (one member, one vote) and participation in decisions affecting their societies. In other than primary societies the administration should be conducted on a democratic basis in a suitable form.

3. Limited Interest on Share Capital

Share capital should only receive a strictly limited rate of interest, if any.

4. Return of Surplus to Members

The economic results arising out of the operation of a society belong to the members of that society and should be distributed in such manner as would avoid one member gaining at the expense of others. This may be done by decision of the members as follows:

    (a) by provision for development of the business of the co-operative;
    (b) by provision of common services; or
    (c) by distribution among the members in proportion to their transactions within the society.

5. Co-operative Education

All co-operative societies should make provision for the education of their members, officers, and employees, and the general public, in the principles and techniques of co-operation, both economic and democratic.

6. Co-operation among Co-operatives

All co-operative organizations, in order to best serve the interests of their members and their communities, should actively co-operate in every practical way with other co-operatives at local, national, and international levels.

This list of six principles replaced a list of seven originally adopted in 1934.

Though the principles say co-operatives "should" do this and "should" do that, they were presented to the International Co-operative Alliance as "universal" and "inseparable" principles. In other words, there might be other kinds of principles that apply to this type of co-operative or that, but *these six principles apply universally to every co-operative,* and any organization that fails even one of the six tests is not, according to the 1966 commission, a genuine co-op.

There are several important points concerning these principles. First, co-operatives are owned by those who use them, not by investors whose interest is to make a profit from them. In a consumer co-op, the consumer's interest therefore predominates. This is why trading surpluses, if they are distributed, are returned as refunds on sales, not as dividends on the initial capital put up by each member. If the surplus remaining at the end of the year is returned in proportion to patronage, then each member gets back exactly the amount of the surplus that came from his or her purchases. In this way, no other person profits from that member's transactions with his or her society. After the refund, the member has paid *exactly* what the goods cost to obtain and deliver. The co-operative system, in the opinion of many of its supporters, therefore eliminates all profit, speculation, and exploitation of consumers. It achieves what the Catholic church once called the "just price" for every product it handles.

Furthermore, a member gets only one vote no matter how many shares he or she purchases. This is because the co-operative is an organization of people, not an accumulation of sums of capital. Profit-oriented businesses respond to consumers' needs only to the extent that the competitiveness of the marketplace requires them to do so in order to turn a profit. A co-operative responds to consumers' needs no matter what the state of the economy because the members, through the democratic control structure, determine its policy and supervise its operations. For this reason among others, co-operatives are held to be an excellent remedy to monopoly situations. Unlike a profit-oriented company, they will not take a profit when they can get it, but instead, under the consumers' control, return the surplus to the member consumers.

It is also important that *consumer* co-operatives, the first co-operatives to spread widely, were the ones that decided the principles and philosophy of co-operation. It was argued by the British movement and by the ICA that consumer co-operatives were the purest and most ideal form of co-operative. This is because everyone is a consumer, so a consumer co-operative can represent a general interest. A co-operative of producers can only represent a minority— those who produce a certain commodity. In the view of many co-operative thinkers, this meant that the self-interest of the members of a consumer co-operative was very nearly identical with the general interest of the community, as long as the co-operative was open and did not discriminate in its membership (the first ICA principle).

There are other principles, "rules," and "methods" that have been put forward at various times, especially for consumer co-operatives. These include honest weights and measures; sale of goods only at market prices; no advertising or gimmicks; no credit sales; and "continuous expansion."

Consumer and Producer Co-operation

The British co-operatives were urban and working-class, and this pattern was repeated in a few other European countries. Ian MacPherson, a leading historian of co-operatives in Canada, has pointed out that it was the miners and urban classes of Canada who founded the first consumer co-operatives. From the 1860s to the 1880s, the centres of co-operative development were the mining districts of B.C., Alberta, and Nova Scotia, and the big cities of Halifax, Montreal, Winnipeg, and Toronto. After the turn of the century, more co-ops emerged in these areas, sponsored and inspired by labour organizations such as the Knights of Labour or the Trades and Labour Congress. But although the first consumer co-ops were urban or working-class, these did not last, falling victim to economic downturns such as that following World War One, and failing to re-establish themselves thereafter. Professor MacPherson tells us that the early co-operatives had "short life and minimal impact," and that the working class never caught on to the British idea that co-operation was essential to their economic interests.[3]

There was also a second pattern of co-operative development, one represented in central and northern Europe rather than in Britain. This was the co-operative organization of farmers for marketing their products, purchasing their farm inputs, and providing credit for agricultural improvement. Such agricultural co-operatives were pioneered in Germany by Friedrich Wilhelm Raiffeisen from the 1860s onward. Raiffeisen is remembered as one of the founders of the credit union movement, which came to Canada when Alphonse Desjardins led in the creation of the first *caisse populaire* (people's bank) at Lévis, Québec in 1900. Most credit unions in western Canada, however, were created after 1944. Another influential European example was provided by Denmark, where farmers created a comprehensive system of co-operatives of all types, including consumer co-operatives serving agricultural needs.

As events turned out, it was the farmers and rural Canadians, especially in the three prairie provinces and in Québec, who built a powerful and diversified co-operative movement overshadowing the accomplishments of urban workers. From the turn of the century onward, co-operation in all of Canada, particularly in the West, acquired a distinctly agricultural orientation.

Western farmers have tended to think of themselves more as producers than as consumers. Their greatest economic interest is the marketing of their crops or livestock and the prices they receive for them. This is also the sphere in which they have the greatest expertise. When farmers began to consider co-operative buying, they thought not so much of groceries, the first line carried by the Rochdale Pioneers and the foremost concern of the early urban consumer co-ops, but rather, of the bulk commodities they needed for their farms: binder twine and barbed wire, oils and greases and fuel as they acquired power machinery, and a few more general consumer goods like coal and apples. Farmers turned to consumer co-operation almost as soon as they began co-operating, but con-

Learning co-operation by practising it: a barn-raising bee in the early days of prairie settlement. Farmers in western Canada quickly discovered that building an economy and local communities were co-operative endeavours. By working together they could make their dreams into realities, and shape their society—towns, farms, and businesses— to suit their own needs. (Provincial Archives of Manitoba N7657)

sumer co-operation remained, for some time, secondary to co-operative marketing. Professor MacPherson notes that rural co-ops before 1914 were hampered by "inadequate understanding of co-op principles. They tended to be afterthoughts of men and women who had organized marketing co-ops."[4] One could also add that they were hampered by the lack of any enabling legislation and by the hostility of merchants, particularly wholesalers who refused to sell to them.

As the following chapters will show, the agrarian movement provided important general support for all kinds of co-operation, but in certain cases and in certain periods it also limited and frustrated consumer co-operatives. It is not that farmers or their leaders discouraged consumer co-operatives; quite the reverse. All kinds of co-operation were seen as desirable. But the greatest efforts were, until the 1930s, devoted to producer co-operation, and consumer co-operation of the Rochdale model remained little appreciated or understood. The exception was an influential minority of farmers and rural leaders, many of whom had direct knowledge of the European principles and accomplishments.

The agrarian viewpoint generally led farmers to look for big centralized co-ops operating cheaply and with little capital paid in. This was appropriate for marketing their products, and they had the expertise to do such things well on a large scale. Big, specialized co-operatives suited the feeling of class identity among western farmers, and also suited the specialization of their crops which, in the case of wheat, had to be sold in a big way, on international markets, to gain maximum benefits for the producers. The Grain Growers' Grain Company of 1906 (now United Grain Growers—UGG) was one such large, centralized instrument for farmers, organized as a joint stock company because legislation and the grain trade did not permit genuine co-operative organization at that time. The prairie wheat pools created in 1923-24, which are true co-operatives, have also tended to be much more centralized than the consumer co-operative model.

Rochdale principles of consumer co-operation, brought to the western co-operative movement by influential British, Danish, and Scandinavian leaders, envisaged small, localized, unspecialized stores serving all the regular needs of the average consumer. Share capital was to be substantial to give the store enough capital to carry the necessary inventories. Prices were not generally to be below the prevailing market levels. This was to give the co-op financial leeway, for a dangerous tendency of co-ops was to starve themselves of capital or to cut their margins too closely and thus end up with a loss at the end of the year. It was much safer for young, growing organizations to sell at market prices, earning healthy margins, and then return the excess as a patronage refund at the end of the year when all expenses were known. Selling at prevailing prices was also intended to avoid price wars with more powerful and better-established competitors who could put the co-op out of business. And Rochdale-type co-operative stores had to be developed very gradually, to give the members, directors, and managers time to learn the basics of shopkeeping, and to knit together as democratic units with the loyalty of their members.

Many misconceptions had to be unlearned, and many consumer co-operatives had to fail as businesses before these lessons were understood. Only then did the powerful and competent retailing system maintained today by co-op members begin to take shape.

Conclusion and Questions

We might ask to what extent the Co-operative Retailing System has, over the years, been shaped by producer attitudes and expectations. How successful has it been at broadening from its agricultural roots, and how hard should it try to do so? Everyone is a consumer and co-operatives are open to all, but are there practical limits that restrict our consumer co-ops more to the rural population?

We could also ask whether consumer co-ops today do or must strictly follow the original Rochdale style: local democracy; good capitalization raised from the membership; market prices; gradual growth through education of members and member loyalty, as opposed to speculative growth through advertising and facilities designed to capture passing trade from competitors. Or have tendencies toward centralization changed the picture, tipped the balance toward ambitious projects requiring big capital, toward price-cutting competition instead of patronage rebates, toward growth by competitors' methods instead of by education in co-operative philosophy? Have co-ops outgrown some of the Rochdale principles? Have they refined and perfected them? Or have they and their members not finished learning them?

PART TWO: ORIGINS, 1914–1931

Introduction to Part Two

It is customary when looking back on the early history of consumer co-operatives in western Canada to stand in awe of the hard work and idealism of the pioneers. These far-seeing and largely anonymous individuals formed and patronized their co-ops faithfully, ignoring offers of better prices from competitors. They put up with scorn and derision from opponents of co-operation. They sacrificed their time without financial reward, and, when necessary, mortgaged their farms to save the co-op from creditors. Starting from nothing, they built a movement.

This view of the pioneers of consumer co-operation is a myth in the best sense of that word: something that is truer than fact because it inspires and educates, because it communicates the essence of the past, the lessons that are important to us here in the present. It is true that a tiny handful of pioneers did these things. That tiny handful determined which co-operatives would survive, and in what form. It is also true that the vast majority floundered, ignorant of the philosophy of co-operation, concerned only with prices and willing to take a cheap price wherever it could be found. Under these circumstances, co-ops came and went like the dust on the prairie winds or the fish in the Pacific ocean currents.

It is vitally important to see the accomplishments of the pioneers in the context of their times, for only when we understand why the many failed does it become clear why the few succeeded. Failures contain as many lessons as do successes. The first three decades of the twentieth century were not especially happy ones for consumer co-operation in the West. That the idea survived at all is the true legacy of the pioneers—and a tribute to what a committed minority can accomplish in a difficult and hostile environment.

*   *   *

11

3

False Starts and
Broken Dreams, c. 1900–1926

The settlers in the western Canadian interior quickly discovered that they were dependent on a national and international transportation and marketing network that was, as they saw it, dominated by a few big interests. In a region with little industry of its own, they were at the mercy of shippers and sellers, while their own products were largely sold on international markets in which they were unprotected from price fluctuations. Every aspect of this system came under criticism, from the elevator agent whose scales were dishonest and whose dockage of grain was arbitrary, to the rail companies that determined rates and availability of cars, to the buyers and sellers of grain in world markets. Farm organizations began to argue that farmer-owned facilities and companies were the answer to their grievances, and the co-operative movement in the West was underway.

Farm Organizations and Early Co-operatives, 1900–18

In the first years of the twentieth century, farmers in western Canada began to organize. By 1909 each of the three prairie provinces had a single political and educational organization for the grain farmers of the province: the Saskatchewan Grain Growers' Association (SGGA), the Manitoba Grain Growers' Association (MGGA, renamed the United Farmers of Manitoba in 1920), and the United Farmers of Alberta (UFA). The United Farmers of British Columbia was formed in 1917 (for a timeline of events, see Appendix 3).[1]

Encouraged by these agricultural organizations, farmers also took to organizing businesses. At first these were local buying clubs and co-operative elevators. Then in 1905, E. A. Partridge of Sintaluta, Saskatchewan, took matters

Opposite: *Founders of the United Farmers of Alberta, 1909. The new UFA took on both the political/educational and economic functions of its two predecessors, the Alberta Farmers' Association and the Society of Equity. From 1921 to 1935 the UFA formed the government of Alberta, and starting in 1932 it developed a central purchasing co-operative for farm inputs. The UFA withdrew from politics in 1935 and from educational work in 1948, continuing since that time as a farmer-owned central purchasing agency. (Provincial Archives of Alberta A10729)*

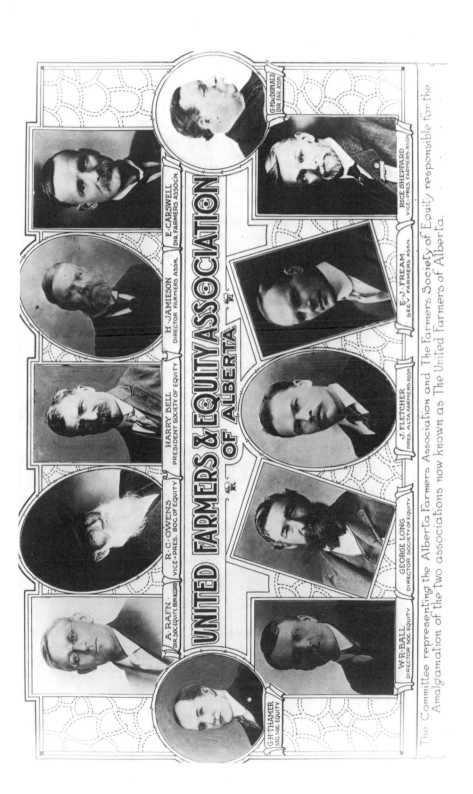

UNITED FARMERS & EQUITY ASSOCIATION OF ALBERTA

G. MacDONALD
DIR. FAIR. ASSN.

E. CARSWELL
DIR. FARMERS ASSOCN.

RICE SHEPPARD
VICE-PRES. FARMERS ASSN.

H. JAMIESON
DIRECTOR FARMERS ASSN.

HARRY BELL
PRESIDENT SOCIETY OF EQUITY

E. J. FREAM
SEC'Y FARMERS ASSN.

R. C. OWENS
VICE-PRES. SOC. OF EQUITY

J. FLETCHER
PRES. ALTA. FARMERS ASSN.

A. RAFN
DIR. SOC. EQUITY. BON ACCORD

GEORGE LONG
DIRECTOR SOCIETY OF EQUITY

W. R. BALL
DIRECTOR SOC. EQUITY

G. H. THAMER
SEC. SOC. EQUITY

The Committee representing the Alberta Farmers Association and The Farmers Society of Equity responsible for the Amalgamation of the two associations now known as The United Farmers of Alberta.

a step further when he visited Winnipeg to study the activities of the big grain-trading companies. Partridge reported that year to the farmers' conventions at Brandon and Moose Jaw, and proposed the creation of a farmer-owned co-operative marketing organization for the West. While he received a skeptical reception from the organized farmers, a town-hall meeting in his home town in January 1906 endorsed the idea, leading to the creation of the Grain Growers' Grain Company (GGGC). Shares sold briskly and the new company became a success. In 1917 it amalgamated with the Alberta Farmers' Co-operative Elevator Company to form United Grain Growers (UGG).

The Saskatchewan and Alberta Co-operative Elevator Companies, founded in 1911 and 1913 respectively, were government-sponsored initiatives in response to the continuing pressure of organized farmers concerning grain shipping and handling. While they had, like the UGG, features resembling those of a co-operative, such as limitations on the number of shares any individual could hold, and efforts to involve local members in decisions and in profits, the co-operative elevator companies were, like the UGG, essentially joint-stock companies. The Saskatchewan elevators, like the government elevators in Manitoba, later became part of the wheat pools that were organized in 1923–24.

The co-operative elevator companies and the UGG had entered into supplying the farmers and buying clubs with bulk farming inputs. By 1917 the UGG handled 3,000 carloads of bulk farm needs, and the Saskatchewan Co-operative Elevator Company handled 1,500.[2] In another development of future importance for co-operative wholesaling, the Saskatchewan legislature in 1913 and 1914 passed amendments authorizing the SGGA to act as a marketing and purchasing agent for registered co-operative associations and for Grain Growers' locals. The result was an extensive wholesale business with more than $300,000 sales in 1914.[3] It was from their political and marketing organizations—centralized joint-stock companies in the first instance—that farmers learned to co-operate as consumers.

One Manitoba farmer who joined the GGGC in 1906 later recalled what it was like in those early years. The Grain Growers' Association conducted publicity campaigns to promote consumer co-operation. Then it was up to the local people:

> Somebody took a horse and rig and boned the farmers individually for to join this and to get started . . . and then . . . they started co-operative business. We used to get in a carload of apples every fall in Cordova and whenever we wanted anything particular like seed grain we'd all go together and get a carload in and we had quite a co-operative venture.[4]

An Alberta farmer stressed that farmers' concerns were practical:

> People didn't come into the co-operative movement on a theory, but they went into it as an answer to a problem. When you found you had been hooked for your groceries . . . or your coal or anything, you said, let's

get together and bring a carload of coal in. It was a co-operative effort [to] unload the coal then. . . . We brought in . . . a carload of apples and a carload of coal, unloaded right at the station. . . . and so people were meeting an immediate need.

"Meeting an immediate need" by improvised means, with farmers' educational organizations promoting the idea and farmers' joint-stock companies doing the wholesaling, is a good characterization of how consumer co-operation caught on in the West.[5]

The First Consumer Co-operative Societies

The 1890s and early 1900s saw one wave of co-operative buying activity; a second and greater wave came alongside the inflation during and after World War One. By this time, the pressure of the organized farmers had resulted in legislation being passed that enabled the incorporation of consumer co-operatives. Alberta, in 1913, passed the first effective co-operative legislation in the West, and the other provinces soon followed. In the wake of this legislation, consumer co-operatives multiplied and blossomed—and were cruelly cut down, especially in the post-World War One depression, but also throughout the prosperity of the 1920s.

The first two associations to take advantage of the Alberta Co-operative Associations Act were Huxley and Stettler, both of which incorporated in July 1913. Neither survived. One of the incorporators at Huxley explained that the

Griffen Creek Co-operative Association (about 1919). Many early co-operatives started from scratch, creating a brand new service in a location where no services had been offered before. Building the co-operative was part of building the community. (Glenbow-Alberta Institute NA–1856–2)

co-op failed because "the wholesales would not sell goods to them."[6] The supervisor of co-operative activities, writing in 1948, noted that 165 co-operative associations had been founded in the ten years from 1913 to 1923. The first fifteen of these had *all* failed. Only eight of the first hundred, and only sixteen in all, were still operating twenty-five years later. That meant a survival rate of less than one in ten.[7]

Figures for Saskatchewan show the same pattern. By the end of 1914, one year after the legislation was passed enabling co-ops to be formed, there were 102 co-operative associations reporting to the government's Co-operative Organization Branch (including community halls, livestock associations, and others, but mostly consisting of co-operative purchasing societies). The number of associations reporting increased every year to 350 in 1919, and the number of members of those associations from 2,850 to 18,248. Then the growth reversed. Every year from 1921 onward there were fewer active co-operatives, until the year 1928. In that year the number and membership of co-operatives bottomed out, and consumer co-operatives finally began to work together as a system by founding their own wholesale.[8]

The first two waves of consumer co-operative activity had receded with little widespread and enduring effect, not only in the West but across Canada. Meeting immediate local needs was not by itself a basis for long-term strength or stability. One federal government official, writing in 1925, reviewed the progress of consumers' co-operation to that date, and concluded that "the consumers' Co-operative Societies of Canada have laboured under the disadvantage of lack of communication and absence of opportunity for the discussion of common problems."[9] They were isolated and did not work together. Further, she emphasized, *"the desire to effect a saving in buying commodities has been the only motive of most of the members and there has been little knowledge of the principles of co-operation."* The emphasis on price alone, and not on philosophy or education, had left the early co-ops weak and divided from each other.

George Keen and the Co-operative Union of Canada

In those days the only body bringing consumer co-operatives together was the Co-operative Union of Canada (CUC). Founded in 1909, the CUC was the brainchild of an old British co-operator, George Keen, who, as general secretary ran the organization from his home in Brantford, Ontario. While today the CUC, renamed Canadian Co-operative Association in 1987, brings together all kinds of co-operatives, until the 1930s it was primarily a federation of consumers' co-operatives, and for them it played a critical role.[10]

It might be assumed that one middle-aged co-operator working from his house on the far side of Canada would have little effect on western Canadian co-operatives. But such was not the case. In the early days before co-ops had their own wholesales, Keen served a crucial role as advisor, inspector, educator, prophet, and business analyst for co-operatives throughout the West. Starting in 1923 he made annual trips to western Canada to speak to consumer co-operators and visit their co-ops, and he arranged for many of the CUC congresses in those years to be held in the West. The Saskatchewan commissioner of co-operatives, W. Waldron, wrote in 1926 to the Co-operative Union in Manchester, England, concerning Keen: "His is a life devoted to the co-operative movement but with a minimal recompense. His salary is inadequate, his organization cannot afford office facilities." T. W. Mercer, the head of the British Co-operative Union, replied, "In my opinion Mr. Keen has never been properly treated by Canadian co-operators. His understanding of co-operative principles and their application is remarkable."[11]

In 1923 a co-operator by the name of Robert Wood, secretary-treasurer of the co-operative society in Armstrong, B.C., wrote to Keen. Wood's complaints were in many ways typical of that time. He protested that, "owing to the . . . need for close economy," his society could not afford the CUC's affiliation fee. His co-op was in trouble in part because of previous failures by businesses that had been "co-operative only in name." "As a result the people of this district look on anything co-operative with suspicion." Because of the "scarcely disguised opposition," few customers would commit themselves to buy shares. The co-op was therefore "seriously hampered by lack of capital."[12]

Keen's responses to Wood grew out of a lifetime of understanding of small, struggling co-operatives. As Keen put it, "this Union has, from coast to coast, had long and painful experience" of co-operative failures. Keen observed that the "profit" figures for Wood's co-op were not so bad, for the lines being handled; the problem was the rapid expansion of its nonmember trade, which, because nonmembers did not buy shares, left it with too little capital to handle that trade. Ultimately, though, he warned, "there is really no hope for the movement on this continent unless co-operative societies are prepared to co-operate with each other." In Keen's opinion a co-op that could not afford to join the union, that could not afford to co-operate with other co-operatives, or that could not afford to educate its members, was doomed to be another of the consumer movement's many failures.[13]

Keen maintained consistently, throughout a voluminous correspondence covering decades, that consumer co-operatives must start small and grow slowly, through constant education and membership growth, so that capital, member loyalty, and experience and competence of managers and directors all grew in step with sales volume. Co-operatives should pay attention to good business principles and trade at market prices, only on a cash basis, to ensure they made enough to cover their overhead. Only at the end of the year, when actual overhead was known, should the surplus be returned to members as patronage refunds. In this way risks were minimized. Further, co-operatives, as he emphasized to Wood, should co-operate with one another. One way to do so was to join the CUC and share their experiences. Keen edited a publication, *The Canadian Co-operator,* which published monthly statements of sales and expenses

George Keen, General Secretary of the Co-operative Union of Canada, 1909–44. Keen played a pivotal role in the formation and activities of the CUC, the national educational and lobbying organization for Canadian co-operatives, and he had a lasting influence on the consumer co-operative movement in the West. (Public Archives of Canada C–51906)

from member co-operatives. Co-op directors were encouraged to compare their performance, especially cost ratios, with other co-ops in order to identify problems before they became serious.

Keen agreed with many that bad management was often a problem in early co-ops, but he refused to let the matter rest there. He affirmed on many occasions that bad management was ultimately the fault of directors who did not do their jobs. As he put it, there were many reasons why co-operatives failed,

> but my long experience teaches me that behind them all is the failure of directors to understand and to discharge their duties, and behind that again, a lack of knowledge of and devotion to co-operative philosophy, which would impel them to become efficient, and to be conscientious and self-sacrificing in the discharge of their duties.

"It seems almost impossible to get societies to see that money spent in co-operative education is not only money well spent but absolutely imperative for the welfare of the movement."[14]

Robert Wood was rapidly persuaded of Keen's philosophy, and within a few years became a regional vice-president of the CUC and was advocating it to other co-operatives in B.C. In 1929 he wrote that he had visited a struggling society in Tappen:

> They said that with the exception of members of the Board low prices were the only consideration to their members and customers, and I told them plainly that if this were the case failure was only a matter of time and as forcibly as I was able urged that their real need was to educate their members and patrons.

As long as a quick return in the form of low prices was members' only concern, the early co-ops would continue to struggle with too little capital, too little member loyalty, and would continue to fail.[15]

One reason Keen was not always listened to was that he was frank and insightful, while local directors resented outside advice and preferred to listen to their own managers. Keen rarely beat around the bush, as, for example, when he wrote to the Kamloops Co-operative Society in 1923:

> I notice that you meet fortnightly. Weekly meetings are preferable. . . .
>
> You will note from the Business Bulletin that your operating expenses are the second highest; namely 16.73%. . . . Personally I am afraid you have considerably over-estimated your gross profits and that in consequence you may be in a position of false security.
>
> . . . . You will need to look into your expense ratio very carefully to see what economies can be effected.

Under Keen, the CUC performed some of the business information and supervision functions later assumed by the co-operative wholesales. The case of the Fernie Industrial and Provident Co-operative Society illustrates some of the difficulties. The co-op refused to follow Keen's advice, and when he was proven right, the organization left the CUC. A director told Keen that the CUC's advice had got the directors into trouble with the manager.[16]

The nature of Keen's advice, and the nature of the reception to it, both tell us a lot about the shortcomings of the early co-operatives in the West. Of course, not all co-ops that had short lives "failed"—many made savings for their members, provided services during a crucial period of settlement when services were rudimentary, or gave their members and leaders valuable experience and personal development. Yet alongside all the transitory co-ops, there were a few that were striking successes even in terms of operations and longevity, and those few durable economic successes were critical for the development of the co-operative movement and especially of its wholesales.

Leading Retail Co-operatives, 1914–26

Manitoba was the only province where the oldest incorporated co-operative association survived. This was the Moline Co-op, which grew out of a resolution in early 1914 by the local MGGA. Ten farmers met on 24 March 1914, to found the association, which did $6,442 in business that first year, most of it associated with the GGGC elevator. Moline was later important as one of the eight founding members and one of the leading supporters of the Manitoba Co-operative Wholesale. But it started small: until 1920 it operated a few afternoons per week out of an old schoolhouse.[17] One of its managers, Bob Matthewson, went on to the staff of the Manitoba Co-op Wholesale and eventually of Federated Co-operatives Limited.

Another Manitoba co-operative that grew out of an MGGA local was the Minto UFM Association. Although the co-op did not apply for a charter until 1927, it had its origins in a January 1918 meeting of the Minto farmers. The MGGA local handled "flour, apples, coal, fence posts, twine, etc.," with W. F. Popple acting as its secretary for $125 per year. Popple was possibly the Minto Co-op's greatest contribution to the co-operative movement, for he went on to head the Manitoba Co-op Wholesale through its most difficult years.[18]

Several of the early Alberta co-ops also played crucial roles in the later developments of the system as a whole. Undoubtedly the most important of these was Killam, registered 8 December 1914 under the name of Willow Hollow Co-operative Association. This was the oldest successful co-operative in Alberta. At a schoolhouse meeting in Willow Hollow school district in 1914, former Lancashire man William Halsall presented a paper on the Rochdale philosophy of co-operation, and by the end of the meeting twenty-two people had subscribed ten-dollar shares to form a co-operative society. Seven years later the co-op moved six miles into the town of Killam and changed its name. Under Halsall's leadership to 1938, the co-op branched out into groceries, dry goods, hardware, lumber, fuel oils, livestock, and even banking of members' deposits (in 1927 the co-op started Alberta's first credit union). Not to stop at this, Killam Co-op added a 16,000-egg incubator in 1927, a cheese factory in 1935, and a co-operative egg- and poultry-marketing service in 1938. Killam Co-op was one of a few that stood out with comprehensive stores and community service institutions. Its significance to the movement as a whole was great, for in the mid-1930s it saved the Alberta Co-op Wholesale from collapse, subsidizing it with cash and donated services while Halsall ran the provincial wholesale out of Killam Co-op's facilities.[19]

Wetaskiwin Co-op, founded in 1917 out of an earlier carlot buying club, was also part of the strong nucleus of co-operative retailing in Alberta. While Killam contributed William Halsall to the movement, Wetaskiwin sent its manager, A. P. Moan, to serve as the first manager of the Alberta Co-op Wholesale Association.[20]

Saskatchewan had thirteen co-operatives founded in 1914 that lasted for at least fifty years. These were Bethune, Borden, Davidson, Elbow, Hafford, Kindersley, Laporte, Lemberg, Lewvan, Lloydminster, Melfort, Wilton (at Lashburn), and Young.[21] Of these, the Davidson, Lloydminster, Melfort, and Young co-ops played especially important roles in the development of the co-operative system as a whole. Each of these four established a large and success-ful store and contributed greatly to the provincial wholesale.

As in many of the other cases mentioned here, farmers in the Melfort area had been getting together to buy binder twine, barbed wire, and apples in bulk before any co-op was organized. After the provincial co-operatives act was passed, eight people met on 22 January 1914 and decided to found an official co-operative. In its early years the co-op was plagued by poor attendance; one meeting was attended by only two people. Two years after its founding, they discussed quitting. The minutes noted: "It was finally decided that we dare not go back. All we could do to protect our own interests was to go ahead and try to get a vastly increased membership and a capital big enough to place the asso-ciation on a working basis." In 1918 they were able to hire a full-time manager, and they chose wisely in Robert McKay, who later piloted the Saskatchewan Co-operative Wholesale Society through its most critical years in the 1930s.[22]

Davidson Co-op was founded after an SGGA Local met in April 1914 and called for the creation of a consumer co-operative. Like so many early co-ops, it started with little: a $325 weigh scale and a tiny office beside the tracks, where orders were received in carload lots. One report claimed that in 1915 the David-son Co-op was the first in the prairies to own petroleum tanks.[23] By 1918 the co-op was able to convert an old implement office into a grocery store, and in 1919 built an ammonia cold-storage plant that permitted it to handle fresh meat. By 1920 Davidson Co-op had hardware, a tinshop, dry goods, and home fur-nishings, and in 1926 it opened a co-op bakery. Davidson was one of the two strongest co-operatives in Saskatchewan, and its loyalty and volume were essen-tial to the development of the Saskatchewan wholesale in the early years. Its manager, W. H. Ketcheson, an ardent proponent of co-operation and of "buy-ing British" from the British co-operative movement, also managed the Saskatchewan Co-op Wholesale Society in its first three years.

The co-op that competed with Davidson to be Saskatchewan's largest in the early years was Lloydminster, which, like Davidson, had both farming and old-country roots. The Barr colonists contributed to the founding of the co-op in June 1914. Its first premises were located in a stable purchased for $300, but after only four years it bought out a private merchant and entered the grocery business. Like Melfort and Davidson, Lloydminster had a remarkable manager, C. G. Davidson, who also contributed greatly to the wholesale's development. And like Davidson Co-op, Lloydminster had continuity: in fifty years only thirty-eight people served on its board of directors.[24]

The Young co-operative was also large, successful, and a leader among prairie co-operatives. Like the others it grew out of an SGGA buying club. It was one of the first to establish a co-operative library, one of the first to affili-ate with the Co-operative Union of Canada, and it was one of George Keen's most regular hosts on his visits to the West. It set up a model and very active education committee in 1920, one of whose objectives was the ambitious "[c]onciliation of the conflicting interests of the capitalist, worker and consumer, and the equitable division among them of . . . profit." One report recalls that "it was regarded as a duty by directors that they should visit schools in the area and lead discussion about co-operatives and the co-operative movement in general." Like many others, Young Co-op had an old-country manager with a deep philosophical understanding and commitment, "Andy" Allison, who served as manager and secretary from 1915 to 1947.[25]

These few early co-ops stood out for a number of reasons. Most had exceptional managers with deep understanding of co-operative philosophy; many of them went on to assume leadership positions in the provincial wholesales. Not a few of them were old-country co-operators (mainly English and Scottish) with substantial backgrounds in the movement, and in most cases they were supported by boards of directors who also had a commitment to and some understanding of co-operative organizations. These few co-ops grew rapidly, retained the loyalty of their members, and were a driving force behind the creation of the new co-operative wholesale societies of 1927–28.

The Growing Need for Consumer Co-operatives

Up to 1928, Canada was an underdeveloped country insofar as consumer co-operation was concerned. Few co-operative associations existed, and even fewer worked together. In 1927 the International Co-operative Alliance reported just fourteen co-ops affiliated to the CUC, by far the smallest national movement of any affiliated to the ICA—with the sole exception of Yugoslavia, which had six. Even tiny Estonia had 277 affiliated co-operative societies. Still more dramatic was the matter of co-operatively owned wholesales. Canada was one of a very few countries with no affiliated co-operative wholesale. Estonia, Georgia (USSR), Lithuania, Latvia, and Japan all had co-operative wholesales, but Canada did not, not even at the provincial level in any province.[26]

For several key reasons, this backwardness was becoming a more and more urgent problem for Canadian farmers and co-operators during the 1920s. On the one hand, farming in the 1920s was becoming a more complicated business. The introduction of power machinery meant a need for equipment, parts, service, fuel, and lubricants. Farmers' fixed costs went up, but their incomes, derived from fluctuating world markets, remained variable. Technology exposed farmers to a cost-price squeeze, giving them a more urgent interest in consumer co-operation in order to keep prices down. Like the industrial labourers of Rochdale, farmers faced their own "industrial revolution," and needed to mass their purchasing power to control consumption and alleviate their economic dependency.[27]

And, on the other hand, the 1920s saw the advent of the chain store, the travelling salesman, the mail-order house, and concentrated industrial concerns of all types. Consumers saw these concentrations of economic power as threats to their own independence, for if a few big concerns drove the many small shopkeepers out of business, consumers would be exposed to profiteering and monopoly pricing. The growth of chain and department stores only increased farmers' suspicion that they were not getting a fair deal from private traders. One co-op manager wrote in 1929 that a Red & White store had just opened in his town. "It is obvious," he stated, "that, in a few years, there will be few absolutely independent retail merchants. Each may own his own business, but he will be tied up as to the source of his supplies." If private business was undergoing this development, then co-operatives would have to cope with it as well—and that meant an increasingly urgent need to tie co-operatives together into their own system.[28]

Discussion of co-operative wholesaling, for farmers especially, was therefore in the air in the 1920s, even before retail co-operatives were themselves widespread or well developed. Keen wrote, "I feel we are on the eve of large developments in Canada, and they are giving me considerable anxiety."[29] The reason for his anxiety was that, although organized farmers were increasingly promoting consumer co-operation, their understanding of its principles was not necessarily great. There was still a major difficulty in spreading an understanding of Rochdale principles beyond the small circle of a few philosophically committed, generally old-country managers, directors, and government officials. If the principles of retail co-operation were not yet understood, how could farmers move on to wholesaling?

Organized farmers persistently forwarded proposals which could be characterized by four main features: little or no share capital, pricing at cost, no particular devotion to local control or member democracy, and intertwining with the organized farmers' movement (for example, sales limited to members of the farm organization, or directors elected from its locals instead of by the co-op's own patrons). In such cases, officials like Waldron in Saskatchewan wrote back to explain to the farmers that such arrangements were neither legal nor desirable: they would leave the co-op with no capital and no margins, and with insufficient member loyalty and education. They would violate co-operative principles.[30] Farmers advanced such views based on experience with marketing pools that had to start big to survive, and with the floating of large joint-stock companies; such proposals also reflected a desire to give their members service at the lowest possible cost. The problem was that these ideas were not appropriate to consumer co-operatives.

Though the need for co-ops, and especially the need for retail co-ops to band together, was acute, problems such as these inhibited further development. The problems of co-operative unity and education were greatest in British Columbia, which explains why that province proved unable to found a co-operative wholesale until 1939, a decade later than the prairie provinces.

Limitations to Co-operative Development: the Case of British Columbia

Co-ops in B.C. were divided among three regions, the Coast, the south-central Interior, and the Kootenays. The coastal co-operative societies, with the exception of the strong Sointula fishermen's co-op, were almost entirely "associations of dairy farmers . . . distributing seed, feed, and supplies," as one B.C. co-operator described them in 1929. The south-central co-ops, including Armstrong, Revelstoke, Penticton, Tappen, and Arrowhead, were a more promising base for collective efforts, but the last three of the co-ops named here were in financial trouble in 1929. The third group, including Natal, Fernie, Creston, Nelson, and Cranbrook, were predominantly mining and railroad workers' co-ops. Several of these were in trouble as well. The social, economic, and geographic differences among the fishermen, farmers, and workers who formed B.C.'s co-ops were greater than those among groups in other provinces, and the difficulties of transportation and communication more severe. There was no nucleus of strong societies to lead the way,[31] nor was there the strong government support for consumer co-operatives, such as that enjoyed by Saskatchewan and, to a lesser extent, Manitoba and Alberta. Keen complained that the Registrar of Companies in B.C., who was in charge of co-operatives on the side, took "no interest in, and may be opposed to, co-operation." The farm movement and co-operatives in B.C. clearly did not command the same public attention or government interest as in the prairies.[32]

Armstrong Co-operative Society store in Armstrong, British Columbia (1920s?), one of the strongest and most influential consumer co-operatives in B.C. Robert Wood, who started as secretary-treasurer of the Armstrong society, became a regional vice-president of the Co-operative Union of Canada in the 1920s. It was Wood who called the conference in 1938 that led to the establishment of the British Columbia Co-operative Wholesale Society. (Provincial Archives of British Columbia C–3477)

Nevertheless, as the other western wholesales began operations in 1928–29, there was an effort to create a co-operative wholesale in B.C. as well, with co-operators discussing the project with the United Farmers of Canada, British Columbia Section. The United Farmers clearly had the initiative in this project. A leading B.C. co-operator wrote, "as far as I can see . . . there does not seem to be any means of either stopping it or guiding it," because officers of the UFC were "obviously using this, and some other matters to advertise the efforts of the UFC," with little regard for co-operative principles or for the long-term stability of the wholesale they wished to form. The "considerable personal following" of the UFC leaders made it impossible to stop them, yet "seeing that the UFC Locals must be in a poor state of organization as yet, and with hardly any resources[,] they are taking almost impossible chances."[33]

This was precisely the same problem consumer co-operators in other provinces were experiencing: efforts to speed co-operative development and form wholesales became bound up with the politics of farm organizations, where individual and institutional interests shaped the policy, and led to impressive but risky and poorly financed schemes. The B.C. effort went as far as issuing an invitation to subscribe for shares in December 1929, and appointed an acting manager. However, while the co-operative with the largest volume in B.C., the Fraser Valley Surrey Farmers' Co-operative Association of Cloverdale, backed the provisional wholesale, the Egg Pool and the powerful Fraser Valley Milk Producers declined to support it. Personal differences and UFC politics led to bitter divisions, among which the efforts of co-operators to advocate Rochdale consumer principles went unnoticed.[34]

The political problems that prevented B.C. from organizing a co-operative wholesale in 1929–30 were a reflection of problems throughout the entire West in those years. Since B.C. had the additional problems of geographical disunity and occupational diversity among co-operators, it was not likely that such problems could be overcome.

In the last half of the 1920s, the few strong co-ops that existed did start to work together and founded their own wholesales. This was a crucial development. Until 1928 the number of viable retail co-ops was declining. When they joined together and founded their own wholesale—began to work together as a system—the decline was reversed, and genuine co-operative development began to occur. From 1928 onward a great many successful co-ops were founded, co-ops that survived the bad times that were to come.

Conclusion and Questions

It has been said many times that retail co-operatives are the foundation of the Co-operative Retailing System; the wholesales that have existed over the years have existed only to serve local retail co-operatives, to fill the demand that the local association has mobilized. This being said, the difficulties facing co-operative wholesaling in the 1920s should be obvious: commercially successful retail co-operatives were few, scattered, and not comprehensive in the goods they handled, even in the prairies where they were better developed than anywhere else in Canada. They had the support, however, of farm organizations, and they had a handful of leaders with a clear vision of how consumer co-operation worked. With this they entered into the ambitious business of co-operative wholesaling. Was this premature? Should the co-operative movement have developed the retails first, and a wholesale much later? That would have been the Rochdale model. Or was the formation of the wholesales, perhaps, the best way to strengthen the retails?

4

Manitoba Co-op
Wholesale, 1926–1931

During his western trip in 1928, George Keen concentrated on the province of Manitoba. His tours and discussions left him with the following impressions:

> I found the societies in Manitoba were not as advanced in co-operative understanding as in Saskatchewan. I did not visit any which could be regarded as successful or as stabilized as, say, Davidson, Young, Lloydminster, and Melfort.

Elsewhere Keen ranked the western provinces in order of their "intelligence, understanding and appreciation of [co-operative] philosophy" as Saskatchewan first, followed by Alberta, then B.C., then Manitoba. In fact, with the exception of B.C., it was in exactly the reverse order that these provinces opened their co-operative wholesales.[1]

Manitoba Co-operative Associations and the Need for a Wholesale

More so than the other provinces, the Manitoba co-operative retailing movement was based on carload buying clubs and bulk commodity co-ops, rather than on stores with inventories, elaborate premises, or full-time managers. Nevertheless, although Manitoba had few well-developed stores, it had no lack of general co-operative ambition. Manitoba became the first province in Canada to get a co-operative wholesale up and running. Organized in 1926, incorporated in 1927, Manitoba Co-operative Wholesale Limited (MCW) opened its doors and began operations in early 1928.

This was not a full-fledged wholesale in the usual sense of the word: the co-op wholesales in those days did not generally have warehouses or inventories of goods. They merely grouped the orders of member co-ops and placed these combined orders with suppliers, obtaining volume discounts by doing so. In other words, the so-called wholesale was a broker, living off commissions on orders for goods that never actually went through its own hands. But humble though this beginning was, it was a huge step by consumer co-operatives toward the creation of an actual retailing *system*.

Because it was based on bulk commodity associations rather than on stores, a few key commodities were the backbone of the whole retail movement in Manitoba. Chief among these was petroleum. Reviewing the progress of their wholesale decades later, Manitoba co-operators recalled two important forces that had led them to create a more formalized and effective co-operative system. The first was the increasing mechanization of farms, requiring petroleum products that were difficult to handle. The second was the opposition of profit enterprises.

"It was impossible," they recalled, "to apply the buying club method to handling of [petroleum] products because voluntary help was not always available during the rush seasons."[2] With mechanization, farmers needed oil and grease during the harvest itself when none of them had time to unload, weigh, and take delivery of it. And unloading petroleum products was much more complicated and difficult than unloading other goods. Petroleum, however, offered sensational savings. Many petroleum buying clubs had sprung up in the 1920s, especially around Winnipeg, as the 1954 annual report recalled when looking back on the history of MCW:

> These clubs were in no sense true co-ops. With no buildings or other fixed assets, and with only voluntary help, they had a will-o'-wisp quality of here today, gone tomorrow. Selling strictly at carload cost, they were accused with some justification of price-cutting. . . .
>
> Opposition soon developed. . . . Local merchants resented the "unfair competition" and put pressure on wholesalers. Buying clubs found margins growing smaller, and experienced increasing difficulty in obtaining supplies.

Then in the mid-1920s, the federal government, under pressure from the commercial lobby, amended legislation governing explosive materials in such a way as to prohibit unloading of petroleum tank cars directly into drums. This was a body blow, in the opinion of co-operators, to the buying clubs, which owned no tanks and had no capital with which to buy them.[3]

As a result of the business lobby and of the expensive equipment involved, petroleum buying was moving out of the reach of farmers' buying clubs. But farmers still needed petroleum products and there were still great savings to be had. The incorporated co-operative association seemed to be the answer, since it could raise capital, erect tanks, and hire staff. By 1927 there were about half a dozen such formal oil co-ops in Manitoba. As the volume of co-operatively marketed petroleum products grew, however, private suppliers reacted against the co-op movement. "Suddenly these small Co-ops found it very hard to buy supplies at any price," Manitoba co-operators recalled later in reviewing their history. This, together with the other developments noted above, led them to consider forming a co-operative wholesale[4], but it took three years of organization before the wholesale was operational.

In December 1925 at Boissevain, the United Farmers' local in Souris district unanimously passed a resolution urging the formation of a central purchasing organization. E. D. Magwood, George Brown of Deloraine, and Roy W. Johnston of Croll took the lead in carrying the matter forward. At the January 1926 UFM convention in Brandon, delegates from locals which did co-operative buying met in the basement of the convention hall one hour before the convention "to discuss the advisability of establishing a central buying agency."[5] Magwood, Brown, and Johnston were appointed as a committee to survey the UFM locals and develop a plan.

In March 1926 the committee of three decided that any "central buying agency" that was formed would be organized as a co-operative, that it would be incorporated under the Manitoba Co-operative Associations Act, and that any locals it organized would be separately incorporated, also as co-operatives. These were key points, but they were not so quickly or firmly established in the other provinces (see chapters 5 and 6). This decision established consumer co-operation according to the federated structure, still used today, of autonomous retail co-operatives owning their own wholesale. A circular was sent out, and Magwood travelled from district to district discussing the plan.[6] Finally, on 29 July 1926 the provisional board of directors met for the first time, reaffirmed "that the basis of organization be the local trading unit with consumers [as] members or shareholders in the local," and decided to apply for a charter.[7] The development of by-laws and a memorandum of association took over a year, but on 17 November 1927 the charter was granted.

The first general meeting of shareholders in Brandon in February 1928 showed that only $477 had been spent in three years of organizational work. MCW was very much the product of volunteer work by organized farmers.[8]

The Early Years of MCW: Price Wars, Printing Plants, and the Struggle for Existence

"This new Wholesale looked far from promising," Manitoba co-operators recalled twenty years later, "even to those who had helped organize it."

> Its main difficulty was lack of capital. The few Locals established at that time could put up only $1,300—hardly enough to gain the confidence of suppliers or banks. It had a very small volume to offer and so could not bargain for prices or discounts, and, of course, had no credit rating.

While fourteen locals supported the wholesale and sixteen expressed interest by the time of the first general meeting, only eight were legally organized as co-operatives and eligible for membership. Homewood, Grunthal, Minto, Moline, Oakville, Rosebank, Sperling, and Thornhill were the eight associations upon which hopes for co-operative wholesaling rested.[9]

Almost immediately, the fledgling wholesale encountered problems with suppliers. Johnston, writing in 1929, said MCW received "a very cool reception" when it approached the oil companies. "With the very large capital that the oil companies had at their backs, and the very limited amount of capital in the Co-operative Wholesale, it may have appeared like a joke." Joke or not, the oil companies did more than ignore or obstruct the new farmers' company. Almost as soon as its offices opened, MCW became embroiled in a vicious gasoline price war. The Winnipeg *Tribune* on 28 February 1928 reported a three-cent drop in gasoline prices, as much as five cents in rural areas. In those days gasoline was about thirty cents a gallon, so these were large decreases. "The greatest cut went into effect in the southern portion of the province"—which is where the petroleum clubs and co-ops were most active. The *Tribune* reported that "the immense increase of co-operative buying" and "the prospects of new companies coming into the Manitoba field" were the main reasons given by dealers for the price cuts.[10]

Manitoba co-operatives suffered severely from the price war. Where co-ops had been able to pay patronage rebates of five cents per gallon, now their gross margins were less than one and a half cents. The co-ops, and the wholesale, survived by absorbing the losses and by tough organizational work. Co-operators were convinced that the gasoline war ended in 1929 only because new co-ops at Glenboro, Wawanesa, Brandon, Minnedosa, Neepawa, Hamiota, Solsgirth, Kenton, Ewart, and Hartney gave the co-operative system a broad enough base and a large enough volume to discourage the oil companies. "With such a network across the province, the co-operative movement became a force to be reckoned with in the oil business. It could no longer be driven out of existence by local or regional price wars."[11]

An important part of MCW's survival (its early years cannot be characterized by the word "success") was the fact that the United Farmers backed it solidly, and, correspondingly, so did the province's co-operative marketing associations. The UFM conventions, districts, and local secretaries were instrumental both to the organization and growth of the wholesale and also to its survival in the 1928–29 gasoline price war. And through an informal committee of co-operative organizations, Manitoba's marketing co-ops were supportive in principle. The Manitoba Pool had cordial relations with the consumer movement, and showed both an interest in the development of the Manitoba Co-op Wholesale and a friendliness toward Keen and other advocates of consumer co-operation.[12]

But there were limitations to the support that co-operative wholesaling received from the farmers' movement. These became evident in the case of the Manitoba Co-op Wholesale printing plant.

The printing plant was acquired with the idea of providing services to the other co-operatives based in Winnipeg. This would generate enough steady revenue to get the wholesale going. Unable to obtain sufficient volume in actual wholesale business, MCW looked for support from better-established Manitoba co-operatives and attempted to serve them. And having obtained pledges of support from these other co-operatives, MCW went ahead with the purchase of the plant. There are two interpretations of what happened next. Manitoba consumer co-operators later claimed that private businesses deliberately under-quoted the co-op printing plant, even submitting bids below cost in order to discredit MCW and drive its printing operation out of business. According to this version, Manitoba marketing co-operatives, influenced by these bids, decided the MCW printing plant was inefficient and uncompetitive, and they declined to support it. It is also possible that, since printing is a technical business that has nothing to do with either wholesaling or farming, that MCW lacked the expertise to scrutinize the plant and ensure it operated efficiently. Whatever the case may have been, Manitoba Co-op Wholesale, already struggling, was stuck with an expensive white elephant. In 1929 it left the printing business, swallowing a loss of $5,000. The wholesale was on the verge of collapse.[13]

George Keen later claimed that he had spoken to Manitoba co-operators about the purchase of the plant, "strongly challenging the wisdom of such action." Keen repeated his consistently maintained co-operative philosophy that

> a co-operative wholesale did not create, but satisfied, a demand for merchandise. There was no organized co-operative demand for printing in the province. It is the function of the retail society [not the wholesale] to foster and develop demand.

In Keen's opinion, only after retail co-ops had developed their own strength and mobilized the demand for a product—as in the case of petroleum products—should the wholesale leap in to supply that need. The purchase of the printing plant was a speculative effort, based on insufficient capital and member support, and did not fit Keen's model of gradual growth from the bottom up through education and membership loyalty. Perhaps the printing plant was a desperate measure, gambling on the support of other co-operatives, but it was not consistent with consumer co-operative purposes, and its failure made matters much worse.[14]

Reduced Expectations, Cost-Cutting, and Stabilization, 1930–31

E. D. Magwood, first president and manager of Manitoba Co-operative Wholesale, told Keen: "We representatives of our associations cannot afford to stand still. We must develop rapidly."[15] That impatience had a heavy cost. MCW began its life with losses, and before the first year of operation was completed, Magwood resigned. He was replaced by Walter F. Popple, who then faced a very difficult financial situation. Petroleum was subject to fierce competition by better-capitalized private companies, while volume in other commodities was so low that it was difficult to get deals from wholesalers and manufacturers. The co-operative movement in Manitoba was too shallowly rooted to support a wholesale easily. Years later it was revealed that "a good many products had to be handled through the MCW office without any commission, in order to build up volume."[16]

Two years of operations had placed the Manitoba Co-op Wholesale in a situation of crisis. When they were most needed, Popple and the directors who supported him now came into their own. Under Popple's leadership in 1930, with just ten member associations, two office staff, and one part-time fieldman, the wholesale "settled down to a period of rigid economy."[17] Popple began what was nearly a one-man campaign against credit trading by the wholesale and its members, in order to establish finances on a firm cash basis. In the midst of the Depression he preached to the delegates assembled at annual meetings, exhorting them as their president and manager to follow co-operative principles, which then included trading only on a cash basis, being loyal to the wholesale, and undertaking co-operative education. Ian MacPherson has characterized Popple as "a dynamic individual with utopian co-operative convictions," and this is surely an accurate judgment. Popple tried to popularize the co-operative philosophy by urging all locals to affiliate to the CUC, and by organizing annual meetings of Manitoba societies to coincide with Keen's western tours.[18] Popple's energy, faith in co-operation, and advocacy of business sense and co-operative education were essential to MCW's eventual success.

Popple's qualities alone, however, would not have been enough. It took the courage of a small group of directors to save the wholesale in 1930:

> The situation was desperate. The bank would not give any credit to finance operations. As the only way out, the Directors, individually, signed a guarantee for $15,000. We cannot overemphasize the courage and wisdom of those early directors. Had they not been willing to sign these guarantees, there might have been no Wholesale today—and perhaps no local Co-ops. . . . These directors might have lost their farms. . . . Good businessmen would call them foolhardy but they had great faith in the co-operative way of business and the years have proven how right they were.

Hampered by an insufficiently-developed co-operative movement, by a lack of co-operative understanding, by fierce private opposition, and by key business mistakes, co-operative wholesaling in Manitoba was saved by just eight men, farmers all, who did understand and who risked what they had to make it work.[19]

When the Manitoba wholesale was forced by its poor finances to discontinue its field service in October 1930, Popple and the other directors continued the work of attending annual meetings of co-ops and UFM locals to promote consumer co-operation. They had some success, but it was uneven. A total of 45 locals were affiliated to MCW by the end of 1930. It is noteworthy that only 2 of these were more than three years old—Killarney (1920) and Moline (1914). Most were not only new, but very small, ranging from Winnipeg Beach with 31 members to Brandon with 268. The average membership was just 88. A few locals bought most of the wholesale's turnover. Brandon, with $29,900, and Hamiota, with $28,108, each accounted for about 10 percent of MCW's total sales to members. Thirteen large associations, representing about 1,500 individuals, bought 68 percent of MCW's sales to members in 1930.[20]

If a few generally newer and smaller co-ops and locals carried the wholesale, it was true that many of the older and better-established co-ops stayed out. Of thirty-five such nonaffiliated locals, at least five were founded in the period 1916–20. One, the Workers and Farmers Co-op of Winnipeg, had 345 shareholders and did over $94,000 in annual sales, nearly half again larger than Brandon, the largest affiliate. Eleven nonaffiliates whose sales were reported did over $294,000 in turnover, more sales than MCW itself made in 1929. One reason the wholesale could not serve many of these co-ops was the narrow range of goods it handled: MCW survived by concentrating on a few bulk farm commodities in those early years, but not all retails handled these commodities. Those that did not seemed to have little need for the wholesale.

The narrowness of the wholesale's base was reflected in its financial statement. MCW reported a loss of $539 in 1929, and though it made an earning of $6,407 on operations in 1930 (based in part on cuts in expenses ranging from a 23 percent cut in salaries to an 84 percent cut in publicity), that entire earning was swallowed by the accumulated deficit of $7,777, which included a loss of $1,144 on the printing plant in 1929 (see Appendix 4 for sales and savings of all wholesales). The wholesale's total assets in 1930 were $16,983, of which $14,200 consisted of accounts receivable—a dangerously high proportion. High accounts receivable translated easily into many bad debts—especially during the Depression when money was scarce—or at the very least tied up the wholesale's scarce capital. Eighty-eight percent of the capital subscribed by members, in fact, was not paid, giving the wholesale only some $1,545 to work with.[21]

Under strict economies and Popple's firm leadership and co-operative inspiration, MCW gradually turned the corner. By 1931 its sales had declined to $274,321, but it eliminated the accumulated deficit and managed for the first time to retain a net saving of $950. Thereafter the Manitoba wholesale showed an earning every year for nearly a quarter of a century, until amalgamation in 1955 with the Saskatchewan wholesale. Understandably the losses of 1928–31 were glossed over as the wholesale became more and more successful. As the 1954 *Annual Report* noted, "Even though your Wholesale was incorporated in 1927, we have only listed figures starting at 1931 as that was the first year that a deficit did not show on our books."[22] But the difficult times, overcome by co-operators who learned from them, were the base upon which the future successes were built.

Conclusion and Questions

Was MCW formed prematurely? Did its initial losses and disappointments amount to a failure, and if so, why did they occur? To what extent do co-operatives learn from such failures?

Co-operatives are democratic organizations based on the education and participation of ordinary people. As such they have the disadvantages of democracy and, sometimes, of inexperience. They may take a long time to discuss and respond to problems and market challenges. Apathy may limit their achievements. They may, especially in the beginning, base decisions on an unclear understanding of co-operative principles and business methods. But as democratic organizations they are also supremely flexible. They can survive disasters that would finish off an organization that existed only for profit, because their directors and members are willing to make sacrifices and learn. In many cases, setbacks that cause members and officials to learn more about running co-operatives are not, in the long view, failures at all, but rather strengthen the movement even if the individual co-operative is found no longer to be needed by its members. The experience of the Depression also seems to indicate that a democratic structure will bring forth leaders when it needs them, in a time of crisis—the directors who mortgaged their farms, for example, or the leader like Popple with his stern warnings about credit, costs, and the necessity of co-operative education. Co-operators should ask themselves which are greater, the costs of democracy—or the benefits.

5

Alberta Co-op
Wholesale Association, 1926–1934

Alberta shared many of Manitoba's problems in 1928, if not necessarily to as great an extent. It did have a few centres such as Killam, Wetaskiwin, and Edgerton that provided both a strong economic and philosophical base for consumer co-operation, and which promised a diversified and steady volume for any wholesale that could be created. But such centres were few. As in Manitoba, it was more a question of relying on organized United Farmers' locals than upon well-developed, independent retail co-operatives. But Alberta had an additional and very serious problem: unlike Manitoba, the producers' organizations were not very supportive of consumer co-operation. Eventually, not only the UGG, but also the UFA entered the farm supplies business. The Alberta section of the CUC did not have wheat pool fieldmen promoting consumer co-operatives. And the UFA effectively deprived the co-op wholesale of the petroleum business that proved so fundamental in Manitoba as well as in Saskatchewan.

No other province better demonstrated the importance of co-operation among co-operatives than Alberta in the early years, where the consequences of the failure to co-operate were made strikingly evident.

Co-operative Buying and Alberta Farmers

Alberta did, from a relatively early date, have provincial organizations that brought together co-operatives for mutual support. The 1923 Alberta Co-operative League was one, founded by eight of the more successful consumer co-operatives at a meeting in Wetaskiwin. The league provided for regular meetings among the co-operative store managers and facilitated collective purchasing by them. Then in 1928, using moneys from the Wheat Board Money Trust (the provincial share of the surplus left when the federal Wheat Board was discontinued in 1919), the first Alberta Institute of Co-operation was held. The institute developed as a set of simultaneous educational sessions in Olds, Vermilion, and Lethbridge where speakers were brought in and discussion occurred relating to all aspects of the co-operative movement. Speakers at the institute advocated consumer co-operation, but as the record shows, understanding of the special principles of consumer co-operation did not penetrate very deeply.

Retailing in Alberta (about 1915): the Andrew Reid store in Ponoka. A few years after this photograph was taken, the Reid store was bought out by the Ponoka Co-operative Association, which became one of the strongest consumer co-operatives in the province and a vigorous supporter of co-operative wholesaling. (Glenbow-Alberta Institute NA–2839–32)

One difference seems to have been that the farmers' movement in Alberta had more expansive aims with respect to consumer co-operation. Henry Wise Wood, president of the UFA and chairman of Alberta Wheat Pool, asked the first institute the following question:

> Why do we organize as a producing class to solve our consumptive problems? You cannot organize all the consumers in one big organization. Everybody is a consumer and you cannot organize them. Really the reason we are organized as producers is because we have to have a common interest and it is that common interest that makes it possible for us to organize an organization to deal with consumptive problems.

Wood's speech indicated a powerful belief in organizing farmers as producers into one large movement, a movement that would also include co-operative supplying of farmers' needs. This belief tended to contradict efforts to establish consumer co-operation as an equal and autonomous branch of co-operation.[1]

There could be no doubt that co-operative buying was seen as strictly secondary to the great co-operative marketing enterprises. The power and political importance of these enterprises was made clear in 1929 when J. E. Brownlee, the premier of Alberta, urged Alberta's farmers and co-operators to strive toward the construction of a "co-operative state." The 1929 institute proceedings contained forty-five pages of addresses on pooling of wheat, and twenty-six on livestock and dairy pools. Consumer co-operation rated only a single article seven pages in length, under "Other Examples of Co-operation," which the editor pointedly introduced as "[striking] a new note" at the institute.[2]

By 1930 consumer co-operation rated its own chapter in the institute's proceedings. The editor noted that consumer co-operation was now seen as necessary for farmers' interests, and referred to "the growing realization that . . . to achieve ultimate success, [co-operation] must be such as to encompass the entire socio-economic field." This realization made the UFA vitally concerned with consumer co-operation. As Amos P. Moan, head of Alberta's new co-op wholesale, noted, the UFA's interest had shaped the course of development of co-operative wholesaling in Alberta:

> The Consumers' Committee of the United Farmers of Alberta . . . encouraged us. . . . The trade of a few hundred locals would give us volume; and coupled with the trade of fifteen stores a large volume would be assured. So after careful deliberation the stores agreed to organize a wholesale.

Encouraged by the prospect of UFA support, Alberta co-operators had embarked on an ambitious plan.[3]

Large Dreams: 1928–30

On 23 April 1928, Alberta Co-operative Wholesale Association Limited held its first general meeting in Edmonton. There A. P. Moan of Wetaskiwin was elected president, W. Halsall of Killam, vice-president, and T. Swindlehurst of Edgerton, secretary. Later in the year when Moan resigned to become manager, Halsall became president. These men represented Wetaskiwin, Killam, and Edgerton co-ops, probably the best-developed in the province in terms of both finances and philosophy. At that first meeting the wholesale announced that it was acting temporarily as an agent for the stores in placing orders, "but eventually a distributing centre will be established in one of the cities." Orders were invited from UFA locals and co-op stores alike for Brantford binder twine, as well as for "chocolate, vinegar, overshoes, underwear, etc." At that first meeting the earlier Alberta Co-operative League was wound up and its assets absorbed by the wholesale, but only after "heated discussion" and after Halsall urged that it be retained to carry out educational work. Halsall, a persistent, long-time advocate of co-operative education, was defeated, as he would be on several more occasions in the following years.[4]

The ambitious plans of Alberta Co-op Wholesale had to do with its powerful friends. The Co-operative League had already met in March with the premier of Alberta, two other cabinet ministers, the presidents of the Wheat Pool, the Livestock Pool, and the Dairy Pool, and the secretary of the Poultry Pool. This group discussed in detail the setting up of a co-operative wholesale society. Later in the summer more meetings occurred which gave the wholesale's leaders the impression that "both the UFA and the Government are taking a deeper

Hauling farm fuel from a UFA depot (1924), under one of a variety of joint purchasing plans operated by the UFA on behalf of its members. In the days before mechanization, coal and wood were major items among farmers' purchases, alongside other consumables such as binder twine, flour, apples, and salt. (Provincial Archives of Alberta NA-4187-33)

interest in our work."[5] When the ACWA executive met in October 1928 they decided to commence operations on 1 January 1929 and to obtain warehouse as well as office space. Noting that a "large amount of education will have to be done," they requested a $1,000 subsidy from the Wheat Pool funds. With official and UFA support and with such subsidies in sight, hopes were high. "The delegates dispersed," said the minutes, "feeling that another epock [sic] making period had been added to the Co-operative Movement of Canada."[6]

George Keen issued urgent warnings. "I hope that you and the Board have thoroughly surveyed the situation," he wrote to Moan in November 1928, "particularly the relation between the profit on trade immediately in sight and the operating expenses." Keen was afraid ACWA was starting too large and too fast, with too expensive a setup and too little business assured. "In the incorporation of these wholesale societies we ought to take the minimum of chance. If they are successful from the start they will stimulate the whole Movement. On the other hand if any loss is shown in the initial stages the same will have just as discouraging an effect."[7]

Keen's specific warning was to be cautious in relations with the UFA and the government, particularly as these were looking into ambitious schemes to work with private promoters or buy out private stores to create co-operative chains quickly. While the wholesale was in the process of organization, discussing its by-laws with the government, the marketing committee of the UFA was talking to manufacturers about supplying goods to their locals, and looking to the new wholesale to do this for them immediately. The government, in the meantime, was offering loan guarantees. "The Movement should assume full responsibility for its own business obligations," wrote Keen. Government involvement should not go "beyond its legitimate field" or it could do "more harm than good." As for the help of the producers' organizations, he wrote the following:

> There is a vast difference between marketing organizations and consumers' societies. . . . while the former centralize operations and hire highly paid service from capitalist undertakings upon which they depend for success, consumers' societies must rely upon local initiative, the cultivation of the co-operative intelligence of individual members, and a comprehensive social vision.

Swindlehurst told Keen, "You are very much disappointed with the outcome of our efforts in Alberta," but maintained, "we cannot look into the future, and see the consequences of our actions, but blindly grope our way."[8]

In January 1929, Halsall reaffirmed that the policy of the new wholesale was "to deal with the UFA and to this end it is desirable to work in conjunction with the [UFA] marketing committee."[9] In April the executive met with representatives of the UFA and the Wheat Pool "for the purpose of devising ways and means whereby the Co-op Wholesale may serve efficiently the UFA locals." At that meeting the UFA representatives requested copies of all correspondence between the wholesale and UFA locals, and suggested UFA representatives be invited to all Alberta Co-op Wholesale meetings. Clearly, the UFA did not intend to stay at arm's length from the wholesale. As an immediate measure to promote "the rapid development of Consumers' Co-operatives," and especially to help locals not yet ready to incorporate as co-ops, those present resolved to incorporate a "Northern Alberta Co-operative Association" in Edmonton to act as a wholesaler. Although ACWA representatives were in the majority at this meeting and on the board of the new association, they deferred to H. E. G. H. Scholefield and A. F. Aitken, two of the three UFA representatives, and agreed that these men be the president and vice-president, respectively, of the new wholesale.[10]

The co-op wholesale was not united about the course it was following. At a meeting of managers at the Corona Hotel in Edmonton on 13 May 1929, Moan announced that "the executive of the C[o-operative] W[holesale] S[ociety] and the UFA are to meet the Government on Saturday the 18th to talk over the matter of finance for the consumers' movement." Halsall, the president, explicitly disagreed with what his manager had just announced. He "strongly protested the idea of any governmental assistance . . . expressing his opinion that if the UFA wish to have retail stores, they themselves ought to furnish the capital." The majority either followed Moan, or were, perhaps, intimidated by the UFA's demands and enticed by the government's promises. The best that Halsall and Swindlehurst could manage was a motion to invite George Keen to speak to Alberta co-operators about the principles of co-operation.[11]

Moan, in his manager's report to the Alberta Co-op Wholesale annual meeting at Olds Agricultural School on 27–28 June 1929, stated that while ACWA "started out to supply the needs of our stores," it was now thought that it should go after the orders of the UFA locals. "My time has been spent almost wholly on this work," he told the delegates.

> Our problem at the present time is the financial question, as we have not the money to put in large stocks. . . . it is up to you to say if we shall ask the Government for assistance. I suggest that we ask them for $20,000, this will be a very small sum for a Wholesale but it will get it started.

"The right method," he admitted, "is for each trading Association to incorporate and help with subscribing some capital," but too few were in a position to do so immediately. Moan did say the wholesale would have to concentrate on a few lines to start with, noting that to open as a comprehensive wholesale would "take $100,000 or more."[12]

Later in the meeting, however, Scholefield of the UFA "expressed at some length his disappointment at the slow progress being made." He went on to say that a meeting of the UFA board was to be held the next week, "and we shall have to give the reason why we cannot buy from the Co-operative Wholesale. There are other bodies in the province . . . from where our locals could get their supplies." Following the criticisms of the UFA representatives, a delegate "moved a vote of censure on the Wholesale Board and asked them to resign in a body," but the motion failed with no seconder. Halsall spoke against Scholefield, against rapid expansion, and against government subsidies, but the delegates were plainly swayed by Moan or intimidated by Scholefield's thinly veiled threat. The meeting voted to give service to UFA locals on the same terms as to actual co-ops, and to "explore every avenue to provide the necessary capital" for the wholesale—authorizing Moan to talk to the government.[13]

Although Halsall was re-elected president at the first meeting of the new board, he had been defeated on the key decisions that led to the wholesale concentrating its services on UFA locals instead of on co-operative associations. He did, at least, carry the day in a series of motions promoting co-operative education, and instructing locals to sell at more than the wholesale price in order to preserve some margin and some security.[14]

Lumber and Liabilities

In the fall of 1929, in a series of meetings held at the legislative buildings in Edmonton in conjunction with discussions with UFA and government representatives, the ACWA board made some fateful decisions about expansion. At the January 1930 annual meeting they reported a $15,000 bank loan, the acquisition of stocks of groceries and dry goods and a warehouse to contain them, and the opening of a branch in Calgary, about which they commented: "This action was taken because of representation from the UFA executive that these locals in the South were requesting that service be given." They also reported that ACWA had contracted with the lumber firm of Pettepher and Pederson for two million feet of lumber on a cost-plus basis "and have the option of buying the entire output of their mills on the same basis, and by reason of this contract the Wholesale is in a position to supply lumber to their members at wholesale prices." The wholesale was expanding rapidly to meet the role required of it by the UFA, the need immediately to serve UFA locals and farmers with goods on a province-wide basis. At the meeting, Halsall resigned, and virtually dropped out of the affairs of the wholesale for the next four years.[15]

The UFA continued to press the co-op wholesale to consider changes to its structure and operations that would permit it to expand faster and meet the UFA's needs. At the board meeting on 11 March, Aitken moved that the board "survey the whole construction of the Consumers' Co-operative movement." While this implied planning and co-ordination, the next day he reported to a meeting of co-op directors and managers that an Oil Pool had just been incorporated. The creation of a separate UFA-sponsored central oil organization ensured that the Alberta Co-op Wholesale would be shut out of the lucrative oil trade.[16]

In April and May 1930 the wholesale already appeared to be in trouble. Circulars to members were cut back, cheaper premises were inspected at the Farmers' Supply on the south side of Edmonton, and problems were encountered trying to move the lumber for which the wholesale had contracted. The bank refused to honour the wholesale's notes to Pettepher and Pederson "until orders were received, and the lumber began to move." By June matters were getting tense; ACWA had committed itself to sell or pay for all two million feet of lumber by 30 November, and with spring building season over, too little had moved.[17]

Over the summer, ACWA abandoned its warehousing and mail-order activities, turning these over to the Farmers' Supply so that Moan could "devote as much time as possible to the sale of lumber." In spite of this, on 15 October Moan reported that only half a million feet of lumber had been sold. Unless one and a half million feet could to be sold by 30 November, ACWA would have to come up with the cash to pay for it. ACWA plainly did not have the cash, so a motion was made to approach the government again "in regard to giving a guarantee to the bank until such time as the lumber can be disposed of." On 9 December the premier himself met with the board and "talked over the general situation in the Co-operative movement." The wholesale had failed to meet its obligation to the lumber company and negotiations were under way.[18]

The ACWA financial statement for the year ended 31 December 1930 revealed a company that should have been ordered to cease trading. Assets were $58,620 but liabilities exceeded this by $9,739. Some $33,000 of the assets, moreover, consisted of lumber stocks that could not be sold, whereas the $33,000 debt to Pettepher Pederson and Company was already a month past due. Even aside from lumber, the wholesale was running a general operating deficit of $3,513.

The 1931 directors' report began with the statement, "It must be admitted that the results are very disappointing. . . . Our membership must hold us severely to task for failure to accomplish even a fair measure of success." They noted that "in an effort to secure volume from the [UFA] Locals prices were cut to costs with very little success in securing volume."

> We have made mistakes in attempting too much with too little capital and especially in the case of lumber by obligating ourselves too heavily. . . . These policies which proved to be so unprofitable were carried out with the object of securing and controlling a provincial volume, and of rendering a service and a saving to the organized farmers.

They went on to urge amalgamation into "a Provincial Co-operative Association with centralized control and management" as a way out of their difficulties. It was, however, wishful thinking to suggest that the UFA would consider amalgamation with an organization as bankrupt as the ACWA now was.[19]

A special members' meeting on 26 February urged the premier of Alberta to bail the wholesale out. In a special statement Moan argued that the government should help the wholesale on the basis of "justice" and of "public welfare." Edgerton Co-op, meanwhile, forwarded the resolution that it was "not satisfied to have the UFA executive exempt from liability in regard to lumber contracted for." According to the minutes, "the attitude of the UFA executive in regard to setting up an opposing buying agency was discussed and condemned."[20]

At a special meeting between the wholesale and the UFA on 25 May, Premier Brownlee chided the UFA. "What I should like to have seen," he said, "was for the UFA to have taken into consideration [that] the C[o-operative] W[holesale] S[ociety] [was] already functioning, and it would have been better if they had met with the CWS executive to talk the matter over with them prior to going into the question of co-operative buying." If the UFA had not already committed itself to other suppliers, the premier would have suggested they "retire from the field, [and] give their support to the CWS in every way possible."[21] But the UFA was not now about to do so. In January 1932, J. R. Hanning, president of ACWA, reminded the UFA executive of what he saw as its responsibility for ACWA's predicament. Norman Priestley replied (according to the minutes) that "the UFA were definite in their decision that there was nothing further to be done, and that they would pursue the policy they had started with, and that [ACWA] could not be of any use to them at present."[22]

The lumber fiasco was not wrapped up until mid-1933, when the Royal Bank finally sold the lumber for $11,000, one-third of what the co-op wholesale had paid. The wholesale then argued that, since the bank had not given notice before selling ACWA's lumber, it must forego any further claim for the remaining $21,000 owed on the lumber account. This left unpaid only the original $15,000 bank loan. The annual meeting in 1934 heard that the Wheat Board Trust had agreed to liquidate the entire debt in return for ten cents on the dollar. The co-op's contribution consisted of $772 already paid by ACWA plus $728 advanced by the Killam Co-op. With the wholesale's most serious debts finally removed, the entire board of directors resigned. The manager resigned, and Swindlehurst quit as secretary. William Halsall now returned, as if from exile, to take both their positions and run the wholesale part-time out of his own co-op at Killam.

The wholesale was by no means in good shape. Financially it was in a shambles, still owing lesser amounts to other creditors and unable to pay them. Killam essentially subsidized it to keep it going. Directors charged their expenses to their own co-ops because the wholesale had no money to pay them. In 1935 Gaudin, the vice-president, tried to resign, and even resorted to nominating someone else for his own position, but to no avail. Every individual willing to serve was desperately needed. The only thing ACWA could carry on was education, and this it proceeded to do under Halsall's leadership. Halsall had not even been back as an officer of the wholesale for a single meeting when his characteristic ideas began to reappear in the motions in the minute book: hold a two-day co-operative school, bring in George Keen to address it, appoint an education committee. Within one year the wholesale found the resources to rejoin the CUC, and persuaded Alberta Wheat Pool to do the same. A provincial section of the CUC was organized for educational work. Radio and newspaper campaigns were undertaken to publicize consumer co-operation. Although ACWA was crippled, these activities laid the basis for future rebirth.[23]

One province was left, and one wholesale. In Saskatchewan co-operators might yet snatch success from a situation that appeared, initially, more ominous and threatening than either Manitoba's or Alberta's.

Conclusion and Questions

What lessons should be drawn from the demise of Alberta's first attempt to get a co-op wholesale up and running? Should we blame it on bad management? Or is the combination of centralization, over-expansion, and lack of education always a dangerous one for co-operatives, regardless of management? In other words, was the problem lack of business skill, or lack of co-operative understanding—or the absence of co-operation from farmers' organizations?

Perhaps what undid the Alberta wholesale was not incompetence in the usual sense, but an excessive desire to serve the organized farmers' movement, and a failure to follow an independent and autonomous path of co-operative development. The directors of that era meant well and were sincere, but followed the lead of others instead of following co-operative principles. The fact that the UFA itself had little regard for the kind of co-operative principles represented by the co-op stores and their wholesale, and the fact that the Depression caught the wholesale at the worst possible moment in its overly ambitious expansion program, ensured a complete failure. There was no possibility in Alberta even for the kind of emergency rescue that Popple and his board carried out in Manitoba. There, the wholesale had been badly hurt by the campaigns of its enemies and by an unwise business decision. In Alberta the wholesale was essentially killed, not by its enemies, but by its friends.

6

Saskatchewan Co-op
Wholesale Society, 1925–1931

Saskatchewan, which Keen had argued possessed the widest and deepest appreciation of co-operative principles of any province in Canada, was the first to start discussing the formation of a co-operative wholesale, and the last of the three prairie provinces actually to create one. The reason was that, as in Alberta, the organized farmers' movement got into the act. Unlike Alberta, however, in Saskatchewan the advocates of consumer co-operation did not follow the lead of the United Farmers, but instead played a tense political game of negotiation and compromise. The outcome was that the Saskatchewan wholesale both retained control of co-operative wholesaling of all types, preserving the independence of the consumer movement, *and* also secured the support of the United Farmers and their locals for its efforts.

Saskatchewan Grain Growers and Concepts of Co-operative Trading

In 1914 the SGGA set up a Trading Department to act as a purchasing agent for Grain Growers' locals. While initially there was some success, the department soon developed problems with credit sales and with seasonal and fluctuating demand. A large carryover of binder twine into 1919, caused when farmers cancelled their orders because crops were poor, contributed to a $45,000 loss when the price of twine fell. The Trading Department continued to run deficits to 1923, and had insufficient reserves to cover this kind of setback. This led to what the SGGA euphemistically referred to as an "impairment of capital"— in other words, the department had lost much of the money put into it. One writer has given over-extended credit, insufficient capital and reserves, disloyalty by locals, mismanagement, and insufficient attention to the Trading Department by officials in other branches of the SGGA as the reasons for the failure of the venture.[1]

The difficulties in which the SGGA Trading Department found itself by the early 1920s should have been proof of the superiority of co-operative ownership to ownership as a service department of a farmers' association. A co-op wholesale would not (according to co-operative principles) operate on a credit basis, would require capital contributions from every patron, would develop member loyalty through education, and would be scrutinized at every level of operations by its customers. To realize this, however, required a certain familiarity with the idea of a co-operative wholesale society on the British model, a federation of co-operatives to serve their own needs where the organizational responsibility was at the local level, not the central. It was a simple idea to create one warehouse to send orders out to all farmers. It was a more complicated idea to incorporate the locals, rather than the central, as co-operatives, and run each of them according to co-operative principles—more complicated but, according to the advocates of the idea, more successful. Saskatchewan had more than an average number of advocates of the co-operative idea, including Andy J. Allison of Young Co-op, Harry W. Ketcheson, the manager at Davidson, C. G. "Scotty" Davidson of Lloydminster, and Robert McKay of Melfort. From his first trip in 1923, when he stopped off in Saskatchewan on his way to the Alberta Co-op League meeting in Wetaskiwin, George Keen found a warm and enthusiastic reception from Saskatchewan co-operators. Keen also developed a close working relationship and friendship with W. Waldron, who took over in 1923 as Commissioner of Co-operation and Markets in the Saskatchewan Department of Agriculture.

Under the encouragement of Waldron and Keen, both having old-country co-operative experience, and with exceptional managers such as those mentioned above, Saskatchewan co-operatives began discussing the formation of a wholesale in the summer of 1925. At the government-sponsored Conference of Co-operative Associations in Regina on 29 July 1925, attended by Keen, a resolution was adopted "that a co-operative wholesale association be created." A provisional committee was elected, with Ketcheson as chairman and Waldron as secretary, to discuss the proposal with Keen and work out a detailed plan. The plan they developed was to raise capital by having co-operative associations subscribe shares, with the aim of eventually buying out the Trading Department of the SGGA. The debenture holders of the SGGA would be given debentures in the new wholesale, and would elect two-fifths of the board of directors until the co-ops had raised enough money to pay back their investments.[2]

Just as the co-ops were proposing to buy out the Trading Department, however, the SGGA began to take an interest in revitalizing and expanding it.[3] The SGGA convention in Saskatoon in January 1926 received a report of "a very successful year's operations in the Trading Department," and was told "steps have already been taken to increase the volume of business."[4] Waldron had thought a tentative arrangement had been reached with the SGGA to reorganize, separate, and possibly rename the Trading Department, but nothing had been done. No resolution to this effect had been introduced at the SGGA convention.[5] Instead, in May 1926 George Edwards of the SGGA sent out a circular in which he admitted that "the Trading Department went through a very difficult time following the War, with the result that there was some impairment of the capital subscribed." But he now maintained "there is no doubt that we have turned the corner . . . with the support of our Locals and members, the impairment of capital can be made up in a reasonable length of time. . . . undoubtedly the total impairment can be wiped out in a very few years if we receive the support of those who believe in co-operation." To accomplish this, a "supreme effort" and a "vigorous selling campaign" were needed. "Buy . . . through the organization which you yourselves have created," he told the organized farmers of the province.[6]

As in Alberta, the organized farmers were a potent political force who had now realized the potential of collective buying, but who appeared to have no patience for the long, laborious development of local co-operatives.

Co-operative Wholesaling—by the Farmers or by the Co-ops?

In February 1926 Waldron wrote that the SGGA was intent on "developing their Trading Department and proceed[ing] entirely on their own lines."[7] The issue was who would control the wholesale. At a meeting of co-operative store managers in Regina in July, Waldron reported that the SGGA insisted on "at the very least a large majority of the directors" in any reorganized wholesale.[8] Keen noted that "the intervention of the SGGA was not solicited by the associations," but had the effect "to defer indefinitely the establishment of what was in contemplation," namely, a true co-operative wholesale. The Trading Department he could not recognize "as being in any sense co-operative." "Underneath the whole thing," he told Waldron, "is a poverty of real Co-operative Spirit. I feel much discouraged."[9]

Waldron encouraged the co-operative association representatives to undertake a counter-campaign, especially as in the summer of 1926 the SGGA was in the throes of a merger to form the United Farmers of Canada, Saskatchewan Section. He wrote to Ketcheson, "it seems to me that, before the new farmers' organization definitely settles the policy of its trading department . . . three or four of those in authority should meet to talk things over" and come up with a plan to popularize collective buying "on a truly co-operative basis." One way that Ketcheson and Waldron both hoped to promote co-operation was by encouraging contacts with the British co-operative wholesales, and possibly even by requesting some assistance from them.[10] While Ketcheson was on a visit to England he arranged that his own Davidson co-op should act as distributor of Co-operative Wholesale Society products. This "Buy British" campaign backfired, however, when the SGGA heard of Ketcheson's effort and established its own contacts with the British co-ops, in order to sell the same goods by mail in competition with the retail co-ops. Ketcheson wrote to the manager of the Trading Department, Brown, protesting that the department was encroaching on an area the co-ops had developed only with "considerable expense and a good deal of effort."[11] Keen described the SGGA/UFC leaders as "interested only in institutional success" for their own organization.[12]

In August 1927 the UFC leaders developed a new burst of enthusiasm for centralized buying after they met with Aaron Sapiro, the American co-operative lawyer and consultant. Sapiro, better known for his advocacy of wheat pools, "stressed the necessity for centralized buying, and [a] standardized system of selling." He recommended the formation of a Saskatchewan Wholesale Cooperative Society with one million dollars in capital, the shares to be held not only by co-op stores but by incorporated farmers' trading units and by the UFC.[13]

In spite of efforts by Ketcheson, Keen, and Waldron, the issue of how to organize co-operative wholesaling in Saskatchewan was still in doubt at the start of 1928. Waldron reported on 9 February that "UFC members wish to do away with patronage dividends and sell goods at cost plus wages. They evidently wish to adopt the Pool idea as far as possible." He went on to suggest that the UFC was deliberately keeping him and the "experienced managers" of existing co-ops in the dark and taking control of co-operative development.[14] "They will also organize many new points. In this connection I may say that it is UFC members they desire." Waldron claimed to have evidence that there was a plan to buy up the shares of non-UFC members and exclude them from co-operative buying. "In some cases they make it so objectionable for a non-UFC shareholder that he leaves anyway. It is *not* Co-operation."[15] To both Waldron and Keen, these tendencies toward centralization and linkage to the UFC violated the principles of openness to all consumers and political neutrality. This in turn artificially restricted the potential volume of consumer buying, and linked the wholesale's fortunes to a single farmers' organization and a single head office, instead of the broad grass-roots base they envisaged. Then, as the UFC convention at the end of February approached, a report claimed that W. M. Thrasher, secretary of the UFC, had developed "an elaborate scheme" for a "co-operative chain of stores" across the West.[16]

The UFC convention in February-March clarified little, in Waldron's opinion, both because of a closed door policy that kept the deliberations secret—the contentious issue of compulsory pooling dominated the conference—and because of vague resolutions.[17] The 1928 UFC convention did decide to transfer the assets of the Trading Department to a "Co-operative Wholesale Society," and they supported this decision with rhetoric about how it would contribute to the formation of a "Co-operative Commonwealth." But the new society was not necessarily going to be co-operatively owned by autonomous retails; the proposal as it emerged was to have a board of directors composed two-thirds of representatives of the UFC and UFC debenture holders; co-operatives would have only three seats of nine. W. H. Beesley of Moose Jaw, representing the Trading Department, was the president of the new co-operative wholesale, and W. Laird of Handel, representing the UFC, was the vice-president. The co-operatives had only Ketcheson on the wholesale society executive, as the third, untitled member. This was a wholesale on the UFC's terms, which in 1926 had demanded "at the very least a large majority" on the board, and not on the co-ops' terms, for they had suggested only 40 percent representation for the organized farmers and the debenture holders together. Ketcheson told Keen that "co-operative representatives on the Board have decided to give it a fair

Delegates to the 1928 convention of the United Farmers of Canada, Saskatchewan Section, decided to separate the UFC's Trading Department, a farm supply business created in 1914, from their political and educational organization. This decision was a key step in a battle that lasted from 1925 to 1929 over whether consumer co-operatives or the central farmers' organization would control the co-operative farm supply business in Saskatchewan. The Trading Department was eventually taken over by the Saskatchewan Co-operative Wholesale Society and became the nucleus of Canada's largest co-operative wholesaling operation.

trial," even though the UFC's intentions were far from clear and the power lay solidly in its hands.[18]

The spring and summer of 1928 were characterized by anxiety and tension in the consumer co-operative movement in Saskatchewan. Waldron's efforts to promote co-operative principles had rewarded him with "an offensive reception" from the UFC, and put him in hot water with his superiors in the government—he was compelled to withdraw from the Co-operative Trading Associations conference. Keen was forced to tread on eggshells in regard to Saskatchewan, and seriously considered avoiding the province altogether on his western itinerary that summer, so as not to become embroiled in messy political controversy. "All this misunderstanding and confusion is giving me considerable embarrassment," he wrote. Ketcheson was under attack in his own co-operative, likely from UFC sympathizers opposed to his stand. The three chief promoters of a co-operatively owned co-operative wholesale, Waldron, Ketcheson, and Keen, were at least partially neutralized by politics while the question of the future direction in Saskatchewan hung in the balance.[19]

At the Lloydminster Congress of the Co-operative Union of Canada, agreement was reached for the first time among the co-op stores, the United Farmers, and the debenture holders in the Trading Department. At the first annual meeting half a year later, Ketcheson looked back to this congress as the decisive step in the process of settlement concerning the transfer of the Trading Department. Representatives of the English and Scottish co-operative wholesales were in attendance, along with CUC members, adding to the occasion.[20] But the struggle over the character and policy of the new wholesale was not quickly resolved.

The UFC's sponsorship and participation led to a rash of incorporations of co-operatives in the fall of 1928. Waldron and Keen worried that the UFC was encouraging incorporations that were too small, based on a single UFC lodge, and which had too little capital. Some, for example, authorized a total capital of only 100 one-dollar shares. "How can they hope to accomplish anything worthwhile on such an amount?" asked Waldron in despair. "What interest will be engendered to see that the association is successful if each individual's financial investment is only such an infinitesimal sum?" He also worried that few UFC lodge secretaries seemed to be organized enough to be managers of a business. On all of these points, Ketcheson, Davidson, and McKay lobbied to persuade the UFC representatives on the wholesale board that the judgment and experience of co-operators dictated a different approach. And they had some success. Frank Eliason, one of the representatives of the UFC, wrote to Waldron that the Saskatchewan wholesale had adopted an official policy of discouraging one-dollar shares, encouraging only one incorporation at each town or shipping point, and asking that locals consult the wholesale before applying for incorporation.[21]

In 1929 the wholesale, which had registered as a joint-stock company under the name of Saskatchewan Wholesale Society Limited, secured incorporation by act of the provincial legislature as Saskatchewan Co-operative Wholesale Society (SCWS). Coming up to the UFC convention in February of 1929, it remained a hybrid of representatives of the Trading Department, the UFC, and the co-ops.

It seems likely that the patience, persistence, and above all the business experience and knowledge of Ketcheson, McKay, and Davidson were paying off. They were having success in influencing the future of the wholesale, even with a minority of the votes. In addition, the UFC was embroiled in controversy over whether to enter politics, and appeared deeply divided between factions arising out of its two predecessors, the SGGA and the Farmers' Union. Undoubtedly these struggles distracted the UFC's attention from consumer co-operation. At a board meeting in early February, Ketcheson was chosen as manager of the new wholesale, which seems to be a tribute to the respect the co-op managers had earned.[22] The last straw, if it was needed, was the revelation two days later that the manager of the Trading Department, Alex Brown, had been arrested for embezzlement.

The Regina *Leader* reported on 11 February 1929, that the Trading Department manager had been arrested in Saskatoon for appropriating some $5,408, the proceeds of thirty-five carloads of coal, for his own use. Apparently Brown, the manager, had secretly controlled the Livingstone Coal Company, with which the Trading Department did business. Large shipments of coal had been delivered to the company, and the Trading Department had omitted to charge for them. The Livingstone company then sold the coal and Brown kept the proceeds.[23] This was a good scam for Brown while it lasted, but its discovery threw the trading efforts of the UFC into complete chaos. When the books were investigated, the situation was found to be disastrous: the auditors had permitted uncollectable accounts receivable to be carried on the books, thereby concealing the size of accumulated deficits. A chartered accountant hired by the UFC was unable to determine if accounts had been fraudulently made up, or if they had simply been so incompetently handled that no records were kept to prove delivery of goods, billing for goods, or receipt of payments for goods.[24]

The Trading Department had never been an impressive success. In 1928, assisted no doubt by its illicit giveaways of free coal to the Livingstone company, the department had run up another loss, this time of $16,804. When, on top of this, its manager was arrested for corruption, the Trading Department's credibility was reduced to nil. Under such circumstances the UFC directors' original idea of asking for $25,000 from the co-ops for the UFC's "goodwill" appeared a little ridiculous, and eventually, when the state of the accounts receivable was realized, the UFC had to write down its sale price of some $80,000 by about $20,000.

By contrast, Ketcheson, Davidson, and McKay radiated competence in that they were professional managers of very large and successful co-operatives. Once the society was incorporated, the Trading Department taken over, and Ketcheson installed as manager (in the last half of 1928), the scales began to tip toward firm control by the co-ops. The three-and-a-half year waiting game played by the Saskatchewan retail co-ops had ended in a victory. As if to clinch it, the new president of the UFC, George H. Williams, held Keen's approval for his "genuine co-operative interest and understanding."[25] The co-ops had not only won control of their own wholesale; perhaps even more importantly, they had earned the respect of the organized farmers and retained their support.

Saskatchewan Co-op Wholesale under Co-op Control

At the SCWS first annual meeting in April 1929, Andy Allison, C. G. Davidson, Robert McKay, and J. G. Mohl—the representatives of the province's strongest co-operatives—were all elected to the six-member board, with Allison subsequently chosen as president, Davidson as vice-president, and McKay as the third executive member. Ketcheson, of course, was manager. This was a decisive victory for the co-operative societies, and a sign that they had taken complete control of the wholesale, as they had hoped to do four years previously. Saskatchewan's new co-op wholesale immediately took out membership in the CUC and offered twice the membership dues required.

B. N. "Barney" Arnason, who started work in 1929 with the Co-operation and Markets Branch of the Saskatchewan agriculture department, vividly recalls the early leaders of SCWS. President Andy Allison was "a quiet, unassuming, courteous, friendly man, an efficient manager who maintained a close relationship with his members." In 1932 Allison asked the auditor for Young Co-op to adjust the depreciation and bad debt allowances in order to make sure the co-op showed a net loss for the year of five dollars. "He said with a smile that this . . . was intended as a lesson for [the members'] own good," says Arnason, to remind them that their co-op faced difficult times and needed their support.

All co-ops faced difficult times and needed member support, as Ketcheson quickly discovered in trying to manage SCWS. The negotiations over the absorption of the Trading Department proved complex, related to problems determining its exact accounts receivable and liabilities. The UFC, saddled with debts and political divisions, was not as great a help as Ketcheson had hoped for. "I have been continually worried over finances since I came," wrote Ketcheson. "I was assured the UFC would get behind the C.W.S. but with all the trouble and dissension in the Board the Bank is inclined to put the lid down." There was a serious lack of co-operative understanding and education among the UFC lodges who were interested in buying from the wholesale.[26] As if this was not enough, Ketcheson found himself facing competition from the UGG for the business of both co-ops and UFC locals. Serious friction resulted. The board of the Saskatchewan wholesale took a leading role in forcing the UGG to resign from the Co-operative Union of Canada at the Winnipeg congress in 1929.[27]

Ironically, Keen, the consistent and ardent advocate of consumer co-operative principles, disapproved of the attack on UGG. Used to accepting compromises and tolerant of those who were tolerant, Keen was grateful for the UGG's generous financial support of the CUC. But co-operators in Saskatchewan, who had to fight daily at that time for co-operative principles, and who engaged in direct competition with the UGG in the field, were not so tolerant.[28]

The Saskatchewan wholesale's first year of operations disappointed Ketcheson, but for the times they represented a considerable achievement. With twenty-nine members and $2,900 in capital, SCWS transacted $635,474 in sales in 1929, and managed to pay 6 percent on share capital and 1 percent on purchases. By March 1930 Ketcheson was able to report that the wholesale to that point had paid $40,000 to the UFC for its assets—two-thirds of the purchase price. In April he reported that the wholesale had developed a lucrative oil department which had alleviated the wholesale's cash-flow problems.[29]

Ketcheson, however, continued to be frustrated. He had problems with his staff, with a series of resignations and with difficulties in obtaining accurate monthly statements. He was also in trouble with his old co-op at Davidson, whose new manager, "Jock" Wilson, was one of the independent breed of local managers.[30] As early as the February 1930 board meeting there were expressions of dissatisfaction with Ketcheson's bookkeeping, monthly statements, credit policy, inventories, and general office supervision. Finally, after the February 1931 annual meeting, President Davidson "on behalf of the Board complained on the continued lack of organization and harmony in the organization." A motion was passed that "the Board has lost confidence in the Secretary-Manager," and Ketcheson resigned. Robert McKay was unanimously appointed to replace him.[31]

Ketcheson's "zeal" and "uninhibited drive," as his qualities were later described, had been essential to achieving the organization of the wholesale under the control of co-operators, but as the Depression deepened, other qualities were called for.[32] It is difficult to say precisely what caused Ketcheson's problems, but two points are clear. A board loaded with the expertise of successful co-op managers carefully scrutinized his performance, provided close instruction, and removed him unanimously when, after fair warning, matters did not improve. The board had both authority and expertise, and used them. Second, under McKay there was no evidence of similar dissatisfaction. The office, the books, and the monthly statements were evidently handled to the board's satisfaction, and McKay's economies and business sense carried the wholesale through the Depression.

Bob McKay, says Barney Arnason, was "a tall, rangy man, quiet, rather reserved, but with a fine sense of humor." As a manager he was "a cautious individual," which was to prove an asset. "He had a keen mind, good business sense, and held his own in negotiations" with suppliers, adds Arnason.

Following Andy Allison, C. G. Davidson was president of SCWS through most of the Depression. Arnason calls "Scotty" Davidson "one of the most colourful characters . . . in the co-operative movement," a man who was "immaculately dressed, polished in his manner." To some he appeared "caustic," and "more of a businessman" than a co-operator, but as president of SCWS after Allison, his business experience and connections proved useful, helping SCWS to find suppliers and obtain goods on credit when funds were short.

The 1931 financial statement reveals a wholesale that did, indeed, require careful management and supervision. With $488,174 in sales, SCWS had over $60,000 in assets, but over $50,000 of these were in accounts receivable, deriving in part from credit business and also in part from old Trading Department notes that had so far proven uncollectable. The wholesale did have a surplus account, but had little in the way of working capital with which to carry its twine inventories. It relied instead on lines of credit from the bank, which had to be a risk with a commodity as unpredictable as twine. Finally, over $15,000 was still owed to the UFC for the original purchase of the Trading Department. The Saskatchewan wholesale was healthy enough, but could not afford risks. It lived on low-risk commission sales, carried the lowest possible inventories, and operated with minimal staff and office space. It remained successful because it lived within its means. Substantial growth would come later.

Conclusion and Questions

By 1931 all three prairie wholesales had faced considerable difficulties. Two of three were still functional, if reduced to a skeleton basis for the duration of the Depression. In every case important lessons had been learned, and the wholesales had survived their first changes in personnel. In Manitoba and Saskatchewan they had come into the hands of strong managers with deep commitments to co-operation, who would guide them through to eventual expansion.

Which was the more important: that capable managers had finally been found, or that they were managers with understanding of and commitment to co-operative principles?

Lessons had been learned about how fast to expand, the need to follow rather than lead the local retails in organizing demand, and the importance of co-operation among co-operatives. Perhaps the most important lesson of all concerned the need for co-operative education so that retails would be founded on sound principles, would support the wholesale, and would have, in turn, the support of their own members.

All three wholesales may have been, as Ketcheson feared, premature; but by the courage and sacrifice of a very few, and by patience as well as by desperate improvisation, they survived and began, slowly, to take root.

PART THREE: FOUNDATIONS, 1931–1938

Introduction to Part Three

In the 1910s and 1920s, the pioneers of consumer co-operation in western Canada had founded co-op stores in widely scattered locations, and buying clubs in somewhat more. These in turn had taken the first tentative steps to co-ordinate their purchases through co-operative wholesales—wholesales not yet advanced enough to have warehouses or stock significant inventories. Through these stores, buying clubs, and tiny wholesales, the rural population of western Canada was beginning to learn the principles and practices of co-operative buying. But only the surface had been scratched. Consumer co-operation was still a fragile thing; if anything had happened to blight the movement at this point— if there had been, for example, a repeat of the failures of 1920–28—consumer co-operation might well have declined and perished, becoming only a quaint and rustic piece of prairie folklore, remembered alongside barn-raising bees, threshing gangs, and village blacksmiths as part of the western farm heritage.

But what happened, in fact, was the Great Depression, which had far-reaching and fundamental effects upon western Canadian society. One might expect to find that the crushing poverty of this era, poverty that devastated whole towns, would have weakened and undermined community-based institutions, including consumer co-operatives. But the opposite was true. In the bleakest depths of the Depression, consumer co-operation at last sank its roots into the populace. The despair of the thirties about the state of the economy and of society, fed and nurtured co-operation as the spring rains nurture the soil.

*   *   *

7

Depression and Co-operation, 1931–1938

Stories about the devastating effects of the Great Depression of the 1930s, especially its effects on farming communities, are numerous and well known. The stock market crash of October 1929 ushered in an era of chaos in world markets, including high unemployment, low demand, falling prices, and tariff wars. In the prairies, in particular, environmental factors reinforced the crushing effects of the Depression: drought, heat, wind, dust, disease, and grasshoppers caused crop failures year after year. The combined result was a disastrous fall in farm incomes, with huge numbers of farmers driven off the land, and with whole sections of rural western Canada becoming depopulated. As population fell, towns decayed, and many died.

Economic Hardship and the Need for Consumer Co-operation

For obvious economic reasons, the initial effect of the Depression on co-operatives was negative. The prairie wheat pools, flagships of the western co-operative movement, collapsed and had to be bailed out by governments. They survived, shorn of their actual pooling function which was taken over by a federal wheat board, and cut their activities back to grain handling, farm policy, and some farm supply sales. The infant co-operative wholesales were hard-hit, with the Alberta association failing, and that in Manitoba coming close to a similar fate; Saskatchewan cut back and survived. Plans for co-operative wholesaling in British Columbia were put on hold for the better part of a decade. And individual consumer co-operatives suffered greatly, for farmers who had no money could not pay for purchases. Falling sales or rising credit trading (which, although illegal in some provinces, was widely practised) ruined many local co-ops. If economics were all there was to co-operatives, this would have been the end of the story. To a purely economic organization, hard times such as those experienced by farm communities in the 1930s would have meant disaster.

But co-operatives are not purely economic organizations; they are societies of people, flexible and responsive to their members and able to organize their customers. Because attitudes and beliefs, not just spending habits, affected co-

56

operatives, the crushing effect of the Great Depression rebounded to their advantage. A fundamental change in attitudes began slowly to strengthen consumer co-operation.

The Depression was a formative experience for many of those who became involved in co-operatives and led them in their expansion during the following decades. Morris Jevne, later involved with ACWA, FCL, and Interprovincial Co-operatives, says the "prime reason" he became involved was, "I was growing up during the Depression. I thought certainly there must be an alternative to the misery I saw around me." He recalls, "there was a need at that time," and to meet this need people began to consider "collective action versus competitive action."

The change from competitive to collective attitudes was not easy. It involved putting aside assumptions acquired during the booming 1920s. One writer, recalling how the Depression hit Mennonite communities in southern Manitoba, observed that in the 1920s farming "had become a business for profit rather than a way of life." People assumed that if they worked hard as individuals, prosperity would come to them. The Depression proved that assumption to be a lie. No matter how hard you were willing to work, there was suddenly no hope of quick success.

> This inability to "work their way out" came as a rude shock. For the crash had given lie to this as well as many other beliefs which had been held as irrefutable—that a man could by his own efforts support himself and his family; that only the shiftless and lazy were unable to find employment; that farming was a secure occupation. . . . in the space of a few years the people's faith in this traditional philosophy had been destroyed.
>
> There was now general agreement that a solution to the problems of the times was beyond the ability of the individual.

As a result, the new ways of the 1920s—hard work, individualism, one-crop specialization, and mechanization—were discredited, and the communities in question were forced back to pre-World War One traditions of co-operation in which farming was seen as a way of life rather than a profit-making business.[1]

Further efforts at producer co-operation, however, offered little hope. Farmers had organized their marketing co-operatives, but the Depression had cut them down. There was little that could be done if there were no good crops to sell, or if international markets kept prices low. Consumer co-operation, on the other hand, could be expanded and could make the most of what farmers did receive. In 1931 the Alberta Co-operative Wholesale Association board of directors observed, even as their own organization was failing, that in the long term "co-operative buying offers greater hope of securing economic independence for farmers than any other line of action."[2] The problem for co-operatives was to survive until the long term arrived, until consumers could rise above short-term, individualistic perspectives to grasp the need to make a commitment and work together.

Tomahawk and District Co-operative Association store, Alberta (probably late 1930s or early 1940s). The co-operative store movement, dealing in general consumer goods and food (as opposed to the bulk farm supply business), was particularly strong in Alberta and formed the basis for the Alberta Co-operative Wholesale Association.

In early 1932 Robert McKay told George Keen that even in Saskatchewan "the Consumers' movement can not be considered successful. The mortality rate amongst Co-operative Associations has been very high." McKay attributed the failures to excessive granting of credit and insufficient capitalization, observing that "the average Co-operative Association in its initial stages is usually sadly undercapitalized."[3] Both of these problems—too much credit and too little capital—had to do with the lack of money in western farm communities. They were also related to a lack of commitment and loyalty by the membership, who typically had been reluctant to put money into the co-ops even in good times, and eager to take it back out in patronage rebates. In the 1930s when money was scarcest, the need for loyalty, commitment, and re-investment began to be more clearly seen.

Survival Tactics for Co-operatives

In these circumstances, with retail co-operatives, like many kinds of businesses, closing their doors, it was a remarkable achievement simply to keep the co-operative wholesales open. By 1932, only the fourth year the prairie wholesales had been in operation and the third year of the Depression, the three wholesales had aggregate sales of $981,414. Virtually all of this was in the form of commissions earned by the wholesales acting as buying agents on behalf of their member co-operatives, grouping the orders of locals and then taking a portion of the savings made possible by ordering in larger quantities. The wholesales wisely did not, with the exception of Alberta, enter into actual warehousing and handling of their own goods. Yet even the first move of grouping purchases was an essential step on the road to developing an integrated system of co-operatives.

Avoiding the carrying of inventories and running on a shoestring, Walter Popple in Manitoba and Robert McKay in Saskatchewan weathered the worst of the Depression and kept the infant wholesales intact. The Saskatchewan Co-op Wholesale Society had been in the black from its first year of operation, and by 1932 Manitoba was as well. Their net surpluses of $7,336 and $6,954 in that year seem small by present standards, but to achieve any surplus at all was no easy matter.[4]

The lessons for local associations were similar to those for the wholesales. Associations that had to carry inventories, which is to say those that operated stores, suffered badly from the Depression, while bulk-commodity-purchasing associations did well. Not having to carry stocks of goods or pay much for rent or facilities, the bulk associations could start small and operate with next to nothing. Figures for Saskatchewan in 1930–31 show that co-operative stores experienced a sharp decline in sales, while carlot buying associations largely maintained or increased their sales. The difference was most pronounced in the southern part of Saskatchewan, where the Depression hit hardest. From one year to the next, the sales of the twelve store associations in that region fell from $668,916 to $285,061, while the sales of fifty-odd carlot associations increased from $223,350 to $367,974, surpassing the total sales of the co-op stores.[5] The Depression therefore represented a setback in the development of actual co-operative stores, and shifted the consumer movement in the short term decisively toward relatively informal local buying clubs. Under difficult economic conditions, these required less capital and proved to be easier vehicles for mobilizing community buying power.

A 1938 study classified 61.3 percent of all Saskatchewan co-ops as either petroleum or heating-fuel (in other words, coal and wood) co-operatives. While consumer co-operatives had only 7.6 percent of the total retail volume of the commodities they handled at the points they served, in petroleum products, twine, coal, and wood they were estimated to command more than 20 percent of their local markets. Specialization and minimization of capital requirements were the policies that brought most co-operative associations through the Depression.[6]

Co-ordination and Co-operative Development: the Role of the Wholesales

Although these policies ensured the survival of the co-ops, they also created a problem for the wholesales; a co-operative movement cut back to the bare bones did not have enough volume to make wholesaling profitable. If the wholesales were to work, and return to the member associations the savings they needed to keep going, more volume was essential, and furthermore, new and existing co-ops had to be kept viable. It was out of necessity that the co-op wholesales became involved, during the Depression, in financing, auditing, managing, and even creating local co-operative societies. The creation of chains of centrally owned stores had been discussed by the farmers' organizations in the late 1920s, but had been rejected—in part because of the vigorous opposition of committed co-operators who believed it violated basic principles of co-operation, and also because, in practice, it did not work.

The alternative approach, if one wanted to be systematic about co-operative development and co-ordination, was the contract approach. Like the chain-store idea, this, too, was pursued furthest in Alberta. In 1930 the manager of the Alberta wholesale reported that six co-ops had agreed to "go on a contract basis with the Wholesale and pledge their entire volume of business" in all products the Alberta Co-op Wholesale Association could handle. By surrendering their autonomy in purchasing to the wholesale, locals could achieve greater savings on their orders and allow the wholesale to build up its volume and also the capital required for further development. This attempt did not save the Alberta wholesale from the difficulties it was already in. But in 1938 the contract approach, the "Alberta method" as other co-operators called it, did put the reorganized wholesale on its feet again. A. H. Christensen, supervisor of co-operative activities for the provincial government, explained that under the purchasing plan the wholesale "puts at your disposal expert knowledge in buying and selling" for the price of "one-half of one percent on your Purchases." The plan was tied to building up investment in ACWA and was intended to give the wholesale the working capital needed to provide new services. It played a major role in the revitalization and success of the Alberta wholesale.[7]

The wholesales were also driven to take over some retails directly in order to save them from going out of business. This, too, was motivated by the concern to ensure that the wholesale had sufficient volume to function effectively. The Manitoba wholesale, for example, was compelled to step in and take over the operations of the Glenboro and Birtle associations in the mid-1930s. These two associations had been among MCW's strongest supporters, and it could not afford to let them go out of business. Accordingly, they were bought out by the wholesale and, since it proved difficult to reorganize them as co-ops, they were run for a number of years as direct "sales agencies" of the wholesale. By 1936 the wholesale had invested over $7,000 in them, and was still running losses on both totalling nearly $350 that year. This represented nearly 17 percent of the wholesale's total assets invested in two money-losing co-ops. It was undoubtedly painful to invest money in the midst of the Depression, only to make further losses, and particularly when the wholesale was so tiny and had so little to work with in the first place. But the added volume was necessary to enable the wholesale to make money on its other operations—and it preserved a co-operative presence in the two locations against the day when good times returned.[8]

Of all the provinces, Saskatchewan had the strongest central involvement in the creation and supervision of local co-operative associations, both in the

1930s and later. This began in 1932, when, as manager McKay described it, the Saskatchewan Co-op Wholesale Society became concerned with "the unsatisfactory manner in which twine had been distributed through UFC Lodges in the past." Many of the lodges were "losing interest," an expression of the declining vitality and poor finances of the UFC during the Depression. Accordingly, McKay tried "an experiment" in 1932, distributing twine through Pool elevator agents. "This method worked so satisfactorily that negotiations were entered into with a view to making this method general." The result was the affiliate plan developed in 1933–34.[9]

The affiliate plan was essentially an effort to mobilize sales in bulk commodities, thereby giving Saskatchewan Co-op Wholesale Association a big boost in volume and viability. The idea of the plan was to have the central co-operatives and farm organizations step in where interested co-operators were too few, were not well enough organized, or had insufficient capital to create their own association. The wholesale paid for any necessary facilities, consulted with local customers as an advisory board, and conducted the management and especially the accounting for the affiliate local. Usually a United Farmers or Wheat Pool group served as the nucleus for such affiliates; very often a Pool fieldman did the organizing and a Pool elevator agent acted as secretary. Over time, savings credited to the affiliate were to be retained to build up share capital, until the affiliate could be organized as a co-op and own its own facilities. The approach worried George Keen, who feared that it might "degenerate into direct sale through local agents by the Wholesale to individual farmers, or unincorporated groups, similar to the defunct Trading Department of the SGGA." If this was the result, there would be no comprehensive local societies with their own democracy, education, and autonomy, but only another version of the chain-store idea, controlled by remote central institutions.[10]

Government regulations spurred the development of the affiliate plan. When pressure from retail merchants led the federal government to require coal vendors to have permanent sheds, this put an end to the old carlot coal orders where local farmers shovelled coal out of the rail car into their wagons. Sheds were now needed, and where local groups could not erect them, the wholesale did, and permitted the local to pay for them gradually out of patronage rebates.

The affiliate system was definitely good for the wholesale's business, providing it with volume and markets. It is not quite so clear how good it was for co-operative development, but some affiliates did go on to become autonomous co-ops. The Saskatchewan commissioner of co-operatives, B. N. Arnason, reported in June 1935 that thirty-six new co-operative trading associations had been registered in the previous twelve months. Arnason went on to observe that "the majority of the trading associations were incorporated as a result of the arrangement between the Saskatchewan Co-operative Wholesale Society and wheat pool committees at the various points."[11] More than fifty years later, Arnason thinks back to the affiliate plan and calls it "perhaps the greatest contribution that Bob [McKay] made" to the co-operative movement.

The real test, however, was not only whether co-ops were incorporated, but whether they became viable and grew. In 1945 it was calculated that 53 co-operative associations that had previously been bulk-commodity affiliates now operated general stores, out of over 300 co-operative associations that were members of the Saskatchewan wholesale at that time. This was an important addition to the co-operative movement. But it was also observed that "too many of the affiliates appear to be simply marking time. . . . there is a grave danger, unless something is done, of local interest waning to the point where it will be uneconomical to continue operating." The directors argued further that "centralization has been carried too far and . . . a gradual process of decentralization . . . may be in the best interests of both the locals and the federation."[12]

The affiliate plan, by providing audit and other services to affiliated bulk associations, was also meant to make local management more reliable. The low level of development of the consumer movement meant that managers played an absolutely fundamental role in co-operatives of that era. In 1932 Thomas Swindlehurst, secretary of the Alberta wholesale, acknowledged that "management in the co-operative movement of our Western Provinces means far more than we sometimes realize." He explained that managers were left with the key role because of the deficiency, at the beginning of the 1930s, of education among directors and members:

> We are helping to build a foundation of the greatest movement of the future. Our directors are mostly elected from members that have made very little study of consumer co-operation. The few that have are giving most of their time and energy to fostering the producers' side, and we find it very difficult to get them interested in any form of educational activities. Therefore . . . it is up to us to foster some form of education among ourselves.[13]

Under these circumstances the co-ops that survived were those that had honest, scrupulous, and competent managers. There was no controlling and knowledgeable membership or directorate to ensure that every co-operative had such a manager; those who did not were at the mercy of whomever they picked, and if they chose badly under the difficult conditions of the Depression, they rarely got a second chance.

Co-operation and Loyalty among Co-operatives

At the end of 1930 the manager of the Alberta Co-op Wholesale Association commented on the refusal of the Alberta Wheat Pool to join the Co-operative Union of Canada, which is to say, to support an organization dedicated mainly to promoting consumer co-operatives. Amos Moan of ACWA attributed the Alberta Pool's refusal to "a swelled head." Moan gave almost an impression of satisfaction that the once-mighty pools had over-estimated themselves and been brought low by the Depression. Everyone now had to admit, he wrote, that "purchasing could not be neglected" if farmers were to be helped.[14]

Fortunately, in Saskatchewan especially, any such acrimony disappeared during the Depression. By 1932 the Pool and the co-op wholesale in Saskatchewan were working closely together in a contractual partnership. Pool fieldmen carried out general co-operative education and helped organize many new co-ops, with the wholesale contributing to the Pool field-staff budget. In addition, the Pool's elevator agents assisted with the Saskatchewan Co-op Wholesale Society's affiliate plan, as already described above. The help of the Pools, as well as of other farm organizations and co-operatives, meant that in many communities the development of consumer co-ops "piggybacked" on established rural organizations.

This systematic approach to co-operative development was mainly a Saskatchewan phenomenon, for in that province both the Pool and the government provided solid assistance. In 1936 Popple of Manitoba reported "considerable increase in business through Co-operative Elevator Associations throughout the Province." He went on to claim that "possibilities for the Wholesale increasing its volume through this channel cannot be overestimated." However, the co-operation between the Pool and the co-op wholesale seems to have been less or later than in Saskatchewan.[15] In Alberta matters were much worse. Although William Halsall reported in early 1935 that the Alberta Pool seemed to favour a Saskatchewan-type arrangement, he was afraid that the wholesale's bad relationship with the UFA would undermine systematic country distribution. By April any opportunity had passed. Halsall reported that "the UFA, UGG and the Wheat Pool have recently joined forces and are distributing bulk commodities wherever there is a UGG or a Wheat Pool elevator. The UGG are going so far as to handle these commodities where there is already a Co-operative Store." The producers' organizations were distributing farm commodities, and consumer co-ops would not be systematically promoted at their elevator points.[16]

Still, even in Alberta the wholesale was able to demonstrate some success by 1937. Based on the loyalty of just seven co-operatives that bought 87 percent of the wholesale's volume, ACWA finally achieved a surplus of $644.45. Ponoka and Killam co-ops together accounted for 42 percent of the volume. Their loyalty was rewarded. With its lumber inventory and debt problems eliminated by 1934, with sales and surpluses increasing by 1936, and with a new manager in Dave Smeaton and a reorganization in 1938, Alberta was at last back on its feet.[17]

Manitoba, too, had improved its position. From a 1.3 percent net saving in 1934, to 2.6 percent in 1935, to 4.6 percent in 1936, it exhibited a steady gain. It earned more than $25,000 in commissions in 1936, over 90 percent of this on the three product categories of petroleum, twine, and coal and wood fuel.[18] Popple stated in 1937 that it was "very gratifying to be able to present to our

Fisher Branch, Manitoba, Ukrainian Farmers' Co-operative annual meeting (1940). Consumer co-operatives are community institutions that embody some sort of common bond. In western Canada this bond was frequently strongest where the residents of a community shared a common culture or ethnic background. Besides Ukrainian co-operatives there were also, among others, co-operatives with distinctively Finnish, Norwegian, and Mennonite memberships. (Provincial Archives of Manitoba N5590)

delegates at each Annual Meeting a Financial Statement showing considerable improvement over the previous years, despite the difficult economic conditions." Keen praised the Manitoba organization, saying he appreciated "the great services you have rendered to the Movement by your devotion, well-directed energy and sound practical judgment in overcoming the effect of initial errors of policy and placing the Society on a strong footing." Keen identified the loyalty of co-ops to their wholesale as the key ingredient of the success in Manitoba.[19]

And a great development had taken place in British Columbia. While a bitter internal struggle in Vancouver contributed to the decline of the urban consumer movement in the 1930s, farmers' and fishermen's co-ops, organized and developed during the Depression, provided the backbone of new strength.[20] In 1939 a Conference of B.C. Co-operatives on Collective Buying was convened, attracting fourteen societies with 2,170 members and over one million dollars in combined volume. The largest volume of sales, by far, was in feed (over half the total), reflecting the strong development of the co-operative movement in the Fraser Valley and other agricultural areas. Groceries and hardware were next, indicating a relatively well-developed store movement. The conference determined to establish a Co-operative Wholesale Society of B.C., which came into existence the same year. In its initial stages it was guided by the examples, experience, and advice of the earlier prairie societies.[21]

Conclusion and Questions

Of the lessons that might be drawn from the experience of co-operatives during the Depression, three, perhaps, are of special interest. The first is the importance of co-operative education in providing an impetus for the movement. Why was it during the Depression, when co-ops had the least to work with, that the significance of education began finally to be widely understood? Is co-operative education more important during bad times than in periods of prosperity?

Second, it is worthwhile to observe that co-operatives survived the worst economic crisis western Canada has ever experienced by cutting back to what they could do best, cheapest, and in the largest quantities. They were forced to put aside their dreams of fully stocked stores and capital-intensive developments, and work with simple carlot buying associations and commission-agent wholesales. Are there lessons in this for co-operative development today? Should the cities, for example, be further penetrated, not by big multi-purpose co-ops with their own facilities, but by small buying clubs, specialized co-ops, and intensive educational campaigns?

Third, what is to be learned from the co-operation among co-operatives that was so important to the consumer co-ops in the 1930s? Is this, too, something that happens only when times are bad? Perhaps there are other kinds of co-ops today that merit help, in the same way that consumer co-ops were helped by the older marketing co-ops during the Depression.

8

Consumers' Co-operative Refineries Limited, 1934

The most amazing and possibly the most important episode in the history of the consumer co-operative movement in western Canada was the development of Consumers' Co-operative Refineries Limited (CCRL) at Regina. The story is amazing because, under the desperate circumstances of the Depression, a small group of farmers with no experience and little money entered the oil business, ultimately taking on the giants of the private oil trade. It is important because petroleum became the dynamo of the Co-operative Retailing System, the lucrative commodity that powered the system's expansion and sustained it down to the present day. Tony Dummer, who started in the drum yard of the refinery in 1940 and went on to become a senior manager of Federated Co-operatives Limited, says that too few people recognize that "without the Co-op Refinery . . . we would not have the type of co-op movement we have today in western Canada. It provided the cash flow that made a lot of things possible." "If it wasn't for the Refinery," he emphasized, with a touch (but perhaps only a touch) of exaggeration, "we wouldn't have anything."

Petroleum and the Need for Co-operative Action

Petroleum has shaped the history of consumer co-operation in the West. Alberta's wholesale, which, due to competition from the United Farmers, handled no oil, failed in the 1930s and developed weakly thereafter, its co-op stores struggling with low-margin goods like groceries and dry goods. For both Alberta and B.C., their eventual amalgamations with FCL were (as one former division manager commented) "marriages of necessity. Federated couldn't let them fold." But the Saskatchewan and Manitoba wholesales, which had oil, progressed powerfully and dramatically. When they merged it was a dovetailing of two similar operations based on similar commodities. They added together their sales volumes in the goods they both handled, and multiplied the savings through the increased efficiencies of larger-scale operations.

Oil also affected the character of the local co-ops. Twine, coal, and so forth could be handled without a store, with little more than a shack, in fact, in which orders could be arranged, and a trackside frontage where members could unload the cars when they arrived. In Saskatchewan, at least, the Wheat Pool Elevator agent often made the shack unnecessary, and ran the co-op out of the elevator. But oil required expensive tanks, and expensive tanks meant locals had to raise capital; these developments necessitated a more formalized structure with larger shares and a permanent facility that began to serve as the focal point of the co-op. The handling of petroleum products therefore contributed to the growth of a more formalized consumer co-operative movement.

Petroleum products required this kind of concentrated effort because of farmers' needs during a period of depressed farm prices, increasing mechanization, and increasing concentration of the oil industry. The fall in farm prices from 1929 to 1931 put a squeeze on farmers to reduce their input costs, on the heels of the mechanization that had occurred in the 1920s. One history of the refinery noted that "petroleum . . . was the principal item of expenditure to the tractor farmer;" the price of tractor fuels, therefore, became a crucial concern and led to the establishment of oil co-ops. Most notable, for the history of CCRL, was a concentration of about ten such co-op associations in the area around Regina. In 1931 they could buy wholesale supplies easily from four companies: Imperial Oil in Regina; Northwest Stellarene in Coutts, Alberta; Maple Leaf Petroleum, also in Coutts, Alberta; and Sterling Oil Refineries in Moose Jaw. But between 1931 and 1934 Imperial Oil bought out Maple Leaf, and both of the other two were purchased by the British American Oil Company. Instead of four regional suppliers, there were now only two large multinationals. "Within three months" of the last takeover, claimed co-operators, "the wholesale price of gasoline was increased." This meant retail margins declined, and independent dealers were caught in the squeeze. They could not turn to American sources because duties on imported gasoline, raised to 3.7¢ per gallon in 1933, made this uneconomical. Co-ops (and all independent retailers) were now prisoners of an oligopoly.[1]

Origins of the Co-operative Refinery

The refinery that accomplished so much was started with only "a hope and a prayer," as one manager puts it. It must have appeared at the time as a desperation measure. The Saskatchewan wholesale was at that time in difficult circumstances, according to an official history of CCRL from the later 1930s, and was "not in a position financially to lend [its] aid to the building or promotion of a Refinery." Consequently "the organization was carried out apart from that body." In fact, even moral or personal support by SCWS leaders was conspicuously absent at first. Harry Fowler, a leading force behind CCRL and later president of FCL, wrote in 1936: "At the inception of our organization [CCRL], the Wholesale Society was not extremely friendly to the organizing of a refinery, conscientiously feeling that such an enterprise would not be successful."[2]

Canning CO-OP motor oil in the oil and grease warehouse at the Co-op Refinery (about 1940?). With the increasing mechanization of agriculture, oils and greases, along with petroleum fuels of many kinds, became important commodities for consumer co-operatives across western Canada.

It was with no support from established central institutions, and only as a result of the initiative of the grass roots and of local co-operatives in the Regina area, that CCRL came into being.

On 29 March 1934, twelve farmers met in the Sherwood Rural Municipality office on Cornwall Street in Regina. Representatives were present from eight rural consumer co-ops around Regina: Sherwood, Wilcox, Riceton, Sedley, Pense, Milestone, Grand Coulee, and Kronau. They met, according to the minutes, "To Discuss the Advisability of Building an Oil Refinery in or near Regina for the Purpose of Supplying Petroleum Products to Bona Fide Farmers in the District Adjacent to Regina." Their discussion revealed an intimate understanding of both co-operative share structures and the political process for lobbying the government, experience presumably gained from their prior involvement in the farm and co-operative movements. Harry Fowler distinguished himself by moving the first two motions, first, that the meeting "bring all the pressure it could bear on the Provincial Government for the passing of a gasoline bill in the interest of, and for the protection of the farmers." Parallel to this political effort to solve their problems, the farmers also resolved to create a refinery association, and Fowler moved to set the par value of the shares at $25, "and that each subscriber be urged to purchase . . . [o]ne share of stock for each quarter section of land operated, with a limit of not more than eight shares to any *one* subscriber." This, they likely hoped, would be both affordable in difficult times, and enough to pay for a very expensive undertaking.[3]

The minutes of this early meeting reveal that the farmers who founded the refinery, though novices in the oil business, were not novices in co-operatives or in politics. They had experience and education and understood how to organize people for a goal. In subsequent weeks they incorporated their new company and progressed with their organizing activities. Public meetings were held in ten towns in the region, jointly organized by the provisional refinery board and the local co-ops.[4] These seem to have raised local response. It was later reported that 150 people attended one of these meetings at Riceton, and no dissenting vote was cast with respect to the refinery proposal.[5]

In July the form and nature of the refinery were discussed, and once again Harry Fowler made himself known as an initiator and an instigator, including an instigator of controversy. Fowler's concern was evidently to strengthen the refinery by tying it formally to the local co-ops, creating an integrated co-operative structure with firm local roots, rather than just an independent central refinery. For this reason he proposed an "Organization Advisory Committee" for the refinery, consisting of representatives of the local retail associations. According to the minutes he also "presented a memorandum indicating that, in his opinion, the stock should ultimately be held by the Local Co-operatives themselves." Fowler wanted immediately to make the refinery what is now sometimes called a second-tier co-operative, a co-op owned by local co-ops rather than by individuals, and so tied into the larger co-operative movement. The consensus of the meeting was that Fowler's idea "was not practicable at the present time . . . it was agreed that there was merit in Mr. Fowler's suggestion and it might be looked upon as an ideal to be aimed at in the future." This was not the first time that one of Fowler's ideas was rejected as ideal but not practicable. As in other cases, he did eventually get his way. In the summer of 1934, however, the need to raise a lot of capital was urgent, and as co-operatives could not provide it, there seemed to be no alternative to continuing to sell shares to individuals. Fowler, not one to accept this lightly, arranged that all the shares he sold in his Wilcox area be designated as purchased "in trust" by individuals on behalf of the Wilcox co-op.[6]

Then lengthy discussions began with respect to "cost, volume, etc. of various types of plants." The choices were a full-fledged cracking plant that could take heavier oil, or a smaller skimming plant that would do straight distillation of a lighter oil. A problem immediately arose. Even a small skimming plant producing 200–500 barrels a day was quoted as costing between $16,500 and $40,000, and so far the provisional board had only $697.50 in cash (less $559.21 in organizing expenses), and only $6,075 in shares subscribed. It must have appeared doubtful that a small group of farmers could afford to enter the oil business, but the board was adamant. On 9 August it unanimously declared that the minimum it would accept would be a 350-barrel-a-day skimming plant which could later form the nucleus of a cracking plant. They thought big, for their resources.[7]

Stock subscriptions were severely limited, however, by bad crops in southern Saskatchewan, and also by hail. Southern Saskatchewan was among the hardest-hit regions in the prairies. This was the era of the Bennett Buggy, when farmers who could not afford gasoline for their automobiles hitched them to their horses instead, and used them as wagons. It was not the easiest time for farmers to come up with share capital to purchase an oil refinery.

If anyone should ask how a large co-operative venture is organized, the lesson provided by CCRL would seem to be: meetings, meetings, meetings. After all the local and central meetings from March to October of 1934, the pace only quickened. Ten critical meetings were held in November and December, most of them lengthy and detailed, to determine what kind of plant to construct, how to pay for it, and where to locate it (both Regina and Moose Jaw made bids). In these deliberations the organizers had the help of some expert advice.

The refinery superintendent who advised the first board of directors was O. B. "Burt" Males, who had managed the Sterling Refinery at Moose Jaw but had resigned when it was bought out by British American. Males was of immense assistance in bringing inside technical knowledge of what was needed and how to get it. Fowler later wrote that "without a man of his honesty, integrity and technical skill, the Co-operative Refinery would never have gotten off the ground."[8] And many others have paid similar tribute to Males's skill as a manager and his knowledge of the petroleum industry. Fowler was a person who dreamed large and who could get people excited about his dreams. Males could watch out for the bottom line and take care of the practical requirements. The combination of the two of them was a classic example of the promoter and the pragmatist, the visionary with the ideas and the nuts-and-bolts expert—a combination that has produced success in many retail and wholesale co-operatives over the years.

On 31 December, after nine months of meetings, the refinery executive was finally ready to engage Males formally as superintendent.[9] The plans Males designed drew a bid of $56,000 from a local iron works, which, as Fowler recalled, "did not provide for an office or any frills or working capital."[10] The directors literally built as big as they could afford, with Males cutting down costs in ingenious ways: a boiler bought from a local brewery went into the refinery, and a thirty-six-inch-diameter smokestack became the refinery's fractionating tower.[11]

In the fall of 1934 the new directors had also chosen their officers. E. E. Frisk became president, and the only contested position was that of secretary-treasurer—a position won by Harry Fowler, the idealist, activist, talker, and organizer who had already made himself so evident in the early meetings. The board also asked Fowler to be the first manager. He recalled later, "I think perhaps they felt my experience in the bank and in private business was such that I would be reasonably satisfactory."[12]

It is more likely the board also chose Fowler for his character and talents, and not just for his experience, but it is true that his experience was varied.

Dorothy Fowler recalls that her husband "had a pretty tough time getting started in the world." With no education and a poor homestead, he came to Wilcox with the Bank of Nova Scotia. He resigned from that job, possibly because a bad knee interfered with standing at the bank desks, possibly just because (as he himself later put it) he "could not see that banking was the kind of life that I would like." He entered a partnership to operate local grain elevators on a lease-purchase arrangement; that came to an end in an elevator fire in 1928. Thereafter, Fowler and his partner George Munro (later manager of Sherwood Co-op) went into "every business you could think of"—insurance, oil, machinery—"they sold everything you could think of in a little town in the Thirties," says Dorothy Fowler. A house fire in 1930 wiped out that business, and was also a personal tragedy as the Fowlers lost two children—this was Harry's second tragedy; he lost his first wife in childbirth. The first thirty-five years of his life constituted a classic, tragic hard-luck story. But Harry Fowler was also the kind of person who, in romantic hard-luck stories, overcomes all obstacles. In 1931 he gave up on profit business, and took a position as secretary-manager of Wilcox Co-op. That got him involved in the movement.[13]

Fowler became a grand figure in the co-operative movement because of his ability to think large, to lead by word and example, to communicate with ordinary people. He was a self-educated man who "owned more books than anyone in town" and who gave talks on evolution in the United Church basement. He was a vigorous, energetic, and successful debater with little apparent fear of controversy—just the sort of person who came into his own in a democratic social movement, which is what consumer co-operatives were becoming in the 1930s. Colleagues associated Fowler with "long-range vision," remembered him as "an eloquent and forceful speaker," and were struck by his "deep philosophy."[14] Or as an FCL manager recalls, he was "the guy with the crazy ideas." The same person added that Fowler was "*the* powerhouse of the co-operative movement. He was instrumental in everything with the name co-operative on it." Perhaps the most perceptive tribute to Fowler came from Premier T. C. Douglas of Saskatchewan:

> Who else would have the gall to even think a group of farmers could take on the giants of the oil industry and win! . . . Little wonder that many of his contemporaries, particularly those with responsibility for the total co-operative system were nervous about the visionary in their midst. . . . A visionary who was always coming up with difficult and often seemingly impossible goals to be achieved. . . . No one working with H.L. Fowler could ever rest comfortably upon his oars.

Another co-op organizer is quoted as saying, "Harry was never a good businessman. Thank Heavens he wasn't! If he had have been, there never would have been a Refinery."[15]

Consumers' Co-operative Refineries Limited in 1939, shown here four years after it started operations. To create this refinery took a massive financial and organizational effort on behalf of Regina-district farmers in the midst of the Depression. It went on to become a powerhouse for the Saskatchewan and later western Canadian co-operative wholesales, and a tremendous generator of savings for co-operative members.

The First Year

On 27 May 1935, just over fourteen months after the first organizational meeting, production began. Records indicate 6,095 gallons of crude were processed that day, and some 65,040 over the next three weeks as production reached the maximum the tiny refinery could handle. Indeed, the refinery filled all available tanks after the first week and Males, disgusted, had to shut it down temporarily for lack of storage capacity. In addition, working capital was desperately short. This was temporarily alleviated in June when an important agreement was reached with Saskatchewan Wheat Pool to have the refinery supply 180 Pool elevators with gasoline. This was not only badly needed sales volume; the Pool agreed to pre-pay $5,000, giving the refinery working capital in the meantime.[16]

A seven-day line of credit with the railway was frequently stretched, sometimes to three weeks, and directors resorted to what were later recalled as "unorthodox and slightly unethical" methods of delaying payments to creditors. The president, whose signature was required on company cheques, was mysteriously unavailable on several occasions. He lived out of town, explained refinery staff—and that kept the wolves from the door for an extra few days. Fowler called around the local co-ops with desperate pleas for money, requesting advance payment of their purchases so that the refinery could use the money in the meantime. On one occasion the refinery was in a serious predicament: it had no cash to take delivery of a tank car of crude oil. If it could process the crude, it would have the cash it needed; but without first having the cash, it could not obtain the crude. The story is told that one of the directors, S. J. "Sid"

Gough, went to the local railway agent and slapped the deed to his farm down on the agent's desk as security. The agent released the tank car, and no one knew until years later that Gough had put his farm on the line to get it.[17]

By this combination of financial juggling, emergency measures, hard work, and support by retail co-operatives, the refinery was kept running through its first season. By the end of 1935 it had twenty employees. The board voted to treat them with "fairly generous consideration"; in those days this meant that Superintendent Males got a monthly salary of $331.83; Secretary Fowler, $198.50; and eighteen workers, $60.00 to $123.80.[18] The workers were seasonal, for the refinery did not have markets for year-round production. But even operating below year-round capacity, the first year of production for CCRL was a magnificent success—as perhaps it had to be for the refinery to survive.

By the end of its first year—a year in which it operated for only six months—the refinery had made $253,011 in sales. By August 1936 farmers had subscribed $32,802 in shares (and, of course, had paid up considerably less than that amount), but the refinery had accumulated savings of $28,306—nearly an 86 percent return on share capital in a single year. The dividends declared were 6 percent on capital and nearly 10 percent on purchases—for example, 2 1/2¢ a gallon on gasoline, and 1 1/2¢ on tractor gas. This was an impressive performance in the first year of operations, and one that must have turned many farmers' heads.[19]

It certainly turned heads in the Saskatchewan Co-operative Wholesale Society. With the refinery a proven success, the two wholesales embarked on what was to be an immensely rewarding partnership. As Fowler put it, "since the first year's operation, Mr. McKay and his Board have changed their view point . . . and are co-operating with us to the fullest extent." On 17 January 1936, two SCWS directors attended a refinery board meeting and agreed that SCWS would act as a broker for refinery products for a brokerage fee of up to 1/2¢ per gallon, and would purchase and accumulate stock in CCRL the same as local retails did—setting aside 3¢ per gallon purchased in a share capital account.[20] While SCWS handled relatively little gasoline at first, within six months of this agreement it became by far the largest distributor of refinery kerosene, grease, and other secondary products. Over time it immensely aided the Co-op Refinery in developing a distribution network: Fowler pointed out in 1936 that of twenty-five new oil locals organized in the spring of 1936, "more than one-half . . . are under the auspices of the Wholesale Society."[21] Because of the refinery's commitment to working with local co-ops, and with the wholesale society, and to tying all of these together into an integrated network, handling each other's products, owning each other's shares, attending each other's meetings, the co-operative movement in Saskatchewan was immensely reinforced. One suspects the influence of Harry Fowler lay behind this consistent loyalty and support toward other co-operatives.

Price Wars, Crude Oil Supplies, and Expansion

Corresponding to farmers' sudden enthusiasm for co-operative oil was the sudden hostility of the oil giants. Before one year of operations had been completed, the board of the refinery was informed that "the major oil companies had inaugurated a price cut at many of the points being served by the Refinery, and that their price cut did not go beyond the confines of Refinery distribution." This was a regional price war apparently launched by CCRL's two multinational competitors in an attempt to regain their volume in the Regina area, and to reverse the runaway success of the co-op refinery. The challenge was serious. The price cuts were substantial enough in certain areas—as much as 5¢ per gallon according to Fowler—to eliminate the local co-op's margin on some major products.[22] The threat was that the local would suffer and would either lose money or be unable to pay a rebate. While the wholesale was not directly threatened, it needed the volume these locals represented, and it stood up for them, allowing a special dividend of 1 1/2¢ per gallon "to each local where evidence was produced that a price cut was being offered to their members by the major oil companies."[23]

Nor was the competition with the profit companies limited to market competition. Lobbying, government regulations, and import duties were also weapons by which the oil business and the Regina refinery engaged each other. Farmers had to look to politics to back up their economic self-help. The Co-op Refinery, like the oil co-ops that had preceded it in searching for oil supplies for

A Consumers' Co-operative Refineries truck takes a load of fuel out of the loading bays at the refinery for delivery to co-op members (1939 or 1940s). Serving, at first, mainly co-operative associations in the area around Regina, the refinery quickly expanded its distribution as farmers became eager to purchase petroleum products from their own refinery and to share in the savings it generated.

farmers, liked to look south of the border for cheap oil, rather than to work through the large Canadian oil companies. Just as lobbying by the oil companies had led to prohibitive duties on importation of American gasoline, frustrating the western oil co-ops and creating the circumstances that led to the creation of the refinery, so too, now that the refinery was producing, an additional duty was proposed on the American crude it used. An extra 1/2¢ duty proposed for imported crude was a serious threat to the new refinery, and Fowler enlisted the help of George Keen and the CUC to help fight the proposal in Ottawa.[24] Fowler also made a personal appeal to Prime Minister R. B. Bennett, which Fowler later claimed played a role in reducing tariffs on petroleum products in 1936.[25]

As the directors of the refinery began to realize both the potential of the business they had entered into, and the seriousness of the competition, not only in the marketplace but also in the halls of government, their thoughts turned more urgently to expansion. The skimming plant had only been in operation for a year (and not a twelve-month year), but with the threat to the supply of the kind of petroleum it needed, and with consideration of the greater profit margins involved in the processing of heavier crude, they decided in July 1936 "that the energies of the Association should be directed toward the building of a Cracking Plant," and to this end they called a special shareholders' meeting.[26] It did not prove possible to add a thermal cracking unit, however, until 1940.[27]

The dividends declared in 1936 were not, under the circumstances, as great as in 1935, but there was still one cent per gallon on gasoline and 5 percent on capital—rebates that were a graphic demonstration to farmers of the savings they could make by owning their own refinery.[28]

The history of the refinery thereafter was one of nearly continuous expansion. The new thermal cracking unit constructed in 1940 tripled the capacity of the refinery to fifteen hundred barrels per day, and full twelve-month operation began. In 1942 capacity was increased again to two thousand barrels per day, and sales topped $2 million, on which savings of nearly 12 percent were made. Concerned about secure crude oil supplies safe from the control of profit companies and from import regulations, the refinery began to invest in oil exploration in Saskatchewan.[29]

The refinery's massive growth in sales was paralleled by and contributed to the growth in the sales of the Saskatchewan Co-op Wholesale. The two became ever more closely integrated as the refinery distribution area grew to match, more or less, that of the wholesale. Many oil co-ops bought their oil through SCWS, and many established retail co-ops added oil as a commodity and began to sell CCRL products. The membership of the two organizations, except for the old individual shareholders in CCRL, became more and more congruent. Not surprisingly, amalgamation was discussed, and in 1944 it became a reality— but that is a story for a later chapter (Chapter 11).

Conclusion and Questions

The biggest question raised by the early history of Consumers' Co-operative Refineries is simply, could it be done again? The refinery, important though it was, came about only because individual consumers and local co-ops were prepared to take a risk and devote a lot of time to something that was by no means a sure deal. Could other co-operative enterprises or expansions come about in this way, or is the help of a large central co-op now necessary? At the time the refinery was created, existing co-ops would not help—they were too conservative and had their own interests to protect. Should an established co-operative take such a risk to develop a new enterprise? And if not, who will take it?

Perhaps only a few years after 1934, it would have taken millions, not tens of thousands, of dollars to break into the oil industry. With concentration of ownership increasing and technology becoming more elaborate, CCRL may have entered the industry at the last possible moment, given farmers' meagre resources.

And what of people like Harry Fowler?—how often can an organization find an individual who is both a visionary and persuasive enough, some of the time, to influence hard-headed managers? These factors suggest there will be few repeats of the dramatic events of 1934.

On the other hand, it may be (as many co-operative visionaries would argue) that a large enough, well-educated enough, democratic enough people's movement will always find some way to meet its needs and goals; if not by buying a refinery, then in some other way; if not by finding a Harry Fowler, then by finding some other individual with some other talent. The trends of mechanization and oil-industry concentration were pushing people to do something about petroleum, with or without a Harry Fowler. The refinery is an example of how things that are considered necessary, even if unlikely from a financial point of view, can be done if people are organized.

9

Origins of a Movement: Co-operative Education and Ideas, 1931–1939

The phrase "co-operative education," though it constitutes one of the six fundamental principles guiding all co-operatives, has no precise definition. Certainly in the 1930s, when the need for education of all types was desperate, co-operative education had a multitude of meanings, from training in accounting for staff members of retail co-operatives, to study groups on co-operative history and principles, to co-operative youth camps, to publicity aimed at convincing the general public of the merits of co-operation. At that time no distinctions among these functions were necessary, since all of these needs were equally urgent, and since, with the limited resources of the co-operative movement, such functions were frequently performed by the same individuals. These different types of educational programs had not yet acquired the specialization that characterizes them today.

For the 1930s, the best way of defining co-operative education is to say that it was the activities that made co-operatives into a popular movement. Deepening members' understanding of how co-operatives worked, helping directors and staff to perform their jobs more effectively, winning new support in more communities, drawing all co-operatives of all types together into a single cause: these were the activities that constituted "education." They were intended to overcome the individualism of members and the isolationism of individual co-operatives, and to link people and organizations together into one movement—a movement being a large part of the population that is united by ideas and goals, and which grows, aims to grow further, and to change conditions through its growth.

Co-operative Activity and Community Action

In 1935 Walter Popple, president and manager of Manitoba Co-op Wholesale, spoke to his delegates about co-operative education, urging them to recognize its importance:

> It is my intention to keep this subject before our delegates because I believe it is the lack of education that is most seriously retarding the progress

of the Co-operative Movement in Western Canada. Plans must be agreed upon, whereby we may prove to people outside of our Movement that the saving of dollars and cents is not our only objective, but that the social benefits are of infinitely greater importance.

Popple urged that local retails follow up a conference resolution that every local establish an education fund.[1] And he raised the same question two years later. Education, he wrote, "is the most important subject confronting the Co-operative Movement in Canada."

At each Annual Meeting the question apparently receives sympathetic consideration by our delegates . . . but as far as we know, with the exception of a very few locals, no definite policy has been adopted for educating the people of the communities along the lines of the democratic principles of co-operation, the only sound basis on which we may hope for our organization to survive.

Popple emphasized organization of study groups, membership in the CUC and the Manitoba Co-operative Conference, use of the Co-operative Promotion Board, activities of the United Farmers of Manitoba and United Farm Women, as means for conducting education. He argued it was "time . . . for us to forget many of the petty grievances which tend to keep our people pulling in opposite directions." He issued an "urgent message" to unite in support of co-operative education.[2]

Co-operative education found a ready audience in the Depression because the economic threat to local communities encouraged people to look for local, community solutions. A good example of the trend to local action and education is provided by the Rhineland Agricultural Society founded in Altona, a Mennonite community in southern Manitoba, in 1931. The Depression had hit southern Manitoba hard: 626 of 1,240 farmers in the Altona district had lost title to their farms through foreclosure or bankruptcy; a further 455 were so heavily in debt they were obliged to pay one-third of their crop to their mortgage holders; only 159—less than 13 percent—retained clear title. In direct response to this crisis, five friends, including two farmers, a businessman, a school principal, and a teacher, met and called a civic meeting to establish the Rhineland Agricultural Society. The best known of the five was J. J. Siemens.[3]

One week after the founding of the agricultural society, the Rhineland Consumers' Co-operative was created. It is probably not too much to claim, as one writer has done, that the Rhineland Co-op, supported by the agricultural society, exerted "a vast influence on the communities of Southern Manitoba."[4] Altona became the hub of co-operative development in the region, home of the area's largest and leading consumer co-operative, of Altona Co-operative Vegetable Oils, and of many educational activities. For the Rhineland Co-op, success was associated with a prolonged and intensive educational effort. In 1935 it set a fixed proportion of its surplus aside for education; in 1939 it even

A meeting at Rhineland Consumers' Co-operative, Altona, Manitoba (about 1935). Rhineland Co-op was a leader in the co-operative movement in southern Manitoba in the 1930s and 1940s. It led in the creation of the Federation of Southern Manitoba Co-operatives in 1941 and had a model program of co-operative education, publishing, and community activities. (Provincial Archives of Manitoba Rhineland 1)

engaged its own educational fieldman who helped organize discussion groups, "folk schools," new co-ops and credit unions, contests and fair displays, and who also assisted in organizing the 1941 Federation of Southern Manitoba Co-operatives. This commitment to education included internal affairs; traditionally, Rhineland directors had always been closely involved with management, and there was an on-going emphasis on education and recruitment of members. It was probably well that the co-op had this basis of education and involvement to draw upon, for it started with no working capital and no credit, and with fierce opposition from more conservative Mennonites who decried the "radical," "evil," "outside" influence of the co-op, and denounced its leaders as agents of Moscow.[5]

In Winnipeg, circumstances were much different; an urban co-op could not build on either the farm organizations or the bulk farm-supply business. But here, too, education was a key to the development that began to take place in the 1930s. In a passage replete with lessons for urban co-operative development down to the present day, Christine White, organizing secretary and director of Red River Consumers' Co-operative in Winnipeg, recalled how the co-op came into existence:

> About the end of 1936 a little group of people began coming together, in downtown Winnipeg, to talk about Co-operation. Some of us had been

members of Co-operative Societies in Scotland and England and Denmark. . . .

We . . . decided to form ourselves into a study group to meet regularly, and consider in detail the actual problems and difficulties. Right away we uncovered some very interesting facts. We found out, for example, that the reason so many Co-operatives have failed, was that no preliminary study had been made. . . . Another thing we found out was that—in the city at any rate—the old method of "starting small" would no longer do. Business is now so well organized, there are so many rules and regulations . . . that the days of the "Bedroom Store" are gone forever. It is no longer possible to start with a few members. . . . Success demands thorough understanding of principles and methods, and a group strongly organized.

Our group came to the conclusion that Fuel would be the best commodity for us to start with. It was something everybody needed, could be delivered in any part of the City, and in many ways appeared to be suitable. However we were taking no chances, so instead of starting right in with a Co-op, we tried our apprentice hands with a Buying Club.

In ten weeks this put us in touch with hundreds of co-operatively minded people and then we decided to go right ahead with preparations for a Fuel Co-op.

In March 1937 the provisional board of directors then set targets of $2,000 capital and 400 members to be achieved by 1 September. White commented that this "took plenty of organization work . . . for we had to get Committees in every section of the City." The buying club and then the share-selling campaign served as opportunities for co-operative education and organization of members. By the time the co-op started up, wrote White, "We knew where to find lay men and women, who knew something about Co-operation, who had been 'educated in advance.'" The co-op met its target, got its charter, immediately joined Manitoba Co-op Wholesale, and in its first season (1937–38), after two years of organizational work, had 538 members, did $45,000 in turnover, and paid a rebate of 2.5 percent.[6]

Much of the education upon which co-operatives were based in those years was the type that occurs through personal contact in small communities, through shared experience and need. Neighbours talked as they shovelled wheat for their co-op elevator, or unloaded coal brought in by their buying club, or hammered together a community hall. All of this was education, and it prepared the way for co-operation to become a movement.

Often the nature of the experience and the need were highly local. The Fram Co-op founded near Kinsella, Alberta, in 1937 provides one example of this. In the worst of the Depression few farmers could afford cars, and many who did had no money to operate them. As a result, farmers in the hills south and west of Kinsella discussed the need for a country store within easy reach, and this need for local services led to the creation of Fram Co-op. There was a further community tie: the eleven signatories of the memorandum of association, farmers all, bore five different Norwegian surnames—one family name occurred five times on the list. Co-operation was firmly rooted here in family and community structure, reinforced by shared ethnicity and by traditions brought to Canada from the old country, and finally brought together by the community's need for service. [7]

These varied community experiences and local lessons in co-operation were tied together into a movement by a new factor that emerged in the 1930s: more formal and more systematic agencies of co-operative education than had ever existed before.

The Agencies of Co-operative Education

As a result of the Depression, farm, government, and co-operative agencies began to pull together to promote co-operation. As they did so, a popular movement began to take form in the rural West. Provincial co-operative conferences supported co-op education, as did federations of agriculture. Leading consumer co-ops and their wholesales were members of the CUC, and producers' co-ops were being pressured to join. As membership grew, provincial sections of the CUC were founded, leading to intensified action on co-operative education. Manitoba's Co-operative Promotion Board and the Wheat Board Money Trust in Alberta used the invested proceeds of the 1919 federal wheat board's surplus to sponsor education about co-operatives. Government and university personnel were at the service of these organizations. And, of course, there were the fieldmen of the major co-operatives, especially of the wheat pools.

In the activities of all these educators and agencies, consumer co-operation received special emphasis. In the 1930s it was the phase of the co-operative movement whose time had come. Typical of the day is part of a radio broadcast paid for by the government Co-operative Promotion Board in Manitoba, broadcast on 8 February 1937—an excerpt which would still serve consumer co-operatives well if aired today:

> Outwardly, the co-operative looks just like any other place of business and inside, too, it has the same appearance, except that on some of the goods you may see a co-op label. Prices, too, are pretty much the same. A stranger might go into a co-op store and if he had not seen the name outside, not know the difference. But to the member it is very different. He is one of the owners of the business. He has helped supply the capital necessary to equip and stock the store. He wants to see it succeed. He tries to get his friends and neighbors to join and increase the turnover because that will be beneficial to him and them as well. And then—and this is an important point—he knows that any surplus that results from the operation of the business will not be profit but will be returned to him as a patronage dividend. . . . If the turnover is large and the business had

been economically conducted it will be something worthwhile—three percent, five percent or perhaps ten percent.

That speech was part of a long program by J. W. Ward, registrar of co-operative associations for the province of Manitoba.[8]

A diverse cadre of popular educators and organizers lay behind the co-operative education of the 1930s and 1940s, and a few of the more prominent were government officials. By 1934 W. Waldron of Saskatchewan had retired, but Keen wrote to him to say he had been convinced "as to the value to our Movement of a sympathetic interest by government officials."

I had a striking illustration of this fact in my itinerary this year. Of the three western conferences, the largest attended and most productive were those of Saskatchewan and Manitoba, in the order named. Both have the advantage of the active, intelligent and sympathetic interest of government officials all the time in the promotion of the success of the movement.[9]

The official of whom Keen approved so heartily, Waldron's successor, was B. N. Arnason, whose service to co-operatives in Saskatchewan was longer and, if anything, more distinguished even than Waldron's. Ironically, Waldron had written of Arnason in 1932: "He is a Swede or Icelander, I forget which, but he's quite a decent fellow and will do all he can to keep things together [in the Co-operation and Markets Branch]. Unfortunately he has had no experience whatever and his knowledge is all obtained from books."[10] Despite such apparent handicaps, by 1937 Keen observed that Arnason was "more or less in charge of co-operative education" in Saskatchewan, and he recommended Arnason's example to other provinces.[11]

Dorothy Fowler recalls that Arnason and the Conference of Co-operative Trading Associations, which began in 1934 with Arnason as secretary, played a crucial role in co-operative education. She remembers that besides Arnason there were two other regular speakers. One was Walter Francis, a young lawyer who had worked for the university's extension department, and who later became a partner with Gauley and Company, a law firm with which FCL (and its predecessors) has maintained a close, longstanding association. The other was Harry Fowler. "I called them the 'three musketeers,'" says Fowler, "and their wives the 'co-op widows.'"[12] Under the leadership of such individuals the conference took a keen interest in education, striving as early as 1935 to set out a provincial plan of action.[13]

Alberta at that time had only the one musketeer, William Halsall, to promote co-operative education. Halsall did what he could, but without as much help from retail associations, farm groups, universities, and governments as was available in Saskatchewan. At the end of 1936 Halsall wrote that "the great need of the co-operatives in this Province is an experienced man who can exercise constant supervision" over the activities of co-operators.[14] In 1937 A. H.

The Saskatchewan Conference of Co-operative Trading Associations, 1939. Started in 1934 under the leadership of B. N. Arnason, the annual conference quickly became an important meeting for discussion of co-operative ideas, practices, and projects.

Christensen was appointed supervisor of co-operative activities in Alberta, and fit the bill.

Christensen was a Dane who had nearly seventeen years experience in Danish co-operatives. Halsall observed that he was "very quick and intelligent and gives me the impression of being a sound co-operator." Most important in Alberta, where both the UFA and Social Credit had tried to sponsor co-operative schemes to their own advantage, Christensen was a strong believer in a nonpolitical co-operative movement. "My own understanding of proper education along Co-operative lines," Christensen wrote, "is, that it should result in the rising generation realizing true Co-operation is non-political. . . . A correct educational foundation laid on Co-operative principles will teach our young people to *think* for themselves, and not to run with the mob."[15] When the Alberta wholesale was successfully reorganized in 1938, ACWA's secretary, Edward Petersen, manager of Wetaskiwin Co-op, gave Christensen "the credit of stirring us into action . . . he has given us unstinted and effective assistance ever since he took office."[16] By the end of 1938 Christensen had overseen a new act, tougher enforcement, new initiatives in co-operative education, a revitalized wholesale with a new purchasing plan, and meetings pushing co-ops to join ACWA and the CUC.[17]

Manitoba Co-op Wholesale had a particularly strong contingent of field workers, another important part of the educational effort of the 1930s and 1940s. Of these the one whose name probably appears on the most minutes of local meetings and in the most newsletters from the 1940s onward is Don Slimmon. "Don had a natural ability to organize," recalls a former region manager. "He seemed to have the ability to go out to an area, talk to a number of key people, have a meeting, and organize a co-op. He was real good at that." Slimmon recalls that a week as a field worker for the wholesale was a week full of meetings and of getting his hands dirty helping out the retails—"take stock all day Sunday, install a new manager on Monday." To judge by the record, he then organized new co-ops and credit unions on Tuesday through Saturday. The era was characterized by a free-wheeling style that involved making difficult on-the-spot decisions—like hiring or changing a manager—along with the local board. Similarly, to organize a new co-op, he would contact the Pool agent and other key people, talk them up, call a meeting, and get it rolling.

Others also added to the educational framework enjoyed by the consumer movement in the 1930s and 1940s. The provincial co-operative sections or federations of agriculture had some employees who often played a key role in communications. Several universities got into the act. The extension department of the University of British Columbia became active in co-operative education, and the University of Saskatchewan sponsored "short courses for co-operators" during the summer. These brought in provincial experts—Robert McKay to teach merchandising, W. B. Francis on legal problems, Arnason on organization, Keen on history and philosophy and duties of directors, Fowler on financing and the economic significance of co-operatives, Professor Gordon on adult education and study groups, to quote from the 1938 course.[18] St. Joseph's College at the University of Alberta hosted schools for Alberta co-op store managers, directed by the university's extension department along with the Alberta wholesale.[19]

Local study groups contributed greatly to the development of the co-operative movement. The Terrace Co-op in B.C., for example, owed its origins to discussions sponsored by the KitsumKalum Farmers' Institute in 1938, where participants learned the principles of co-operative store operations. The advent of World War Two delayed matters somewhat, but in 1939 the federal government asked the University of British Columbia to administer funds for education in co-operative principles. By 1941 the UBC adult education department had several active field workers. One of them, Art J. Wirick, later secretary of the B.C. Co-op Union, spoke at Terrace in May 1941. With the war winding down in 1944, public meetings were held and provisional organization took place; the co-op was set up in 1945, and it opened in 1946.[20]

In Manitoba the great promoter of study groups from 1939 onward was the Manitoba Federation of Agriculture (later Manitoba Federation of Agriculture and Co-operation), which brought together all the major co-operatives in the province to take over the educational work previously done by the UFM, the Manitoba Co-operative Conference, and the Co-operative Promotion Board. The MFA provided assistance with organization of co-operatives, supplied speakers for meetings, trained people in speaking skills, ran courses, and helped women's groups. In 1940–41 it arranged 291 official visits to 190 meetings whose combined attendance was over 12,000 people. It held five folk schools for youth, three co-op schools, and seven leadership days; it ran a library; and it conducted 435 study groups with 4,287 members, as well as distributing 9,000 study-group pamphlets. The Manitoba legislature voted $5,000 to pay for study-group materials, and the courses offered included among other topics, Homemaking, Wheat Studies, Public Speaking, Foods and Health, Consumers' Co-operation, Rural Leadership, Soil Conservation, and Our Health. They also tuned into and discussed radio programs such as CBC's "Farm Radio Forum." Unification of the many different educational efforts in the MFA provided a boost to the study-group program; only 17 groups functioned in 1937–38 and only 58 in 1938–39, but after the formation of the MFA this increased to over 200 in 1939–40 and to the 435 noted in 1940–41.[21]

J. W. Ward, the government registrar, commented that "study group work . . . has resulted in a greatly increased interest in the co-operative movement. This has brought many additional members to the established co-operatives and a steady increase in the number of new associations."[22]

All of these activities were also supported by a lively co-operative press. Each prairie province had a newspaper put out by the producers' co-operative or co-operatives. Manitoba had the *Manitoba Co-operator,* Saskatchewan had *The Western Producer,* and Alberta had *The Cow Bell* (later amalgamated with *Co-op News*). However, consumer co-operators were repeatedly disappointed by the inadequate coverage they received in the producer co-operatives' newspapers. The exception to the rule was Alberta's *Co-op News,* formed by a fusion of the Alberta producers' and consumers' papers in 1942. Edited by J. Russell Love of Northern Alberta Dairy Pool, who became president of the Alberta Co-op Wholesale Association, *Co-op News* gave disproportionate emphasis to consumer co-operation, especially in its editorial pages. By the 1940s Russell Love emerged as one of the leading publicists for consumer co-operation in the West.

In 1939 Saskatchewan Co-op Wholesale Society and Consumers' Co-operative Refineries began producing the *Co-operative Consumer,* a newspaper devoted entirely to consumer co-operatives. They also collaborated to prepare ten thousand copies of a pamphlet on the principles of co-operation for distribution to school teachers.[23] In 1941 the *Consumer* became more than just a Saskatchewan paper, when Manitoba Co-op Wholesale began to distribute it as well. It was not an advertising medium in the modern sense, but a full newspaper with news, features, columns, editorials, items picked up from wire services, reports on local co-ops, and other items with serious informational content.[24] Its editor from 1942–43 until the 1960s, E. Forrest Scharf, became a strong influence for co-operative education in Saskatchewan, both through the press and through the co-op union.

The limitations of the educational activities of the time should also be noted. Jack Trevena, who attended co-operative educational sessions from the late 1930s onward, recalls that many consisted simply of speeches by the experts of the time on the history of co-operation. The standard of education was not high or consistent, there were no reference texts, and nothing fancy about the structure of the meetings. Practical methods were rarely discussed. And Trevena recalls that the "experts" of the time could not even agree on how many Rochdale principles there were. "We'd listen one week to one of them who'd tell us there were seven co-op principles, and he'd list them. But then the next week, the speaker would tell us there were only four. . . . We asked him what the difference was, and he said, 'those others aren't principles—they're just methods.'" In view of the frustration caused by so simple a matter as finding out how many co-operative principles there were, Trevena prefers to characterize the co-operative education of the time as "the near-blind leading the blind."

However unsystematic, the co-operative education that began to emerge in the latter part of the 1930s had one very effective feature: a great deal of personal contact. The agencies described above, from the wheat pools to the government to the new provincial co-operative unions, went out into the countryside and spoke at local meetings and to local people. Radio broadcasts and publications supported this effort, but there is no doubt that a great deal of the co-operative education that counted happened on the spot. This kind of education communicated not just ideas but *values* that helped knit the movement together. From about 1937 onward, co-operation was more firmly supported than ever before by a decentralized, grass-roots educational and organizational campaign. Established co-operatives, governments, and universities provided the funds and personnel for an educational process that was, nevertheless, localized and community-based. This was a broad, interrelated ferment of activity, with Wheat Pool field staff founding consumer co-ops, wholesale staff founding credit unions, town-hall meetings drawing in those who had never been in a co-op before, and neighbours discussing co-operation with each other as they socialized or worked together. Every effort reinforced the others to produce a web of organizations, institutions, and social contacts supportive of co-operatives in local communities.

Co-operation and Women

In conjunction with this widespread educational effort, the co-operative movement did not just expand geographically. It also expanded socially, and most importantly, into the 50 percent of the population so far least affected: women. As organizations associated with the business or production end of farm living, co-operatives until the 1930s had been organizations led by and sustained by farm men. This began to change, in part because of the growth in the consumer movement. Co-operatives were increasingly prominent in the home or consuming end of farming, and this may (as some co-operators have suggested) have given farm women the opportunity to take part without breaking with their traditional roles as homemakers. However, women began to become involved in co-operatives that still dealt mainly with commodities like oil and lumber.

This seems on the face of it to have little to do with their traditional roles. Probably the biggest reason for the increase in female participation was not that co-operatives were now involved in "female" areas of economics, but rather that the expansion of the co-operative movement took co-operation beyond economics and made it a community affair, associated with lifestyle, values, family, and far more than the instrumental world of production. Consumer co-ops rounded out the co-operative movement, and (together with the co-operative education of the 1930s) generalized it into a cause for the whole community.

Canadian co-operators, knowing that Britain had a strong Women's Co-operative Guild, had long wanted to get women involved in the movement. George Keen wrote in 1921:

> I feel that the Guild Movement should be exclusively under the control and direction of women. For some years past I have done what I could to foster initiative and our guilds are of considerable service to the individual societies. At present we have not yet reached the stage of national or provincial federation.

That stage was not reached for another two decades.[25] In 1932, however, Keen arranged for Fanny M. Eddie of Regina to address the CUC congress concerning women's guilds. Eddie was once a vice-president of the British guild, and went on to become the president of the Saskatchewan guild, the first provincial guild to be founded, in 1940.[26]

The first local guild in Saskatchewan had been founded in 1918, but had not lasted. The real increase in interest in guilds came from 1934 onward, as the development of the refinery in Regina created increasing interest in co-operation as a movement. Dorothy Fowler claims that the refinery was much more welcoming of women than either the Wheat Pool or the Saskatchewan Co-op Wholesale. "Women were people and were accepted as such by the refinery board and management," recalled Fowler in a speech in 1984.[27] "Many women attended the Annual Meetings of the Refinery," stated a history of the Saskatchewan guild. "These women were not only tea-ed and dined, but a bit of educational work was introduced during the gatherings." The Regina guild, re-founded in 1935, took the lead in this.[28] One reason for the involvement of women in the refinery may have been the impetus provided by Harry and Dorothy Fowler. Dorothy Fowler recalls, "We worked more or less as a team. He could talk to the men and I could talk to the women." They travelled together to meetings and Dorothy was a full participant. This set a tradition whereby women were invited to meetings and encouraged to stay to learn about co-ops. The tradition was passed on to SFCL after the 1944 amalgamation. "These people believed they were equal. They thought they had a job to do and they went out and did it."

Perhaps the Depression, with its crushing effect on families, had required farm women to be stronger, and this carried over into the co-operative movement. Possibly it also drove home the importance of economics in traditional areas of female concern. In any case, as the co-operative movement became a community movement its importance was evident to women, and participation increased. World War Two could only accelerate this by thrusting still greater responsibility on women while their husbands were away. The Guild Creed united personal with social goals:

> For Ourselves: Freedom and growth of character.
> For our Children: A higher social order, economic opportunities
> and security.
> For the World: Peace among nations and a common goal—
> the welfare of mankind.

The beginning of lasting organization, by linking guilds into a provincial federation, was credited to the Saskatchewan Conference of Co-operative Trading Associations, which had arranged a special women's section in 1939 where Keen spoke on the role of women's co-operative guilds, and experts discussed the co-operative movement. Five locals existed at that time. Other women's groups also participated in the founding and the on-going operation of the guild, however, including the Homemakers, the Regina Council of Women, and the women's section of the United Farmers. This, too, reflected the way in which co-operation was becoming a community concern.[29]

The other development that strengthened women's support of co-operatives was the co-operative press. The *Consumer*, in particular, took articles on co-operatives, how they functioned, and what they did into the homes of thousands of members. It was no longer necessary to chat on coffee row with the men, or when unloading rail cars, in order to pick up news and information about co-operatives. Women were specifically invited to meetings through the pages of the newspaper and told what went on there. There were also special women's sections designed to attract their attention to the paper.[30]

This was also true in the other provinces where guilds were not yet so well organized, and not federated into a provincial organization. In the *Co-op News* Mary Hope Spencer's "Co-operative Women's Section" provided an entertaining mix of serious discussions on topics like the war effort, romantic diversions about exotic people or places, practical tips on topics like health insurance or crafts, occasional poetry, and educational possibilities for personal development.

In becoming so broad and integrative, the co-operative movement also became ideological—not in the sense of acquiring a partisan political ideology (though that did happen for many individual co-operators), but in the sense of acquiring an ideology of its own, a comprehensive set of interpretations about how the world worked, what was wrong with it, and how to fix it. This ideology and the energy of the co-operative movement overlapped with some of the trends toward political protest in western Canada in the 1930s.

The Political Implications of Co-operation

The most obvious political association of co-operative activity was with the Co-operative Commonwealth Federation (CCF), if only because of its name. Founded in 1933, the CCF promised to create a "Co-operative Commonwealth" (a phrase used by consumer co-operators for decades) in which co-operatives would guard "against the too-great domination [by] the state." The CCF specifically singled out consumer co-operation as a "higher function" than the producer side, and though it affirmed the need for a localized, co-operative basis rather than a state-owned basis, it also promised to place "the credit of the nation" behind groups of consumers to help them construct their co-operatives.[31] George Keen frankly called the CCF's name "an embarrassment to us . . . a misnomer, and an awkward title," for he regarded the party, at least at first, as a standard state-oriented socialist party.[32]

Others disagreed. J. S. Woodsworth of the CCF wrote, "I hope the time will soon come when, in Canada, the co-operators will follow the lead of the co-operators in Great Britain and realize the need for more definite political action." Robert Wood, from Armstrong Co-op in B.C., insisted that in his experience co-ops encountered a wall of "uncompromising hostility" that was in any case political, from those committed to the established parties, and that therefore any new party would only help. "Personally," he wrote, "I believe that the spread of the socialist propaganda of the CCF will indirectly forward the spread of the ideas in which we believe more effectually than we can forward them purely as co-operators." However, Wood also wrote that he was "personally unable to visualize the CCF . . . as a political party." This was an interesting comment, for it indicated that those who saw a relationship between the CCF and the co-operative movement did not see the CCF as a political party, but as a protest and social reform movement.[33]

It may often be forgotten, however, that it was not only with the CCF that the co-operative movement became entangled. The situation in Alberta was much more complicated, for the CCF was not the only co-operatively based party active in the thirties. Even earlier a United Farmers of Alberta government, and then one led by Social Credit, had each launched its own consumer co-operative initiatives. Again, each party involved claimed to be more than a mere political party, and instead claimed to represent a broad farmers' alliance. Henry Wise Wood of the UFA claimed to offer the world "a system to take the place of the old party system—a system based on co-operation . . . and to take the place of the present hopeless political system that is based on the principle of dividing the citizenship against itself."[34] As part of the systematic promotion of this philosophy of co-operation, the UFA not only erected the large centrals that competed with the co-operatively owned Alberta wholesale; there were also constituency co-operative associations which donated funds to the UFA while it was in politics, and which kept the minutes of their political conventions and co-op annual meetings intermixed in the same minute book.[35] In

1935 the UFA was out of politics, but Social Credit was now in power, and Halsall complained that he feared becoming "entangled" with the new government, which also emphasized a populist sort of economic reform: "we had enough of that with the UFA."[36]

In some localities co-operatives were associated with communist groups. This was particularly true of Ukrainian miners and trade unionists in northern Ontario and Winnipeg, and of the Finnish fishermen of Sointula. Though the co-operative movement did not approve of such connections (the co-ops involved were usually expelled from the CUC, for example, when their political connections became clear), it is another expression of the fact that co-operatives were tightly bound up in the needs and aspirations of local communities. Where those needs and aspirations were strongly linked to a particular political persuasion, especially political protest, co-operatives had similar associations.

The relevant point is that as co-operation became a broadly based movement in which large numbers of people enthusiastically believed, with organization and education to give it form and focus, it could not avoid having some political implications. In the cases noted here, the political parties that espoused co-operation were parties that themselves aspired to be popular movements, and which, like the co-operative movement, promised reform, regeneration, and prosperity. In this sense the co-operative movement was linked not to any one political party, but to the reform impulse that was a part of several different farmers' and workers' protest parties of the 1930s.

Conclusion and Questions

By about 1938, educational campaigns were coming together in every single western province, assisted by government and co-operative functionaries and field workers, by university extension specialists, and by educators and publicists. The history of the grass-roots aspect of the period, of co-operative philosophy and education in the 1930s and 1940s, leaves one large question: to what extent are consumer co-operatives, even today, coasting on the strength of that amazing wave of co-operative idealism that began to sweep the rural West half a century ago? How many of the most loyal co-op patrons today are those who experienced that era, or whose parents and local communities have passed on a little of that heritage intact? And was this a one-time phenomenon, never to be repeated? What was necessary to make it happen?

The crucial point, it was suggested in this chapter, was the personal contact and experience of working together within the local community, which tied into the educational campaigns by the various agencies. Co-operative education has become a great deal more specialized and professional since the 1930s, but has the personal dimension, the dimension that linked education into a people's movement, been forgotten? Long-time co-operative educator Harold Chapman, first head of the Co-operative College of Canada in the 1950s, observes that today "we send out a newsletter, and we assume that will do the same thing for them [the members] that standing in a boxcar shovelling coal together did." If this personal dimension cannot be provided today, what implications does that have for co-operatives? "If people *aren't* going to be in the boxcar together shovelling coal," asks Chapman, "what are we going to substitute?" What will get people talking to one another? An institution can perpetuate itself—that is the job of an institution—but what are co-operatives without a movement or purpose to sustain them?

PART FOUR: MOVEMENT 1938–1950

Introduction to Part Four

From 1938 to 1950 co-operation truly became a movement in western Canada —a force of people organized for change by the ideas and values they held in common. Within the co-operative movement, consumer co-operation came into its own, perhaps even leading the movement as a whole in growth, dynamism, and numerical strength of its followers.

The story of 1938–50 is the consummation of the work that had been done during the Depression. It was an era of rapid, confident, and seemingly boundless expansion, when the benefits of the education and organization of the Depression era were cashed in. Consumer co-operation touched almost every farming community and most towns; it involved men, women, and children. Expansion in sales, numbers of co-ops, facilities, and numbers of members were expressions of the popular movement that carried co-operation forward, especially in the rural areas of western Canada.

* * *

10

Co-operative Growth and Diversification, 1938–1950

In the years from 1938 to 1944 the consumers' co-operative movement in western Canada turned the corner. Established co-operatives began at last to show impressive growth in number of members and in sales and savings on their behalf. New initiatives and new kinds of co-operatives laid the basis for an integrated and comprehensive co-operative movement encompassing everything from farm machinery to insurance—a movement increasingly able to satisfy all its members' major needs as consumers through co-operative channels. When economic restrictions were loosened in 1944, this opened the floodgates for a consumer movement that had spent five years amassing capital, new structures, and new plans.

Co-operative Business under Wartime Conditions

There is no doubt that wartime regulations created many headaches. "In some instances," noted the Saskatchewan wholesale's annual report for 1941, "the effect of some of these regulations has placed the Wholesale at a decided disadvantage as compared to competitive business." Government quotas, for example, were considered an "unfair handicap" for an "expanding business such as that of the Wholesale." Moreover, imports were restricted, leading to shortages of supplies in many goods. The consumer co-operatives had frequently depended on American suppliers, including American co-operatives, for lubricants, washing machines, car batteries—and these were now either unavailable or more highly priced. Quotas for Canadian production were based on previous years' purchases from Canadian sources. This left the co-op wholesales entirely without supplies in several lines.[1]

But wartime limitations were also "an opportunity for the Wholesale and the local organizations to consolidate their positions, whereas previously there was a general tendency to expand to an almost dangerous degree and much faster than sound financing justified." Now co-ops *had* to sit back and build up their bank balances, their capital accounts, their educational campaigns, while waiting for the day when they could go ahead and build new facilities. Locals were advised to "avoid over-expansion, the over-building of inventories, and the over-extension of credit. They must place more stress on education, without which our whole movement will lack strength and be ill-prepared" for the end of the war.[2]

It is important to remember that co-operatives are not just economic institutions. In many ways it was the *psychological* impact of the wartime experience that was decisive. World War Two was a gigantic struggle that consumed many lives, including the lives of many western Canadians. It is in the nature of such events to make people look for causes, and the cause at that time was the fight against fascism, in favour of democracy. Robert Wood, in his speech convening the conference of British Columbia co-ops that led to the founding of the B.C. wholesale in 1939, stated (even before war had broken out) that "competition and individualism" had been discredited during the Depression, leaving the world with a choice between "two forms of collective action . . . that favoured by the fascist states, under which collective organization is effected and controlled from the top down . . . or that . . . which is essentially organization from the bottom up, controlled . . . by the individuals comprising our [co-operative] memberships for the benefit of humanity at large." Co-operation, to Wood and other co-op leaders and publicists, was the answer to the deficiencies of prewar individualism as well as the challenge of fascism.[3]

Later, during the war, A. B. MacDonald of the CUC told the Saskatoon Board of Trade that "the present world struggle might well be the funeral dirge of the competitive economy." Co-operation must replace it.[4] Others saw the philosophy of co-operation reflected and proven in the co-operation of the United Nations to beat Hitler and his allies.[5]

This kind of thinking became more pronounced when the question of victory seemed decided, and the new question arose of what the postwar social order in Canada would be. Russell Love noted in 1945 that "in a very short time, hundreds of thousands of Canadians will be returning to civilian life. What will the post-war world have in store for them?"[6] Love argued, in his many speeches and publications of that era, that the capitalist system had solved the problem of how to *produce* wealth. What remained was the co-operative organization of the economy to *distribute* it fairly. "The rugged individualism of pre-war days with its wasteful economic strife and its ruthless competition, and its fear of insecurity and unemployment must give way to a new order of mutual understanding and co-operation designed to substitute peace for violence, construction for destruction, and abundance for scarcity." He continued:

> The co-operative movement with millions of members scattered throughout 39 countries . . . has one clear cut common objective—that is to secure a higher standard of living for the masses of the people, through a more equitable distribution of the national income. . . . We believe that . . . through the mechanics of the co-operative movement, the common people can recapture the ownership and control of their own destiny.

The war heightened the sense of a society working together, determining its future, and fighting for democracy. All this, in turn, gave a powerful impetus to co-operation.

The war years must have been an inspiring time for consumer co-operators in the West. Russell Love was president of ACWA, and James McCaig, remembered by Barney Arnason as "a good organizer, a fiery speaker, a strong believer in the social as well as the economic benefits of co-operation," was president of SCWS. Until 1942, Walter Popple, another philosophically committed co-operator, was head of MCW, and his successors, D. J. Wallace and Wilfrid McSorley, were perhaps even better and more inspiring speakers. In B.C., Robert Wood, though aging, was still the honourary patron of the new wholesale, and S. F. Ricketts, then its secretary, was beginning a long career as a co-operative publicist. And, of course, Harry Fowler was secretary-manager at the Co-op Refinery. The western consumer movement has seen great speakers and inspiring proponents of co-operation since those days, but it seems unlikely that there have ever been so many of them at one time.

As part of the tremendous feeling of confidence and optimism, the certainty that co-operation was an unstoppable people's movement, it is only fitting that many statements of the Rochdale principles during the 1940s added an eighth to the customary seven: "continuous expansion."[7] It was held to be a guiding philosophy that co-ops should expand without bounds until ultimately all of society was transformed.

Growth and New Initiatives: the Provincial Wholesales

Wartime conditions permitted some growth and many new beginnings for the co-op wholesales in the West. This was true in B.C., where the B.C. Co-operative Wholesale Society was incorporated in the fall of 1939, and opened its Vancouver office in September of 1940. By 1944 its membership had increased to twenty-six co-ops. Although it was initially unable to undertake much warehousing, it did earn some revenue from a brokerage business, similar to the other wholesales in their early stages.[8]

The sales and savings statistics and significant developments for all of the wholesales are outlined in the appendices to this book. In general, all the wholesales grew steadily from 1938 on, enjoying their best economic advances since they had been created.

Alberta Co-operative Wholesale Association was reorganized in 1937–38 and found a firm base of thirty-five member societies who contracted to purchase *all* possible supplies through the wholesale. A new head office was opened in Edmonton under a new manager, David Smeaton, an experienced retailing man who had served many years as a purchasing agent in both private and co-operative sectors. Alberta was back on its feet, and Dave Smeaton was a welcome addition to the leadership of the western consumer movement.

Saskatchewan continued to lead Canada in co-operative strength. This was based in part on a powerful movement of local retails: from 1934 to 1943 the number of active retail co-ops in Saskatchewan increased from 281 to 679. Their paid-up capital doubled, assets quadrupled, membership increased to five times what it had been in 1934, sales to seven times, and net savings grew to *nineteen times* what they had been in 1934.[9] At the heart of this expansive consumer movement, both the refinery and the wholesale prospered. Again, the turning point was 1938, when the Saskatchewan wholesale's volume surpassed $1 million in a fifteen-month sales year.[10]

Like the others, the Manitoba wholesale also increased its sales steadily from 1937 on, reaching not quite $1 million in 1941, the last full year of Walter F. Popple's management. Under Ed Chown, MCW broke the $1 million barrier in 1942 and the $2 million mark in 1944. One employee, who was later a manager for FCL, gives Chown "a good chunk of the credit" for this growth. "He was aggressive in developing new products and new services. The Forties were the era of Ed Chown."

As the co-operative wholesales grew, they also branched out into new products and into new economic functions. The central co-operatives acted first to secure greater control of those commodities for which demand was best mobilized: petroleum (through the refinery), feed, coal, lumber, and, increasingly, general store goods—groceries, hardware, and dry goods (clothing).

Coal for co-op members from the Hy-Grade coal mine near Drumheller (late 1940s). Saskatchewan Co-operative Wholesale Society purchased an interest in the Hy-Grade mine in 1940, and in 1945 it was taken over under 100 percent co-op ownership. Until oil and natural gas replaced coal in home heating, the Hy-Grade mine, together with the nearby Empire mine, constituted one of the most important manufacturing enterprises of the Saskatchewan wholesale and later of FCL. The mine was closed in 1962.

Trucks from Sherwood Co-op (Regina) take delivery of the first shipment of lumber from the co-op mill at Canoe, British Columbia (1945). The Canoe lumber mill has remained a highly successful operation for western Canadian consumer co-operatives over the years.

Alberta was the first to enter into feed production, marketing its Co-op Maid feed for the first time in 1939. In 1942 Saskatchewan Co-op Wholesale Society acquired what one co-operator describes as "an old tin shed over on Duchess Street" in Saskatoon, for the purpose of starting up feed production. "They bought an old bread-dough mixer and a shovel—that was their feed-mixing equipment." In 1943 the Manitoba wholesale also began producing CO-OP Feeds.[11]

Expansion into coal production came in 1938. Although coal was one of the wholesales' biggest commodities in those days, they had difficulty finding reliable supplies from profit companies, who did not like selling to the co-ops. Then a group of unemployed miners began to operate an abandoned mine in Lethbridge. SCWS offered financial help to the miners, who willingly agreed to supply their production to the co-operatives.[12] In 1941 SCWS's interest was switched to the Hy-Grade Mine at Drumheller, and in 1944–45 both the Empire Mine and the Hy-Grade Mine were purchased by the Saskatchewan wholesale to be operated as subsidiaries.

Other expansions in productive enterprises also stand out. These include the purchase by SCWS of a flour mill at Outlook in 1939; the refinery expansion that came on stream in June 1940; the merger of SCWS with the refinery in 1944 to produce an integrated producing and distributing organization (Chapter 11); and the purchase by the new Saskatchewan Federated Co-ops of a lumber mill at Canoe, British Columbia, in 1945.

Expansions in warehousing of goods also came at this time. In 1941 MCW began wholesaling its own goods. And in 1941–42 SCWS opened a grocery department, and for the first time, the co-op wholesale stocked its own inventories of grocery and related products for delivery to co-op stores. The growth in store goods was attributed to the fact that the bulk-purchasing associations were diversifying their activities. Local co-ops now wanted to move into every kind of goods their members could use, and this on-going development of the local co-ops into all-around retails provided the volume necessary for the wholesale to diversify its own operations.[13]

In addition, from 1938 onward the western co-operators were involved in other projects, outside the range of activities of the wholesale itself, that would be consolidated in later years. One of these was farm machinery. In 1936 and 1938 federal and Saskatchewan government studies had looked at the implement industry and made proposals for co-operative solutions. Then, in 1939, the Co-op Tractor manufactured in St. Paul, Minnesota, was brought in for sale to Saskatchewan farmers. This started an involvement in farm machinery that was pursued further when Harry Fowler, his old business partner George B. Munro, and others, founded Canadian Co-operative Implements Limited (CCIL) in 1940. B. N. Arnason was the organization secretary. In 1941–42 some 50,000 farmers subscribed $10–20 each in CCIL district locals, although due to wartime restrictions no manufacturing could be undertaken until 1944. Second, in 1938, a life-insurance plan was introduced for employees of the wholesale. This was one of the first moves in a large number of co-operative initiatives in insurance, superannuation, finance, trust companies, mutual benefit associations, and credit unions over the following years, including, in

Farmers try out the CO-OP tractor in the field (1939 or 1940). Saskatchewan Co-operative Wholesale Society imported CO-OP tractors for the first time in 1939, ordering them from National Farm Machinery of Indiana, a farmer-owned machine company. Co-operation in purchasing CO-OP tractors helped lay the basis for Canadian Co-operative Implements Limited (CCIL), which in 1946 purchased the Cockshutt factory in Winnipeg and began producing its own equipment. (Photograph courtesy Harold Benson)

1940, the creation of the Saskatchewan Co-operative Credit Society. And third, in 1938 a joint purchasing committee for binder twine among the three prairie wholesales laid the basis for later interprovincial co-operation.[14] In 1940 Interprovincial Co-operatives was founded, about which more is said in Chapter 12. The wholesales and their personnel, but Saskatchewan's Fowler in particular, were closely involved in all these developments.

As the wholesales made better earnings, they also hired more staff, and their managers had more time to devote to working with the retails. It was no longer a case, as in the Manitoba Co-op Wholesale in 1937, of three people running a tiny office and preoccupied with making ends meet—one manager, one bookkeeper, and one secretary. Now there was money for warehouses, delivery men, audit departments, and full-time field workers. It became possible, toward the end of the 1930s, for the wholesales to play larger leadership roles in co-ordination of buying and also in co-operative development.

Capital, Sales, and Co-operative Development

Up until the last half of the 1930s, successful co-operatives had paid out as much as possible of their annual surpluses as patronage rebates to members, after setting aside portions of their surpluses for mandatory reserves, educational projects, and other miscellaneous purposes. Consistent cash payments year after year had impressed many members. Unfortunately, paying out surpluses in this way meant that the co-ops did not accumulate much capital. To make matters worse, most of them had little share capital to start with, since under the circumstances of the Depression, when most had been founded, it was not possible to raise much money from sales of shares. As pressure grew for more elaborate facilities, more lines and larger inventories, both local retails and the second-tier co-ops that serviced them needed more capital.

The plan that financed much of the expansion of the late 1930s and early 1940s was the Revolving Door Plan developed by Harry Fowler at Wilcox Co-op and at the Co-op Refinery. The plan retained the main feature of patronage rebates, crediting surpluses to members in proportion to their purchases, but it withheld payment of those rebates for a number of years. The member still owned them and would eventually receive them in cash, but for a certain period the co-op had the use of them for investment in expanded services. At Wilcox and at the refinery the revolving door was a five-year period: the refunds for 1935, for example, would be received by the member in 1941. The revolving door, in effect, meant members contributed working capital in strict proportion to their purchases, so that the burden was fair and the co-op's financing grew as sales increased. The main alternative was to have members subscribe for more expensive shares, perhaps $25 or $50. But in this case the small member and the large one would pay the same amount. This was presented as less fair and undesirable considering co-op principles.[15]

With variations, all the wholesales and many of the retails had adopted such plans within a few years. The Saskatchewan wholesale adopted it in 1939 and announced that the revolving-door method of building up local capital replaced the old affiliated plan of building it up by loans from the wholesale.[16] The result of the plan's wide implementation was that as the retail economy improved, the co-ops, and especially the centrals, had capital with which to finance expansions, inventories, and new product lines.

It was a sign of the times that the refinery, which was the first large co-op to promote the revolving door, also quickly outgrew it. Temporarily retained patronage rebates did not supply quite as much cash as the refinery needed for investment in new technology to crack heavier crude oil. Accordingly, the refinery made use of another device: the selling of co-operative savings bonds, and its subsequent expansion and modernization in 1939–40 was financed by the first Petroleum Expansion drive, which mobilized co-op members' savings to improve the facilities they owned. Typically, such bond issues for co-operatives require extensive educational campaigns and can only succeed where the membership is well-informed and highly supportive. The success of the refinery's drive, and later the success of similar drives by local retails, are another sign of how firm the support for co-operation was becoming in those years.

But since the shortage of capital was one of the great bottlenecks of the expansion that was beginning, other imaginative solutions were attempted. The Saskatchewan Co-operative Credit Society founded in 1940 was intended to serve as a kind of "co-op clearing house" to take in surplus money and funnel it into retail development, lending funds to retails for expansion. This also helped out the wholesales' finances by reducing credit transactions with their member co-operatives.[17] The point illustrated by the credit society is an important one: effective capital for co-operative development could be obtained not only locally through revolving-door or bond schemes, but also on a movement-wide basis through agreement and planning among co-operatives. This was an era of great improvisation and of making do with inadequate resources; better co-operation among co-operatives was one way of reducing these limitations.

Just as the leaders of the Saskatchewan wholesale and refinery recommended the use of the Co-operative Credit Society to solve the wholesales' credit problems, so too they recommended that local co-ops encourage the formation of credit unions in their communities to solve the credit problem at the local level. Credit business meant high accounts receivable, which tied up a co-op's capital and at the very least inhibited its ability to expand. Working capital was so short that in some cases credit granted to members put the survival of the co-op at risk—it might have so much money out in accounts receivable from members that it could not meet its own accounts payable. Along with the upturn in the economy, the advent of a large credit union movement in the West solved one of the worst and longest lasting financial problems of consumer associations: namely, credit business.

The wholesales, their employees, and their members therefore promoted the infant credit movement. Sherwood Credit Union, the story goes, was started out of a shoe box in a desk drawer in the Co-op Refinery office. Fieldmen like Don Slimmon in Manitoba, though their salaries were paid by a co-op whose business was wholesaling, took salaried time to organize credit unions in local communities. Many stories could be told of communities where the co-op association and the credit union shared a building, a president, or a manager—and sometimes they shared them with the Wheat Pool, too. Leaders in the consumer co-operative movement looked beyond the growth of their own organizations, to imaginative new ideas and new departures from the basic co-operative idea. This was part of what made co-operation a movement. Those involved believed, and discovered in fact, that each kind of co-operative could reinforce the other.

The other side of developing the consumer movement was the question of sales volume. A series of meetings among Saskatchewan store managers between 1938 and 1940 discussed ways to co-ordinate buying, expand the services and volume of the wholesale, and develop new co-ops. B. N. Arnason of the government Co-operation and Markets Branch challenged the co-op managers at the January 1938 meeting to find new ways for "linking all Co-ops together more firmly" and achieving real "co-ordination of buying power." These remarks had a great effect on the meeting; following his speech the agenda was changed by adding "Co-ordination of Buying Power" as item number zero at the top of the agenda. A motion was passed recommending study of "a wholesale distributing house" stocking its own goods to "co-ordinate the buying power of existing co-operatives" and to help in the development of new stores. This idea was not unanimously supported. Even Robert McKay, manager of the wholesale, argued that store managers should only buy from him when he could offer a better price than private businesses. And C. G. Davidson, manager of Lloydminster co-op, who dissented from the motion passed by the meeting, "strongly advocated that the utmost caution be used" in efforts to co-ordinate the stores.[18]

Managers resisted the adoption of the Alberta Plan of contract buying. A 1940 meeting noted that "in Alberta they had been successful in getting the store managers to adhere to this plan, the same measure of success had not been obtained in Saskatchewan." The store managers consoled the directors and the wholesale manager that they should not be too disappointed, that "with patience and a little time, . . . perhaps by tackling one line of goods . . . at a time, eventually the whole could be co-ordinated."[19]

Another approach to the need for volume in store goods, the need for co-operative development, and the need for central supervision and co-ordination, was the associated stores plan of 1939. McKay argued this plan was necessary because "for various reasons the movement to date cannot be considered a success." The development of the bulk-purchasing associations into real co-operative stores, a development needed to secure volume in different commodities for the wholesale, was proceeding too slowly. McKay therefore suggested that the wholesale step in and, in areas it chose, line up a hundred interested members and one interested private merchant, buy out the merchant with the wholesale's funds, and hire him back to run his store "on a Co-operative basis, in return for a salary to be agreed upon and interest on his investment." The plan further stipulated that these stores would function with "no local share capital, but with a membership fee and the 'Revolving Door' plan of retention of profits": one half of the surplus would be paid out at the end of each year as a patronage dividend, "the balance would be retained and set up to the credit of each member." When the capital accumulated through retained surpluses equalled the amount of investment in the store, it could be reorganized as an autonomous local co-op.[20]

This seemed like the easy way to start co-ops: no commitment needed by members, no capital. All new members had to do was buy, and their shares and ownership would accumulate automatically out of the accumulating savings. The wholesale would provide ample money, and an experienced private merchant would provide expert management. Like so many "easy" plans for creating co-ops, however, this one was viewed with suspicion by George Keen. He argued vehemently that autonomy could not be forced on people; that co-ops where members made no financial commitment and had no co-operative understanding would lose their support and fail; and (above all) that self-interested private merchants could not be trusted to run their stores on a genuine co-operative basis. McKay replied that in his experience ownership of shares had no effect on the loyalty of customers. "As long as the desired results are being attained for the consumer the nominal ownership is immaterial."[21]

The advent of World War Two tipped the balance in favour of McKay's plan. Directors had already argued at the 1940 annual meeting that the growth of the wholesale and the development of locals could only take place in one of three ways: through the Alberta Plan of contract buying, through the 1939 plan to buy out private merchants, or through "a Co-operative Chain of Stores." Since the Wartime Prices and Trade Board forbade expansion by starting new stores, buying existing stores was a necessary option.[22]

In 1944 a Toronto newspaper reported that the prairies were "afire with enthusiasm for co-operation," "burning with the same intensity as in the days when the wheat pools . . . were devouring all opposition that stood in their path." The reporter referred to the Associated Stores campaign in Saskatchewan, which in his eyes meant the co-ops had "adopted the early chain-store technique of cut-price competition which compels private owners to sell out to them in the main at the co-operatives' price." By his figures, 171 Saskatchewan retail stores had changed to co-operative ownership in only six months.[23] This report may have sensationalized what was happening, but it seems the associated stores were a success in promoting the transition from a commodity-based movement depending on bulk buying of a few products, to one which was store-based, offering more comprehensive local services. They did not necessarily come about with the same degree of centralization that McKay had proposed in 1939, however. With the sharply increased sales and savings of the war years, many local bulk co-ops found it possible, after all, to raise locally the capital necessary to purchase a store. In 1946 the management of the whole-sale reported, for example, that the new general merchandise business opened by Spalding Co-op had become Store No. 99 under the Associated Store plan. The Spalding store required $10,100 for the inventory, $2,500 for the building, and $500 for the fixtures—all of which were paid for through loans and share capital raised by the members in Spalding. At Sturgis, in the meantime, mem-bers were canvassing for funds and had raised $10,000. Unlike during the Depression, substantial amounts of money could now be raised for expansion from ordinary co-op members.[24]

The parts of the associated stores plan that worked, then, were those that called for central auditing and supervision, and buying out of private merchants to acquire facilities, inventories, and expertise. The idea of establishing associ-ated stores purchased and owned by the wholesale, without local share capital, does not seem to have been the rule. The rough compromise of the 1940s was that operations might be centralized, but ownership would not be—a compro-mise that has characterized most of the subsequent history of the system.

Income Tax and Co-operatives

The question of financing for consumer co-operatives was also related to another issue current in the mid-1940s: namely, taxation of co-operatives.

One consequence of the growth of co-operation was that it aroused the hostility of private merchants. This was true in 1908, when lobbying by the Retail Merchants' Association led to the narrow defeat of the first national co-operative legislation proposed for Canada, and it has been true through most of the following eighty years. Where it has come up most frequently—and it seems to do so at least once every decade—is in the question of what taxes should be imposed on co-operatives. The contention by private retailers has been that co-operatives enjoy a tax holiday, which some have said explains their success. This is not true. Co-operatives pay normal sales and business taxes, and also pay income tax on their own income which is directly equivalent to that paid by profit corporations. A federal royal commission in the 1960s heard many arguments that the alleged disproportionate growth of co-operatives was the result of tax advantages, and it found it was not so.[25] In fact, as will be described below, the protestations of merchants have led to many restrictions on co-operatives over the years, and to the imposition of at least an equal tax burden on co-operatives and their members.

The major difference between income tax for a co-operative and for a profit corporation lies in the treatment of patronage refunds. It is a fundamental belief of co-operators that the savings distributed to members should not be included in the co-operative's taxable income, because these savings are merely returning to members (of a consumer co-operative) what was theirs in the first place. Following the essential purpose of patronage refunds (Chapter 2), each member gets back precisely the portion of the co-op's earnings that came from his or her own transactions with the co-op. If members are paid any other kind of earnings, these are taxable just like corporate profits. If the co-operative retains savings and does not allocate them to members, then these constitute part of the co-operative's income, which is taxed like a profit corporation's income.

Co-operatives have argued that patronage refunds to members are equivalent to providing a volume rebate on the member's purchases, something done by an immense number of companies and (though strictly regulated) not considered taxable. The main difference between a patronage refund and a volume rebate is that the amount of the patronage refund is not determined until the end of the year when the co-operative knows how much money it has.[26]

The principle of the nontaxability of patronage refunds, with some kind of definitions and restrictions, was established from an early date. The year 1944 was a key point, however, in the further evolution of the tax debate.

The wartime growth of the co-operative movement drew attention to co-operatives and led to the 1944 appointment of a federal Royal Commission on Co-operatives and Taxation under Québec justice E. M. McDougall. (One of the members of the commission was B. N. Arnason, whose inclusion is a tribute to the recognition given to both the Saskatchewan government and Arnason in the area of administering co-operative legislation.) The new provincial sections of the CUC were instrumental in encouraging and organizing co-operatives to make submissions to the commission, and this activity provided a new focal point for the co-operative movement. It also helped secure a set of recommendations from the commission which, as J. T. Phalen later wrote, "were acceptable to co-operatives, but not to the opponents of co-operatives."[27]

In 1946, after the commission had reported, the government drafted legislation which introduced new provisions that co-operatives believed imposed extremely unfair burdens on them. A year later, after nationwide protests through Members of Parliament and the CUC, co-operatives claimed to have modified the worst features of the new legislation, though they were still not pleased.[28] The legislation as enacted in 1946 included a provision that earnings from business with customers were generally taxable where those people were *not* members of the co-operative. Co-operatives did not greatly object to this provision, since they have never believed sales to nonmembers should be encouraged—a co-operative trading with a nonmember is really in the same economic relationship with that person as a corporation dealing with a customer. Second, however, patronage refunds to members were made taxable unless paid out within twelve months—they could not be kept tax-free in reserves—or unless the member in question had applied for more shares, or unless a special by-law had been passed authorizing that the sum be retained as a "patronage loan" by the member to the co-operative. This started a long debate between co-operatives and governments about how patronage refunds ought to be paid. Needless to say, these provisions resulted in some hurried improvisation by co-operatives, and the adoption of many special by-laws. Of particular concern, however, was a third feature: a provision that the taxable income of a co-operative could not be reduced through paying out patronage refunds to less than 3 percent of capital employed. This had the effect of limiting how much of the earnings of co-operatives was distributed as patronage refunds to members. It established a minimum amount, based on the capitalization of the co-operative, on which the co-op would have to pay income tax.[29]

The 3-percent provision was criticized vehemently by co-operatives as "a strange, abstruse, complicated and unprecedented method of applying an income tax law." Among other objections, they claimed that it discouraged the building up of adequate reserves, pressured co-operatives "to adopt unsound methods of financing and operating," effectively forced them to make income when they preferred to distribute savings to members, and discriminated against small co-operatives.[30] Joe Dierker, a lawyer deeply involved in the taxation discussions, later wrote that he was not sure that there ever had been any logical basis for relating taxation of patronage refunds to capital employed. Dierker recalled that "one gentleman, who was closely involved in the original drafting of that provision," stated, "'We just wanted some more tax dollars from co-operatives.'"[31] It took twenty-five years until, after another royal commission (the Carter commission of 1962–67, which studied the whole income tax system), a white paper, and extensive lobbying, the taxation of 3 percent of capital employed was eliminated.

There are many reasons why governments might want to support co-operatives, including the fact that they are controlled by Canadians and keep earnings in local communities, as do small businesses; in addition, unlike any other form of business, co-ops spread those earnings, as well as the feeling of ownership, widely and equitably throughout the community. Nevertheless, despite these reasons, governments are not particularly supportive of co-operatives, through tax exemptions or otherwise. Far from it—co-operatives have had to fight for recognition and consideration from federal governments, have had to organize to counter hostile lobbies, and have operated under close and at times suspicious government scrutiny and supervision.

Growth of Retails: the Great Postwar Expansion

The postwar years saw the greatest expansion of co-operative retailing ever. Using the sales volume of the wholesales, corrected for inflation, as an index, co-operative sales more than tripled in the ten years from 1945 to 1955. By contrast, it took until 1971 to triple again (see Appendix 5). More important, co-operation was spreading into new communities and involving more and more people.

During the forties and fifties, hundreds of new co-operative associations of all sizes were founded, and old ones expanded. The wholesales, and especially their field staff and retail services personnel, were instrumental in this development. It is impossible to describe what every retail did at that time, but a few examples from one area of western Manitoba will illustrate what was going on throughout the West.

Don Slimmon, an MCW fieldworker for the region, recalls in his book *People and Progress* that for the co-operative movement the 1940s were the Roaring Forties. Slimmon describes no fewer than thirty new co-ops formed in his district in the five years between 1944 and 1949, most of them in 1944–45.[32]

In the spring of 1946 a new co-op was opened in Boissevain, Manitoba, with around 150 members supplying $4,645 in shares and $4,180 in loans, and with the Manitoba Co-op Wholesale kicking in $3,000 for the equipment necessary for a petroleum, feed, hardware, and flour outlet. In 1949 the co-op bought out a grocery store, and in 1955 it erected a building for its lumber, hardware, feeds, and bulk oil operations. Sales hit $251,286 that year.[33]

At Brandon, meanwhile, the co-op whose office was said in 1932 to be "so small there is no room to turn around; you walk in and back out" was ready in 1945 to purchase a downtown lot and in 1946 to build a new outlet for farm supplies. Part of the new building was rented out to Co-op Implements and the co-op store manager served as the CCIL agent. By 1953 the Brandon Co-op went into groceries, and in 1956 it built a new store.[34]

In Gladstone, the Manitoba Pool elevator agent promoted the formation of a consumer co-op, and on 28 February 1946 the co-op was organized in the Pool elevator office. Ed Chown, manager of the wholesale, and Don Slimmon attended, as did sixteen local farmers. Those sixteen soon raised $3,500 in share capital. "It took all that sum to buy the co-op's first petroleum storage tanks," claims a write-up of the Gladstone Co-op's history, "so none was left for the purchase of fuels to fill them." As so many times before, the co-op worked because directors pledged their personal assets to give it working capital.[35]

The same was repeated throughout scores of similar districts across western Canada. New co-ops were founded. Old ones added new lines, especially groceries and dry goods, to make themselves into comprehensive and well-rounded store associations.

What went along with this growth was that consumer co-ops increasingly became focal points of their communities. An article in 1955 argued that co-op stores should see themselves as part of the web of church, educational, municipal, patriotic, fraternal, recreational, social, service, health, and occupational clubs and societies that provide a framework for rural and town life:

> There was a time when the Co-op Store was rather a separate part of the community. It was a new thing, and in many cases was set up in protest . . . so, of course, the other local merchants and businessmen in town took rather a dim view. . . .
>
> But is this as it . . . really should be? Should not the Co-op Store have grown up enough today that it is taking a more active part in the life of the community as a whole?

The author argued that co-ops should take up their community responsibilities by sponsoring contests for school children, staging social events for local residents including nonmembers, advertising both co-op prices and philosophy, developing women's guilds "to spread the Co-operative story," encouraging directors to serve in other community associations, developing good relations with the local press, and exchanging fraternal delegates with other organizations. This was a vision of co-ops as the hubs of their communities. It was a reality in many places, and still is in some.[36]

Bruce Arnott, a former fieldworker, remembers being welcomed wherever he went because of a sense of family among co-op members. "If you were in the Co-op you were readily accepted. You got the feeling people were glad to see you, and you were glad to lend a hand." Being a co-op member was in some circles also an expected thing. Sometimes there was even a "self-righteous feeling that everybody should do this," and criticism of neighbours who wouldn't join. "It was hard," he observes, "to draw the line between a business activity and a social one. It all blended together." All of this was part of the sense of the co-op being a movement that would expand indefinitely. "There was no feeling of just staying as you were. There was always that inner drive to keep on growing. There were always more people to win over, more services to provide, if not this year then maybe next."

In 1954 president W. McSorley of the Manitoba wholesale noted the role of the co-op in promoting intercultural harmony, bringing together for common goals different ethnic groups that did not usually mix. "Many of you will recall, as I do, examples of boards of directors whose roster might read in some such fashion as: 'Bodalski, Friesen, Laval, McTavish, Olson, O'Reilly, and Smith.'" By virtue of their ability to unite the interest of *all* people as consumers, co-ops had become unifying forces in local communities—centres of what McSorley called "home-town spirit."[37]

Conclusion and Questions

The tremendous expansion of the postwar years has never been repeated in the same way. In recent decades co-ops have grown in volume, membership, and facilities, but not in number. In the 1940s co-operatives penetrated new communities. They held continuous expansion to be a principle. They devoted time and energy to activities with no immediate payoffs for their own organizations —like open-ended educational endeavours, or sponsorship of new kinds of co-operatives, or, sometimes, sticking with money-losing propositions in the belief that increased loyalty and commitment would soon make them profitable. Was this just unrealistic idealism? Or did it provide the basis for the most successful period of development of new co-operatives and expansion into new communities that the consumer movement has ever seen?

The wholesales also grew, expanding in volume, and taking important steps to move from distribution into production, just as in 1928 they had expanded from retail into wholesale distribution. While the movement spread, as it were, horizontally into new communities, the wholesales grew vertically to integrate more economic functions, and to provide more services. Within the course of just a few years during the war they entered into the manufacture of feed, coal, and lumber. What permitted them to be so daring, and to succeed in enterprises with which they had no experience? Was this, too, a consequence of the confidence they derived from being part of a vital, growing movement, and of the support they received from their members?

Perhaps the controversy over income taxes and co-operatives was also a sign of their strength as a movement, a sign that business lobbies now considered them enough of a threat to warrant concern. Is it necessary that growth of co-operatives results in confrontation with profit-oriented competitors, and in political struggles?

11

Growth, Amalgamation, and Professional Management, 1944–1950

The union of the Co-op Refinery and the Saskatchewan Co-op Wholesale in 1944 was one of the most important events in the history of co-operative retailing in the West. Canada's two largest and most effective consumer-owned wholesaling and manufacturing co-operatives joined to create a single and even more powerful organization, one that combined their tremendous savings (tremendous relative to the sums co-operatives had previously worked with) and their complementary functions of manufacturing and distributing. From this union came a body that was recognizable as the forerunner of today's FCL; it was another step toward the creation of an integrated retailing system among co-operatives.

Saskatchewan Federated Co-operatives Limited, 1944

In March 1944 the directors of the refinery and of Saskatchewan Co-op Wholesale passed resolutions in favour of amalgamation, and on 13 March they met in joint session to discuss in detail how the by-laws for a merged organization would work. There were several stumbling blocks. Harry Fowler of the refinery mounted a one-man campaign against the wholesale's district system for electing directors, arguing that it should be modified to include "proportional representation." John Sinclair of the wholesale board, from Limerick, spoke against Fowler, and no other directors supported Fowler's ideas.

The question of a name for the new organization aroused greater division. The wholesale vetoed Co-operative Enterprises Limited, which had been proposed by a CCRL representative. According to the minutes it was Fowler who suggested Federated Co-operatives Limited or Saskatchewan Federated Co-operatives Limited. But once again there was resistance from the wholesale. John Sinclair replied to Fowler that "we should stick as closely as possible to the present Saskatchewan Co-operative Wholesale Society name." A straw vote was held in which Fowler's two suggestions tied with Saskatchewan Co-operative Society Limited. Among the names eliminated were Saskatchewan Central Co-operatives Limited and Saskatchewan Co-operative Wholesale Society. In the end, Fowler's suggestion, Saskatchewan Federated Co-operatives Limited (SFCL), was adopted in the tie vote because more directors chose it as their second choice. By compromise, the new organization now had a name.[1]

On 8 June 1944 SCWS and CCRL held a joint special meeting at the Bessborough Hotel in Saskatoon. There W. B. Francis, solicitor for the wholesale and an old and trusted participant in its decisions, told the delegates:

> Many of you think of these as two instruments, for most part serving the same people, owned by the same people and controlled by the same people. . . . in recent years, these two great instruments each performing the function for which it was created, have grown side by side and with ever increasing harmony. The question was bound to arise: . . . Why are these two great organizations which serve us, and which we own and control, not welded together in one even greater organization?

The arguments involved were the same as in all the subsequent amalgamations that led to present-day FCL. On the advantages side were the elimination of duplication, pooling of leadership, stronger financial position, and greater coordination with elimination of conflicting policies. On the disadvantages side were "loyalties to the present organizations . . . especially among the men who pioneered these organizations . . . there is a danger of losing something of value, even if only sentimental, if the organizations should be merged." Control would be more remote.[2]

As in most subsequent debates of this type, the co-operators involved chose size, strength, and power over sentiment, though there was discussion. For example, because the SCWS charter had, through successive amendments from 1929 to 1944, become broader, it was proposed to retain its charter and do away with CCRL's. Therefore SCWS would become the parent co-operative, and vote its shares in the refinery as a wholly owned subsidiary. All CCRL shareholders (except individuals) would become SCWS shareholders instead. Two delegates objected. One said that this was actually equivalent to SCWS taking over the refinery. He was right; but since, by and large, the same people owned both, this was not a problem for most of those present. Another CCRL delegate grumbled that the financial position of SCWS was not as good as that of the refinery—which was likely true, since petroleum products, in which the refinery specialized, were the most lucrative of any products handled by the co-ops. But, nevertheless, the amalgamation carried.[3]

The 1944 amalgamation of Consumers' Co-operative Refineries and the Saskatchewan Co-op Wholesale was an historic event. It created a kind of super co-op within Saskatchewan, a powerful, united co-op (in comparison to other co-operative organizations) with tremendous sales volume, economies of scale, and reinforcing functions in production and distribution. Other co-op wholesales had entered into production of goods, but only in small ways. Now, with oil, Saskatchewan saw a union of co-operative production and distribution, adding the margins at the production end to those at the distribution end in the savings that could be achieved. This was the first co-operative that was vertically integrated in a big way, and in that integration lies a key part of the origin of the co-operative system of today.

However, the merger had one other incidental effect. Harry Fowler, who had strongly supported the amalgamation, did himself out of a job. He went to Indiana to manage a co-operative farm machinery enterprise. Only when he found himself "too idealistic for the Americans," as Dorothy Fowler recalls, did he return to become manager of Tisdale Co-op. He re-entered SFCL—as an ordinary local manager, for the time being.[4]

The Growth of Co-operative Wholesaling, 1944–50

The grass-roots development of retail co-operatives meant that all the provincial wholesales grew, accumulated capital, and increased the range of the goods they handled and the services they provided to local retails.

In Manitoba the wholesale grew from just over $2 million in sales in 1944 to over $5 million in 1950. Net savings did not increase as quickly or as steadily, which is a sign of the adjustments that were taking place. Savings increased from $140,000 in 1944 to $199,000 in 1948, but then fell again. Meanwhile, Manitoba Co-op Wholesale acquired a new head office and bought out its oil supplier, Penn Oil Companies Limited, to form an oil division, and in 1945 established a hardware department. By 1949 MCW had a new feed plant, as

Manitoba Co-op Wholesale's warehouse at Vine and Whyte Avenue in Winnipeg (1952). As the sales volume of the co-operative system increased, so too did the warehousing and distributing activities of the co-op wholesales. There was a constant struggle to keep up with growth. (Photograph courtesy Reg Boulet)

well as new dry goods and grocery departments. It also established a construction department to help both the wholesale and the retails with their ever-more-rapid expansions, and an insurance department to help consolidate insurance on the growing number and value of co-operative premises and facilities.

Alberta also showed steady development. Its sales broke the one-hundred-thousand-dollar mark in 1940, the two-hundred-thousand-dollar mark in 1943, and were close to six hundred thousand by 1947. Perhaps more importantly, for a wholesale that had had great difficulty making savings in the 1930s, its net savings increased as well, reaching and then hovering around the fifty-thousand-dollar level from 1943 to 1947. It acquired a warehouse in Edmonton in 1945, and in 1946 entered into an agreement with the United Farmers of Alberta to distribute Maple Leaf Brand petroleum products. Finally, in 1948, an expansion program was embarked upon, and management service and audit departments were opened to support local retails during their own growth. The course of this expansion program is discussed in Chapter 13.

In British Columbia the wholesale was, with the lifting of wartime restrictions, finally able to undertake full operations. With less of a base than the other provinces, however, the B.C. wholesale was more sensitive to the emerging trends of retail concentration and integration. In 1945 it set up an associated store plan to spur systematic retail development, since gradual development from below was proving too slow to cope with change.

Saskatchewan Federated Co-ops adopted an ambitious five-year expansion plan in 1946, and for the first few years the targets were largely met. Sales increased from $6.7 million in 1945 to $17 million in 1950, while savings peaked at $831,000 in 1947. During the war years a dry-goods department was begun, and a second grocery department was opened in Saskatoon. Meanwhile, the Empire and Hy-Grade coal mines were purchased outright, as was a lumber mill at Canoe, B.C. In 1946 SFCL acquired a new headquarters on Avenue D in Saskatoon, greatly increasing its office and warehouse space. Following this expansion, the year 1949 saw some consolidation, as management was restructured, and the Outlook flour mill was closed in favour of the new Saskatchewan Wheat Pool mill in Saskatoon.

A sustained effort was made throughout this period in crude oil exploration, as SFCL attempted to ensure an adequate supply of crude for the refinery in the face of increasing concentration among suppliers. Drilling rights were acquired for large areas in Saskatchewan that remained largely unproductive, since the technology of the day could not economically exploit the heavier oil found in the province; but SFCL also bought wells in the Turner Valley field in Alberta, and in 1948 struck oil near Princess, Alberta. The target of the 1946 five-year plan was never attained, but, nevertheless, production amounting to 12–15 percent of the refinery's requirements was obtained in the hands of SFCL, providing some measure of security.

In all of this, consumer co-operatives were sustained by the ideas and philosophy that had emerged by the end of the war years, an optimistic

Head office building for Saskatchewan Federated Co-operatives Limited and later FCL, 1946–1970. This building on Avenue D in Saskatoon was purchased from the T. Eaton Co. in 1946. During World War Two it had served as an army warehouse, and as a result of some untold military incident, it acquired a bullet hole in the plate glass of the front door that remained there throughout SFCL's and FCL's occupancy.

philosophy of improvement and of building a fairer and more prosperous society.

Formalization of Staff and Structure

The charter of the Saskatchewan wholesale, now carried over to SFCL, gave the organization power to "carry on in accordance with co-operative principles the business of wholesale purchasers, procurers, shippers, vendors, and dealers of and in goods . . . of every kind and description, used in agriculture and farming or by consumers," and to manufacture or process the same, "including hardware, lumber, building materials, fuel, machinery, farm implements, binder twine, dry goods, and groceries."[5] This extremely broad charter was the result of the expansive dreams of early co-operators, and of nearly two decades of lobbying governments to obtain legislative improvements. From 1944 onward, the new organization began to take on many of these tasks and become more like what had been envisaged. In so doing, its product lines, services, and subsidiaries multiplied, and in proportion to this diversification, so too did its staff and management. In SFCL's early years, two subjects dominated its directors' meetings: how to organize and operate its manufacturing and processing subsidiaries, and how to organize management and staff.

In the fall of 1946 there was a strike in the Alberta coalfields, and by virtue of its ownership in two mines, SFCL was involved in the labour dispute. At the August board meeting manager McKay reported widespread problems with the work force, and the meeting was interrupted by President George Urwin to report the miners' demands: a forty-hour week, wage increases of $2.50 per day, and a deduction of five cents per ton of coal for a Miners' Welfare Fund. For virtually the first time, the wholesale had to discuss a general labour policy. The directors discussed "the possibility of participation by Labour in the earnings" as one way of helping the miners—the idea being to share operating surpluses with the employees, as an alternative to increased wages.[6]

The debate about the Alberta miners reveals several things. First, co-op leaders now had responsibilities of an order they had never possessed when their wholesales were small brokerage and accounting offices with few employees. Bigger management decisions were now required. Second, the SFCL board seemed sympathetic to the miners. After all, co-ops in this era believed their mission was the improvement of the standard of living and economic power of ordinary people, and felt they should pursue this even in their capacity as employers. Third, the board indicated a reluctance to consider wage increases, and a desire instead to look for more imaginative ways of accommodating the miners' concerns—such as "participation in the earnings."

The board also paid attention to such seemingly minor touches as Christmas presents. At first each staff person was given a turkey; later, when the staff grew too numerous for this to be practical, each was given five dollars.

At this early date there seemed to be little divergence among ordinary staff, management, and directors. "If you were part of the co-op, member or employee," recalls one co-operator, "you belonged to the co-op family. It wasn't employees or directors or owners." Staff were expected to be interested in co-operatives, and attended evening seminars to learn about co-operative history and principles, and about other kinds of co-operatives. SFCL instituted labour-management meetings in order to further its relations with its growing staff; in August 1946 the main concern voiced by labour was "the desire . . . that these meetings be made more interesting" by inviting directors to discuss SFCL departments. "Particular interest was shown [in] petroleum expansion."[7]

However, relations became more formal over time. In the fall of 1946 SFCL was negotiating with the unions in its various departments and subsidiaries, with the goal of reaching one master agreement to cover the Saskatoon and Regina offices as well as the mill and the refinery. The union draft proposed to include Sherwood Co-op in the bargaining unit as well, with (as McKay saw it) "the obvious intention . . . to prepare the way for later bringing in other local co-operatives." This was "very strongly opposed" by management, emphasizing the autonomy of the local retails.[8] There were many points of negotiation on both wages and benefits, but the two greatest problems were the promotion schedule and the wage schedules. McKay noted in November, after agreement had been reached, that "we have gone a long way to meet the demands of our employees, but in doing so we are not likely to find ourselves any too popular with our competitors, nor possibly with some co-operatives." Saskatchewan Federated Co-ops had willingly agreed to what it believed was an industry-leading contract that would put pressure on other employers, retails included, to increase their own payment schedules.[9]

The move toward more formal staff structures came earliest in Saskatchewan, where the fusion of the two large second-tier consumer co-ops and the multiplication of retails put the greatest pressure on the old ways of doing things. It went together with another fundamental change: the emergence of specialized, professional, internally developed management.

Changes in Management: New Structures, New People

The postwar expansion meant a great change in the co-operative wholesales, and by 1950 all of them had changed their management, in part to accommodate changing needs and circumstances. This was most complex in Saskatchewan Federated Co-ops, with its great range of operations. Robert McKay, manager of the Saskatchewan wholesale for fifteen of its eighteen years, resigned late in 1946, and this began a long period of casting about for a management structure suitable for a large co-operative wholesale and manufacturer.

Upon McKay's resignation, President Urwin "outlined the progress of the organization . . . and was of the opinion that the ramifications of the organization . . . being of such a diversified nature, no ordinary business manager could qualify for the position. He personally had been wondering if the present setup of placing the entire responsibility on the shoulders of one individual was the correct one." Following Urwin's reasoning, the directors proceeded to appoint four managers, all responsible directly to the board. Harold L. Benson was appointed production manager, R. F. Stephenson was distribution manager, E. T. "Ted" Mowbrey became treasurer, and Harry Fowler was offered the position of secretary "in charge of organization and public relations." All four managers were paid the identical salary, $4,800 per year, a further sign of their strict equality in the eyes of the board.[10]

The appointment of four equal co-managers was a sign not only of the increased complexity of the organization, but also of the board's confidence in its own ability to act as the co-ordinating agency for management. In particular, Urwin, as president, must have been more than willing to play a key role. Urwin was a full-time president, on the spot in the wholesale office where wholesale managers made decisions, and closely involved with operations. One of its former members calls SFCL's management by committee a "very awkward type of thing, but it seemed to work, in a way."

By the early 1950s the management committee had evolved into a different kind of structure, dominated by three distinctive personalities. Stewart had become treasurer, and he, along with Fowler as secretary and Urwin as president, formed an executive team. Stewart recalls that Urwin and Fowler were both "very hard-working, well-read, knowledgeable men." Fowler was "a top-notch conversational/promoter type. He could sell the Eskimos snow." And it is worth noting that, as secretary, Fowler was in an excellent position to use these talents in promoting new projects. He could free-wheel in devoting time and energy to new kinds of co-ops and new ideas. Urwin, Stewart continues, "was the guy who had the first nickel he ever made—and a very successful farmer. If you wanted money, you didn't go to George Urwin." But although Urwin "wouldn't spend a nickel, . . . he wasn't afraid to spend a million overnight. He wasn't afraid of big money." Urwin may have been "a hard-nosed, English businessman," but he was also "a man of vision."

The Saskatchewan Federated Co-operatives Limited management team (about 1954). Left to right: Dave Stewart, treasurer; Harry Fowler, secretary; George Urwin, president; Ben Pawson, distribution division manager; Harold Benson, production division manager.

Another FCL manager recalls that Urwin was "a very conservative individual. He ruled the delegate body with an iron hand. At the annual meeting, when George got up [to speak], that was it."

As for Stewart, as an ex-General Motors employee who had studied assembly-line techniques, he was the up-to-date business administrator, the one who controlled inventories and costs, personnel, productivity, and budgets. He recalls that when he came to Saskatoon, inventory was in "a heck of a mess." As in personnel and other areas, the wholesale had outgrown its old procedures, and Stewart was one of a few with experience in large business operations. As he tells it, the Saskatoon warehouse had ten thousand items with fifteen clerks writing down every nut and bolt in and out on ledger sheets. "The first thing I did was tell them to throw out all the books." In place of ledgers, Stewart says he introduced a system of tags to put on the bins; when the bin was nearly empty the clerk gave the tag to a buyer who ordered more. Only two or three stock-takers were needed to check the bins. "They had nobody who thought about these things. . . . Good co-operators, but they had no background. Then we started hiring people who knew what they were doing."

Undoubtedly the emergence of a more professional attitude among managers was a crucial change, but in fact it seems it was less common to hire experienced people than to develop them. One senior manager of Saskatchewan Federated Co-ops and of FCL argues that "one of the basic philosophies of our personnel department" was always to find a place for people—"we develop people internally." Tony Dummer, who was present during the reorganization and expansion of SFCL's Personnel Division in the 1940s, lists many people hired in his day who "never worked anywhere else." Many had arrived on the ground floor with no experience or knowledge of co-ops—"I'm a Nova Scotian originally and I didn't know the back door from the front door of what a co-op was about," observes one—and for a large number the co-op was their first job of any kind. But they learned. Dummer is a good illustration of his own policy, for he began by cleaning oil drums and ended up as an executive assistant. Another went from messenger boy to retail accounting and, eventually, management of a division; a third started as a fieldman and climbed up through the locals' services division into senior management; a fourth began as a part-time clerk in high school and went on thirty years later to be manager of his region. These managers developed from within left their mark on the system.

The Role of the Centrals in Retail Services

The increasing concentration in the wholesale of people with many years' full-time experience in the consumer co-operative movement resulted in a much more critical examination of management, including the activities of local managers. One long-time retail manager, later an FCL region and senior manager, comments that in those days boards had the attitude that "almost anybody that had a bit of education and knew how to figure and was a hard

The co-operative movement was kept going by meetings: Harry Fowler addresses an outdoor meeting in Swift Current, Sask. (1950s?).

worker could be a co-op manager." In his estimation, and he was a former Safeway employee, there was "a big difference" between the standard of management at local co-ops and at their chain-store competitors. "I was very thankful I had my Safeway experience—in those days the co-op didn't give you much training."

Another long-time refinery and FCL employee remembers that financial planning for the retails was one of the greatest needs in the 1940s and 1950s. "Since they were all autonomous, there was a lot of waste that took place . . . many, many unwise moves were made that cost us a lot of money. We wouldn't have survived if not for the cash flow from the Refinery."

An ex-fieldman remarks that one reason for the problems with managers was precisely that members were so supportive and loyal. Members would ignore enticements from competitors and stick with the co-op because they remembered its past successes and believed in its future. This must have helped many co-ops survive bad management, but it also helped preserve many of the local managers who were "very naive and very unskilled. They thought that if you just ordered something and put it on the shelves people would buy it because it was the Co-op." As the competition grew keener in the postwar boom, this naiveté became dangerous.

Yet another FCL manager who started in those years recalls that in the late 1940s the various provincial wholesales had many "messes on our hands" as a result of local managers appointed during the war, when manpower was short and the selection was poor. Changes of managers became frequent. "There were stock problems, cash shortages. The whole idea of professional managers as we have them today just wasn't there."

From these and other views it is clear that in the eyes of central managers, untrained and erratic local managers constituted one of the biggest problems confronting the co-ops in their rapid growth after the war. The wholesales' reporting, supervision, and accounting began in those years to help the locals become more efficient.

Centralized auditing for retails was one aspect of this help. It had long been done for the different kinds of affiliate and associate co-ops, and the audit departments were now expanded as more and more autonomous co-ops, too, were encouraged to have their accounting done centrally. This could catch problems with management before they became fatal.

Another kind of service for the retails was the effort to improve managers through better training and communication. In the Manitoba wholesale, for example, there was a Public Relations and Publicity Department under Gordon Leckie. This department organized co-op tours in the western provinces and in the United States, to help directors and managers become familiar with other parts of the movement. It produced managers' and directors' bulletins, and provided training courses and seminars for senior managers. It sent out "Co-op-ograms" (newsletters) to retail members, and assisted with meetings, drives, campaigns, and so forth.[11]

These different kinds of help for retails were delivered with the aid of the large field services that were characteristic of the 1940s. The Manitoba wholesale, proportionate to its size, probably had the most extensive field service of any of the wholesales. "We had seven fieldmen based out of Winnipeg," recalls a former MCW employee, "each with a car—a very expensive deal when you look back at it." But in times of rapid growth, and with the great need to watch local management, this was a necessary service. It was also an important part of what kept the movement going and sustained its growth. A former MCW fieldman remembers that in that job he became "a multi-purpose co-op field-man. . . . One thing we were taught was that it was a *movement,* and that we as co-op workers should take an interest in other aspects of the movement. If Co-op Implements was having a problem, or any co-op, . . . we should do what we could to help them."

It was not easy for a co-operatively owned central to provide these kinds of management services to fully autonomous retail co-ops. "We had a difficult job in Federated," comments a former manager.

> We were the central organization owned and controlled by the retail co-ops. *They* owned and controlled *us,* but because we, by and large, had the expertise and the specialized people, the retails had to rely on us. . . . You had to make some tough decisions from time to time. So here they own and control the Wholesale, and there's the Wholesale doing something that . . . isn't what they'd like to see us do.

This dynamic tension between ownership and control on one side, in the autonomous locals, and managerial expertise on the other, in the central, has remained with FCL ever since. It is substantially the product of the growth of the 1940s and 1950s, when the central became large enough, and the need for managerial expertise great enough, that the central could begin to play an important role in the life of the locals.

Conclusion and Questions

The development of the wholesales, and especially of SFCL, from 1944 onward, epitomized two trends in the consumer co-operative movement: first, the trend toward vertical integration, toward expanding from distribution into production, and from wholesaling into retail services; and second, the formalization and professionalization of management. Together, these trends accentuated more and more the operational side of the consumer movement, as opposed to the ownership and representational side. The seeds were sown for a new duality between directors and managers, between philosophy and practicality, between long-term and short-term goals, membership and efficiency.

Co-operatives have tried to minimize this dualism, or turn it to their advantage, through the approach of viewing board and senior managers as a management team, an approach epitomized in SFCL's management committee of President Urwin, Secretary Fowler, and Treasurer Stewart. Have co-ops—retail and wholesale—been successful over the years in making the management team idea work? Was there too much board interference in management in those days? Or have directors lost an important part of their influence since the days of Urwin and Fowler?

It also seems that the professionalization of the wholesale staff went together with criticism of local managers, and efforts to improve management at the local level. To what extent did the development of professional staff in the wholesale mean a power struggle with local managers? In such a relationship, where central managers are critical of the proficiency of local managers, who (keeping the members' interests in mind) should win?

PART FIVE: CONSOLIDATION 1950–1961

Introduction to Part Five

In the true "movement" stage of consumer co-operation in the 1940s, the kind of growth that had occurred had been growth in people—retail co-operatives multiplied, spreading into new communities and touching more and more of the population. But this kind of growth was already beginning to slow by about 1950, when the next era, the era of consolidation, set in, corresponding to changes in western Canadian society as farms grew larger and rural areas lost people and services. Growth now meant not new co-ops, but bigger ones with better facilities and more well-rounded services.

With these changes, a second pattern became apparent: the further development of professional management in the consumer co-operative system. A different kind of central wholesale began to emerge. The 1944 merger between the refinery and the Saskatchewan wholesale had created a kind of super co-op in Saskatchewan that combined manufacturing and wholesaling, and which, with growing resources, began to branch out into a comprehensive range of commodities. The 1955 merger with Manitoba created Federated Co-operatives Limited, and ensured that this kind of development became one which crossed provincial boundaries. The 1961 amalgamation with Alberta Co-op Wholesale Association consolidated FCL as a regional trading unit, and set the stage for discussions with B.C. about a further merger. During this period the decisions were made that led to a single Co-operative Retailing System for western Canada.

*   *   *

12

The Second Amalgamation: Origins of Federated Co-operatives Limited, 1955

In 1954, President Wilfrid McSorley of the Manitoba Co-op Wholesale, addressing the last annual meeting of that organization before its amalgamation with SFCL, reviewed the history of the consumer co-operative movement in Manitoba. He divided it into three phases: The Years of Survival in the 1930s, The Years of Expansion in the 1940s, and The Years of Consolidation in the 1950s. He also linked these three eras to Manitoba's three general managers, W. F. Popple, E. B. Chown, and C. B. Fraser. "Many problems seem to follow after a period of rapid expansion in any organization," observed McSorley. Under Fraser's stewardship in the 1950s, McSorley explained, the job was to tackle these problems, to develop strength in finances, personnel, and service to member co-ops, and to consolidate resources.[1] What McSorley said about Manitoba applies more generally to the whole consumer movement in the West.

Manitoba Co-op Wholesale management group (1953). General Manager C. B. "Bun" Fraser is seated in the middle of the front row.

Social and Economic Change

In 1952 the Saskatchewan government set out the terms of reference for a Royal Commission on Agriculture and Rural Life. This commission was to look into "the problems involved in present day trends in agricultural production," farm capital and credit, and rural transportation and services.[2] The commission reported that in 1951 average farm size hit 550.5 acres, and for the first time in Saskatchewan's history, more than half the population was not involved in farming.[3] What this meant was that small farmers were disappearing, and population base and level of services in rural communities were declining. The postwar era also saw an increase in car ownership and improvement of the road network, including keeping highways open throughout the winter. These changes, too, contributed to larger trading areas and the closure of many services in smaller communities.

Parallel to these changes, the co-operative movement was losing some of its momentum, due, perhaps in part, to having reached some of its limits, but also due to prosperity and changing attitudes. A 1953 article on consumer co-operation in Alberta's *Co-op News* commented on problems in attendance at annual meetings:

> Should a heading appear in the paper, "Co-op in Difficulties," the chances are the meeting would be a well-attended one, all members turning out to see just what was ailing their business. More usually, however, during the past few years at any rate, is the heading which reads, "Small Meeting Following Successful Year."
>
> It seems that when everything is going along smoothly, with adequate sales, when the road is smooth, co-operative members are prone to be apathetic.

The statement is one which could probably also have been made, in many communities, at any time since 1953.[4]

In Manitoba the number of co-op members grew by sixteen thousand in the three years from 1945–48; by seven thousand in the next three years; and by less than two thousand in 1951–54. Membership actually fell in 1954 for the first time since the war.[5] In Saskatchewan the number of co-op associations which were members of the wholesale fell steadily from 535 in 1949 to 431 in 1954, at the same time that retail sales increased sharply. This indicates the ongoing consolidation among co-operative associations.[6]

And together with this economic rationalization, business was getting bigger, and the nature of the competition co-ops faced was changing. "Big business is getting *better organized* and *bigger,*" members of the B.C. Co-op Wholesale Society were told in a special 1951 report on co-operative retailing. Chains still handled a lesser volume than independent retailers, claimed the report, but they were growing faster. Co-ops faced "increasing competitive pressure," especially in the cities where co-ops, "which, on the average, have not kept fully abreast of these changes, find it relatively difficult to operate." Co-ops in B.C. were told that "possible disaster" was facing the consumer movement "unless a realistic adjustment is made to modern conditions." During the greatest period of prosperity B.C. had ever known, eighteen co-operative outlets had closed, versus only six new ones created, in three years.[7]

McSorley's final report as president of MCW indicates the growing awareness of changed conditions, as well as showing how the imminent merger of Manitoba and Saskatchewan organizations was expected to help co-ops deal with these changes:

> Our movement was born in depression and adversity. We have lived to see a continuing day of prosperity. . . . If our co-ops are to grow under such conditions, we must pay proper attention to smart and up-to-date service and facilities. No longer are consumers interested only in costs, as they were forced to be in the "Dirty Thirties." We [must] give as good—or better—service as private companies.
>
> Certainly if we wish to expand to reach all consumers, we must stress service. For example, development of co-ops amongst urban people has become one of our aims. If we are to succeed, we will need Co-op Centres and equipment of the most modern design, operated at top-grade efficiency. To meet this challenge, our FCL will have the volume and resources to give intelligent leadership. That will be a major benefit from amalgamation.

But McSorley also reiterated the historic faith and optimism the co-operative movement had developed, hoping it could be re-introduced in the new age:

> Many signs of disaster loom large before us—H-bomb stockpiles, growing private monopolies in the production and distribution of basic needs, apathy amongst democratic citizens who feel that big governments are far removed from the ordinary people. These portents cause many people to become pessimists or cynics.
>
> In this dark world picture, co-ops shine with a light of hope for the whole human race. We have a theory of Mutual Aid which unites in harmony the basic doctrines of ancient religions, and the findings of modern social science. But it is not a theory "up in the clouds" of interest only to idealists and dreamers. The essence of the co-operative method is simply—it benefits mankind, and *it works.*
>
> Our success in MCW is one more proof added to the Rochdale story, the Danish story, the Antigonish story, the Wheat Pool story. With such a history behind us, we look ahead to the future of FCL with courage, with conviction, and with confidence.[8]

The Second Amalgamation: the Formation of FCL, 1955

In the spring of 1954 Russell Love of Alberta argued that the wholesales of the different provinces should amalgamate. He claimed that

> provincialism and isolation have retarded the growth and expansion of consumer co-operation in the past. Other types of businesses have found it necessary to disregard provincial boundary lines and treat the Prairie Provinces as one trading area. It would appear that the time has arrived when the major co-ops must also regard the prairies as one trading area.

From the beginning, therefore, the terms of the debate were such that the unification of all the provinces (and B.C. was considered) was envisaged as a possible long-term goal.[9]

The ambitious plan of so broad an amalgamation was rejected, however, as an immediate possibility. Dave Stewart, treasurer of SFCL at the time, remembers that some wanted to push quickly for a grand amalgamation—"once you get something rolling, it's hard to stop"—but he saw his role as to slow this down. Finances and personnel, especially retail personnel, limited how quickly such amalgamations could be carried out. And there was a specific objection to amalgamation with Alberta: co-operative sales in Alberta remained divided between the Alberta Co-op Wholesale Association and the stores it serviced, and the UFA Co-op's bulk commodity points. In 1956 President George Urwin noted that "there are two consumer co-operative groups operating as separate entities in the province of Alberta, sometimes in competition with each other. Because of this," said Urwin, "Federated is not interested in any merger that does not include both the Alberta Co-op Wholesale Association and the United Farmers of Alberta Co-operative."[10]

But Manitoba was another matter. Manitoba Co-op Wholesale was stronger in the bulk business than in the store business, and could therefore offer a large volume in high-margin goods. Saskatchewan Federated Co-ops could use this volume, for by 1954 the most recent expansion of the Co-op Refinery had been completed, and an outlet for the increased capacity would help to increase savings. Several ex-managers from that era claim that the 1955 amalgamation with Manitoba was based mainly on petroleum considerations; as one put it, the amalgamation "was fuelled largely by the desirability of utilizing the full volume of the refinery in Regina." Saskatchewan and Manitoba, one with a refinery and the other with successful bulk petroleum co-ops, complemented one another. "No two Co-op Wholesales on the continent were more alike in all respects," the Manitoba directors told their delegates, "from their philosophic outlooks to their dollars-and-cents position."[11]

Beyond this, the Manitoba wholesale was also in much better shape financially than any of the other provincial wholesales, apart from Saskatchewan itself. MCW had in 1954 only one-quarter the sales of SFCL, but because the

Co-operators celebrate the success of the latest refinery expansion drive (18 August 1954). Even more people turned out in 1960 for the refinery's 25th anniversary when nearly 40,000 co-operators are estimated to have visited the site, a powerful demonstration of the strength of the co-operative movement and of its pride in the refinery.

Manitoba wholesale concentrated on relatively few products, its earnings were high, and it had a relatively large amount of capital at its disposal.[12] There were also geographic incentives: eastern Saskatchewan was better served from Winnipeg for goods from central Canada. Manitoba co-operators, for their part, hoped for a leap in economic power and in service through amalgamation with Saskatchewan.

Discussions between the two provinces began early in 1954, and it quickly became apparent that the boards and managers of both organizations were in favour. The Manitoba directors reported that amalgamation was "readily accepted as a logical and inevitable move."[13]

Late in 1954 some of the Manitoba members grew alarmed as rumours of the impending amalgamation spread. A story in the Minnedosa newspaper reported local members were concerned that the Saskatchewan wholesale would overwhelm its counterpart in Manitoba, and that Manitoba shareholders would lose control; that the secret negotiations between the two boards violated the principles of grass-roots democracy; and that it might mean divorcing Manitoba co-operatives from their provincial organizations and federations, including the Federation of Agriculture and Co-operation. C. B. "Bun" Fraser, manager of MCW, intervened to tell the press "there has been no secrecy and it isn't a sell-out."[14] Despite these reassurances, however, Bill Parker, president of the Manitoba Pool, was reported to be strongly opposed to the loss of identity entailed in amalgamating with Saskatchewan.

When the shareholders' meetings were finally held, no dissenting votes were cast. At the Manitoba meeting, 151 of 162 possible voting delegates were present, representing 118 of 129 member associations. Only one abstained.[15] "We did a really good job of having meetings and talking it over," recalls "Smokey" Robson, then an MCW field serviceman.

There were regrets and mixed feelings. Don Slimmon, who, as one of MCW's fieldmen, had been involved extensively in the grass-roots organizing of the 1940s and 1950s, is one of those who expresses reservations about the ultimate effects of the merger. The concept of the new organization, he argues, was that of a pyramid or a hierarchy, not of decentralized decision-making in the locals, "on the spot." When SFCL's approach was extended to Manitoba, the head office began to do more and more. This meant that co-ops "lost the drive and the responsibility that local people had," and, as Slimmon sees it, bureaucracy and red tape took over where democracy had once prevailed.

Another former MCW employee, answering the question of whether co-operators in Manitoba felt they were losing something, says, "yes and no."

> There was the feeling of wanting to stay as you were, to keep growing; the feeling of loss of identity . . . but at the same time [there was] the practical side of it—more efficient operation, better buying power. . . . The feeling was that it was the way to go; things were getting bigger.

An ex-manager concurs that some people were concerned: "There were certainly a few people who felt they were being swallowed up by a big colossus." But "there was more money available for expansion. We were able to do things because of the economies of scale that we in Manitoba previously couldn't do because we were small." One of these things was urban co-operative development—very soon the new FCL had made a commitment to the expansion of Red River Co-op in Winnipeg.[16]

The amalgamation of 1955 was also in many ways an amalgamation between equals. For the first joint board, George Urwin of the Saskatchewan wholesale became president, and Wilfrid McSorley of Manitoba became first vice-president. Harry Fowler of Saskatchewan became secretary, and J. J. Siemens of Manitoba became associate secretary. Assigning top management of the new organization was a slightly more complicated matter. Dave Stewart of Saskatchewan recalls, "Once we were amalgamated, there was a problem. Who was going to manage the Wholesale? Me or Bun Fraser?" As with the presidency and other offices, the approach was to compromise. "They made us both managers! We were 'co-managers'. Can you run a business that way?"

Fraser recalls that he and Stewart were "completely different people." Stewart was the financial type, and took charge of finance, accounting, per-

The boards of directors of Saskatchewan Federated Co-operatives and of Manitoba Co-operative Wholesale at the meeting in Saskatoon on 23 September 1954 which laid the basis for the merger that formed Federated Co-operatives Limited in 1955. Officers are seated, left to right: J. J. Siemens (secretary, MCW), C. C. Hunt (vice-president, MCW), W. J. McSorley (president, MCW), George Urwin (president, SFCL), L. L. Lloyd (vice-president, SFCL), W. E. Mills (SFCL), and P. Robertson (SFCL).

sonnel, and manufacturing, while Fraser says he "was the 'people' type. . . . I loved working with retail co-ops. I loved merchandising." He took charge of retail services, merchandising, and public relations. As a result of their differences, he says, it was a "pretty ideal situation." "We got along pretty well," agrees Stewart. Their first report claimed "we have been able to select the most successful operating techniques from each organization."[17] But Stewart also shakes his head, thinking of the co-manager system. "I always think back on those days and wonder how we made it."

Many of MCW's managers entered senior posts in the home office of the new organization, taking responsibility for services provided throughout FCL's area. The retail services and educational functions of FCL benefited particularly in receiving new Manitoba personnel, perhaps because these areas had been among MCW's special strengths. At the senior management level, the melding of the Manitoba and Saskatchewan wholesales was smooth.

The Challenges of Bigness

The amalgamation of 1955 was the first serious challenge to co-operators' provincial loyalties. The old farm movements and farm co-operatives had virtually all been organized on provincial lines. Grain Growers, United Farmers, and wheat pools had set their sights on their provincial capitals and had become powerful political as well as economic institutions in their provinces. This provincially-oriented attitude was deeply imbued in their organizations, as evidenced by the fact that Manitoba Pool opposed MCW's amalgamation with Saskatchewan, and that the UFA in Alberta at that time resisted close co-operation with out-of-province and non-farmer-oriented co-operatives. By contrast, the creation of FCL as an interprovincial co-operative wholesale was another expression of the basic idea that consumer co-operation was for consumers of all kinds, everywhere. Consumer co-operatives were not just agricultural organizations intended to serve a specific farming population, and were not restricted by provincial boundaries.

Dave Stewart told the author that the Manitoba amalgamation was "the one that determined the future," the one that proved that "being a big co-operative in [one province] wasn't the only thing we required to serve the members." The year 1955 was "the breakthrough, the turning point" when "we got away from the parochial attitude. That provincial attitude was a big problem." Gordon Sinclair, then a Manitoba retail director but later president of FCL, agreed. The amalgamation involved "a deliberate effort to erase boundaries," with districts crossing borders and, at the first annual meeting, with delegates mingling in the hotel and placed with strangers from other regions. He recalled that "pulling people together, erasing long-standing boundaries, was a very deliberate effort to make a Co-operative Retailing System that belonged to Western Canada, and to get rid of provincialism." FCL was a recognition that "when big things have to happen, the big issues take priority over the hometown loyalties."

In 1955 it was no longer possible in Saskatchewan or Manitoba for the wholesale to refer to "serving the people of the province," to the opinions of "Manitoba" co-operators or the purchasing habits of "Saskatchewan" consumers. At about the time of the merger, FCL managers and directors began to refer to their market and constituency as "Federated-Land"—the first printed reference the author found was from Bun Fraser in 1956, though it is said that Harry Fowler originated the term.[18] Now, says Sinclair, " 'Federated Land' is all of Western Canada, right from the Great Lakes [to the Pacific]—it's kind of a wonderful feeling."

Consumer co-operation acquired a regional identity stronger than the provincial loyalties of the old farmers' movements. It became a kind of co-operative or organizational patriotism, a higher-than-local allegiance. Did this also threaten to take it further from the grass-roots? At the very first meeting of FCL's shareholders in June 1955, Harry Fowler presented the issues succinctly: "We are living in an era of vast and rapid change. Bigness is the order of the day." The first challenge of the day was that "we must meet the threat of 'bigness' by being big ourselves." But, Fowler continued, there was a second challenge. Some co-operators had told FCL that "Federated is expanding too fast now"; some local directors claimed, "Federated is becoming a monopoly." Fowler felt that such comments showed something was wrong. The second challenge of the day, therefore, was to conduct "an educational program . . .

to create a full understanding that the Co-operative Movement is a 'bridge' not a 'barrier' to economic democracy."

> We have not fully met the "challenge of the day" if we only achieve bigness, utility of capacity, efficiency and service to our members. The simple fact of ownership of these vast facilities from the local co-operative store to the timber berths of British Columbia, to the oil wells of Saskatchewan and Alberta, to the coal mines in Alberta, is not enough. There must be knowledge of this ownership. There must be a recognition of the fact that ownership is more than receiving patronage refunds on goods bought. There must be a recognition of responsibility that these things are ours, and must be controlled by all who participate in the benefits.

With these words Fowler laid out a dual, long-term program that could be considered a constant down to the present day: on the one hand, to become as big as necessary to compete in large markets, head-to-head with horizontally and vertically integrated profit firms; and on the other hand, to remain in touch with members and to preserve their perceived and real ownership and control.[19]

National Co-ordination: the Growth of Interprovincial Cooperative

When the first provincial wholesales were founded in 1928, the idea of forming, instead, a single interprovincial wholesale was also discussed. This proved impossible, partly because many of the problems of that time were provincial in scope and did not lend themselves to cross-border solutions—such as the problem of relations with the provincial farmers' organizations. The managers of the wholesales consulted with each other on placing joint orders, however, and as early as 1935 discussed joint orders for twine and other common goods. By 1938 this activity was becoming regular.[20] It led, ultimately, to the creation of Interprovincial Cooperative Limited (IPCO) in 1940 as a "third-tier" co-op—a co-op run by a federation of provincial co-operative wholesales, later including co-operative wholesales from every region of Canada.

IPCO was unable to become functional until wartime restrictions were lifted. By 1948 it had $4.401 million in sales, and entered into manufacturing with a bag factory in Montreal. The goods distributed under a CO-OP label by IPCO included car, radio, and flashlight batteries; binder twine; brooms; grain grinders; milking machines; oil and greases; shingles; turpentine; and washing machines.[21] Actual production by IPCO was expanded in 1951 by a coffee and tea plant in South Burnaby, B.C., and in 1953 by an agricultural chemical formulating plant in Winnipeg, Manitoba. In 1956 it entered the automobile supplies field with CO-OP tires.

Interprovincial Cooperative became one of the best examples of the co-operation that had developed by the end of the war between producer and consumer co-operatives. One of its chief functions in the beginning, alongside joint ordering for its member wholesales, was to serve as a vehicle by which com-

Co-op representatives inspect the factory that bags CO-OP "Indian Brand" fertilizer, first marketed by Interprovincial Cooperative in 1955–56. Present are representatives of FCL (Jake Fehr, left), IPCO (Bill Silversides and Al Cushon, next from the left), and Alberta Co-operative Wholesale Association (Bruno Holdfelt, fourth from the left).

modities produced and processed within the broad co-operative movement could be marketed under an official CO-OP label through retail co-ops. IPCO was a major seller of products from the Saskatchewan Wheat Pool flour mill and flax-crushing plant opened in Saskatoon in 1949; of CO-OP vegetable oil products from Altona; of CO-OP jam produced by the B.C. Fruit Growers; and of CO-OP salmon from the B.C. Fishermen's Co-operative Federation.[22]

The dreams and ambitions of Interprovincial Cooperative were extensive. In 1944 a comprehensive plan was formulated for organizing co-operative production so as to reconcile the interests of consumers and producers. Three different options were outlined. Co-operatives would agree that some commodities would be under exclusive producer ownership, in which case IPCO would buy the product at market prices, or act as broker for the producer and take a commission. Other products were to be produced in facilities jointly owned by IPCO and by producer co-ops, according to agreements they would reach over time. In this case IPCO would negotiate a commission or would split operating surpluses with the producers. Third, other products would be placed under "direct" consumer control through the IPCO board, and the entirety of the surplus would be returned to consumers. This 1944 interprovincial plan reads like a blueprint for a self-sufficient co-operative economy, covering all steps from manufacturing to retail sales, reconciling the interests of producers and consumers, and determining fair prices and returns by a consensual system of on-going agreement and negotiation among co-operatives.[23]

One tangible result of this policy was that Saskatchewan Federated Co-operatives Limited got out of the flour-milling business and left it to the Wheat Pool. Although the Co-op Mill at Outlook had had satisfactory results under wartime conditions, this was only because 75 percent of its production was taken by the British Ministry of Food. Only a quarter of production could actually be disposed of through the co-operative marketing system in Canada. Moreover, the mill was antiquated and expensive to run. An agreement was therefore reached with Saskatchewan Wheat Pool in 1945 to close the Outlook mill, have the Pool open a new one, and market the product through IPCO.[24] When the Pool mill opened in 1949 this started the drive to sell CO-OP flour, perhaps the biggest of all the early CO-OP label campaigns.

In the 1940s and '50s IPCO represented a vision even broader than both FCL and western Canada.

Conclusion and Questions

The formation of FCL was deliberate adaptation to a new era. Efficiency, savings, market power, bigness to compete with bigness (as Fowler put it) were the essence of the new ideas of that time. But Fowler had laid out two objectives, and although he called them "orders of the day," they are still relevant three and a half decades later. He had argued that co-ops must get bigger. How well has the system followed this prescription?

FCL has grown, amalgamating with Alberta in 1961 and with B.C. in 1970. Large organizations like the UFA Co-op remain outside (Chapter 13), and other provinces remain separate. In some of them, notably Ontario, there is very little co-operative presence in urban centres. Are there further possibilities for "bigness" here?

IPCO is the existing agency for co-ordination with these other provinces and other co-operatives. It is today a commercial success in chemical formulation and product procurement. Although it operates the chemical formulating plant in Winnipeg, IPCO has not yet fulfilled the dreams and aspirations of the 1940s for expansion of co-operative control over production and processing. Nor is IPCO integrated with its members as a system in the way FCL and its member retails are organized. This suggests consumer co-operation could expand further into manufacturing, perhaps even into a national-level third-tier co-op to replace IPCO's looser federation.

The second task proposed by Fowler was to undertake education that would preserve the member's genuine sense of ownership. Is this still an important goal today, or are price and service all that consumers want from a co-op in today's competitive environment? Do members need to be reminded (as they were in the forties and fifties) that every dime spent in a co-op is a contribution to consumer power and to their future savings; while every dime spent in a competing outlet is lost to them? Do they need to be told to buy CO-OP brands to increase consumer influence in the marketplace, to increase the prospect of future savings, to increase the wealth retained in their own communities? In what other ways ought they to be reminded of their ownership status and responsibilities?

Fowler's questions, and others like them, are still being asked by the Co-operative Retailing System today. That is one constant from 1955 to 1988. But another set of constants are equally obvious, including the co-operative pride, the optimism about expansion, and the organizational patriotism that reached a new stage through the 1955 merger. This is no longer a farmers' pride or a provincial patriotism, but has become embodied in an institution that extends beyond provincial boundaries. Since FCL's creation, consumer co-operation in the West no longer has a provincial character, but one which is regional and perhaps even national. That, too, has remained an essential part of the culture of the system down to the present day.

13

Alberta Co-op Wholesale and the Third Merger, 1951–1961

By 1950 Alberta co-operators had built a large consumer movement. If the volume of the United Farmers of Alberta Co-op and the Alberta Co-op Wholesale had been combined in a single organization, Alberta would have been stronger in co-operative wholesaling than Manitoba. The UFA, headquartered in Calgary, and ACWA, in Edmonton, possessed distribution networks serving large numbers of farmers and rural people who purchased co-operatively. But the two were divided by policies and personalities.

In policy terms, the UFA stood for service to farmers and concentrated on farmer members, farm communities, and farm supplies. It was structured without autonomy for local outlets—a single organization to serve a single constituency, the farmers of Alberta. ACWA was organized along the lines of the other co-op wholesales, serving a diverse array of autonomous locals which, in turn, aspired to serve all consumers in all commodities. The UFA and ACWA were different enough that they could not unite, but also similar enough to overlap and compete. ACWA was involved in some farm commodities, like feeds. And the UFA, though it concentrated on lucrative, high-volume bulk farm commodities, since the early 1940s had owned a chain of sales outlets that sold groceries and general merchandise.

In the 1950s, ACWA's growth and the possibility of interprovincial amalgamations changed the picture. More co-ordination, even amalgamation, was discussed.

Expansion and Crisis: ACWA, 1948–52

Buoyed by its successes, ACWA embarked in 1948 upon a fateful program of massive expansion. A special shareholders' meeting that year approved the program, and authorized $1 million in preference shares to finance the expansion. New management service and audit departments were created by the wholesale to help member retails manage their growth. In 1949 a feed plant was purchased in Edmonton, and a branch warehouse was established in Calgary to extend services to the southern part of the province. In 1950–51 new warehouses were also built in Edmonton and Calgary. And it was in 1951 as well that ACWA made its greatest leap, purchasing the UFA's entire chain of twenty-one retail outlets. This purchase was a significant step forward in co-ordinating ACWA with the UFA, for it ended competition between the two in the store business. It expanded ACWA's distribution network, extending it into the heart of major cities like Calgary. The takeover of these outlets and their direct management by ACWA typified the aggressive, everything-at-once, wholesale-led and wholesale-directed expansionist philosophy of Alberta co-operative leaders.

Had there been a greater number of experienced managers in Alberta co-ops, or had this expansion been undertaken a few years earlier to catch the peak vitality of the co-operative movement, it might possibly have gone into the record books as a daring success. But that was not how things worked out. ACWA expanded just as the era of postwar economic consolidation set in, just as the farm economy entered a difficult phase and rural communities began to be rationalized. In addition, it expanded in capital-intensive ways—brand new warehouses, block purchase of the UFA stores—when it had a weak capital base. The Alberta wholesale, following its difficulties of the 1930s, its competition with the UFA, and its lack of petroleum earnings, simply did not have the solid financial base enjoyed by the other prairie co-op wholesales. It had none of its own money to commit to the purchase of the UFA stores, relying instead on an additional $280,000 preference share issue, a $250,000 bank loan, and $180,000 to be paid gradually "out of retail sales." As it turned out, the actual valuation of the stores was greater than expected, so that even more money had to be raised from shareholders and committed from future sales than originally planned.[1]

Sales jumped with the expansion, but earnings fell. Sales broke the million-dollar mark for the first time ever in 1949, but even though these sales were nearly three times as great as those from 1945, the net savings were barely half as much. In 1950 ACWA had nearly $2 million in sales, but only negligible savings. And in 1951, with the purchase of the UFA stores, sales jumped to $2.7 million—but ACWA's financial statements showed a deficit of close to $400,000.[2] In January 1952 the directors reported that 1951 "will be remembered as a year of extreme difficulties and acute adjustments." Huge increases in accounts receivable and advances to locals were "crippling the finances of ACWA." The large operating loss that year was traced to past mistakes, including over-valued inventories, underestimated bad-debt expenses, accounting adjustments, and other problems. Some $25,000 was lost on punch-card accounting equipment that had to be thrown out in 1951 when it proved useless.[3]

With the expansion program foundering, president J. Russell Love asked Saskatchewan Federated Co-ops to recommend a new manager. This search led to the appointment on 1 August 1952 of E. T. (Ted) Mowbrey, former treasurer of the refinery and of SFCL. One of the first things Mowbrey did was to arrange financing from the Saskatchewan Co-operative Credit Society (SCCS) for the over-extended Alberta wholesale. Five months later Mowbrey explained to ACWA's creditors the conditions he found when he arrived. If accurate, his comments reveal an organization whose management, accounting, and inventory systems and personnel had not developed in proportion to the increased volume.

> The condition and organization of the warehousing were chaotic. Office and accounting records were worse. There was insufficient co-ordination between the various departments and almost a total lack of control over physical inventories; transfers of stock between the various wholesale warehouses were improperly recorded or not recorded at all; accounts payable were not balanced and in many cases could not be reconciled with the actual account as shown by suppliers. Accounts were overdue and suppliers generally were demanding immediate payment. Some suppliers had insisted on C.O.D. shipments.

Because of this situation, Mowbrey reported that most of his time at first had been taken up negotiating with credit managers in the various supply houses, and then he had negotiated increased loans from the SCCS—nearly one million dollars by the time of his report.[4]

The creditors to whom Mowbrey reported in December 1952 were nearly all of the major co-operatives of Alberta and Saskatchewan, including the UFA, the SCCS, Saskatchewan Federated Co-operatives, the two Wheat Pools, the United Grain Growers, and the Northern Alberta Dairy Pool. Together these co-ops had kept ACWA afloat, paid off its bank loans, and financed its greatly expanded capital requirements. Now they were owed far more than the Alberta wholesale, with its modest savings, seemed capable of ever repaying. Some of the Saskatchewan co-operators present, notably R. L. Stutt, representing the chief creditor, SCCS, objected to the large and "unexpected" demands for capital from ACWA. There was considerable discussion of selling off ACWA assets, notably the new Edmonton feed plant, in order to pay the creditors. But Alberta co-operators—led by ACWA's sometime competitors—the UFA and the UGG—stood up for the indebted wholesale. George Church, president of the UFA Co-op, stated that he was "vitally concerned with the effect that the liquidation of the Wholesale might have on the whole co-operative movement in Alberta"—and especially on holders of ACWA preferred shares. Church and J. E. Brownlee, president of United Grain Growers, persuaded the others to wait until 31 March 1953 and give ACWA another chance to get its house in order.[5]

As it turned out, the plug was not pulled on ACWA. The 1952 financial year showed another sales increase and some savings, while 1953 brought large increases in both categories. Including its retail sales, ACWA in 1953 had more than $4.5 million in sales, and made more savings than in almost any previous year. The sales total, at least, was respectable, equal to almost two-thirds of Manitoba Co-op Wholesale's volume in the same year. With signs of some progress, ACWA's creditors in the co-operative movement were patient. Major help from producer co-operatives and Saskatchewan Federated Co-ops, and especially from Saskatchewan Co-op Credit Society, enabled ACWA to survive 1951–52. It was then that Russell Love's thoughts turned to amalgamation with other provinces; but SFCL and then the new FCL insisted the first step must be amalgamation with the UFA Co-op.

Amalgamation Attempted: ACWA and the UFA, 1954–58

The UFA Co-op was the direct heir of the Alberta farm movement of 1909–35, though it had undergone a major transformation since that time. In 1935, after a crushing election defeat at the hands of Social Credit, the UFA had retired from politics. After that date there were no more UFA political candidates or constituency organizations. In 1948 the organization further abandoned its social and educational functions, leaving these to the newly formed Farmers' Union of Alberta. What was left was the UFA's commercial activities, begun in 1931–32 when Norman Priestley, George Church, and others had formed a committee to organize and systematize the purchasing activities of UFA locals. In recognition that the commercial endeavour was now the heart of the UFA, the name was changed in 1948 by adding the word "Co-operative." The main purpose of United Farmers of Alberta Co-operative Limited was now the ownership and control of its subsidiary, UFA Central Co-operative Association.[6]

In 1948 the UFA Central Co-op consisted of three components. Most important was a petroleum division which operated 148 agencies for Maple Leaf products. The other components were the stores division, twenty-one outlets with about $2 million in sales, and a bulk-sales division specializing in twine, fence posts, and coal, which had much lower sales than the other divisions. The total sales in 1947–48 were some $4,868,000, or nearly eight times those of ACWA. By 1951 the UFA store business had reached the point where there was pressure to create a separate wholesale, which would then be competing with ACWA. UFA Co-op decided to sell out to ACWA rather than compete, and concentrate on the more remunerative petroleum division. In March 1957 it bought the assets of Maple Leaf Petroleum, for whom it had acted as an agent since 1935.

Originally the UFA and ACWA had been divided by many fundamental principles, but by the 1950s these specific differences had mostly been eliminated. The UFA had ceased to be a political organization, it had adopted a share-capital structure, and it offered patronage rebates—in fact it even had a revolving-door plan to use retained savings to create capital, just like the other co-operative wholesales. The only important structural difference remaining was the membership basis: UFA Co-op had individual memberships in a centralized organization, while ACWA was owned by autonomous local co-operatives.

Although ACWA extended feelers toward the UFA Co-op in promoting a broad amalgamation in 1954, for several years little happened. It appears from

Board of Directors of Alberta Co-operative Wholesale Association (mid- to late 1950s). Although it attempted for several years to bring about a merger with the United Farmers of Alberta Co-op, personalities, politics, and differences over whether to serve exclusively farmer needs or also general consumer needs kept the two apart until 1961, when ACWA finally merged with FCL.

the record that UFA Co-op resisted or ignored ACWA's overtures, seeing no moral or economic necessity to unite with its smaller cousin. Then in 1957 Love began to make more public statements regarding a possible amalgamation, apparently creating some concern or confusion among UFA Co-op members about what was really afoot. The Farmers' Union of Alberta discussed a resolution favouring the merger of the two co-ops and appointed a committee led by its president, Arnold Platt, to investigate the matter. At the UFA Co-op's annual meeting in the fall of 1957, delegates discussed the matter at great length and asked their board to "make a clearcut statement of our policy in connection with amalgamation and to publicize it as widely as possible."[7]

It seems from these initiatives that Love and ACWA were trying to force the issue, to use public agitation to bring UFA Co-op to the bargaining table. They did at least force the board of the UFA Co-op to take a public stand and explain its position on amalgamation. A memo to the UFA Co-op board, apparently from late 1957, suggests that UFA directors had been silent on the amalgamation issue for two reasons. First, they "did not want to make it more difficult for ACWA either to operate or finance"—meaning they did not want to state publicly their criticisms of ACWA's financial position and thereby create a lack of confidence in the association.[8] But second, the directors perhaps feared that "public controversy on the matter might intensify a feeling . . . that it was not logical that two co-operatives should compete for the loyalty of the farm people." This in turn might lead to a decision to "clear the matter up once and for all by amalgamating the two groups even at some considerable sacrifice." In other words, if the matter became a public issue, a question of farm politics and principle rather than of business, the UFA Co-op directors were afraid that amalgamation would be approved. They did not want to discuss it, but were forced to simply because "ACWA have embarked with remarkable success on a propaganda campaign designed to bring about amalgamation whether our delegates and board agree to it or not."

The stage was set for a public clash of wills between Russell Love and George Church, both dominating figures in their organizations, and both reluctant to concede gracefully.

At the January 1958 annual meeting of ACWA, both Love and Church spoke to the delegates about the amalgamation. Love argued that ACWA was now on a "sound basis" financially after the "embarrassing" over-expansion of the early 1950s.[9] He then once more presented his 1954 vision of "one strong, effective regional co-operative wholesale, serving all of the co-operators in this great natural trading area." George E. Church's address then spelled out publicly why UFA Co-op refused amalgamation. First, Church referred to organizational structure.[10] UFA Co-op, with its twenty-five thousand individual members, could (according to Church) serve farmers better because it could sell in small communities where there was insufficient volume to sustain an independent local co-operative. Second was what Church called philosophy, namely, the UFA's emphasis on serving farmers. He claimed that "the farm philosophy has been incorporated in our organization as an integral part of our merchandising policy," and that members felt the UFA Co-op's farm education and policy role would be "weakened through amalgamation" with ACWA. Finally, Church argued that the "disparity between the financial position and earning potential of the two organizations . . . provides the single biggest obstacle in the way of amalgamation." He described UFA Co-op's philosophy as a stable "pay-as-you-go" policy contrasting with ACWA's risky debts. Church proceeded to give ACWA advice on its financing and merchandizing policies, advocating simplification, retrenchment, and getting out of the nonfarm-oriented grocery business.

Russell Love published a rejoinder to Church, but the details of the argument are less important than the simple fact that the UFA Co-op firmly refused amalgamation. Perhaps Love's most pertinent argument was that ACWA had done no worse, compared with UFA Co-op, than the wholesale departments of the other provinces had done in comparison with their petroleum departments. What he was suggesting was that it was the products handled, not the skill or wisdom of the two organizations, that differed. The distinction between them was simply groceries versus gasoline. And Love also argued cogently that, while the margin on groceries was lower than on gasoline, the turnover was higher and the capital needed was much less. With groceries the savings on volume might be lower than for gasoline, but the savings relative to capital were greater—and groceries were something everyone needed. To abandon the grocery business was therefore absurd.[11]

Arnold Platt of the Farmers' Union of Alberta (FUA), who had in the meantime been reviewing the whole question, disagreed with Church's assessment of the obstacles to amalgamation. In his report to the 1958 FUA convention, Platt argued that the membership and finance questions could have been surmounted by determined negotiators. Though based on association memberships, ACWA provided (since 1957) for individual members; and though based on individual members, UFA Co-op provided for associations to be members. There was room for compromise. While UFA Co-op was, indeed, better financed, Platt also noted that ACWA was well enough financed to cover its liabilities.[12]

Platt did not compare the proposed Alberta amalgamation to the 1944 amalgamation in Saskatchewan, though he could have, and this was a comparison used at least once by Love. When Saskatchewan Co-op Wholesale and the Co-op Refinery had amalgamated, the refinery had been much better financed than the wholesale, just as UFA Co-op's financing was superior to that of ACWA. This did not stop amalgamation in Saskatchewan. The Co-op Refinery had originally been based on individual shareholders, just like the UFA Co-op, whereas the Saskatchewan wholesale had always been based on co-operative

E. T. (Ted) Mowbrey, manager of Alberta Co-operative Wholesale Association, points out some of the first CO-OP tires to be installed after Interprovincial Cooperative's entry into the automotive supply business in 1956.

associations. This did not stop amalgamation in Saskatchewan. But then, Saskatchewan had Harry Fowler and other co-operators who had been working for ten years before amalgamation to synchronize the two Saskatchewan co-ops and to promote their merger. Alberta had no such movement-wide vision leading its co-operatives.

Discounting the organizational and financial characteristics, Platt said the remaining factor identified by Church was the most important: philosophy. While both UFA Co-op and ACWA were presently controlled by farmers and served farmers, only the UFA Co-op was committed to "complete farmer control" as a permanent organizational principle. The UFA handled goods only for farmers, and only farmers could be members. ACWA's structure, however, based on local stores handling general consumer goods, meant "there is nothing to prevent the control of this organization passing into the hands of essentially urban people."[13] Here Platt went to the heart of the UFA's philosophy, a philosophy that went back to 1909 (or earlier): farmers must be united and must have absolute control of co-operatives. "As a farmer," he said, "I am not much more interested in producing cheap food for a consumer controlled co-operative than I am in producing for a chain store." Platt quoted American precedents for the view that the consumer co-operative movement must remain solidly under the control of farmers.

UFA Co-op grew out of Alberta's agrarian tradition. Direct membership by all farmers in a single united organization was preferred to any sort of federated structure or generalized consumer interest in which farmers' power might be diluted. Elsewhere, Norman Priestley went so far as to argue that the Rochdale co-operative model was a "foreign" one, alien to the farmers of Alberta, who had discovered a better co-operative pattern more suited to their needs. Underlying all the other issues was one irreconcilable item: the choice between a producer-controlled consumer co-operative movement united by agrarian interest, or an expansionist consumer movement with the potential to breach the barrier between town and country.

Amalgamation Accomplished: ACWA and FCL, 1958–61

At the Federated Co-operatives Limited annual meeting in January 1960 the FCL board reported that UFA Co-op "is not prepared to merge" with ACWA. This necessitated a change in FCL's policy. The board was now prepared to recommend a merger with ACWA alone, with approval in principle at the 1960 annual meeting, final details in January 1962, and with the amalgamation intended to be effective on 31 October 1962. The board was able to present a relatively favourable view of ACWA's finances, although it was true, they admitted, that "FCL assistance will be required to finance new premises." "At the same time, however, the Province of Alberta, with its population of over 1.2 million—greater than Manitoba or Saskatchewan—appears to offer a wide field for co-operative development."[14] Based on this information, approval in principle for amalgamation was endorsed by the FCL delegates. Less than one week later, ACWA delegates, hearing Love speak of the need for bigness and the ways a larger FCL would promote co-operative development, also approved the merger plan.[15]

In fact, the merger took place rather more quickly than expected. One year later the FCL directors gave the following explanation to their delegates:

> Your Board of Directors can now report that the spirit of togetherness, understanding, and purpose that has prevailed during the past year, along with the hard work and wholehearted co-operation of management and personnel of both organizations, has enabled the two-year task to be completed in a single year.

According to the directors, personnel from Federated's head office had been so successful in co-ordinating management, merchandising, and inventories that amalgamation could proceed immediately.[16]

The glowing language used in the directors' report is not quite the same as the recollections of the staff members involved, who recall the amalgamation as a rescue that was pushed faster than intended in order to save ACWA from going under. The year 1960 was not a good one for the Alberta wholesale. Its net savings fell by more than one-fifth compared with 1959, a dangerous development for an organization so heavily indebted. Its financial statements show that it still owed more than $1 million in long-term liabilities, including $701,000 still owed to the Saskatchewan Co-operative Credit Society. Its ratio of current assets to current liabilities had deteriorated from the 2.3:1 twelve months earlier to 1.5:1, which was significantly less favourable. Working capital was tight and was mainly tied up in inventories and accounts receivable, so that FCL had to advance loans to ACWA for premises, working capital, and inventory financing.[17]

One FCL manager who was involved at the time of the merger estimates that the amalgamation cost four to five million dollars, and thereafter entailed an annual cost for several years until Alberta operations could be fully reorganized. The figures provide some support for this view. While sales increased by some $12 million from 1961 to 1962 for the two combined organizations, the new, three-province FCL earned less money in 1962 than it had earned in two provinces in 1961 (see Appendix 7 concerning FCL's financial performance).[18]

It was also less of a marriage between equals than the 1955 Manitoba–Saskatchewan merger had been. In 1961, the manager of ACWA was retained only as the Alberta branch manager for FCL, and was not promoted beyond that level. J. Russell Love, ACWA president, ceased to be a director and continued only as an honourary president of FCL. His long involvement ended when he was unable to secure election as a director for any of the four districts created in Alberta, an indication of dissatisfaction with his leadership. Love's departure was the end of an era for Alberta co-operators.

With all the changes and all the difficulties, it is important to record the opinion of one co-operator who was a store manager in Alberta at the time of the
merger, and later a manager in FCL: it "certainly" was the right thing to take
Alberta into Federated Co-operatives. This was an example of co-operation
among co-operatives, of saving and preserving the accomplishments of Alberta
co-operators, of short-term sacrifice for long-term potential. Another FCL
manager wryly cited the Alberta amalgamation as an example of co-operative
philosophy taking precedence over business sense. But Harry Fowler called it
"another historic occasion in the life of the co-operative consumer movement
in western Canada. We cannot go on into the future and compete against great
corporate enterprises with a peashooter."[19]

Conclusion and Questions

The discussions between ACWA and the UFA show that not all proposed amalgamations among co-operatives succeed, and that what can frustrate them is
differing policies, organizational traditions, and personalities. What do we
make today of the fundamental difference between the UFA Co-op and
ACWA: whether a consumer co-operative should represent a farmer interest
or a general consumer interest? To what extent does or should the Co-operative
Retailing System remain farmer-oriented? Or does the history of FCL bear out
the view that organization of the general consumer interest, including the urban
consumer interest, is to farmers' advantage?

And what of the eventual amalgamation of ACWA with FCL: was this
excessive idealism? Should FCL have respected its own bottom line and let
ACWA go under? Or is such co-operative idealism good long-term business
sense?

The 1961 amalgamation also ended the last large-scale experiment by a co-
operative wholesale in actually owning and operating retail outlets. In Alberta,
first the UFA and then ACWA had run retail outlets, against the principle of
local autonomy observed by most consumer co-operators. The stores did not
make money for either group. FCL managers insisted that they be returned to
an autonomous basis, and when they were, one store, Calgary, proved a spec-
tacular success (see Chapter 18). The Alberta experience has suggested to some
co-operators that consumer co-operatives really must be organized on the basis
of autonomous locals in order to thrive.

14

The Challenge of Bigness: Co-operative Education and Communications, 1955–1965

Russell Love expressed the opinion in 1954 that the Canadian co-operative movement had become "lazy" and "follows the path of least resistance." This was evident, he wrote, in how it financed its expansions: "Instead of an educational campaign to get members to invest more capital we adopt the lazy way of retaining patronage dividends by a special by-law"—the latter a reference to the modified revolving-door scheme then becoming common, by which patronage rebates were converted into share capital and credited to members' capital accounts.[1] An economist claimed in the daily press that co-ops were "faltering." Dr. Sol Sinclair of the agricultural economics department at the University of Manitoba said co-ops were lacking in enthusiasm in transferring the spirit of co-operation to the upcoming generation.[2] To address such problems, educational and publicity campaigns were made more systematic and more professional.

Relations with the General Membership

The task of communicating more effectively with members had been around for as long as consumer co-operatives had existed. In 1948, co-op managers in Manitoba were told the following:

> Unfortunately there are still a few Boards who believe their only obligation to the general membership is to present them with dividend cheques once a year and to hold an annual meeting which few people attend. It takes a lot more than a dividend cheque if you are going to build a strong, progressive Co-operative. As a matter of fact, we will go a step farther and say that you will have trouble in getting the members to even accept dividend cheques if they have a thorough understanding of their Co-operative. They will insist upon leaving their money in the Co-operative so that it can bring them greater benefits in the years ahead.

Therefore, the managers were told, "a Co-op must concentrate at least 90 percent of its publicity work on selling the Co-op idea. *Once the idea is sold, you can't stop people from buying the goods.*"[3] To do this, directors should talk to members and visit their homes. The co-op should subscribe to a co-operative newspaper on behalf of every member. Year-end statements should have an explanatory format—"your members are not trained accountants"—and should be sent out to everyone, whether they attend the annual meeting or not. The announcement of the annual meeting should be "an invitation—not a notice," and patronage rebate letters should also be used as "one of the most valuable ways of keeping your members informed." In addition, "a Local should send out three or four circular letters, at least, per year," and the annual meeting should be "an annual meeting worth attending," "peppy, well-planned, well-organized," and including "the social angle—a supper before, a musical number during, or a lunch after."

This program of activities to inform and involve members represents an ideal that the co-operative system strove for over the next forty years. The problem was how to ensure these things happened in retails that did not have the initiative or expertise to do them on their own, or which did not recognize the need.

In 1956 George Munro of Sherwood Co-op expressed his frustration with educational campaigns. "We have held meetings in school houses, churches, halls, using films, talks by management on Sherwood, and other speakers. Attendance was in most cases rather poor and audience participation not much better. I often thought they attended and listened out of a sense of duty." Efforts were then made to sponsor youth and women's guild programs, and to increase printed information. "But all this doesn't seem enough. It would appear that when a Co-op is successful the members generally are too content . . . [too ready] to let George do it."[4] The key may also be that as co-ops got bigger and managers got more professional, members had less to *do* at meetings; perhaps the prevailing system was indeed to "let George do it." And Munro also expressed frustration as a manager at having to attend and organize educational events:

> You know, the average manager gets sort of bewildered when he listens to some educational talks. Oh, he listens for a while but he hesitates to speak up during the discussion, and goes back to his business where he feels at home. He knows what his gross should be, what his operating expenses should be and what is over is his net. He knows a lot of other things but he is a little hazy on "media", "motivation", and a few other sixty-four dollar words.

Members attending out of duty instead of interest; managers bewildered by co-op education: this was part of a basic change in the movement. As business grew larger and more technical, members and managers had less to talk to each other about. Members had less knowledge of the business; with less knowledge came less effective power; and with less power, less interest.

Leaders of the wholesales were not blind to the need for improved member relations. Echoing Harry Fowler, Russell Love argued in May 1960 that the "larger co-operative of the 1960s, with increased number of services, will need to take special pains to keep its membership well informed." "There will need to be an aggressive member relations program, employing all the most effective communication techniques," including regular publications for members, brochures, and direct mailings. "The objective of all member relations activities is to strengthen the member's feeling of ownership of, and sense of responsibility for, his co-op. But attaining these twin objectives becomes more and more difficult as co-operatives expand. . . . The member who was on a first name basis with his manager and directors will find this close relationship difficult to maintain as his co-operative grows."[5]

The Co-operative College of Canada

The initiative leading to the creation of the Co-operative College began with the Federation of Southern Manitoba Co-operatives, and with the long traditions of co-operative education in the Altona area of southern Manitoba (see Chapter 9). J. J. Siemens of Altona, who in the early 1950s was vice-president and secretary of Manitoba Co-op Wholesale (MCW), visited the British and northern European co-operative colleges and Folk Schools, and on his return initiated discussions about producing something similar for Canada. In 1951 an organizing committee was formed for an International Co-operative Institute, consisting of J. A. Fehr (chairman), G. W. Leckie (secretary-treasurer), John Harp, and Siemens. All of these people were co-operators from Altona and Winkler, except for Leckie, an educational officer with MCW.[6] Siemens offered a parcel of land on his farm as a site for the proposed institute.[7]

The committee seated here in 1955 is considering an education program for FCL. Left to right: G. W. Leckie (assistant editor of the Co-operative Consumer*), W. A. Johnson (FCL director), C. C. Hunt (FCL director), J. J. Siemens (chairman, FCL director), W. J. McSorley (FCL First Vice-President), L. L. Lloyd (FCL Second Vice-President), and D. H. Fast (manager, FCL Publicity and Public Relations Division).*

When the amalgamation of MCW with SFCL was completed in 1955, the Manitoba project was expanded to a regional one. The Co-operative Institute (renamed Western Co-operative College in 1959 and Co-operative College of Canada in 1972) started up in 1955 under the sponsorship of the Co-operative Union of Saskatchewan, with Lewie Lloyd as chairman, and directed by Harold E. Chapman. Then, in 1956, in conjunction with the trend toward increased specialization and professionalization of staff, FCL identified personnel development as its first priority. "No problem facing our consumer movement today is as important or as urgent as the development of manpower for management positions," said the FCL directors at that time. "Modern buildings, adequate capital, educated members—a co-op can have all these and still make slow progress or none at all, if it does not have a competent manager." The Co-operative Institute was therefore to be expanded and, parallel to this initiative, FCL was to co-sponsor summer schools for co-operators and would offer scholarships at the University of Saskatchewan.[8]

Chapman recalls that throughout the 1950s and 1960s the bread and butter of the Co-op College was its courses for retail and wholesale personnel. According to records, in 1958 the Co-operative Institute conducted seventeen different courses for personnel of local retails, in management, merchandising, accounting, and lumber. These courses were attended by 379 local employees, and, in addition, seventy-nine employees of FCL attended the institute. A further 110 employees of co-operatives were taking correspondence courses. "Particular emphasis has been placed on the selection and training of junior personnel," reported the FCL directors, "to create a force of potential managers for the future."[9] In 1960 plans were announced to construct a permanent facility for the Co-op College in Sutherland, near Saskatoon. The board of directors of FCL approved a three-year, $100,000 construction grant toward the estimated $350,000 cost of the college's new home, in addition to its regular contribution to the College's operating budget. The emphasis on education is perhaps even more evident when it is noted that in the same year this $100,000 grant was authorized, $150,000 was donated to the University of Saskatchewan and $15,000 to Brandon College (now Brandon University). FCL therefore donated $265,000 in special educational grants, beyond the cost of on-going programs, to three institutions of advanced education; this was more than 7 percent of FCL's earnings in 1960.[10]

Many thousands of individual co-operators also contributed to the college's expansion. The women's guilds campaigned for donations, and FCL employees contributed through a payroll deduction scheme.

As the Co-operative College got going, its role also expanded to support not only technical staff training, but also training of co-operative educators. "The College was funded in the beginning to carry out the training program for FCL," recalls Chapman. "But it moved fairly quickly into general and management training for other co-ops, and into co-operative education of fieldmen [of all organizations], and this included education in philosophy and

President L. L. "Lewie" Lloyd of FCL presents a cheque for $25,000 to Principal Harold Chapman of the Western Co-operative College, to help finance the construction of a new residence for the college, and to improve its cafeteria and library (1964). Looking on are FCL director Don Milne from Manitoba, and FCL vice-presidents R. H. (Bob) Boyes of Saskatchewan and Morris Jevne of Alberta.

in . . . basic adult education [techniques]." Chapman observes that in "bringing together fieldmen from all the co-operative organizations," including secretaries and field staff of the provincial co-operative unions, the wheat pools, UGG, and UFA Co-op, the college's activity was supporting co-operation among these groups and a sense of being a common movement. The college also provided leadership and co-operative education to the women's guilds (see Chapter 15). This activity spurred local committees into action in the countryside, and got FCL and retail representatives working together on the local level with Wheat Pool, Co-op Union, Guild, and government representatives to promote co-operative education.

But the ultimate effectiveness of this activity was dependent on local co-operation, and especially upon the support of the individual retails. "The College had the role of training and developing people, including training educators," says Jack Trevena. "But who was providing *co-operative* education"—education of members and the public in the principles and importance of co-operatives? "Nobody was," he suggests, or at least not effectively. The weak link in co-operative education was in delivery to the ordinary member, which was the responsibility of the retails. As the following section shows, this shortcoming was not for lack of trying—or as Trevena adds, "I think the problem wasn't that the people of those times didn't agree" more co-operative education was necessary. "They didn't know how, or what to do. There was a lack of leadership in that area."

But the central wholesales had a major role in one or two particular aspects of member relations through which they tried to help local retails in encouraging member involvement and support. These were in publicity and public relations, specifically, through organizing and subsidizing the public relations federations of the late fifties and early sixties, and through providing the *Co-operative Consumer* newspaper and encouraging retails to distribute it to their members.

The *Co-operative Consumer* and the Public Relations Federations

The *Co-operative Consumer* was the most important single agency for member relations and for general co-operative education of members in the 1950s and 1960s. Subtitled *A Journal of Co-operative Education and Co-operative Development,* the *Co-op Consumer* was edited throughout the fifties and into the sixties by E. Forrest Scharf, known as a co-operative publicist and for his work with the Co-operative Union of Saskatchewan. Under Scharf's direction the *Co-op Consumer* was a diverse and lively newspaper, appearing twice a month with news and editorials gleaned from activities throughout the consumer and co-operative movements.

To give some idea of what the newspaper did, consider that a typical issue in April 1957 consisted of eight pages, of which about one-quarter was FCL product advertising (26 percent). Nearly another quarter was wholesale and retail co-operative news (23 percent), with a heavy emphasis in this case on retails and what they were doing—stories about retails dominated the front page. A further quarter was general co-operative-sector news and editorials, concerning the affairs of other co-operatives and general items affecting all co-operatives (24 percent). Most of the remainder consisted of women's, consumer, and women's guild news, and of general advertisements by major co-operatives promoting co-operation. What readers got, then, was broad co-operative information presented in such a way as to suggest that they should know about the activities of other retails, the wholesale, and sister co-operatives. The message was that co-operation was a movement, and readers received this message alongside FCL product advertising telling them to support the movement's products.[11]

The circulation of the *Consumer* increased steadily as FCL and its affiliates expanded. From 70,000 copies in the postwar period, distribution grew to 137,000 in 1958, 144,000 in 1959, and 155,000 in 1960. There are other indications of the paper's importance at the time: women, especially, followed it closely, and in nine months in 1960 they sent in 10,350 requests for patterns appearing on the women's page. Subscriptions eventually levelled off at around 200,000 when a new format was adopted and mailing lists were culled in 1964. At that time the *Co-op Consumer* had the third highest circulation of any newspaper or periodical in the prairies, following only the *Reader's Digest* and

Free Press Prairie Farmer—although, of course, individuals did not subscribe to the *Consumer;* their co-ops or educational federations did so for them.[12] However, while the *Co-op Consumer* was large, lively, and successful, there was also an identifiable reluctance to commit resources to it. In 1958, for example, plans were drawn up to enlarge the paper to twelve pages, to reserve the back page for articles contributed by each local district, and to increase the price from twenty-five to fifty cents per member per year. Delegates at district meetings would not agree to the increased cost, so this particular proposal was lost.[13]

The notion of district-oriented information and publicity was, however, an important idea whose time had come. The first two District Educational Federations (later known as District Public Relations Federations) were organized in FCL electoral districts seven (Wynyard) and nine (Assiniboia–Gravelbourg) during 1956. Each one had a full-time public relations officer. These initiatives were the results of the Operation People and Operation Onward projects that had been conducted at the time of the Manitoba–Saskatchewan amalgamation with a view to reviewing and improving member relations.[14] In 1957 the success of the first two district federations led the FCL annual meeting to amend the policy so that FCL would subsidize the costs of the local public relations programs. FCL was to pay half of the first ten thousand dollars of each federation's budget, then one-quarter of the next five thousand, as long as the federation had the support of either the large majority of co-operatives in the district, or co-ops with a large majority of the sales volume.[15] The 1957 annual meeting also voted to set aside the back page of the *Co-op Consumer* for use by the PR federations, and from that date, where PR federations were active, readers found the back page filled with news from local co-ops and their districts.

By 1960, public relations federations were active in ten of FCL's fifteen electoral districts, and FCL's grants to the federations were expected to total nearly seventy thousand dollars.[16] With the 1961 amalgamation, the federations were extended to Alberta—and for the first time FCL directors began to imply that the costs were getting too great. Directors warned that the PR federations must start to be self-financing. They "must eventually prove their worth to our Movement. . . . once Federations have reached a point of effectiveness, the need for financial help from FCL should be expected to decline."[17] As central funding declined, the federations gradually became less active, so that by the end of the 1960s their activities were much less in evidence.

During their period of greatest activity the public relations federations made a big impact in many areas, one of which was in supporting women's extension work and guild activities (Chapter 15). Vi Pyett of the Saskatchewan guild remembers, "they did stellar work out in the country. They helped the guilds, and they helped the co-ops." The public relations officers were jacks of all trades who assisted with meetings, publicity, newsletters, promotional and social events—everything consumer and other co-ops, and their related organizations like the guilds, did on the local level, to maintain the momentum of the movement.

The origin of the PR federations and the strength of FCL's commitment to them coincide largely with the influence of Harry Fowler, secretary of FCL from 1955 and president from 1959–63. Fowler was a unique individual in the history of the consumer movement in one important respect: he was a talker, a promoter, and an idea man who had also risen through the management side of the movement. He had the experience, stature, and ability to ensure that co-operative education was well supported. When Fowler moved on to the presidency, he was replaced not by another secretary devoted to organization and member relations, but by a secretary-treasurer. For a number of years thereafter the position was more technical in nature.

The decline of the public relations federations was reinforced by the decline of the provincial co-operative unions, particularly the Co-operative Union of Saskatchewan which took over responsibility for the PR federations in that province in the early 1960s. The co-operative unions were primarily devoted to education and for this purpose brought together all of the different co-operatives and co-ordinated joint efforts, first at the provincial level and then, in Saskatchewan, at the district level. The year 1966 was critical, however, for the fate of the federations and of the co-op unions. Dissatisfaction with the effectiveness and consistency of the federations led to the need for reorganization. FCL objected, however, that it needed one uniform member and public relations program for all three provinces that it served; these could no longer be funded or organized on a district or provincial basis. This corresponded to the One-System approach adopted by FCL in 1966 (see Chapter 16). With FCL's insistence on a region-wide, centralized program, the district reorganization as proposed in Saskatchewan could not be carried out. The Co-op Union of Saskatchewan was reorganized as the Co-operative Development Association, which survived only until 1972, the same year the B.C. Co-op Union ceased to function. No comparable organization has existed since that time.

The decline of the federations was followed some years later by the decline of the *Consumer*. With falling circulation after the mid-1970s and coming under much criticism, the paper was cancelled with the onset of the recession of 1982. Those who observed the struggle over the future of the paper suggest many different factors influenced these events, from rising postage costs to larger retails having their own communications organs, to failure to adapt and provide the right kind of content, to conflicts among the personalities involved.

One of FCL's retired senior managers recalls that a few in the organization were anti-*Co-op Consumer*. They "forced you to change its format and then abandoned it even after they had had their input." He admits to being "one who questioned its role. But you had to question its role because of the pressure from the large retails" who did not subscribe, finding the paper too expensive for their very large memberships. The result was pressure to be cost-efficient, to carry more in-house news and product-related advertising. Bob Matthewson, who worked with the *Co-op Consumer* for many years, observes that it did tend under these pressures to evolve into a house organ, perhaps not quite interesting enough for the average reader. "It got to be a little less 'homespun' than it was at first," he recalls, "and I think it got a bit less interesting. You need that [local] human interest material," like the articles on local retails and those provided by the PR federations, "to keep people interested."

It appears that the goals of the paper were never precisely formulated and agreed upon, and also that the criticisms of the paper were never precisely stated. One of those who was involved on a publishing board for the paper (set up in order to meet legal requirements for special postal rates) comments, "We were never given a reason for terminating the darned thing. We were just never called in again." In 1982, of course, the immediate reason was cost, but behind that lay dissatisfactions never clearly stated, and perhaps, above all, the fact that the paper did not contribute visibly or directly to the "bottom line."

Perhaps a few words should also be added about FCL's subsequent relations with the Co-op College, relations which were also strongly influenced by bottom-line considerations. As time went on the college was heavily influenced by the extension of its activities to a national scale, and also by the development of internal training programs in the larger co-ops. FCL was one of these. Until 1969 FCL continued to sponsor many retail and wholesale personnel who attended the college. Then, when the company's earnings dropped, this was cancelled. When training was picked up later it was done by FCL's own staff. Since 1987 a similar thing has happened for elected retail officials in the system although at its November 1988 meeting the board adopted a policy that does offer some support for elected retail officials who wish to attend outside training courses. But the result is that the kind of training offered is more specialized, and does not offer contact with other co-operatives and co-operators the way the college courses did. "What happened," says Chapman, "was that the *education* part was dropped." The "hands-on" or "practical" training that was kept is, says Chapman, "extremely important . . . but the question is whether there isn't a place for both."

The fate of the co-operative education offered by the college is, like the fate of the provincial co-op unions, the PR federations, and eventually the *Consumer,* a sign of one less tie among all kinds of co-operatives and their members, one more weakening of movement in favour of what was becoming dominant in the 1960s, namely, system (Chapter 16). The educational initiatives of the 1960s did not, it seems, command enough financial support for them to survive the more difficult times that came from the end of the decade onward.

While co-operative education, properly speaking, did not fare well, there were several other initiatives in co-operative communications by FCL. These, too, began in the late 1950s and early 1960s. For example, in 1956–58 a co-operative identification program popularized the new consumer co-operative insignia, the familiar CO-OP within a badge-shaped frame, with a colour scheme based on red and green. This new insignia was to be used as the standard iden-

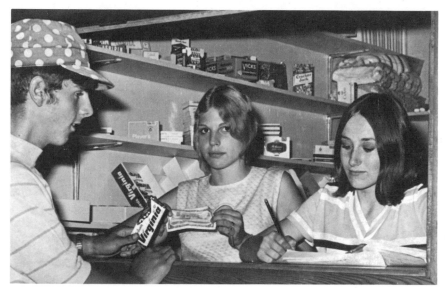

Putting theory into practice at a Co-op Youth Camp (1970). Co-operative youth camps were set up and supported by co-operatives and farm organizations to help teach young people the values and philosophy of co-operation.

tification for co-operative premises and vehicles throughout the consumer system.[18] In 1959 a new centralized advertising program was developed, out of a desire to project a single, coherent, effective image to consumers. FCL began supplying ready-made newspaper advertisements and television and radio commercials to retails.[19] These trends toward improved image and advertising continued throughout the 1960s and 1970s, and have received particular emphasis in the 1980s (Chapter 22).

In all of these cases, centralized image and advertising programs succeeded and persisted, where district-level co-operative education and distribution of materials directly to members declined to virtually nothing in many areas. And, as in the case of the system's relationship with the Co-op College, in-house activities have increased, while outreach activities, and those that involve contact and partnership with other co-operatives, have declined.

Conclusion and Questions

What conclusions should be drawn from the co-operative education efforts of 1955–65, and from their subsequent fate? Was too much done for members and consumers—was it too expensive with too few results? Or was it that not enough was done to make it effective? The ultimate effect of abandoning the approach taken in those years is that it is now up to the retails to perform co-operative education. Is this the best solution?

The loss of the *Co-op Consumer* leaves a hole for many old-time co-operators, who miss the days when they could feel part of a movement, know what other co-ops and co-op leaders were doing. "Once you retire," notes one of them, "the curtain falls. The only reliable information you get is through the Wheat Pool." One wife describes her retired husband's frustration: "He's become an ordinary member, and ordinary members don't know a thing!"

Those retired people who live in the Saskatoon area have the good fortune to be near the meetings of the FCL Co-op Senate, an informal body of retired co-operators which meets regularly with FCL's senior staff. Those outside Saskatoon have no such regular connection. Is the fact that they miss being part of a movement an indication that the Co-operative Retailing System has lost something in its member relations? The disappointment of some retirees may be nostalgia, or it may be a genuine impression that the co-operative system no longer communicates as well as it did in their day. If knowledgeable members who want to be kept informed cannot find the information, what about the great masses of new members who have never been well-informed to begin with?

15

Consumer Activism and the Women's Co-operative Guilds

The women's co-operative guilds were one of the great success stories of co-operative education—"the most significant effort at co-operative education—*education,* not training—that I can recall," in the opinion of Jack Trevena. Through them, new people were brought into the co-operative movement, and new energy and enthusiasm mobilized for its expansion. The guilds provided a link between co-operatives and women, which was important since the co-operative movement had relied so long on the male half of the population. But they also provided a link between co-operatives and communities, for the kind of volunteers who were attracted to the guilds were also frequently community leaders in other charitable, social, and educational causes. "We were so well-known . . . in the small communities," recalls Vi Pyett. "If the Easter Seal or the cancer fund needed workers, we were one of the groups they called upon. And we were a social movement, we emphasized the social part, so they felt free to call upon us." And the guilds specifically provided a link between co-operatives and the growing consumer movement, as shoppers—at that time stereotypically housewives—became more critical and better informed. Increasingly in the 1950s and 1960s the co-operative guilds took on product testing and promotion functions, alongside their basic educational purposes.[1]

Consumer Activism and the Co-operative Code of Ethics

Co-operatives became aware in the 1950s that merchandising practices were changing, and, though they disapproved of some of the changes, they felt under pressure to keep up. FCL's directors claimed in 1958 that "expenditures which stagger the imagination are being made by bigger businesses for advertising and promotion to direct consumer thinking. Methods of attracting attention through packaging, premiums, coupons and gimmicks are becoming so . . . fanciful that the product itself is often relegated to a place of secondary importance." The directors noted that "some say that we should enter into the bid for attention by offering our own premiums, gimmicks, and advertising," but this would be costly to the consumer—every gimmick or coupon has to be paid for through higher regular prices—and "would jeopardize the basic objectives of co-operative endeavour," which involve serving the member's needs in the best way possible.[2]

And it was not only co-operatives that were concerned about these changes. Several royal commissions in the late 1950s and in the 1960s reflected public concern with big business and with prices.[3]

In 1961 FCL's directors received a public relations study and concluded that "consumer co-operatives can best communicate the difference between co-ops and profit-enterprise business by demonstrating, through their daily operations, that *co-operatives are consumer oriented instead of profit oriented* in everything they do and say." Co-operatives would stand for ethical practices, consumer protection (including advocacy of consumer rights in the media and to governments), and education of consumers.[4] As part of this effort a Code of Ethical Standards for Co-operatives was developed, a document that deserves to be reproduced in its entirety:

The Code of Ethical Standards for Co-operatives
1. Purpose

We co-operators recognize that the consumer has certain Rights, and that these Rights should not be violated by the organization. Among these Rights are:

i. The Right to Safety
ii. The Right to be Informed
iii. The Right to Choose
iv. The Right to be Heard

2. Code of Ethical Standards

In recognition of the fact that it is a duty of this consumer-owned organization to respect and protect these Rights, the following Code of Ethical Standards shall apply to all activities of the organization:

A   All claims, statements, information, advice, and proposals shall be honest and factual.

B   Sufficient disclosure of pertinent facts and information shall be made as may be necessary to enable one to make a fair appraisal of the proposal as related to the requirements to be fulfilled.

C   Public decency and good taste shall be duly regarded.

D   Unfair exploitation in any form shall be avoided.

E   Comparisons of co-operative merchandising, products, service, philosophy, principles, and practices, to those of others shall be made honestly and fairly. Unfair disparaging comparisons shall be avoided.

F   Interests of the membership as a whole shall be paramount to the interests of the institution.

G   Equitable treatment of all members shall be diligently pursued.

H   Knowingly persuading or advising an individual into action which may not be in his best interests shall be avoided.

3.   Applying the Code to Practices

Because we agree that the consumer has certain Rights and that we aim to conduct our activities in the interests of the consumer, we shall, therefore, in any or all interpretations or applications of this Code, concern ourselves with human values and not with legalisms. The test as to whether an action adequately conforms to these standards lies in the answer to the question: What is the effect on the ordinary or trusting mind? It is not enough that the discerning, knowledgeable and/or analytical person can make a fair assessment if the ordinary or trusting individual would be misled.

The directors of FCL declared this document official policy for FCL, and encouraged retail co-operatives to do the same for their own organizations. By the end of 1965, 267 retail boards had considered the document, and of these, 260 had adopted it as policy.[5]

Having adopted the code of ethics, FCL attempted to follow through with the related aspects of its program of consumer advocacy and education. Much of this effort was devoted to women's extension work, for women were seen to control the family purse strings as far as general household expenses went, and women were increasingly organized and aware of their power as consumers. The ethical-practices program meant that FCL expanded its staff of home economists (consumer counsellors) from one to four in 1964. It also meant a renewed effort to support the Women's Guilds.[6]

The Guilds and Involvement of Women

Consumer activists told women that they must educate themselves and use their power to curb the excesses of business practice. Mrs. E. S. Russenholt told the Winnipeg Co-operative Women's Guild in 1954 that women could be the most effective group in the co-operative movement to "persistently press upon management the viewpoint and needs of the member consumer." She went on to argue that, since the men in co-operatives had to devote their energies to management problems, it was up to the women to watch out for the member. "The consumer's only safeguard today is her own knowledge of labels, standards, quality and values, which she must learn through experience," the speaker told the guildswomen.[7] Ida Delaney told the Edmonton Co-op Luncheon Club the same year that co-op stores could lead the way in consumer activism. She held that "the co-op store should be a centre of education and information," according to a newspaper account of her speech. "In co-op stores we can learn about both the products and the price. We can also exercise control [of] quality and costs."[8]

Four women's-guild presidents (1950s). The guilds contributed to rural and community leadership by developing the skills and talents of western women. They ran their own local and provincial organizations, administered educational, demonstration, and many other programs, raised money for co-operative projects, and attended leadership and developmental seminars.

But exercising control in co-operatives was not easy for women. In general only one patronage account was held per family, and this was usually in the husband's name. This meant only the husband could vote, and only the husband was eligible for elected office. The whole elected leadership of co-operatives, not to speak of the management, was overwhelmingly male. Dorothy Fowler, president of the Saskatchewan guild from 1954–59, recalls that a manager once refused to give her membership in a co-op "because my husband already had a membership and it would make too much book-keeping." She was not impressed: "I told Harry on him and I got my membership."[9]

In comparison with other kinds of rural organizations, consumer co-ops probably did reasonably well at involving women; but formal involvement in elected or appointed offices was difficult. The guilds promoted ways to get around this. They were instrumental in securing legislative changes that permitted a husband and wife to have separate votes but one patronage account; but though this was legally provided for, many co-ops did not pass the necessary by-laws to implement it. Similarly, many co-ops did not implement another idea promoted by the guilds, the naming of associate directors specifically to represent youth and women. The thinking was that these were groups who had difficulty finding representation through the regular system, so another system ought to be adopted. While some retails did establish associate directors, the practice did not become standard.

Since these measures to obtain greater representation in co-op affairs had only mixed results, the most important activities of the guilds remained those they undertook on their own, in the true spirit of self-help. Guildswomen educated themselves, developed their understanding of co-operatives and their skills for speeches and meetings, and they ran their own independent organizations. These activities were supported by the infrastructure of co-operative education. The provincial co-operative unions, the public relations federations, the Co-op College, and the *Co-op Consumer* newspaper all worked with and assisted the guilds. Though women rarely sat on retail co-op boards, for example, they found an opportunity for involvement through the boards of directors of the district public relations federations. They took courses from the Co-op College on the history of the co-operative movement, on guild leadership, on adult education, on community development, and in many other areas.[10] And they worked with extension specialists hired by FCL and by the co-operative unions.

In the late 1950s, FCL established the position of "Donna Rochdale" to help inform women about FCL's products and policies. "Donna" worked very closely with the provincial guilds in all four western provinces, and took responsibility for several of their programs, including baking demonstrations and product surveys and testing.[11] She was also an associate editor of the *Co-op Consumer,* overseeing its women's page. In her private life Donna Rochdale was Glenora Pearce (later Glenora Slimmon), but she smiles as she says most people who know her from her co-op extension work still call her Donna.

In 1964 the Co-operative Union of Saskatchewan, which had taken responsibility for the public relations federations in that province, hired a women's extension worker, Lorayne Janeson, who worked throughout the province on public relations and women's programs. Janeson, who had been president of the Saskatchewan Co-operative Women's Guild up to 1964, is remembered by one of her colleagues for the "knowledge and dedication" that she brought to her work. The position of women's extension worker survived the reorganization of the provincial Co-op Union, but ceased to exist in 1968 as the Union's successor, the Co-operative Development Association, proved unable to continue with such functions.[12]

CO-OP Labels and the Guilds

One place where the consumer's concern about standards and the co-operative movement's effort to increase savings overlapped was in the matter of CO-OP label goods; it was here that the closest partnership between co-operative retailing and the guilds developed.

The opening of the SCWS flour mill at Outlook began a new phase in the development of the guilds. In 1944 the Outlook guild began to collect recipes for a co-op cook book. Barney Johnsrude, manager of the mill, suggested it include not just recipes, but articles on co-operatives and co-operative education. Published in 1946, the book was reprinted many times.[13] As the mill struggled under SFCL's ownership, and then was replaced in 1949 by a Pool mill which also encountered market resistance to its flour, the guilds became important for marketing CO-OP flour.

Flour was one of the first and most difficult to market of all CO-OP food brands. In 1958 a statement from the Saskatchewan Wheat Pool Flour Mill referred to the difficulties:

> When we commenced operations in 1949 we knew there would be marketing problems. We fully realized we were entering a very competitive field with an unknown product and it would be necessary to break down family prejudices built up over the period of years and handed down from mother to daughter. . . . It was a matter of taking a long range view . . . and having faith in the ability of our Co-operative organizations to eventually break down these prejudices.
>
> It is a good thing we were not too optimistic about the immediate future as we found the task was even more difficult than we had anticipated. . . .
>
> Today, after nine years of hard work, we have been able to break down these prejudices and the demand for our product is increasing each year.

A women's guild cooking demonstration in action (1958). Through demonstrations such as these, guildswomen played an important role in promoting CO-OP label products, especially CO-OP flour from the Wheat Pool mill in Saskatoon. A co-op cook book, first published in 1946 and reprinted many times, publicized the best recipes.

This gives some indication of how tough the battle for consumer preferences proved.[14]

One reason for its eventual success was the activity of the guilds in testing, demonstrating, and promoting of CO-OP flour. Their arguments, recipe books, and baking were a crucial part of what turned the corner for the new product. Dorothy Fowler recalls experiences promoting CO-OP flour in visits to some eighty guilds:

> You'd go to a meeting and ask how many women had husbands who were Pool members. All the hands would go up. You'd ask how many used Pool flour. Not a one. Or maybe three or four out of a whole roomful.

This was a basic educational effort about why people should support their co-ops, a grass-roots organizational drive that took the efforts of hundreds of staff and volunteers.

The greatest savings for co-ops and their members came from certain products, such as flour, not only marketed under a CO-OP label, but actually manufactured by co-ops. As one of the guilds' leaflets from the 1950s reminded readers, purchasing "100% CO-OP products" (i.e., products manufactured by co-ops) meant consumers were buying "not only the *product*—but *ownership* in a mill, refinery, a manufacturing plant, etc." By adding these operations to the consumer movement, the savings on manufacturing would be added to those already made by eliminating profits in distribution. In the mid-1950s the "100% CO-OP products" included CO-OP gasoline and oils, flour, vegetable oil and margarine, lumber, peanut butter, coffee, and tea.[15]

The CO-OP-Label program, however, was also a long-term project, intended to mobilize sufficient consumer buying power in other commodities that co-ops could eventually expand the range of goods they manufactured themselves. "It is through loyal patronage of CO-OP labelled products," FCL reminded its members in 1958, "that sufficient volume can be obtained to warrant the entry of co-operatives into further fields of manufacturing . . . where the greatest savings to consumers can be obtained."[16] Barney Johnsrude, general manager of the B.C. Co-op Wholesale Society, described the purpose of the label program as "to rally sufficient sales volume in our own labeled goods so that the Co-operatives will have control over a specific volume, which can be directed to co-operatively-owned plants when such volume reaches a level where processing and manufacturing can become profitable." Such eventual ownership would mean "the quality of the goods produced can be controlled, the high and wasteful distributive costs (in gimmicks, advertising, needless fancy packaging, duplication, etc.) can be eliminated and the exorbitant profits now going to privately or corporately owned manufacturers and distributors can be returned to consumers." But Johnsrude noted that this kind of program could take a long time. He cited two examples of the CO-OP coffee and tea program, which took a decade to muster enough volume for the co-ops to acquire their own plant; and the agricultural chemical program, which took eight years.[17]

Saskatoon staff members tour FCL premises (1957).

In effect, the development of the CO-OP label was part of the development of a distinctive co-op image. A CO-OP label was to be associated with ownership by the members and return of surpluses to them; "quality products at fair and competitive prices, without adulteration"; factual representation of merchandise; guaranteed refunds for unsatisfactory goods; and courtesy toward customers; in short, "Integrity, Dignity, Reliability, Courtesy, Distinctiveness."[18]

The general label program of the 1950s had three CO-OP labels: red for Fancy or top quality, blue for Choice quality, which combined good standards with moderate price, and green for Standard quality, which emphasized low price. Maintaining this system, however, required "constant policing of the quality" of the goods purchased by the wholesales and marketed under the different labels, and this was one area where the guilds helped. Indeed, they were instrumental in having the label system changed a decade after its introduction. Guildswomen found that the green (Standard) products were giving the CO-OP label a bad name, because consumers were disappointed with the quality. These were abandoned and replaced by the current system which combines quality and low price in a single CO-OP brand.

With the success of the early campaigns, the role of the guilds was made more structured and formalized. In 1956 the Manitoba and Saskatchewan guilds agreed to be "the official consumer group . . . for testing the acceptance of CO-OP labelled goods to be used in the kitchen and home." "CO-OP Testing Forms" were to be sent out from head office, and local women were to rate

CO-OP products against competing brands. Donna Rochdale was to supervise, co-ordinate, and conduct the extension work for FCL.[19]

The CO-OP Label campaign, and the role of the guilds, helped consumer co-operation continue to function as a movement. People were drawn in, educated, and mobilized in support of values and ideas—ideas like concentrating their buying power, eliminating waste and profit, extending consumer control of the economy and of the choices offered in the marketplace. Educators were required to keep this movement going, both volunteers and staff. Ideas had to be explained, support had to be won, and these tasks had to be performed at the local level to be effective. This involved a great deal of energy and activity, much of which, in the case of CO-OP goods and product testing and promotion, was provided by the women in the co-operative movement.

The Women's Co-operative Guilds at Their Height

Not surprisingly, given the triple impetus of consumer activism, CO-OP-Label drives, and managers' desires to increase sales, the 1950s and early 1960s saw the peak of women's co-operative guild activity. FCL's directors reviewed the organization's growth in 1960, and noted that "Women's Co-operative Guilds deserve praise for their interest and notable efforts as champions of the co-operative way and for assisting in its development at every opportunity. It is doubtful if any other type of business is privileged to have working in its support, groups such as our Guilds and their devoted members."[20] In recognition of the usefulness of the guilds, the co-op wholesales donated money to them (on the order of several hundred dollars annually), lent staff people to them, hired extension specialists to work with them, published their newsletters, and co-ordinated many of their programs.

What were the activities and accomplishments of the local guilds? The Manitoba provincial guild reported in 1957 on the wide variety of activities undertaken by guildswomen. Harold Chapman of the Co-op College (then still called the Co-op Institute) had directed a leadership school for women at the annual guild meeting. Leadership schools were a regular feature in those years, training co-operative women to take on leadership roles and educate others. Local guilds had undertaken projects ranging from CO-OP label contests to shopping services to help the housebound. CO-OP Glo-Candle projects perhaps deserve special mention because of their popularity in those years. The idea of the Glo-Candle program was to distribute wax, a by-product of the Consumers' Cooperative Association refinery in Kansas City, Missouri, to local guilds, who would create perfumed, multicoloured, and glitter-speckled candles for parties, celebrations, and meetings. Officials of the wholesale co-ordinated this and other programs. "All guilds," the provincial guild also reported in 1957, "share in the activities fostered by the Provincial Guild Committees on Demonstrations, Testing, Library, and Programs."[21]

Perhaps some specific examples of local activities would also help illustrate the work of the guilds. In 1957 a new guild was organized in Swan Valley, Manitoba, with twenty-five founding members and forty by the end of the year. "The guild," reported the provincial yearbook, "has held nine regular meetings with an average attendance of 21.66 members. Kitchen meetings were held in four homes to test CO-OP granulated soap and CO-OP water softener." Two guest speakers were brought in. The women catered the annual meetings of the dairy and poultry pools, as well as of the co-operative association, sponsored a cooking demonstration at a local fair, and "served coffee and doughnuts at the Co-op Store on three occasions."[22]

Souris guild, also organized in 1957, devoted its first meeting to discussing "arguments one would use to convince others of the co-operative way of life," and at other meetings tested CO-OP white cake mix, salmon, and soap.[23] In Eriksdale the guild raised money for the hospital, served CO-OP coffee and CO-OP cake in the store, and listened to reports on the FCL annual meeting and the CUC congress.[24] Flin Flon, one of the oldest guilds in the province, pioneered with ideas like "Family Day, International Fair and Smorgasbord, and the Co-op Calling Card for newcomers."[25] Virden guild discussed co-operative principles and met with its district representative and its store manager, while Birtle guild, apart from catering the local Manitoba Co-operative Elevator Association annual meeting and the Manitoba Federation of Agriculture and Co-operation youth rally, donated cash prizes to a local horticultural show.[26]

The wideness and broadening or educating aspect of guild programs seems to have been very important in the years when they were at their height. They discussed much more than their local co-op store, relating the co-operative movement to broader community concerns. The Alberta Co-operative Women's Guild discussed "The Problems of Aging—Our Welfare Responsibility," while the Manitoba guild passed resolutions favouring a ban on nuclear weapons testing and calling for safe disposal of radioactive waste.[27] The guilds also defended the broader interests of the co-operative movement, supporting the creation of the Co-op College and raising money for its building program, and fighting in the press for co-operative ideals. The Manitoba guild claimed to have forced the *Financial Post* to retract statements against co-operatives and apologize for two articles.[28] Guilds also maintained liaison with a wide variety of organizations, including the Co-op College, the CUC, local and provincial councils of women, committees on the status of women, the Consumers' Association of Canada, the Red Cross, local welfare agencies, provincial film boards, education curriculum committees, and agricultural organizations.[29] Guild libraries contained books on all topics of social interest, from doctors and health care to international economic disparities, from environmentalism to history of co-operatives.[30] Some guilds even published their own books, like the Swift Current guild which published a book of local poetry and prose in 1964.[31]

All of this activity peaked between about 1960 and 1965. To take Manitoba

Local guildswomen in costume for an International Fair. Guild activities often served a dual role, providing on the one hand for entertainment and socializing, and on the other, for education. International Fairs helped in promoting understanding and in breaking down ethnic and national prejudices, which, in the cultural mixture of western Canada, were sometimes strong.

as an example, the number of active guilds rose to seventeen or eighteen in the early 1960s, then declined sharply. The last recorded annual meeting of the provincial guild was in 1968, and by 1971 the last local guild appears to have been officially disbanded.[32] In Saskatchewan the number of local guilds increased between 1955 and 1965 from thirty-nine guilds with 778 individual members, to eighty-three guilds with 1,252 members. By 1975 there were only eighteen guilds with 228 members.[33] It is estimated at the time of writing that only about a dozen local guilds are active in the area served by FCL, and all of the provincial guilds have been disbanded.

Why did the guilds decline? Certainly their decline coincided with the general decline of public relations federations, co-operative unions, and other educational activities in the field. They were perhaps also products of a specific set of circumstances. As Donna Rochdale reminded women in 1958, "the advent of electricity, automatic heat and many other household labor-saving devices has helped release more of the homemaker's time for community activities. This has opened up the way for you to take a larger part in the co-operatives to which your family belongs."[34] Women were more independent, and looking for ways to apply their talents; some of them turned to women's guilds as a natural way to extend their home- and consumer-oriented experience into good work in the community. Perhaps the next generation of western women were more concerned with careers or other kinds of endeavour, rather than building on experience as homemakers and consumers. Then, too, the general process of economic consolidation undermined many of the small communities where guilds had been active. Better transportation meant women could travel to regional centres where there were more alternatives.

Relations with the managers in the wholesales and in the retails seem to have been ambiguous. Dorothy Fowler recalls that in the early days some managers "didn't want their wives to go to co-operative meetings." Some managers, she recalls, "looked upon us as a necessary nuisance. . . . they were never wholeheartedly behind us"—although she says Harry was certainly an exception. Another co-operator of long experience notes, "I think the retail managers . . . just didn't want them in there rocking the boat. . . . A lot of the managers did not know how to relate to the guilds because they were afraid of them."

Perhaps some of these attitudes also shaped the evolution of the guilds. In 1965 the general manager of one large urban co-operative wrote to the local women's guild, trying to offer advice about what to do to reverse declining membership and growing apathy and frustration among the guildswomen. He suggested that "too much emphasis is placed on Co-op education. . . . Co-operatives have grown in size and complexity. Co-ops also are . . . adjusting to today's competitive world and have to approach the public differently. The younger generation are interested in other things than when the Co-ops and Women's Guilds started. But the guilds have not changed their approach and programs. Perhaps our aims and objectives are too high?" He suggested, therefore, that the guildswomen concentrate on giving tours of the co-op, on organizing children's shows, on helping handicapped women. They should run bingo nights, stage a Hallowe'en party, do hairdressing and make-up demonstrations, discuss teenage problems and child care. He further suggested contests organized to resemble game shows, and discussions on "Is Smoking Dangerous?" "Care of Indoor Plants," "How to Keep Your Figure," and "Traffic Control and Road Safety." "The main thing," the manager said, "is to give something in which the *average* housewife is interested, with Co-op education given by the spoonful at each meeting."[35]

Gameshows, make-up, kids' shows, and co-op education "by the spoonful" are not what the women's co-operative guilds were ever about. If very many managers thought in these terms, looking at the guilds only for their commercial and public relations advantage, and trying to discourage them from conducting co-operative education, then this could be another explanation of why the guilds declined. It may be that their success in educating women was not matched by a corresponding success in educating men.

When the final decision was made to disband the provincial guilds, the guild leaders did this out of a belief that women no longer needed the organizations. Norma Lee (a past president of the Saskatchewan guild) recalls that they wound up the guilds "in the hope that women would be accepted as an integral part of the movement. Sadly it did not occur." The involvement of women through the regular retail board and FCL delegate structures had improved, but not quickly. In 1981, FCL established a Women's Participation Committee, and following its efforts, women have increased from 10 to 12–14 percent of the delegate body at annual meetings. With two women on the nineteen-member board of directors, FCL is further ahead than ever before, and there has been one regional vice-president who was a woman; but otherwise, no senior manager or officer has ever been a woman. This is a slow rate of change for a system whose guiding philosophy has been to strive to represent *all* consumers.

The efforts made by the co-operative system, including by the guilds, were also apparently not enough for a quick revolution in consumer attitudes. Eight years after the start of the public relations federations and three years after the start of the campaign for ethical practices, FCL directors were dismayed to note the continued "lack of understanding" among consumers. They quoted as examples that some highly advertised national brands outsold CO-OP products that were "of equal government grades" but lesser price. Consumers, in other words, still seemed to fall for fancy advertising when CO-OP brands apparently offered better value. Some members, too, were still attracted to competitors by "loss leaders"—products sold at a loss in order to entice customers into the store—"even though it is usually proven that the total cost of a weekly shopping lot is the same or lower in the co-op store, even without taking patronage refunds into account." Still others fell for "contests, draws, and lotteries (which may be technically legal but often violate the intent of the law)." And, claimed the directors, lack of consumer understanding was further evidenced by the fact that co-ops found themselves under pressure to do more advertising and to carry wider selections, even though these measures would increase costs to consumers themselves.[36]

Consumer co-ops, for all the fact that they were well-placed to do so, did not become the leaders of the consumer activist movement. Groups like the Consumers' Association of Canada siphoned off organizational energy and political clout that co-operatives had expected to exercise. And, ultimately, consumers continued to think of their power as lying in their ostensible free choice, where co-operatives had always argued that free choice, which involved advertising, loss leaders, fancy packaging, duplication of brands, and so on, was costly and exploited consumers. Consumer power, in the co-operative tradition, lay not in individualistic freedom to hunt bargains, but in freely given loyalty to their own stores and their own brands, assuring value for themselves by exerting direct control over the store, and building up their savings and market power. In the 1960s, consumerism and co-operativism diverged.

Conclusion and Questions

In their day the guilds served three important functions: first, to educate members (particularly women, but the effort spilled over to the general membership) about co-operation and to develop their leadership skills; second, to assist the Co-operative Retailing System in testing product quality, in determining consumer acceptance, and otherwise to enable consumers to advise on product selection and marketing; and third, to give women a way to be involved and influential in co-operatives, even where by-laws or procedures hindered them from casting votes in their own right at co-operative meetings. What agencies are to perform these functions in the future? The decline of most guilds means that consumers have lost an effective means to participate in the first two tasks, education and product testing and advising. Since co-operatives are about self-help, this is a significant loss. Who now teaches the consumers of food products, for example, why it is to their advantage to support CO-OP brands? And what of the third function—can co-operatives afford to do without the participation and leadership qualities of women, "our greatest untapped natural resource" (as a Women's Participation Committee leaflet from the 1980s describes them)? And if that resource does need to be tapped, what programs need to be put in place to do it?

PART SIX: SYSTEM, 1961–1970

Introduction to Part Six

$\mathbf{A}$t some point, consumer co-operatives across western Canada began to think of themselves not so much as a "movement," but as a "system."

"Movement" and "system" are very different concepts. A movement is defined by the fact that it moves: it is broad, expansive, diverse, loosely organized—and continuous expansion is one of its principles. A movement is also about people; it is something they believe in, and join. It may resemble a political or religious cause. It is a solution, a means for change, an answer. A system, on the other hand, is more neutral with regard to objectives and purposes. A system is defined by the fact that it co-ordinates and standardizes. System is an operational concept, while movement is a small-p political concept relating to membership and leadership—the elected side of the movement, its values and long-term purposes.

"*System*," mutters Don Slimmon, fieldman for MCW at the height of the co-operative movement in the late 1940s. "I hate the bloody word. . . . There's no spontaneity . . . in a 'system.'"

In the 1960s, the concept of system began to overshadow the concept of movement. Western Canadian co-operatives were not unique in this; consumer co-operatives the world around went through many similar changes in the 1960s, due to changes in the global economy. Less well-known than the ICA commission that reported on co-operative principles in 1966 is another ICA commission which reported that same year, a commission examining economic integration. This commission reported that the trends toward integration and concentration of industry had made increased centralization essential for co-operatives, and especially for consumer co-operatives. These economic trends and lines of thinking are one set of factors that made the 1960s the era of system rather than of movement.

Another factor contributing to the change was the retirement of the older generation of co-operators from their leadership positions. From 1959 to 1963 Harry Fowler was president of FCL, and he was succeeded by Lewie Lloyd. These two men imprinted their own stamp on those years, for they were powerful speakers and ardent proponents of co-operative philosophy. Both of them

169

had become involved during the era of the Depression and the war, when economic need and co-operative idealism were at their greatest. They still carried the old fire of those fighting years in their hearts, and when they spoke they could awaken flickers of it in any audience. Fowler, remembers Gordon Wright, who had long experience as a retail and an FCL manager, was "a master at creating enthusiasm. He lived and breathed the Co-op Principles and had a knack of instilling [them] in the minds of other people." A former women's guild president from those years remembers being struck by Lloyd's "fierce dedication." Co-operators still tell stories of Lloyd's speeches, whose length terrorized chairmen and masters of ceremonies who were trying to keep a schedule. On one occasion an alarm clock was set to remind Lloyd when it was time to stop. But even at the end of two hours, Lloyd's audiences were aroused by his fervour and his words. FCL manager Elmer Wiebe remembers him as the co-op movement's "evangelist."

Fowler and Lloyd were men of little education but tremendous faith and flowing words, and their presidencies were the last reflection of the days when consumer co-operation as a popular movement was at its height. In retirement they were still revered as guardians of the movement's values and traditions; with Lloyd's death in 1987 an era truly and finally ended.

*   *   *

16

The Pressures of
Economic Change: "One System,"
1961–1970

On the occasion of the Co-op Refinery's twenty-fifth anniversary in 1959–60, FCL looked back on a quarter century of progress. Directors recalled that "twenty-five years ago, money was our main problem, for we had little." Now that problem had been lessened; consumer co-ops and their wholesale had capital enough for large expansions. "We have learned the techniques of co-operative financing," they concluded, "and need only to continue to do a conscientious job." Also, they recalled, "twenty-five years ago, co-ops were, for the most part, on the back streets—small and humble by today's standards. Now co-ops are moving onto main streets with modern, adequate premises." With money and facilities went a third change. Co-operatives had previously been isolated and independent; now there was "growing awareness of the advantages of amalgamation and consolidation." With this went a need to step up co-operative education. "Obviously there has been a growth in the quantity of our members," they declared. "But what about the quality?" For the future, co-operatives would have to foster "leadership" and "co-operative patriotism" to permit co-ops to draw together and face the challenges of continued integration and consolidation.[1]

With these statements the tone was set for the 1960s. Consumer co-ops and their wholesales would pursue bigness, and attempt to rally members and locals through co-operative patriotism to support a bigger and better-integrated system.

From "Keeping Pace with Change" to "One System"

The slogan for FCL's annual meeting in February 1965 was "Keep Pace with Change," a slogan which certainly summed up the concerns of the time. The kinds of changes meant were the increasing variety of consumer needs, the increasingly technical nature of new consumer goods, the need for larger stores and better-trained staff, the need to cope with rising rural operating costs as populations dwindled, and improving transportation which meant greater centralization both of stores and of wholesale warehousing facilities.[2] In the face of these changes there were two opposing tendencies. The directors observed,

171

A truckload of CO-OP feed goes out (1951). Until the 1960s, all CO-OP animal feeds were distributed in bags.

An FCL truck is loaded at a bulk feed depot (1960s). FCL began bulk feed operations to keep up with the trend toward larger farms and larger feed orders.

"there are some members who are reluctant to admit the need for change and who are more reluctant still to adapt to change." On the other extreme were "others who appear to believe that complete centralization is necessary."[3] FCL's board did not support either of these positions and looked instead for some middle ground between the existing structure of five hundred autonomous retails and the alternative of one single centrally owned co-operative. The proposal they arrived at was "consolidation of activities within local areas" based on amalgamations among neighbouring co-ops. As elaborated by the Managers' Advisory Committee, the plan was that "the 501 retail co-operatives now served by the wholesale would be reduced, through amalgamations, to about 140 larger units."[4] This would permit higher calibre local management, more economical use of manpower, more specialists, the best possible locations for facilities, and region-wide memberships to increase the shopping convenience for members.

These initiatives received support from yet another source, a study commissioned on the recommendation of senior management from the consulting firm of P. S. Ross and Partners, then the consulting arm of Touche Ross and Co., Chartered Accountants, with which FCL continues to maintain a close relationship. The study, begun late in 1964 and completed in early 1965, argued that while the wholesale was "alert and progressive," its structure had outlived its usefulness. As a result of the consultants' report, the management of FCL was reorganized to increase central planning and leadership. Department managers within each regional branch of FCL were now directly responsible to head office personnel, where previously they had been responsible through the branch managers. The new position of chief executive officer of FCL was created, reflecting the fact (as the directors told the delegates) that "ours is now a large organization." Together with these measures, a five-year program was launched to develop long-term planning, market research, personnel recruitment and development, and centralized merchandising.[5]

The other part of the consultants' report concerned the membership side of the organization, and the relationship between the wholesale and its retail members. The consultants reported a "conflict" between the perceived importance of the central as the "key organization" in the whole system, and the fact that it was subordinate to the control of the retails. The consultants said the fact that retails owned the wholesale posed a "psychological" problem in that they would be reluctant to listen to its advice. It was as a result of these concerns that P. S. Ross and Partners introduced the concept of "one system" to emphasize the unity of the wholesale and the retails. As the directors explained it, the purpose was to bring about a kind of revolution in attitudes within co-operatives, to "rid ourselves of concepts of separate functions and individual units, and to think, plan, and act in terms of *one system*."[6]

In conjunction with this change in attitudes, the consultants recommended and the directors proposed the development of "clear, uniform objectives" for FCL.[7] The FCL board believed such objectives were necessary to clear up "uncertainties and a lack of understanding . . . as to the real functions of co-operatives in the total system." These uncertainties included the fact that "managers do not have a common goal toward which they can direct and co-ordinate their efforts. Some feel their job is to maximize business efficiency like hard-headed businessmen, using big savings, no matter how gained, as the measure of success.

Others believe their task is to render maximum service to the members, and still others see the building of true co-operation as the goal." Second, said the FCL board, "some officers of consumer co-operatives also serve as officers of other types of co-operatives or other organizations. With no definition of our objectives to guide them, these people may become unduly influenced by aims, methods, or desires of other organizations." Third, "many people find common denominators in politics, religion, and co-operation. Confusion results when aspects of these become involved in the making of merchandising decisions." Fourth and finally, "because we lack a description of the aims, purposes, or functions, we tend to inject a wide variety of unrelated topics and activity into meetings."

These four points express the fact that the movement character of consumer co-operation was now perceived as an anachronism, a hindrance to unity and effectiveness. Questions of belief and ultimate purposes, sharing of officers with other co-ops, and discussion of topics not strictly related to business were all to be downplayed in favour of strict concentration on unity and on making operations more effective. There was a certain narrowing here, from thinking of the broad co-operative movement to thinking of the narrower retailing system; there was also a strengthening and focussing, a development of clearer institutional identity and roles. "One system" was a philosophy of unity, of loyalty, of organizational patriotism of the sort the directors had called for in 1960.

The Progress of Retail Amalgamations

How successfully were the plans of 1964–65 implemented? Fairest would be to say that progress was made, but not as quickly as had originally been said to be necessary. In 1966 annual meeting delegates noted that neither the plan for local amalgamations of retails nor the plan for voluntary centralization of merchandising "has achieved the desired pace or measure of progress," and they resolved unanimously to "encourage retail co-operatives and their members to support the principle of unity and consolidation," while also stating a commitment "to identify and resolve those matters which hinder the progress of the system towards this end."[8] The vagueness of this resolution is ample testimony to the nature of the problem. What do you do when co-ops have adopted a plan of voluntary amalgamation and centralization, and then not enough of them volunteer?

The slow progress of the plan was not for lack of trying. Discussions were held concerning retail amalgamations, for example, but sometimes the co-ops involved pulled out at the last minute.[9] Retail boards and managers who were not economically hard-pressed did not voluntarily turn their co-operatives over to their neighbours. In spite of resolutions at annual meetings, where delegates were intellectually convinced consolidation and co-ordination were good for the system as a whole, most local co-operatives did not actually follow through with action. It had been proposed in 1964–65 that the total number of co-operative associations be reduced from 501 to 140 or less within five years; but more than twenty years later, in 1988, over 330 remain.

But in spite of the failure to achieve extremely ambitious targets, voluntary regionalization progressed slowly and quietly over the next twenty-five years. Without fanfare or compulsion, certain co-operatives in certain areas have become very successful by doing just what was envisaged in 1964. The Pioneer Co-op in Swift Current, whose branches cover a vast trading area in southwestern Saskatchewan, or Prince Albert Co-op, which operates branches in surrounding communities, come to mind as obvious examples. So does the Delta Co-op in west-central Saskatchewan, also the product of a series of amalgamations, and which, unlike the other examples, covers a large area without a city trading centre at its hub. The Battlefords, Canora, Lloydminster, Outlook, or Portage la Prairie could equally be mentioned. But if one example is going to be picked for the purpose of illustrating this trend, it might just as well be St. Leon Co-op in southern Manitoba.

St. Leon is a small town of some 200 people, a town without even a grain elevator, and just about all contained on a single street. It is also the headquarters of a co-op with three or four thousand members, who do $11 million in business annually. St. Leon Co-op was pioneered by twenty-seven francophones who got together with their parish priest in 1941 and contributed $727 to form the co-operative. It grew and became the hub of the tiny community, the centre of the town's social and economic life—its modern and well-stocked store is at the focal point of the town, across the street from the parish church. "Most of what has happened in this town has happened because of the co-op," says Ray Labossière, manager at St. Leon since 1948. "Without it I think the place would have died."

As neighbouring co-ops got into trouble, St. Leon Co-op stepped in. Labossière recalls, "we took them over because they were in financial difficulties, and we don't like to let co-ops go broke." Now there are nine branches, the furthest one a hundred miles away, and every one of them larger than the parent branch. By all appearances this has not hurt the co-op in the least. "We have no problem with the branches being jealous of the centre!" says Labossière. Savings figures are enviable, and Labossière claims to run one of the largest lumber yards in the system. The success of one small co-operative has been expanded to bring similar benefits to the whole area.

Amalgamation, then, is not to be judged a dead issue. It is still proceeding, and many of the co-operatives leading in it are among the most successful, financially, in the system. It is proceeding, however, at members' own pace, and not the system's.

The slow pace of amalgamations in the 1960s virtually ensured that discussion would return to the centralized model, and that the wholesale would consider taking stronger leadership where retails seemed slow to act. In 1968 President Bob Boyes reminded members that co-operatives "must give up some of their local independence if they want a strong consumer co-operative system." "Surely," he told delegates to the annual meeting, "we do not intend the co-operative movement to be a museum for outdated ideas and methods."[10]

Retail Growth and Democratic Structures

The gradual growth, through amalgamation, of local retails into larger units, plus the growth of the large retails in the cities, raised questions about the democratic participation of members. Could large co-ops communicate effectively with members? Could ordinary people still influence their co-op, and learn by hands-on experience? Several innovations in the 1960s attempted to compensate for bigness.

The answer for many of the co-ops was to adopt a district structure, whereby each branch had its own local committee, elected its own delegates to the annual meeting, or had its own representative on the board of the over-all association. The Yorkton Co-op adopted a delegate structure in 1956 when it amalgamated with the Saltcoats Co-op; as new co-ops merged, each was reorganized as a branch with its own committee.[11] The Pioneer Co-op of the Swift Current area adopted a local branch committee structure in the early 1960s.[12] Both of these systems, however, were informal structures that functioned without being entrenched in by-laws. One of the first, possibly the very first, formalized district system was that set up when four associations in west-central Saskatchewan united to form Delta Co-op in 1961. The Delta Co-op annual meeting as constituted at that time consisted of delegates elected in the local districts.[13]

Considering that area development, including retail amalgamations, remains a priority, and that retails are growing bigger, it is perhaps surprising that so few co-operatives have adopted more elaborate democratic structures. The vast majority still rely on the concept that members will be sufficiently informed to attend the annual meeting—a single meeting for the entire co-op, once a year—and exert their influence on their co-operative by speaking and voting knowledgeably. The co-ops in rural areas that went through amalgamations had to face this problem head-on, and preserve some more intimate involvement for members whose local co-op was no longer going to be autonomous. In many of these cases, a district delegate structure offered a solution. Elsewhere, including where the co-op simply grew without amalgamation, such problems were rarely addressed. This was particularly true in the cities, where considerable growth in membership occurred in the 1960s.

One ambitious innovation for member participation in the 1960s was the Red River Co-op Parliament, an advisory and debating body elected on a district basis within Winnipeg, which debated consumer issues and made recommendations to the Red River board of directors. A number of policy resolutions, both for the local co-op and for submission to FCL annual meetings, came out of the Co-op Parliament's debates. Because of the liveliness of its discussions, as well as the number of people involved, the Red River Co-op

Parliament probably stands out as the broadest member-involvement mechanism devised in any of the major cities, and one of the most complex. As is often the case with such mechanisms, however, they require constant revitalization. The Co-op Parliament served its purpose for the span of a few years, and then declined. No mechanism of similar size or scope is now in place in any of the major urban areas of western Canada. Red River Co-op, it should be mentioned, also had a district structure to provide for the representation of smaller retail units around Winnipeg with which it had amalgamated in the course of the 1960s.

Calgary Co-op also attempted some innovations in democracy, and their fate is instructive. First, in 1968-69, the co-op studied and approved in principle a system of representation which sent delegates elected in local districts to the annual meeting. Then, in 1970, the directors approved an elaborate plan to implement the delegate structure; but the annual meeting rejected it. The few hundred members who attended the annual meeting out of Calgary's tens of thousands decided that an annual meeting of the existing kind was all Calgary Co-op needed. Next, in 1971, the board proposed an advisory council of 200 members, but by 1974, only 55 had been found who were willing to serve, out of 89,196 active members in Calgary Co-op.[14] The factors behind these events are not unique to Calgary. If anything, Calgary is a commercially successful co-operative, and the problem of lack of member involvement may be worse elsewhere. In all the large cities, as well as in many of the smaller centres, average members are not that interested in volunteer participation—they lack sufficient information and motivation. And those who are involved, like the members who scuttled the district system, are too content to commit themselves to major changes.

What is the cause of such apathy? One group of dissidents within the Co-operative Retailing System suggests that it has to do with erosion of local member control due to the greater power of both retail and wholesale managers. Don Slimmon, Hume Compton, Ray Labossière, and others who contributed to a publication called *The Co-op Member Bulletin* in the 1980s, argued that top management had forgotten what the grass-roots needed. Slimmon suggested that local members and boards "have forgotten how to raise hell when they felt they were losing their local autonomy. They have developed a certain awe for positions and offices in this day of tossing around figures like millions and billions." Compton warned of the dangers of "management taking over by default" in retails where the democratic process was apathetic. And Labossière suggested that management had "quite often forgotten the reason for their existence." "We have probably spent too much time trying to systemize the Co-op member/owners," he warned in 1984, "and still expect their loyalty."[15]

Growth and the Problems of Growth

During the 1960s, coping with growth in sales and facilities came to be a preoccupation of co-operatives. Total sales climbed every year and more than dou-

Morris Jevne, president of Interprovincial Cooperative, cuts the ribbon to open IPCO's new chemical complex in Saskatoon (9 July 1964). The new plant took salt, caustic soda, and chlorine as raw materials, and produced ingredients for the herbicide 2,4-D as well as by-products such as muriatic acid and hydrogen.

bled from 1960 to 1968, but savings were more erratic, falling in the aftermath of the 1961 amalgamation, then rising to a record high of over $5 million in 1964, then falling again and hovering at just over $4 million a year until 1969. The failure of savings to increase in proportion to sales is probably an indication of increasing competition and tighter margins, of the fact that sales increased most in low-margin goods, and possibly of some strain and inefficiency in the organization. This, at least, is how senior management analyzed the state of affairs by the end of the 1960s, as will be shown below.

The increase in sales during the 1960s also substantially changed the character of co-ops and of the wholesale. In 1961 the largest volume handled by FCL was in petroleum products—$24.3 million—followed by groceries at $17.3 million. Bulk and farm-supply goods still dominated, as they had since 1928, accounting for 55.6 percent of total FCL sales volume compared to only 39.3 percent for store goods (food, clothes, and hardware). Speeded up by the Alberta amalgamation, by supermarket expansions, and by increasing penetration of large urban markets (see Chapter 18), this picture changed dramatically. By 1967, petroleum sales had increased by 40 percent to $34,471,000, but food sales had increased by 250 percent to over $60 million. Store goods now accounted for more than half of the wholesale's volume—50.4 percent as compared to 43.6 percent for bulk and farm supply goods. Agricultural products, especially chemicals and fertilizers, were also increasing rapidly in importance (see Appendix 6).

This rapid increase in grocery sales, alongside growth in all other products, meant a tremendous increase in warehousing and distribution. Between 1960 and 1967, every major urban centre within FCL's trading area received new warehousing facilities. New office space was also needed, and this was especially true for the home office, still located in the building acquired in 1946 on Avenue D in Saskatoon. The Avenue D building was sold in 1965, preparing the way for the new and much larger head-office building on the present site on Twenty-second Street, completed in 1970.

Most of the new initiatives in the 1960s concerned productive enterprises—above all, petroleum, lumber, and farm supplies. CCRL undertook another expansion drive in 1961, selling a new series of expansion bonds to increase capacity to 22,500 barrels of crude per day. Lumber production was increased by repeated expansions of the mill at Canoe, and in 1965 a new plywood plant was completed on a separate site near the mill. The same year a second lumber mill was purchased at Smith, Alberta. FCL continued to expand in the feed business, opening new feed mills at Calgary and Brandon. A special agricultural department was created in 1964 to handle agricultural chemicals, fertilizers, and twine. Estimating that technological change would lead to a doubling in fertilizer use by the end of the decade, in 1964 FCL persuaded the Alberta and

FCL's board of directors celebrate the start of construction of the new head-office building in 1969. President R. H. (Bob) Boyes is driving the bulldozer. Waving his hat in the background is Boyes's successor as president, Gordon M. Sinclair.

Saskatchewan wheat pools to join in creating Western Co-operative Fertilizers Limited. Interprovincial Cooperative, meanwhile, was dramatically increasing its activity in formulating herbicides, and was moving in a big way into manufacturing of chemical ingredients for agricultural and other chemicals.[16]

These expansions in lumber, fertilizers, and chemicals were costly, and not merely in terms of financial resources. To expand into these products meant hiring and training local staff expert in their use, and the wholesale incurred costs for agrologists on the local staffs of retails, and for organized training programs for local lumber managers. FCL attempted to manage the Smith, Alberta, operation from the Canoe, B.C., site, another indication of a strain on the human resources of the system. The commitments were also extremely large and in some cases risky: the first large IPCO plant manufacturing chemical ingredients from raw materials was only officially opened in 1964, yet by 1968 IPCO was proceeding to quintuple its capacity in order to sell to nonagricultural and nonco-operative markets. In the cases of IPCO and WCFL, these were also joint ventures with other co-operatives, which complicated the management and planning, and in each case these products were to lead to headaches or controversy in the 1970s (Chapter 19).

The Crisis of 1969–70

It was not only in these subsidiaries and joint ventures, however, that growth had strained the management structure and capacity of the wholesale. Bill Bergen, who became treasurer in 1967 and chief executive officer in 1970, said to the author, "I doubt if people realize how close the organization was to financial disaster in the latter part of the Sixties." Bergen recalls that in 1968 he prepared a report for Dave Stewart, then still CEO, in which he argued that given the trends at that time—the prairie economy was in poor shape—FCL had only five years before bankruptcy. The consultants' studies and management reorganizations of the mid-1960s had, according to Bergen, "added considerably to the staff," as had the introduction of new accounting systems. "We couldn't continue," he says, "we were well over-staffed," and the excessive costs were impairing the earnings of the organization. Bergen headed an internal task force which recommended a 25 percent reduction in management staff—nearly 125 people.

This was an acute financial crisis—in all likelihood the worst in the system's history between the mid-1930s, when co-operatives began to fight their way out of the Depression, until 1982. The cuts carried out to meet this challenge were equally dramatic.

Stories are still told about the layoffs. In effect, the entire management structure was erased. Some found they had places in the new structure, and some did not. One of the employees who survived relates that when the dust cleared, he looked around his office area and realized, "I had a job, and nobody else did." Some 18 percent of FCL management positions were eliminated, according to the annual report, in the single year 1969. "It's the difference between making money and losing money," says Bergen, and the only remedy to "one of the lowest periods of earnings the organization ever saw." In 1970 and 1971, even as sales surged strongly, earnings fell disastrously to less than $3 million—1.2 percent of gross sales.[17]

In cutting back the organization to survive the downturn in the economy, there were two clear patterns. One was that the wholesale drastically cut back on the services it provided to member retails, services that had accumulated steadily over the years to include everything from providing decorating kits for retail annual meetings, to maintaining FCL District Representatives (DRs) in each district, to painting retail bulk plants and service stations. In 1965, for example, FCL proudly listed ninety separate services that constituted "some" of the services it provided to member retails.[18] In 1969 a great many of these services were cut, and the retail services division (as one manager of that era recalls) was "completely closed down" with "devastating" effect.

The second area that bore the brunt of the cuts was member and public relations. The Division of Public Relations, as it was then called, ceased to exist as a division of FCL, and no similar unit was re-established for a decade. Many of the centralized functions of the division were taken over by other units— training programs, for example, eventually ended up under the control of personnel officers. But as Jack Trevena, one who survived the cuts, notes, "the people who went were the people in the field. We eliminated all the people who were doing field work, educational work. . . ."

One effect of the cuts, then, was to cut, weaken, or disperse those parts of the wholesale which supported the movement aspect of co-operation. In line with the thinking of the One-System consultants' study, what was preserved in the crisis of 1969 was what was essential to the *operational* system of retailing and wholesaling. Education and publicity had lower priority when resources became scarce. This might have been necessary, though as Harold Chapman notes, the tendency to view education in this way can be counter-productive. "When times get tough you tend to cease to emphasize co-operatives as a movement—and that's one way to make sure you're going to need more restraint."

The drastic cuts in management personnel in 1969–70, along with the appointment of Bergen as CEO in place of Stewart, who had headed FCL's management since it was created in 1955, meant a near-complete change in the organization. If the changing of the guard on the elected side had occurred with Lewie Lloyd's retirement in 1967, the changing of the guard on the management side occurred with Stewart's retirement in 1970. Two and a half decades of stability in top management had come to an end. And it was the second major reorganization in a decade, so that in the opinion of one manager of the time, a "staff morale problem" was emerging. "There was always that anxiety," he remembers: "Are we going to get the axe, or not?"

It was also apparently a difficult era for the board of directors, although less is always said about divisions in a board of directors. Lloyd's retirement had inaugurated an unsettled period for the elected leaders of FCL, perhaps because it was not obvious to whom the mantle of leadership should next fall. Bob Boyes won the presidency, but not by a clear decision of the directors. In what amounted to a Saskatchewan–Manitoba contest, the board was evenly split, according to several who were there, between Boyes and Gordon Sinclair, with the issue remaining undecided even after three ballots and a night of consultations and negotiations among the directors. In the end a name was drawn from a hat, and Boyes became president of FCL. Sinclair continued as vice-president—from 1972 as sole and full-time vice-president—and in his turn succeeded Boyes in 1974. One of the directors from that era recalls, "the board was split right down the centre. The board was not unified at all at that time."

There was ample stress at the close of the 1960s for all the leaders of FCL, elected and appointed alike. A depressed farm economy, complex projects, management readjustments, and a generational change in co-operative leadership all came more or less together in the closing years of the Co-operative Retailing System's fourth decade. At the start of the 1970s the system was to face even greater challenges, as will be recounted in Part Seven. There was too much happening at once.

Conclusion and Questions

The 1960s saw, first through the One-System idea and then through the severe rationalizations of 1969–70, a steady de-emphasis of the ideas and structures that had made co-operatives into a movement. Education, public relations federations, and finally the public relations division fell by the wayside; along the way the provincial co-operative unions declined, and the relationship of the system with the Co-op College became much weaker. Was all this necessary? In bad times co-ops have to cut back to the basics. Is education not part of the basics for co-operatives?

Dave Stewart, who retired as chief executive officer in 1970, raises another question related to the focus on operations and on the bottom line. "Everyone who was in [top] management from my time on," he reflects, "had business—accounting, finance, audit—backgrounds. . . . Does that mean the board of directors is intrigued with people who can quote figures at them? Does it impress them?" If what Stewart implies is true, does this explain the low priority given to educational activities? The period when Harry Fowler—no businessman—was secretary (1946–59), and then president (1959–63), was the period when co-operative education received firm support from FCL. Does co-operative education need another Fowler? Or is the problem that co-operative education is not needed by the members or by the system?

Third, the idea of one system was associated with the need to integrate and compete in order to grow. Some co-operators have suggested that erroneous conclusions were drawn from this assumption of the need to grow, and of the kind of growth that would occur. The system moved heavily into lumber, petroleum, and chemicals, specialized products for the bulk-sales market. Bill Bergen notes, "everybody was expansion-minded, myself included, and didn't realize you could have done a lot more of the kind of development Calgary undertook"—development in groceries and high-volume items, development of urban shopping centres and new members, development of ordinary consumer goods instead of industrial products. "The market potential was there in the urban markets," he says, "but we kept making mistakes." Was the cult of growth in the 1960s excessive? Or was it a necessary response to competition? Did it lead to mistaken assumptions about what kind of growth should occur?

Finally, retail co-operatives should ask themselves how successfully they have addressed the questions about democracy and member involvement that were posed by the expansion of the 1960s. Why, for example, have district delegate systems, or other innovations, been attempted in so few co-ops? Perhaps it is because they are not needed; or perhaps it is because internal democracy has received too little thought and attention.

17

Consumer Co-operatives
and Organized Labour

In the late 1950s and early 1960s, consumer co-operatives in western Canada began to grow beyond the rural, farm-centred environment that had spawned them. The increasing proportion of business done in food, dry goods, and general store goods, already mentioned in Chapter 16, was one part of this change. So was the move to increased consumer education from 1955 to 1965. As co-operatives became more consumer-centred and less farmer-centred, there was greater potential for them to appeal to an urban, nonfarming audience. The great shopping-centre projects that began to become common in the late fifties are another part of the change; Chapter 18 will examine the development of the co-ops in the major urban centres of western Canada. Some co-op leaders naturally assumed there could be an alliance with the urban working classes, and especially with the labour movement. However, the growth of co-operatives into the cities, and the construction of large shopping centres and distribution facilities also increased the role of co-operatives as employers in the retail sector. This in turn contributed to an adversarial relationship between co-operative organizations and the labour union movement.

Labour Unions and Co-operatives

Labour unions and co-operatives share a great deal of the same history, values, and traditions. They had their birth simultaneously among the working classes of the British industrial revolution, and for decades there was no clear distinction between them. Only over time did the idea emerge that labour unions were workers united in their capacity as employees, while co-operatives were the same workers united in their capacity as consumers. Two labour-relations researchers note that co-ops and unions "both developed into social movements which endeavoured to moderate the impact of market competition by means of collective action."[1] In each case the goal of the organization was to increase the power of the members "to achieve the goals of economic or industrial democracy"; and for this reason both could lay claim to "moral legitimacy" because they sought to help the victims of the prevailing economic system.

The difference in the western Canadian case is that the *successful* consumer co-operatives were those organized by farmers, and not so much those organized by workers. Mine and railroad workers had organized co-operatives in the very earliest days of the western Canadian consumer co-operative movement (as recounted in Chapter 3), but these had not become numerous enough to band together, nor strong enough to weather the periodic economic crises during the era of the two world wars. With the exception of B.C., where in some cases fishermen's co-ops played a leading role in co-operative retailing and wholesaling, it was the farming interest that united early co-ops, and it was, and to a large extent still is, farmers who provided the leadership for the movement as a whole. This point should not be over-emphasized, for in spite of their rural base the consumer movement in western Canada was very strongly influenced, through certain key co-ops and key leaders, by the idealistic and social-reformist Rochdale tradition. Although this provided common ground for discussions with union leaders, the farmer/worker split lurked in the background.

Farmers and labour unions have not generally been warm friends. There is a difference in economic philosophy, and not just in rural versus urban culture. Farmers work the hours their businesses take, not nine to five, and put their livelihoods on the line when they buy seed and plant it in the spring. When all manner of risks farmers take with respect to weather and pests are surmounted, then they receive what markets will give them for their crops. In this sense they do not have security, guarantees, or protection, which are the labour union's chief concerns on behalf of its members. But on the other hand, farmers are not usually dependent on a single master who can, if not restricted, arbitrarily hire and fire, change wage and working conditions, and so forth. Farmers take known risks with superhuman elements, weather and markets, but are more independent than most workers with respect to society and other human beings. When they do not believe a market is fair and beyond arbitrary control by individuals, as was the case with the grain markets before 1923, they become as angry and as organized as labour unionists. The grain companies and wheat, dairy, and livestock pools formed by western farmers are the equivalent of the workers' labour unions. It is possible for consumer co-ops and wheat pools to work closely together in many instances, in spite of the fact that they have opposite economic interests as far as food prices are concerned. Why not labour unions as well?

Genuine sympathy for employees had existed in many of the co-ops and wholesales of the Depression and war era. Mention has previously been made of the efforts by Saskatchewan Co-op Wholesale to help unemployed miners in Lethbridge form a co-operative coal mine in the early forties; and of efforts in the postwar era to treat employees with consideration. With the exception of the coal mines and the refinery, co-operatives did not generally have to deal at that time with large numbers of employees. Most retails had only a handful of staff, and most of these were members of local farm families and friends, neighbours, or relatives of directors and managers. There was little distinction between employee and director in the early consumer movement, and no perceived need for labour unions. The idealism of the mid-1940s, the talk of constructing a new social order and restraining the power of big business, inspired co-operative and labour-union leaders to investigate closer relations, especially as co-operatives began to consider the large urban markets.

Contacts between the Organized Co-operative and Labour Movements

In 1950 a panel representing farmers and labour met in London, Ontario, under the auspices of the Canadian Labour Congress, to discuss relations between co-operatives and organized labour. A. L. Mosher, president of the CLC, urged "farm groups, co-operatives and the . . . congresses of labour [to] form a strong central committee to survey their economic situation and find the barriers to closer co-operation." The panel members agreed "that both farm and labour groups should undertake together the job of helping labour to organize its consuming power through co-operatives."[2] As a result of such contacts and points of agreement, co-operatives and organized labour formed the National Labour–Co-operative Committee in 1954 to promote closer relations.

"The Co-operative Movement," declared the Co-operative Union of Canada in 1957, "is in full sympathy with the labour movement." Co-operatives "freely recognize the right of their employees to organize for protection and advancement in accordance with the requirements of the law."[3] Consequently, co-ops made the same pitch to labour unionists that they had made to farmers: co-operate on the purchasing side to improve your position just as you co-operate on the producing side, in both cases to improve your economic position. "Action through co-operatives would help the unionist to control his costs," said the directors, "just as it helps the farmer. Such action can often be more effective than wage increases, because it brings both the immediate benefits of lower costs and the long-term benefits of business ownership." FCL's directors concluded, "because of similarities in objectives, it is natural that labour union members should join the co-operative movement."[4]

The Canadian labour movement responded with its own statement that "labour unions recognize that co-operative participation brings real social and economic benefits . . . making wage gains more meaningful and providing opportunity for development of the skills necessary in democratic living." The CLC also added an unusual phrase: "labour unions . . . recognize that, for well-informed employees, co-operative employment can have values to which the usual criteria do not apply."[5] This seemed to support the idea that co-operatives were different from other employers, and might have different terms or relationships with their employees.

The CLC and the CUC agreed on seven points that ought to govern relations between co-operatives and labour unions:

1.   "Co-operative employees should have wages and working conditions on a level with those enjoyed by employees in comparable profit enterprise."

2.   "Co-operatives should be expected to take the lead in employee remuneration only when costs are not pushed out of line with comparable profit enterprise."

3.   "No obstacles should be placed in the way when employees are contemplating organization."

4.   "Co-operatives are no ordinary employers." Because of their community roots and dedication to service, co-ops offer "unusually satisfactory employment opportunities" to workers.

5.   "Labour unions should endeavour to ensure, on the part of all members, a general understanding of co-operative objectives, principles, and practices."

6.   Co-operatives, similarly, should strive for greater understanding of the nature of the relationship with their employees when those employees organize.

7.   Those involved in negotiations between co-ops and credit unions should not only have understanding of co-operation, labour unionism, and current industry standards, but also "the skills necessary to engage in fair and firm bargaining."

Here was laid out a blending of partnership, consideration for each other's needs and interests, and fair adversarial bargaining within a relationship of trust.[6] It remained to be seen whether the ideals so readily agreed upon by the two national federations could be transferred into practice in individual cases.

One project intended to be a collaboration between the two was the expansion of Red River Co-op in Winnipeg. In 1957–58 Red River was constructing its first downtown shopping centre, one of the most modern in the region, and it was expected that support by labour "should assure success to the new venture in an area that previously has been described . . . as a co-operative desert."[7] In return for the anticipated support by labour unionists, Red River was sympathetic to labour-union organization. The board of the co-op unanimously adopted a hands-off policy under which the choice of a union was left up to employees.[8] Also at that time, Red River Co-op became "one of the first private industry employers to grant three weeks holiday to employees after five years' employment," according to local newspaper accounts. The co-op also instituted a fifty–fifty pension plan (half the cost being contributed by the employer), group insurance, fifty–fifty medical and hospital plans, and a ten-day minimum sick leave allowance.[9] This can only be construed as a policy favourable to organization of employees and to generous benefits for them.

In this it followed in a well-established co-operative tradition, for the co-op wholesales in the West had long favoured generous treatment of employees and had pioneered in the establishment of life-insurance schemes for employees and of the Co-operative Superannuation Society (see Chapter 11 and Appendix 3). Today FCL maintains close ties with The Co-operators Group Limited for its group insurance programs.

The new idea at Red River, besides extending some of the benefits, was an explicit attempt to co-operate with organized labour, and initially this collaboration had some success. One FCL employee remembers that, while Red River had always been "a real, thriving farm co-op," the alliance with labour led to great gains in Winnipeg, which was, after all, the most industrial, the most working-class, and probably the most unionized major city in western Canada. As he recalls, the co-op was successful partly because there was "strong CCF and Labour influence behind it. They did an excellent job of supporting and developing Red River Co-op."

But whether such initial successes could be duplicated elsewhere depended in part on broad negotiations between labour and co-operative centrals. The medium through which this was attempted was the National Labour–Co-operative Committee (NLCC).

Co-ops, Unions, and Labour Relations Policies

In 1963 the National Labour–Co-operative Committee sponsored a conference in Toronto on union-management relations in co-operatives. The conference, involving ten representatives each from leading labour and co-operative organizations—specifically the general managers of all the co-operative wholesales in Canada—was in effect an admission that all was not proceeding smoothly. Barney Johnsrude, manager of BCCWS, told retail managers that the reason for the meeting was that "the Co-operative Labour Relations Committees at both national and provincial levels are not progressing as successfully as had been visualized when this program was launched some years ago."[10] The meeting provided evidence of frustrations on both sides, frustrations that may be taken as indicative of the over-all results of efforts for labour unions and co-ops to work together.

C. B. "Bun" Fraser, assistant general manager of FCL, presented a key paper which outlined five concerns.[11] First, he said, was the problem of "a lack of bargaining skills" on the part of co-operatives. The implication was that retail co-operatives had been taken advantage of in negotiations, and he reported that FCL had, therefore, established the position of industrial relations officer a few months earlier to "work with the management of retail co-operatives . . . giving them training, advice, and guidance." This marked the entry of FCL into its members' labour relations. Second, Fraser objected to unions using "pressure group techniques at co-op annual meetings." Third, he expressed frustration that unions blocked co-operatives' attempts to expand services. He used Saskatoon to illustrate his point, saying that Saskatoon co-op had the only unionized service station, and needed to expand to meet the competition by staying open evenings, Sundays, and holidays. This required an increased proportion of lower-grade employees, which the union would not, according to Fraser, accept.

Fraser's remaining points are equally indicative of basic frustrations. "Management's rights are important," he argued, and the union was "trying to usurp by contract clauses the responsiblility of management." Finally, he objected to strikes or strike threats in co-operatives, claiming they were very damaging to co-ops. "When you strike a chain store," he said, "you merely ask the customers to start dealing with a different chain store. But when you strike a co-op, you ask a member to leave *his own business*." A strike against a co-op was a strike against the member consumers, not against some far-off investors.

Fraser also added some personal observations. "In total," he noted, "I believe that only a very small percentage of union members are supporting co-operatives," although he also believed most managers supported labour unions. "At the same time they [managers] would applaud an increased activity toward organizing many of their competitors. They feel co-ops have been getting rather special attention by the union organizers."

A union representative apparently countered with charges of "conspiracy and collusion" among co-operatives, and it was argued that the policy of organizing co-ops first was "logical in view of the common objectives of the co-operative and labour movements." It was also claimed that FCL visited local co-ops and obstructed negotiations between the local and its union; FCL denied this, and it was suggested that the problems unions faced reflected "the views and attitudes of individual managers only, and not co-operative policy."

The participant quoted here got the impression of "general agreement that NLCC principles are not observed," and sensed "a continual sparring for position and reluctance by both sides to admit credit to the other. I felt a clash between principles and practical economic interest." The one high point, he thought, was the address by Alex Laidlaw of the CUC, who chided co-operative managers for treating employees the same as other businesses do, for failing to accept labour's need for security, and for judging all labour by the minority of bad labour leaders. On the other hand, he also chided labour for not differentiating between co-ops and other businesses, and for not supporting the co-operative movement. "Laidlaw's address was most impressive," read the notes. "I felt it renewed my faith and hope." But he also wrote, "I fear Dr. Laidlaw is far in advance of those to whom the inspiring message was given."[12]

Labour Relations in Consumer Co-operatives

A scholarly study published in 1987 concluded that over the twenty-year period from the mid-1960s to the mid-1980s, labour disputes in the co-operative sector in Saskatchewan became "more frequent and harder fought." By the end of that period, they noted, labour disputes in co-ops, which employ about 6 percent of Saskatchewan's unionized workforce, accounted for 40 percent of the person-days lost due to strikes.[13] The authors identified second-tier co-operatives such as FCL as one source of the increased polarization, claiming that "professionalization and centralization of the labour relations function within the confines of a second-tier co-operative . . . [have] given authority to those who have a purer market orientation, whose beliefs may reflect varying degrees of antiunionism, and who are apt to give short shrift to co-operative values." Local union leaders were found by the authors to resent "central professionals who, to them, represent a more sophisticated and aggressive approach to labour relations than had existed in local co-ops." The result, they assert, is "labour relations structures, tactics and values which are indistinguishable from antiunion profit sector employers."[14] While FCL is named at only one point, it is clear that it is one of the second-tier co-ops included in these comments.

There can be no doubt that a few serious strikes in some co-operatives have inflicted damage on a significant scale within the Co-operative Retailing System. One 1983 strike in Saskatoon (referred to in the study) led to a notable decline in patronage and only a slow return of members and customers after the strike was completed. Saskatoon Co-op subsequently encountered financial difficulties. The failure of Surrey Co-op, one of the largest in the system, was blamed by the manager in part on labour-relations difficulties. He claimed that the co-op's financial difficulties started four years before the bankruptcy with an eight-month strike, and he also said that the co-op's collapse was furthered by the refusal of unionized workers to take pay cuts, and, he speculated, fears by creditors that another strike would occur.[15]

Many other examples can be cited, but it is not so easy to decide what to make of them. In the case of Surrey, for example, one senior FCL manager of the day states that it was the local retail that was determined to take on the union, and that even his personal intervention to pressure the retail to settle with the union did not avoid the confrontation. Another manager of equivalent rank said much the same thing about the Saskatoon strike, that it had been a mistake by the retail to attempt to "break the union" rather than settle for a compromise. Wholesale managers admit that retail managers sometimes pick unnecessary fights and hold unnecessary grudges, but argue that independent retails are difficult to control. "It's very difficult for a lot of people who work in the wholesale," says one retired retail services man, "to get their noses rubbed in what the retail does" in its labour relations.

It is also true that the statistics on increasing strike rates quoted above apply only to Saskatchewan—it would be useful to have similar studies for the rest of western Canada—and that virtually the entire increase in strikes has been since the start of the 1982 recession. This likely influences the statistics. There are also differences between one division of the system and another. Virtually all of the problems have been in the retail sector; and even these have been concentrated in certain operational regions and with certain unions. FCL's own employees have only been on strike once, and managers boast of an excellent relationship with the Energy and Chemical Workers Union at the Co-op

Refinery. If the second-tier co-op, FCL, is behind the increased polarization in labour disputes, why are its relations with its own, direct employees comparatively good?

And within the retail sector, problems have also been posed by the structure of contracts, for many co-ops cover a wider range of job functions and classifications than their competitors. "I don't think there should be a difference" between co-ops and the competition in how employees are treated, says one region manager. "I think over the years there has been a difference: we've tended to treat all employees the same regardless of what industry they're in." For example, he argues, retail clerks are unionized in both FCL and its competitors, but gas attendants in his region are unionized only in the co-op. Because of this, the gas attendants received, he claims, twice as much per hour as the competition paid, and better benefits. "We need to bargain on an industry basis—and be competitive," he asserts. Elmer Wiebe, marketing manager for FCL, observes, "we may at times find ourselves not being competitive in an area such as food where the total industry is organized." The reason, he says, is that the retail co-op's contract may also cover employees in other industries besides food—hardware, lumber, petroleum, feed, farm supplies, anything the local co-op is involved in. "Seventy-five percent of our employees [might be] on the non-food side where very few of the competitors are organized," and on that side there will be a tendency for the co-op to pay higher wages and more benefits. If this happens, the co-op will have difficulty keeping up with the unionized competition in the retail food area, while still remaining competitive.

One pattern that does seem to emerge is that FCL's advisors are very unpopular with the retail unions, and union representatives are equally unpopular with FCL's advisors. In a couple of recent cases described by co-operators, the local union and management decided to settle matters themselves and not to call in outside help either from FCL or from the union. The result was that the contracts were settled within days, without acrimony or work stoppages.

Listening to some co-operators talk about the subject, one is left with the impression that the adversarial relationship has grown larger than either participant really wants. One retired wholesale manager describes the relationship as follows: "You hire the best guy you can get to beat down the workers, and the unions hire the best guy they can get to carry a sling for them. And that's not in the interest of either side." This suggests that collective bargaining in the system has in many cases become a game of posturing in which each side hires and rewards its negotiators for being as unco-operative as possible. "They're better paid for war than for peace," adds another co-operator.

Conclusion and Questions

The discussions of labour and co-ops working together were part of the movement phase of co-operation, when social reform ideals were emphasized. It seems unlikely now that either side is as committed to broad social-reformist thinking as they once were. Today, co-ops and labour unions may, if they work at it, get along; but they are not likely, as had once been hoped, to be recruiting members for each other. Are there ways to overcome or mitigate the adversarial relationship between co-ops and labour unions? Can they help each other? Or is it better to stick as closely as possible to the industrial norms and traditional collective bargaining?

These questions are tied to a more general consideration: do co-operatives have any special obligations for their employees' welfare? Co-operatives have claimed that their system of doing business possesses a special moral legitimacy because it is absolutely and perfectly fair: no person within a co-operative ever exploits (makes a profit out of) another. Doesn't this mean they should also take pains not to exploit their staff? Co-ops in western Canada have rarely complained about paying farmers fair value for their food products, even though this reduces the co-op's earnings. Why should the matter be any different when it comes to paying labour for its services?

There are numerous conceivable alternatives. Some modern management structures emphasize greater employee involvement in regular decision-making—employee advisory bodies or employer-employee councils. In business in general there seems to be a trend toward profit-sharing schemes for employees, arrangements that reward employees in proportion to the company's earnings; some mixed worker-consumer co-operatives in Europe divide surpluses by a prearranged formula between employees and members. Productivity bargaining has been tried by Pincher Creek Co-op, with success. Other co-operative movements that have had to come to terms with organized labour (notably the British consumer movement in the 1920s) adopted procedures for compulsory arbitration of labour disputes in co-operatives—such disputes were automatically referred to a co-op/labour panel. Worker co-operatives could also be a solution: the System already has a guideline stipulating that wages in a retail co-operative should amount to a particular percentage of sales; why not go one step further and turn co-operative stores over to the workers to run on a contract basis for the same amount? FCL is said to have opposed worker co-operatives in the retailing sector; perhaps this could bear review. If one of these alternatives could replace or modify the adversarial system, would it not be more in keeping with co-operative values of democracy and equity?

18

Breaking into the Cities: Calgary Co-op and Its Rivals

$\mathbf{R}$etail co-operatives did not break into the major urban centres of western Canada through partnership with the labour movement, as had been hoped at the time of the formation of the National Labour–Co-operative Committee in the 1950s. But in the 1960s, co-operatives did steadily penetrate the large urban markets of western Canada, at least in the three provinces then served by FCL. The importance of this urban growth cannot be ignored, for today in each of the prairie provinces the one or two largest cities account for 40 percent or more of the population of the entire province. Winnipeg, Saskatoon, Regina, Edmonton, and Calgary have come to dominate their region in terms of population and therefore of consumer markets. Vancouver, largest city in western Canada, similarly represents an immense market. All the major cities, except Vancouver, did eventually develop thriving retail co-operatives. This raises two questions: what were the problems that delayed co-operative development in the cities for so long? And second, how did the co-ops overcome these problems to become successful, after all, in the 1960s?

Finally, however, something has to be said about more recent developments. Today there is still no major retail co-operative in Vancouver, and in almost every one of the other cities the co-ops have encountered serious financial difficulties. In only one city, Calgary, has a big-city co-op lived up to the hopes and expectations of the 1960s—and Calgary was one of the cities hardest-hit by the 1982 recession that laid the others low. Why the difference? The question is of fundamental significance, for without Calgary Co-op or others similarly successful, the Co-operative Retailing System is limited at best to less than half the population of western Canada—and the declining half at that.

Background: Why Were the Cities Late?

There is a curious consistency to the problems consumer co-ops have faced in the bigger cities of western Canada over the course of the last hundred years. Many of the earliest consumer co-ops in Canada were in the cities. But from 1914 onward, urban and rural consumer co-operatives fared quite differently. The urban co-ops were hit very hard by the economic difficulties of the World

War One years and by the postwar depression. They participated once again in the upsurge of consumer co-operation that began in the early 1920s, but then many were cut down again by the recession of 1922–23.[1] At that time the strong southern Ontario co-operative movement was devastated, and with this the leadership in co-operative development was left to the farmers of the rural West. Historian Ian MacPherson wrote about the problems in the cities:

> It was very difficult to kindle the requisite community spirit. The old elites of the towns and cities were customarily opposed to co-ops, while new professional and business elites were preoccupied by their careers and by the economic expansion of the period. The more active working men, moreover, were usually interested in "bread and butter" trades unionism, while the poor were disorganized and disinterested. It was also difficult to appeal on the basis of local interest . . . because somehow . . . communities believed they would share adequately in . . . growth.

In short, consumer co-operatives found no constituency in the cities, no roots among an organized group that needed them.[2]

Co-ops could not rely on the same kind of social and economic foundations in the city that they could in the country. In contrast to the conditions MacPherson described in the cities, farmers' occupational organizations did see co-operation as being in their interest, and they encouraged, subsidized, and conducted co-operative education from which rural co-ops benefited. Rural communities did not believe they would automatically share in growth, and saw co-operatives as essential ways to fight for their local well-being. The spirit of working together so evident in many small towns and rural areas was not evident in the cities, and could not be converted into co-operative membership and loyalty. But how, then, did consumer co-ops manage to penetrate the urban markets?

First Successes, 1944–60

Consumer co-operation spread in the countryside of western Canada in the 1920s, and sank firm roots in the 1930s; but it really only penetrated the cities in the 1940s and 1950s. Perhaps the way in which the Depression hit the urban centres of western Canada, through inflicting unemployment on the working classes and forcing job-seekers to travel from job to job and city to city, was not conducive to co-operation. The Depression drove farming communities together, but possibly split workers apart. In any case, it is significant that consumer co-operation spread to the cities only when it had already grown to the stature of a movement in the surrounding countryside. This is not too surprising, for the prairie cities were much smaller than today, surrounded by the rural areas where co-operation had become a way of life, and intimately connected to the rural and agricultural economy. And not surprisingly, the first two cities to develop large retail co-ops were in Saskatchewan, where the farm co-operative movement was most extensive.

The big news by the 1950s was that some city co-ops could thrive and were proven successes. The chief examples held up as inspirations for other co-operators were in Regina and Saskatoon. Sherwood Co-op in Regina had over $4 million in sales in 1953, earning net savings of half a million dollars for its 14,670 active members. Its manager and a leader in the expansion effort was George B. Munro, who had decided (as one former FCL manager recalls) to make Sherwood "the crown jewel of the co-operative movement." Its new building opened in 1955, a $750,000 palace (by the standards of the time) on the corner of Victoria and Albert. Fifteen hundred people turned out on 22 June 1955 to hear Premier T. C. Douglas open Canada's largest co-operative store, and call it "a monument to the men and women who dreamed dreams and saw visions."[3]

Saskatoon Co-op was not nearly so large, but with some $2 million in sales in 1953, and a membership of perhaps six thousand, it was still a big and very successful co-op.[4]

But as examples of success in cities, both Regina and Saskatoon were atypical cases, for the two Saskatchewan cities were the head offices of Canada's largest co-op wholesale and of Canada's only co-op refinery. Sherwood had purchased both supplies and management from CCRL until 1943, building up a huge and immensely lucrative petroleum volume with a minimum of its own staff or facilities.[5] Saskatoon Co-op began under the Associated Stores Plan of the Saskatchewan wholesale (a management contract) and received inexpensive help from the wholesale offices in town. Its president, E. F. Scharf (editor of the *Co-op Consumer*) told the SFCL board in 1946 that "only through the co-operation of Federated had they been able to take care of the volume of business that they had." Unable to carry inventories on its small premises, Saskatoon Co-op had in effect operated out of the wholesale's warehouses, assisted by the wholesale's staff.[6]

In other words, consumer co-operation had penetrated the two Saskatchewan cities, but not by the normal method of starting small, slowly developing roots among a local constituency, and self-financing growth in a gradual way. Perhaps, then, if there was a lesson in the success of Saskatoon and Regina, it was that co-ops could succeed at least in agriculture-oriented cities, cities containing many farm-raised people, where the wholesale assisted them to start big and grow fast.

While Saskatoon and Regina were, at that time, successful, Winnipeg was laying the basis for impressive future growth. Red River Co-op was conducting an aggressive and forced expansion in the 1950s, which FCL financed in exchange for control of management. Red River's first attempt to open a co-operative store had failed in 1952, and the wholesale assumed Red River's debts in exchange for an equal say in appointing the retail manager. In 1957 Red River signed another management contract with FCL, this time intended to help the co-op get back into the store business in a big enough way to make it viable.[7] The dream soon to be realized was the opening of an up-to-date shopping centre, providing every service and convenience then conceivable, to tackle

A display of CO-OP brand products distributed by Interprovincial Cooperative in the 1950s. Most of the products shown here were manufactured, processed, or packaged in plants owned by IPCO or its member co-operatives. By uniting all stages of production and distribution under co-op ownership, co-operative leaders believed they could pass on to the consumer all of the savings accrued at every stage of producing and selling goods.

head-on the competition in the prairies' largest city. The planned shopping centre was to cost $750,000, one-fifth of which was raised by local shares and debentures; the remaining four-fifths ($600,000) was provided by FCL in a secured loan. The new shopping centre opened in 1958 at Ellice Avenue and Wall Street with thirteen thousand people attending the grand opening. FCL's directors commented that the new centre "brought a climactic end to the description of Winnipeg as a 'co-operative desert.'"[8]

The Red River expansion, the first of several for that co-op, marked the start of a deliberate effort by the co-operative system to promote expansion in the cities. Russell Love dramatized it in his address to the Red River grand opening of 1958: "the big day has come. The time has come to open one of the finest and largest co-op supermarkets in any city of Canada." "For the first time in history," he said, "one hundred and fifty thousand co-operators residing in over five hundred communities . . . have invested a half million dollars in an urban co-op centre that they cannot hope to use. . . . Why has this been done? The answer is obvious. The leaders of Federated Co-operatives . . . being men of vision and action, know that the co-operative movement is destined to go forward and spread into the urban, as well as the rural, communities of Canada."[9]

Red River's development to 1960 is a good example of how intimately the wholesales were involved in many urban expansions. This gave rise to some friction with members who saw the management contracts as restrictions on local autonomy.[10] Co-ops like Red River could not, apparently, raise the vast sums needed for expansion entirely from their own members, through sales of shares and savings bonds. One alternative was to attract new members and wait until the volume and capital provided by signed-up members *was* adequate to finance expansion. But the thinking was that to break into the cities, large, modern facilities were essential to attract the members in the first place, and for this the only possibility seemed to be to borrow. If the wholesale was to finance expansion on such a scale, it could not risk its funds without some considerable control—hence the management contracts. Perhaps this set a pattern for big co-op expansions: urban co-ops got money the easy way, from the wholesale or from financial institutions, rather than the hard way, from their members; and in the process the retail became more dependent on its creditors and on the wholesale, and less on its own members.

Growth in the Cities, 1960–75

In 1959 the FCL board drew delegates' attention to the "increasing need for co-operatives to adapt themselves to . . . population shifts" by expanding in the cities. Expansion was furthered by large amounts of cash available within the system; in seventeen months in 1959–60, FCL made four refunds of nearly $1 million each to its members. The result was a surge of expansion, especially in the cities.[11] Red River's second shopping centre opened in East Kildonan in 1961, and more occurred over the course of the decade. In 1968–69 it enlarged one existing store, purchased another property previously leased, and bought land for a third, new, shopping centre. However, these expansions did not necessarily help its financial position. From 1951 to 1963 Red River's sales multiplied seventeen times, from $224,252 to $3,890,070. But savings fell from an earning of 2 percent of sales to a loss of 1.6 percent in 1963. The co-op got back on its feet, with savings going as high as 3.5 percent in 1974, but then falling again.[12] It remained subject, like many urban co-ops, to fierce competition, relatively weak member loyalty, and debt, a combination that left it vulnerable when another round of expansion in 1978–79 was followed by the recession of 1982.

One of the key problems facing urban co-ops that expanded too much was debt. A 1975 report by the Manitoba government showed that the largest co-operatives in Manitoba were heavily indebted, and members' equity amounted to less than one-third of their total assets. In 1975 Brandon was the most extreme case; local members owned only 9 percent of their local co-op.[13] In Red River's case, the equity base is said to have fallen as low as 7 percent before the co-op was reorganized and stripped of all but its petroleum functions in 1982. These low equity ratios are a sign that the co-operatives were not relying on their own members to finance their expansions, but were borrowing instead. This in turn implies a lack of member understanding and support. In purchasing, too, member support was not strong: the same government report showed that average annual purchases per active member were only $546.50 in Winnipeg, much less than the total amount a family spent at that time on food, petroleum, hardware, and other commodities handled by the co-op. From statistics such as these it appears that urban co-ops were building with borrowed money to attract customers whose loyalty was not reliable.

In 1960 Calgary Co-op opened a second store (see below), which spurred Edmonton co-operators to plan a new supermarket of their own. President Alex Goruk declared, "Here is what we have been dreaming of. . . . A modern Co-op Shopping Centre with wide aisles, a greater variety of food—groceries, produce and meat. Up-to-date refrigerated equipment. . . . dry goods, hardware, household appliances, drugs, farm supplies and other service departments, including a coffee counter and a three-bay service station." This was heady stuff for co-operators in 1960. The grand opening of the new, $750,000 co-op shopping centre on Eighty-second Street and One hundred and twenty-seventh Avenue came in 1961.[14]

Like Edmonton Co-op vying with Calgary, Saskatoon Co-op also tried to catch up to the expansion of its sister city in the province. Emulating Sherwood Co-op's shopping centre development of 1955, Saskatoon Co-op opened a large two-storey shopping centre on a prime downtown location in 1965, moving aggressively into clothing, furniture, and appliances. This department store later burned down, and did not have the opportunity, like many of the grand co-op developments elsewhere (including Regina's), to lose money and be closed.

Don Tullis, secretary-treasurer of FCL at the time, insists that in its expansions "the Saskatoon Co-op Board of Directors just wouldn't listen to Federated," refusing FCL's offer of financing with controls attached. On the other hand, representatives of many retails have been critical of the way FCL allegedly pushed expansion. Feasibility studies conducted by FCL, for example, assumed a given percentage of the market could be won by local co-ops, and did not typically focus on the different nature of the big urban markets, or the problems of winning over new generations of urban consumers in the face of new kinds of competition. Co-operatives that built according to such projections understandably over-built. Likewise, the Construction Department of FCL was criticized in some cases for promoting "grand" facilities with "too many frills," as one FCL director recalls. In short, there are two conflicting views about why excessive expansions occurred, one saying retails pushed them, and one saying FCL pushed them. Individual cases varied, and it is difficult to generalize.

City co-ops had a comparatively easy time of it in the 1960s. The times were mainly prosperous, and competition was, managers from that time generally agree, less than today. While chain stores like Safeway were increasingly dominating the urban retail market, this was a type of competition with which co-ops were familiar. The large discount food chains ("Superstores" and similar operations) had not yet made their impact, and neither had the plethora of integrated and sophisticated hardware and petroleum chains that are present today. And retail co-ops grew in the 1960s with external help. Co-operation did not become an urban movement in its own right, not to the same degree as in the countryside where it was supported by occupational and community interests, by study groups and co-op schools, by networks of field and public relations personnel of various co-operatives and of government departments. The cities were no longer "a co-operative wasteland," but we may infer that they were also not a co-operative stronghold.

The Development of Calgary Co-op

In 1951 the United Farmers of Alberta decided, as described in Chapter 13, to sell their stores to the Alberta Co-op Wholesale Association, and one of these was the UFA store on Eleventh Avenue and First Street South-East in Calgary. Under the management of John Suits, that store became highly profitable, more profitable than many of the autonomous co-ops around the province, and local interest grew in getting autonomy for the Calgary store and thus making it possible for it to distribute its local surpluses to its local customers. At the same time, ACWA was under some pressure from other co-operators to get out of the chain-store business and commit itself to the federated structure of autonomous locals. Discussions of autonomy for Calgary took place in 1954–55.

Much has been written, and more will be added here, about the success of Calgary Co-op, but it is useful to de-mystify its development and point out that its origins were, in their own way, humble, especially as regards member interest and support. When, in 1954, a questionnaire was sent out to the Calgary store's four thousand patrons asking their opinions about local autonomy, only sixty-six replied, and of those, not many more than half were willing to pledge financial support for the idea.[15] It was not, at first, a strong grass-roots movement that led to the formation of Calgary Co-op. But in order to become autonomous, local members had to raise the capital to buy out the fixtures and inventory, and they proposed to raise half of this by selling twenty-five-dollar shares. This was a difficult task. The autonomy drive did not raise as much money as was thought necessary by some, and there were doubts about whether to proceed. But $58,000 was raised, partly with the help of the UFA which permitted direct transfers of old UFA shares to the new co-op, and ACWA helped by assuming the remainder of the $157,000 mortgage. Calgary Co-op came into existence in 1956 with Suits remaining as manager and Gordon Barker, a promoter and organizer who had risen to prominence in the autonomy drive, becoming its first (and for thirty years, only) president. The beginnings of the new co-op were significant: one thousand members and a 3 percent rebate to members on their first year's purchases.[16]

This, too, was not quite co-operative development by the book. The co-op had started with a ready-made store and clientele, and UFA and ACWA had both helped in significant ways. But almost from the beginning there was something a little different about the Calgary store. The campaign for autonomy had revealed apathy and inertia, but had overcome these to raise capital and persuade members that the venture was worthwhile. The success of the autonomy drive was reinforced when the very first year's operations as a co-op were successful and put a rebate back in members' pockets. And that first year set a pattern that dominated the history of Calgary Co-op over the following decades: financing of expansion from within, with minimal borrowing; and a cash rebate to customers every year.

Calgary Co-op grew swiftly and steadily. By 1963, after seven years of operation as an autonomous co-op, its sales were $6 million, and it had sixteen thousand members. The refund to members on their year's purchases was still 3 percent. And in 1963 Calgary Co-op opened its third store, financed, like the previous expansion of 1960, through sale of debentures, $750,000 at 7 percent interest.[17]

As the co-op grew, it also became more centrally involved in Calgary communities and neighbourhoods. In 1964 an education director was added to the staff, and a new public relations officer was charged with assembling a public relations committee to help the co-op. Within two years, this committee's projects resulted in fund-raising and donations for charitable causes, an annual exchange of perennial plants hosted by the co-op, sponsorship of young people to a co-operative camp, Kiddies' Korrals in the co-op stores to mind the children of shopping parents, and a local talent show. All of these projects helped to increase the co-op's service and profile in the community.[18] The community was involved in other ways as well: each expansion was aimed at a new district of the city, and an effort was made to involve community associations in the planning of the new co-op stores. After they opened, they were to remain focal points for their neighbourhoods. Gordon Barker recalls that this worked particularly well with the fifth store, Forest Lawn, opened in 1967: "The Forest Lawn store has been a good store. The manager we had there at the opening was a great guy who believed in people. The people there used to call it their store . . . the Forest Lawn parade used to start on our parking lot; if they had a flea market, it was on our parking lot."[19]

Calgary Co-op doubled both its sales and its membership every four to six years from 1963 to 1978. The number of stores tripled over the same period from three to nine—with the tenth in planning. The co-op now boasted of being "the biggest consumer co-operative in North America."[20] Calgary Co-op had captured an estimated 35–40 percent of the grocery volume of a city of seven hundred and fifty thousand people.

Shown here is the official opening of Calgary Co-op store No. 8 in 1976. One of the secrets of Calgary Co-op's success was the careful planning of its expansions, each of which was targeted at a particular part of the city. In addition, many of the stores were developed in partnership with local community groups.

There is no denying the success of Calgary Co-op, and equally there is no questioning its significance to the system as a whole. At year end in 1987, Calgary Co-op recorded sales of $412 million, which probably represents over one-fifth of the volume of the entire Co-operative Retailing System. Officials at Calgary Co-op estimate that 10–13 percent of FCL's sales are to their co-op. Calgary's savings in 1987 were $20.6 million, and were distributed through a 5 percent refund on retail purchases to over two hundred and eighty-three thousand members.[21] Since, in 1988, the Co-operative Retailing System claimed to be serving seven hundred and fifty thousand people in western Canada,[22] this means 38 percent of the individuals served by the system are members of Calgary Co-op, which is only one of over 330 co-ops in the system. Calgary's phenomenal growth since 1956 has made it a giant among consumer co-operatives.

Calgary Co-op: Why the Success?

Bruno Friesen, now chairman of the board of Calgary Co-op, is quoted as having said, "It's ironic, but of any city where a co-op should not have worked, it's Calgary."[23] "In Alberta," Friesen told the author, "people pride themselves on being individualists." Apparently, a co-op can succeed to match the wildest dreams, even in profit-enterprise country.

And there are other arguments to be made about why Calgary should not have succeeded. Bill Bergen, FCL's chief executive officer through the 1970s, notes that "Calgary should have failed" because of the "antagonism between key people"—a reference, presumably, to the longstanding friction between manager John Suits and chairman Gordon Barker, a friction resulting in Suits's resignation in 1978.[24] The so-called antagonism is significant, because the partnership of Suits and Barker is seen by many observers as the key to Calgary's success. Calgary had two powerhouses, a chairman of the board who was a promoter, an idea man, a "visionary," as one co-operator calls him, seeking growth and mobilizing for new causes; and a general manager widely acclaimed for his skill with people and with safeguarding the bottom line. That the two clashed on occasion is hardly surprising, but the tension between them was a creative tension and a prototype for the kind of tension that perhaps ought to exist between a board and its managers. Calgary Co-op grew quickly, and was well-managed, because of the combination in its critical years of a Gordon Barker with a John Suits.

There is a tendency to treat the appearance of competent people at the retail level as "a fortuitous event," a phrase used by Don Tullis, secretary of FCL in the 1960s and 1970s, to describe the combination of Barker and Suits. In other cities, according to Tullis, you could point to a manager who caused the co-op to founder. "Federated didn't in some cases have the ability to change the manager when he was getting the co-op into trouble," says Tullis, and names examples. Many ex-managers and current managers from the wholesale agree, claiming that success or failure has always been due to the quality of the local management team, which FCL has been unable to affect. "Purely and simply," says Elmer Wiebe, marketing manager for FCL, "co-ops' problems in other centres [besides Calgary] must rest on the shoulders of both [local] boards and management. Leadership was just not there when needed."

Was the presence of a Suits and a Barker then simply a stroke of luck for the system, not to be learned from? Is Calgary's commercial success impossible to duplicate elsewhere? Perhaps, but we should still ask what these local people did so well, and how it might be copied by other local boards and managers.

Pat Bell, treasurer of FCL in the seventies and chief executive officer 1979–83, suggests that in Calgary's case, "the key thing is, they found a niche. They decided they wanted to concentrate on volume. Food would be seventy percent of their business—and they stuck with that. They didn't get carried away." This is an interesting aspect of Calgary's success: it was *not* based primarily on the most lucrative products handled by the system, nor was it based on a broad range of products. The co-op specialized in food, which has one of the narrowest margins. Food, however, despite the tight margins, permits a high volume and tremendous turnover—it can be sold even before the co-op has to pay for it, and the inventory can be turned over many times in a single year. Less financing is needed because capital is not tied up in inventories or accounts receivable. To exploit these advantages, of course, you have to do it well, and concentrate upon it. Next to food, petroleum did play an important role in Calgary Co-op's development, but when the co-op expanded in petroleum, it did so by way of gas bars, not bulk sales. The focus remained on the urban market and the urban consumer.

Other co-ops, says Bell, "didn't find that right mix . . . [didn't] find their niche." Other co-ops (he suggests Edmonton as an example) tried furniture, hardware, and a whole range of products—they "tried to be all things to all people."

Specialization in food and in gas bars may be one reason for Calgary Co-op's success in an urban market, relative to other big-city co-ops. Certainly the "co-op department store" approach does not seem to have worked in any of the big cities; perhaps it is a concept better suited to small-town retailing.

Gordon Barker, the man who presided over much of Calgary Co-op's growth, is restrained and cautious when he talks about it. Thinking back to the first store he says, "we thought that once we had the thing opened we could just sit back and relax. But you can't do that—you either go ahead or go back." Calgary went ahead, but he remembers that the co-op's growth was always controlled. "Always farm for a dry year," he comments, "then if it rains you do well." That conservative policy led to Calgary Co-op owning all its own facilities, wherever possible, and not opening a new store until the last one opened was in the black. The new stores were relatively modest. "There were lots of times when people thought we should have fancier head offices or a little more pizazz in the stores. We never went for that." Stores were also not built speculatively; each one was aimed at a defined district. Barker recalls that as Calgary expanded the co-op had a rule of thumb: one new store for each thirty thousand people. Over-expansion was avoided. For a co-op in a booming city, as Calgary was until 1982, this restrained expansion policy was probably exactly right.

Two other features of Calgary's growth are often cited by co-operators who have been asked to explain the co-op's success. Red McAndrews notes that Calgary's growth was financed mainly from within, by sale of debentures. This meant the co-op had an opportunity to talk to its members—indeed, it *had* to talk to them and persuade them of the co-op's potential for success and of the importance of each expansion. And what went together with this, he observes, is that the co-op always paid a refund, proving its worth year after year to every member. This "wasn't one of the largest factors," he argues, "but it certainly helped." Others think Calgary's regular patronage refunds are even more significant. "That cheque in the mail seems to have an effect on people," says Grant Howard, a former distribution manager in FCL.

It is interesting to note that Calgary has grown so large, even though many annual meetings are poorly attended, relative to the co-op's size. Only a few hundred of its tens or hundreds of thousands of members have attended most of the annual meetings over the years. But then again, Calgary Co-op has paid attention to its members in many other ways. Regular economic contacts with members, from bond sales to patronage refunds, are also opportunities to communicate. The co-op makes a creditable effort in member communications, spending something like a quarter of a million dollars a year on postage to mail newsletters. New members receive well-designed booklets highlighting the by-laws, principles, and policies of the co-op. Calgary Co-op has also paid attention to its community profile and general public relations. Ex-chairman Barker says he is a firm believer "that you take your corporate place in the community. . . . I encouraged our fellows to coach Little League. There's nothing better to get across the idea that the co-op is part of the community." Jack Trevena, long involved in co-operative education, observes, "you go to most general managers and give them money, and they'll spend it all on product advertising. The difference at Calgary is . . . they spend some of it on member education."

In a profit enterprise the relationship between the customer and the merchant ends with the transaction at the cash register; in a co-op it does not. Calgary Co-op has succeeded in creating that feeling of membership and ownership that makes a co-operative distinct from all competitors. The one comment almost everyone makes is, as one former wholesale manager put it, "it's the 'in' thing to be a member of Calgary Co-op." Doctors, lawyers, and oilmen, convinced profit-enterprisers all, are eager to join. This is what it takes to sell two hundred and eighty thousand memberships in a city like Calgary.

Norm Krivoshen, consumer products manager for FCL, adds that the reason urban co-operatives had trouble was that "the co-ops didn't have the capital to compete against the big chains." In Calgary, by contrast, "they have had the resources and took advantage to expand during Calgary's growing years."

Good fortune may be said to play a role in most success stories, and according to some it has been a factor in Calgary. One ex-region manager for FCL notes that Calgary just "never seemed to have a setback." The co-op was founded in time to enjoy the great Alberta boom, and by the time the crash came, more than a quarter of a century later, the co-op was grown-up and strong. "They seemed to expand at the right time." Some point out that the Alberta government curtailed Safeway's expansion during the early 1970s after a royal commission criticized the chain's pricing and practices. Several others comment that competition in Calgary has not been as fierce as in other western cities. One co-operator says that a Superstore in Calgary "will make a substantial difference to Calgary Co-op in the food business." It certainly seems that the large discount chains, and particularly their willingness and ability to absorb initial losses to break into a market, have provided the strongest competition in other large cities. On the other hand, why have the discount chains failed to penetrate Calgary until now? Could it be partly because of the strength of the Co-op?

Calgary Co-op's own leaders generously allow that such claims have some substance to them. Gordon Barker notes that the co-op came in at the right time to expand. And Barker's successor, Bruno Friesen, admits "we haven't had the cut-throat competition here that's been in place elsewhere—although it's coming."

Perhaps the phenomenon of Calgary Co-op will bear further watching, to see if it goes away when we rub our eyes as has been the case with other urban co-operative successes. But there is reason to believe this will not happen in Calgary's case, primarily because the Co-op seems to have succeeded in crossing that crucial generational barrier between the founding generation that makes a co-op successful, and those following whose support must be won in order to keep the co-op going. Young people support Calgary Co-op; it is fashionable to do so. That alone is the sign of a co-op that has not only a past, but also a future.

Conclusion and Questions

What about the other cities? Will the system get back into them? And should FCL help to bring this about? One Manitoba manager thinks it will happen. "Red River," he observes, "is still [one of the] largest retail co-operatives that we have in the system. It's petroleum-based [now] . . . but the organization is still there, and down the road—I may not see it in my day—I think they'll be back in Winnipeg marketing food." A manager in another region comments that the success at Saskatoon Co-op, now under a management contract with FCL, will provide experience for other co-operators in the system "to see if we can compete against the big chains. If that works," he muses, looking to the long term, "I can see us expanding back into the big urban centres." Some have suggested that this kind of project requires the assistance of the wholesale. But assistance such as that given to Saskatoon Co-op is controversial. Is it worth it to the system? The only big-city co-op that is a major success in 1988, Calgary, succeeded without any such help from FCL—it received excellent distribution services, of course, from the FCL warehouse in Calgary, but its management, planning, and financing were basically its own. Is there anything that can be done from outside to create the combination of local management and member support that an urban co-op needs? Even if there was, would it be worth the risk?

There is an alternative view which suggests that the system should concentrate on middle-sized urban centres, where competition is less, where the big chain discount stores don't go, and where margins and savings have always been better. The future of the Co-operative Retailing System could lie in the Swift Currents, Red Deers, Prince Alberts, and Medicine Hats of western Canada. In the long term there is a problem with this, however: something like half the people in western Canada are in the six largest cities, and these are still growing. Is the co-operative system ready to abandon its vision of representing as many consumers as possible, and gaining the benefits that go with high-volume operations?

It is a difficult dilemma. While co-operatives have had many successes in the large cities at various times, the only unqualified and lasting success is Calgary. And that one success was purely locally grown, so that no one is certain how to transplant it elsewhere. Former general manager C. B. "Bun" Fraser muses: "if you could get the right kind of people in the central organization, maybe the retail co-ops in our urban areas should be centrally controlled by the wholesale." But then, he ponders, central control could not have improved Calgary Co-op. "I've been retired for seventeen years, but I still sit here alone at night and stew about these things."

PART SEVEN: CONTROL 1970–1982

Introduction to Part Seven

Sleeping Giant Awakens in Saskatchewan," read the headline in the Winnipeg *Tribune* on 28 June 1974.

"Almost unnoticed," wrote the *Tribune's* business reporter, "a new giant has been emerging in the business world of western Canada—Federated Co-operatives Limited of Saskatoon." "That's right," the story confirmed, "the old alliance of rural co-ops, dealing mainly in farm goods, has become a many-faceted corporation with sales expected to surpass $500 million this year and to reach one billion dollars by 1978." FCL and the Co-operative Retailing System had become not only big, but recognized, a factor to be dealt with in the marketplace of western Canada. But at the same time, the story observed, rapid expansion had led to "severe economic stresses."[1]

This sums up the 1970s: rapid expansion, and scrambling to keep up with change.

Three main factors made the 1970s an unsettled era. First was the fact that growth was outstripping facilities and equipment. Warehouses, local facilities, the trucking fleet—all aspects of the distribution system—needed to expand at once. The same growth also tended to outstrip established decision-making mechanisms, planning processes, and democratic procedures. Operations were much larger and more complex, and the need for better integration among retails and between retails and the wholesale became acute. One initiative to address these needs was the Westland Co-operatives experiment (see Chapter 20). The second reason for the unsettled character of the era was the combination of the FCL management reorganization of 1969 with a generational transition in the board of directors (Chapter 16), which meant that the decade opened with change or uncertainty in both board and management. Finally, there was the economy itself, which from 1970 to 1982 followed a roller coaster of growth, energy crisis, inflation, and recession, punctuated by market disruptions, shortages, labour-management strife, and increasing competition.

Throughout all these challenges, the key issues were those of control: control of growth, control structures for organizations, and the control, by members, of their co-operatives.

* * *

19

Controlled Growth: Inflation, Expansion, and Production, 1970–1982

Bill Bergen, who became chief executive officer of FCL in 1970, recalls that the system faced about eight major challenges in the early 1970s. "Many of the things that happened in the Fifties and Sixties," he claims, "now had to be cleaned up." Bergen's comments are valuable because he identifies most of the main issues on the operating side of the system's activities in the early 1970s.

First, says Bergen, was the need to complete the merger with British Columbia Co-op Wholesale Society, carried out in 1970. Second was the rescue of Interprovincial Cooperative (IPCO) from financial difficulties, carried out in 1971. Third, according to Bergen, was "trying to control the growth of the retail co-ops." FCL tried to put a cap on its retail development and construction departments. "We over-expanded in the Seventies," says Bergen. The problem was not money—there was enough of that—but rather that "you couldn't find the right staff to correct all your problems as you went along." Fourth was development of retail co-operatives in B.C., following from the amalgamation and from the relatively undeveloped co-operative base in that province. Fifth, FCL's feed operations needed expansion and attention. Feed lost money in eight of ten years in the 1970s. Again Bergen comments, "we just couldn't seem to find the right people to bring about the results we were looking for." Sixth was lumber expansion. The Smith, Alberta, mill had been purchased in the 1960s, and according to Bergen "it was another one of those expansions that shouldn't have taken place." "It became a focal point for me to try to convince the board that we should unload that mill." This happened in 1977. Seventh, says Bergen, was oil exploration, cut back in the early 1970s and reinstated after the "energy crisis" of 1973 through Co-enerco. Finally, Bergen recalls the need to consolidate warehousing and computer operations. Once again, he argues FCL over-bought in the 1960s, and had to cut back in the 1970s.

Interprovincial Cooperative

Interprovincial Cooperative Limited or IPCO, as already mentioned in Chapter 16, moved heavily into chemical production during the 1960s, with a concentration on agricultural chemicals and related products. These chemical plants,

Home Office for the Co-operative Retailing System. Since 1970 FCL's head offices have been in this building at 4th Avenue and 22nd Street in Saskatoon.

along with IPCO's older jute-bag, vegetable-canning, and tea and coffee plants, represented one aspect of an old co-operative dream: the expansion of co-operative power from distribution into processing and manufacturing, to create a single, large, vertically integrated system that could return savings from every stage of processing and handling to the consumer at the end of the line. This dream, as pursued in the 1970s, led to serious financial difficulties for IPCO, and this in turn was a serious concern for FCL.

FCL was a co-owner of IPCO alongside the three prairie wheat pools and four other regional co-operative wholesales across Canada. In fact, in 1967, FCL remained IPCO's largest patron and shareholder—at that time holding $586,000 in IPCO shares and $1.1 million in patronage loans—and IPCO was

FCL's largest single supplier. As FCL's 1967 annual report observed, "we naturally have a close working relationship."[2]

IPCO's expansion in agricultural chemicals centred on a five-million-dollar addition to its Saskatoon chemical complex begun in 1967. This expansion was designed to increase by five times the production of caustic soda and chlorine, ingredients used by IPCO's other plants in Winnipeg and Toronto to formulate the herbicide 2,4-D. But the co-op system could not absorb the whole of the expanded production—the excess was to be supplied to a pulp mill in northern Saskatchewan, and this was what led to trouble for IPCO. The deal sounded good: the pulp mill seemed like a captive market. The problem, as some of those involved recall it, was that the Chlor-Alkali plant in Saskatoon was also a captive supplier: it had insufficient markets for its products, unless it could sell to the one pulp mill. The contract that was signed did not even cover the cost of production, and the new facility began to lose money badly. IPCO did not have the capital to handle the losses, it could not negotiate a better contract, and it could not sell the Chlor-Alkali plant. In 1970, IPCO projected a loss of $1.4 million, against an accumulated reserve of $237,000.[3]

On 31 October 1970, FCL was appointed the manager of IPCO and tried to renegotiate the disastrous pulp-mill contract, while also taking cost-cutting measures to reduce losses. Then on 10 December 1970, IPCO was named in a joint action concerning a chemical spill, and was now also burdened with the cost of improved pollution control.[4] Under these circumstances FCL agreed, on 1 February 1971, to take over ownership of IPCO.

"That cost the co-operative movement quite a bit of money," recalls Don Tullis, FCL's secretary at the time. "Basically they were bankrupt." He refers to it as "one of our biggest disappointments."

According to one manager, "the key reason for FCL taking over the operations of IPCO" was "to protect the CO-OP trademarks" that IPCO held. FCL's interest in IPCO was just over $2 million, and IPCO was losing half that much every year. To make the takeover even more difficult, the year 1970 was FCL's toughest ever. The farm economy was in bad shape, sales were falling, savings were extremely low, little capital was available, and other major projects like the B.C. amalgamation were in progress.[5] To take on IPCO and its Chlor-Alkali plant under such circumstances demonstrated a certain faith in the basic idea of IPCO, a certain desire to save something of the co-operation among co-operatives that IPCO represented, and particularly a concern to save the CO-OP label and the united consumer buying power it represented.

Upon taking over sole ownership of IPCO, FCL's strategy was straightforward. The brokerage and CO-OP label business was separated from the production enterprises, all of which were disposed of as quickly as possible, except for the Winnipeg formulating plant which continues to be an important part of IPCO's operations. The Saskatoon Chlor-Alkali complex, now separated into Northern Industrial Chemicals Limited, was naturally the hardest to dispose of. For three years, until 1974, it operated as a subsidiary of FCL, during which time losses of more than $2 million were incurred. The remaining IPCO brokerage business, in the meantime, prospered. In 1970, IPCO, as distinct now from Northern Industrial Chemicals, had only $20 million in sales, but managed a slight net saving at the end of the year. Sales then increased fairly steadily to $71.9 million in 1979, with a positive net saving every year. On 1 November 1979, IPCO was returned to its original owners, FCL being one among them, with an arrangement that FCL would continue to manage the firm under contract, an arrangement that has persisted to 1988.

The rebirth of IPCO is widely hailed as a co-operative success story of the 1970s. Harold Empey, who went in to manage IPCO in the mid-1970s, recalls, "it was really exciting to work with the regional co-operatives and help build that organization up to the point where it was tremendously successful." He also draws lessons from it. "The key to the success of IPCO was giving attention to the main purpose of the organization"—serving the member—"and not letting ourselves get distracted by programs that didn't fit that purpose or by grandiose plans for growth." In the early years, IPCO board and managers "felt that if they were going to supply the members with peanut butter they had to have a peanut butter factory; if they were going to supply them with coffee they had to have a coffee factory; if they were going to supply them with chemicals they had to have a chemical plant." After the reorganization, "IPCO concentrated on 'how can we *best* serve the needs of the member regionals?' It *may not* be through direct ownership in operating a specific plant. It may be through arrangements with others, and we found it was far better to do it that way. It eliminated the capital cost, it eliminated the risk, and gave us a kind of flexibility we never had before."

One of the FCL directors involved with IPCO, however, expresses opinions which may not be in full agreement with Empey. Morris Jevne, who served as president of IPCO from 1966–71, speaks of "limited capacity . . . limited results," because co-operatives have not pooled the resources of *all* member-oriented enterprises into a single, integrated economic unit. This sounds like a vision of an IPCO or a similar national, co-operatively owned organization which is not merely a broker for collective buying of label goods, but something bigger and more powerful. "We should consolidate to the ultimate benefit of the local user," says Jevne, and he suggests that "a conglomerate board" of all co-operatives would achieve "more effective results in the overall social and economic climate of this country." Co-ops' competitors, he notes, are regional or national—local competition is insignificant. The regional or national level is "where the benefits are," because that is where policy decisions are made that affect markets, and that is the level where co-ops should be active.

A Utopian idea? It appears so today. But it is also worth noting that IPCO is not unlike the provincial co-op wholesales in their infancy and childhood: a procurer of goods serving autonomous co-ops with restricted staff, capital, and inventories of its own, and a single manufacturing venture (the Winnipeg chemical-formulating plant). Like some of the early co-op wholesales, it got into trouble (in the late 1960s) when it over-reached itself in capital-intensive expansions. Could IPCO be a comprehensive, nation-wide co-op wholesaling and manufacturing firm in its infancy? And does the 1970 crisis teach us that co-operatives should not try expansions in the field of basic manufacturing, or does it teach us, once again, the old lesson of the 1930s, 1940s, and 1950s— that they should mobilize consumer demand for their products through co-operative channels, before undertaking production?

Challenging Market Conditions: Inflation and Competition

From 1970 to 1979, FCL's sales grew massively, to more than six times their starting level. In ten years of operations, a wholesale doing $183 million in annual volume became one doing more than $1 billion in volume. A substantial part of this was real, rather than inflationary, growth—138 percent growth in real volume in ten years. To give some idea of what this means, consider Appendix 5, which estimates the sales volume of FCL and its predecessors, corrected for inflation. Of the total wholesale volume transacted by the Co-operative Retailing System, $8.8 billion (1987 value) came in the forty-one years from 1929–69, or 26.4 percent of the system's total wholesale volume in its history. In just ten years from 1970–79, sales added up to $12 billion or 36 percent of the total. In other words, even correcting for inflation, FCL moved a greater wholesale volume during the 1970s than it and all its predecessors had moved in the previous four decades. Perhaps this hints at the tremendous growth and adjustment in the organization.[6]

But even so, the great majority of the apparent increase was inflationary, so that as much as 60 percent of FCL's billion-dollar sales in 1979 was the result of accumulated inflation since 1970.[7] The size of the inflationary component created an additional set of difficulties for operations and planning. Rapid price increases mean rapidly-changing market conditions, to which the organization must respond very quickly if it is not to be caught flat-footed. FCL faced constant price increases from its suppliers; it faced uncertainty, unfilled orders, and shortages; and inflation led to work stoppages, as workers fought for wage increases to match inflation rates, which further disrupted supply and transportation.[8]

Inflation also raised the interesting question of whether co-operatives should match competitors' prices when they believed those prices to be excessively inflated. The FCL board noted "a strong public protest against rising food prices" in 1973, and a House of Commons special committee investigating food-price increases praised FCL for its efforts to keep prices down.[9] But how far should co-ops go to undersell market prices? FCL's board and management at that time decided the co-operative system should come out as an inflation-fighter.

Chief Executive Officer Bergen spoke out in the press about the fact that "with inflation business ethics tend to go by the wayside. Some people . . .

charge all the traffic will bear."[10] Bergen also criticized private suppliers who broke "oral and written" contracts, refusing to fill orders at agreed prices and arbitrarily raising prices to match the latest level. By contrast, he said, "the co-operative tries for a normal margin." In 1973, FCL announced a "program of guaranteeing prices, delaying price increases, and establishing prices for some products at more realistic levels," a program which, according to FCL's calculations, saved retail co-ops $1.8 million on the goods they bought from FCL in that single year—an amount which represents FCL's foregone earnings, and a benefit to members in addition to patronage refunds. Retails were asked for their voluntary co-operation in implementing similar policies for their own goods and inventories.[11]

Holding Farm Costs Down

The effort to hold prices to realistic levels was concentrated in the area of farm supplies, where FCL was engaged in competition for the loyalty of farmers who were very concerned about rising costs of inputs such as herbicides and fertilizer. FCL faced increasing competition, especially from high-volume bulk suppliers and from marketing organizations that sold farm supplies as part of an integrated package of services to farmers—including Saskatchewan Wheat Pool, which entered the farm-supply business in a big way in 1969. Although the total market for fertilizer and chemicals was increasing, it was not a simple matter to match such high-volume and integrated competitors. FCL therefore resolved to embark upon an aggressive campaign to expand its facilities and improve its market share in agricultural supplies. In 1972 it began to subsidize fertilizer distribution, paying more than half a million dollars to retails to enable them to sell at lower, competitive prices. These measures meant FCL itself made virtually nothing at all on its fertilizer volume, or lost money when all costs were counted. Similarly in the case of herbicides, FCL had already committed itself in 1972 to sell 15 percent lower than its competitors.[12]

The drive to sell fertilizer corresponded to FCL's investment in Western Co-operative Fertilizers Limited (WCFL), owned jointly with the prairie wheat pools. It also led to friction with WCFL over pricing policy, since FCL wanted the fertilizer co-operative to take on some of the responsibility for ensuring competitive prices at the local level.

Against this background, when inflation became an even greater issue in 1973, FCL "was resolved to avoid any unnecessary addition to farm production costs," and held fertilizer price increases to an average five dollars per ton.[13] By 1978, FCL was paying $1 million more in costs than it received from its fertilizer sales. This was a planned and intentional loss, "leadership for the further development of fertilizer services at retail co-ops."[14] The effect of the fertilizer policy was that FCL found itself underselling competitors by as much as twenty-five dollars per ton. Farmers, recognizing an extremely good bargain, bought out all of FCL's supplies, which had been considered "ample"—and suddenly the system was in the position of being unable to service its members and meet their demands. The directors had to make their first priority for 1975 the development of "a policy to ensure that loyal members are supplied first."[15] Ed Klassen, a director at that time and now First Vice-President of FCL, recalls that the allocation system led to disputes in the countryside—within a family it might be that "one brother could buy CO-OP fertilizer but the other couldn't," depending on their previous year's patronage.

The policy of selling below market prices, muses Klassen, may have been too "idealistic." It led to heavy losses by all parties (including WCFL and the pools), it led to disputes among the membership about allocation, and it meant that FCL did not take the earnings it could have when the market was high, though it was nevertheless stuck with the losses when the market for fertilizer went down.

FCL's agro division did make gains in 1973, and nearly doubled its sales in 1974 to make a whopping 8.5 percent saving, but then suffered a heavy loss again in 1975. Despite high-priority effort, capital spending for agro centres and bulk plants, and planned deficits, crop-supplies operations as a whole lost money again in 1975, 1977, and 1978. Market share in fertilizer did not increase; by 1975, FCL was actually supplying a smaller proportion of the market, even though its tonnage had doubled, than in 1972.[16] Eventually, in 1983, FCL decided to cease handling fertilizer and let retails order it themselves, though it encouraged them to continue purchasing from WCFL and did not, at that time, seek to withdraw its investment in the fertilizer company.

Consumers and Co-operative Production

There was a common thread running through the stories of IPCO chemicals and of co-operative agricultural products in the 1970s: both were fields in which co-operatives tried ambitious expansions in processing and production, and both gave rise to difficulties. Similarly to IPCO with its Chlor-Alkali plant, Western Co-operative Fertilizers Limited, a joint production venture in which FCL participated along with other co-operatives, encountered setbacks when it tried to expand in phosphate rock production. Nor were these joint ventures the only setbacks in co-operative production during the unsettled 1970s. The same pattern occurred elsewhere in FCL's operations—lumber, for example, usually a steady earner for co-operatives, encountered some rough times in the Smith and Revelstoke expansions of the 1970s. FCL's older production venture—the Canoe mill—continued to be successful, but for some reason such established successes could not be duplicated in the new lumber expansions. Likewise feed, at times an extremely successful commodity for the system, did not have an easy time in the 1970s, and some expansions proved especially difficult to maintain.

Before discussing these ventures, however, it is important to state that FCL's most important manufacturing activity, petroleum refining, continued to be

FCL's lumber mill at Canoe on Shuswap Lake, British Columbia. The mill has been owned by consumer co-operatives since 1945, and in the ensuing four and one half decades has been expanded and modernized many times. In 1966 a modern plywood plant, also owned by FCL, was completed just down the lakeshore from the lumber mill.

immensely successful. In 1974 a new series of expansions and modernizations was begun that would take more than ten years to complete. Parallel to the steady rise of the refinery's capacity there was a constant program of expanded distribution, including new bulk petroleum stations and service stations, and, in 1976, the TEMPO program to utilize more of the refinery's capacity by distributing gasoline through a network of independent retailers. In 1980, FCL began discussing the idea of a heavy-oil upgrader to feed into the existing refinery (more will be said about this project in Chapter 22), and in 1981–82 FCL returned actively to the crude-oil exploration and production business with its involvement in the Co-operative Energy Corporation (Co-enerco). All of these ventures in manufacturing have been successful—with the possible exception of Co-enerco, which came just in time to suffer from adverse market conditions.

In fact, with the effects of inflation and of the so-called energy crisis of 1973, combined with the expansion programs, FCL's petroleum operations became even more successful than ever in earning savings. By 1981, petroleum surpassed food as the largest-selling commodity group handled by FCL, a situation that lasted until 1985. In 1981 petroleum earned $43.1 million or 85 percent of FCL's $50.9 million in savings. In 1982, when four other divisions ended up with operating losses, petroleum earnings of $20.7 million turned what would otherwise have been a $10-million deficit into more than a $10-million surplus. Of FCL's $238.6 million in savings over the period 1970–82, $173.3 million, or 72.6 percent, came from the refinery and the crude-oil and petroleum-merchandising departments.

Feed merchandising, on the other hand, suffered losses in eight of nine years from 1971–79. One response was to incorporate a subsidiary—Federated Distributing Company Limited, which handled direct mill-to-farm sales—and to promote the building or acquisition of more feed mills, whether owned by the wholesale or by retails, in order to compete in the bulk-feed business. From 1967 to 1976, six new feed mills were purchased or built, not counting the Prince George mill obtained through amalgamation with BCCWS. Most of these mills were concentrated in small and midsized distribution centres like Melfort, Weyburn, and Lethbridge. This expansion was rewarded by further losses, which were especially heavy in 1974–77 when they ranged from $853,000 to $1.4 million annually. In 1975, the Prince George plant was closed; Lethbridge followed

FCL's Saskatoon feed mill (1970s). Animal feeds are important commodities for many of FCL's member co-ops, and their needs are served by FCL's network of feed mills as well as those owned by local retails.

in 1977; and finally, in 1980, the Otterburne, Manitoba, plant was sold. As of 1980, savings were made on feed, and these became quite large—more than a million dollars a year every year from 1982-87. From 1982-85 feed was the third most lucrative product handled by FCL after petroleum and food.

This rationalization did not occur without controversy being raised from among the members. The feed plants were important to nearby co-ops and to the areas in which they were situated. FCL's board and delegate structures ensure that individual co-ops that are displeased can exert their pressure on a director and raise their complaints in district, region, and general meetings. "No one likes to see *their* mill closed," as one former elected official observed, and the wholesale heard about it from the regions affected.

Gordon Barker, FCL's first vice-president during the early 1970s, recalls the fluctuations of feed-mill operations with a certain amused frustration. "You'd make money one year and miss two, then . . . just as you were ready to sell, you'd make money again." To some extent the fluctuations seem to be cyclical, corresponding to the ups and downs of the livestock industry.

Lumber also had its ups and downs, but in a reverse cycle to feed: lumber made money during most of the 1970s, and in 1980, the first year that feed began consistently to earn savings, the building materials department ceased to do so, corresponding to the onset of depressed conditions in the forestry industry as a whole. It was fortunate for the system that the lumber and feed cycles compensated for each other.

As in the case of feed, it was too much to expect that all of the new and expanded plants would be equally successful. The Canoe operations continued to perform excellently for buoyant markets, working at maximum capacity for much of the period—in 1980 the Canoe sawmill set its fourth consecutive production record, and the plywood plant followed suit. The difficulties were with the Smith, Alberta, mill acquired in 1965, and with the Revelstoke operation acquired in 1979 after the Smith mill had been sold.

The Smith lumber mill was purchased with a great deal of expansion necessary to make it viable, and this FCL was willing to undertake, since as much development seemed to have been packed into the Canoe area as was possible. Conditions, however, were quite different from those at Canoe: the species of trees were different, the local style of logging was different, and Smith was a very small town to which it proved difficult to attract a stable labour force. The Smith mill lost money every year until 1969, when it nearly reached the break-even point, and another expansion was ordered. In 1970 the mill lost $205,000.[17] Further studies concluded that the available timber was insufficient to supply an operation large enough to be economically viable, and negotiations did not result in additional timber berths being obtained.[18] President Gordon Sinclair had to tell the 1976 annual meeting that the mill had been purchased for $500,000 in 1965, and despite $4,000,000 in investments toward development, it had lost money on operations every year except 1972 and 1973, when it received an additional quota of fire-damaged logs at reduced stumpage costs.[19]

Yet in 1977, when the FCL board announced that it intended to sell the mill, delegates objected. A motion calling upon the board to rescind its decision noted that the timber rights contained "some of the best quality timber (if not the best) available in Alberta," and further, that four other operators were active in the same area, all with much smaller quotas, and none of them running at a loss. The motion, which was carried by the delegates, suggested "that the timber available can be profitably harvested and manufactured if managed by people knowledgeable in timber operation in the Northern Alberta area." Delegates were clearly unwilling to believe the mill could not be managed to show net savings.[20] Nevertheless, in 1977, the Smith mill was sold for $4 million. As in the case of the feed-plant closures, the controversy arose from the fact that co-ops in each region wanted their own FCL facilities—in 1975, for example, delegates to the annual meeting approved a motion that FCL should investigate developing forest-products industries in Manitoba to serve the co-operatives in that province.[21] Retails were reluctant to believe the wholesale could not expand in their regions.

The Revelstoke mill was primarily a cedar mill—again, a different species from what FCL was used to at Canoe.[22] One of its attractions was that it came with ample timber limits, but substantial improvements were required, and operational difficulties were encountered early on. The Revelstoke mill's main problem, however, was timing: in 1981, just as it got going, the bottom fell out of the lumber industry. The mill was closed. Pat Bell, FCL's chief executive officer at the time, recalls that in three years "we never did make it pay." "We lost a potfull on it, I think because we went back on our decision not to expand it. And, just when we expanded it, the market collapsed." The mill was eventually closed for good in 1985, and sold in May 1988.

FCL was also involved as a partner in another co-operative production venture. Western Co-operative Fertilizers Limited (WCFL) was started at FCL's initiative after a study of the fertilizer industry in the early 1960s. Farmers' demand for fertilizer was growing, and co-ops—not only FCL, but also the prairie wheat pools, which entered into fertilizer distribution in 1963—wanted to meet this demand. In 1963, therefore, FCL and the Alberta and Saskatchewan Pools formed WCFL, and in 1964 its first fertilizer plant officially opened in Calgary. Expansions followed in the 1960s and 1970s, both at Calgary and in Medicine Hat. Also, in 1976, Canadian Fertilizers Ltd., a subsidiary jointly owned with other Canadian and American co-operatives, opened a plant at Medicine Hat. The CF Industries plant proved to be a great success and an on-going money-maker, but the same cannot be said of WCFL's own expansions, and particularly of its venture at Conda, Idaho, in production of rock phosphate.

As with IPCO's Chlor-Alkali plant, the Conda rock-phosphate plant was a somewhat speculative expansion into production and processing of basic ingredients. Bergen calls it "an IPCO all over again. The management . . . were too expansion-oriented." FCL "opposed in every direction we could," claim Bergen and others, but as only one partner, they could not make enough impact. Wayne Thompson, now chief executive officer of FCL, recalls that the profitability of the Conda facility depended on increasing demand and increasing prices for rock phosphate. FCL (according to Thompson) did not believe these projections were realistic. As it turned out, the price did not increase in the manner predicted, and the Conda plant became a money-losing proposition the day it was opened, and has remained such. Ed Klassen recalls that FCL argued for many years that one of the member organizations should take on the management of WCFL, similar to the arrangement between FCL and IPCO, but FCL was unable to persuade any of the pools to take on this function.

Another production venture in which FCL was involved to some degree during the 1970s was Canadian Co-operative Implements Limited. CCIL had a much longer history than WCFL, going back to the 1940s when it was created as a farmer-owned co-operative with the support and encouragement of the co-op wholesales and their leaders. Over the years, CCIL had been in and out of difficulty, but during the 1970s it was "in" again. In 1975 the major co-operatives, including FCL, got together to set up a funding package to enable Co-op Implements to continue operating, which it has done, as a more than 50-percent privately owned company. According to one FCL manager who was involved, the problem, once again, was an attempt to expand beyond the resource base, and he, too, traces this tendency back to management and how the managers were selected.

Is there any reason why co-operatives encountered difficult times in so many different manufacturing enterprises during the period 1970–82? It could be argued, perhaps, that consumer co-operatives cannot handle the high capital requirements and risks of manufacturing enterprises—and yet this is refuted by the fact that they have done so with remarkable success in one of the most expensive industries of all—oil refining; and other enterprises, like IPCO's Winnipeg chemical plant or ventures like the CF Industries fertilizer operation, remain successful. Could it be argued that the detailed technical knowledge of such industries is too specialized for consumer co-operatives? As one former manager observes, the need for specialized personnel ought not to be a problem for the system: "you can hire *them*." The skills needed to manage a co-op-owned manufacturing plant are not much different than for a profit enterprise. (The real problem, he suggests, is retail co-operative managers, whose job is much different from their profit-sector counterparts.) Perhaps, as many managers tend to say today, co-operatives simply did too much in the 1970s, tried to be "all things to all people," instead of sticking to what they do well. Certainly sticking to what co-ops do well has been the essential ingredient for success in the 1980s (Chapter 22).

Of course, it is also true that if co-ops stuck to what they did well and never embarked on new ventures, FCL would still be a brokerage business with a tiny staff and no inventories, like the provincial co-op wholesales were in the 1930s.

Somewhere along the line, FCL and consumer co-operatives did learn how to do a great many new things to get to where they are today—but the expansion efforts of the 1970s in manufacturing produced, at best, mixed results.

Perhaps one convincing pattern is that the joint-production ventures in which FCL has been involved, thinking of WCFL and IPCO when it had its own management, were unsatisfactory experiences from FCL's point of view. It may be that the structures of such co-operatives are simply too awkward for proper management. Over the long haul, a board composed of delegates from second-tier co-ops, delegates with other primary allegiances, may simply not be effective enough at supervising and participating in management of a complex business, and in setting standards and guiding and controlling the manager.

And perhaps the 1970s, with so much instability and such a tendency to runaway growth, were simply a bad climate for expansion, and especially for speculative expansions—those based on assumptions of increasing markets and prices, rather than on demand already mobilized in co-operative channels. It will be interesting to see, should more stable conditions return after the recession of the 1980s, whether co-operatives are again willing to enter into new manufacturing and processing activities, or whether they have been made permanently leery of extending vertical integration by such means.

Conclusion and Questions

This chapter raises a number of questions in connection with its examination of Interprovincial Cooperative, inflation, agricultural supplies, and co-operative production.

Should the abandonment of IPCO's original, extensive manufacturing and processing ambitions (with the exception of the Winnipeg chemical-formulating plant) be a permanent or a temporary state of affairs? Perhaps it would be useful to co-op members for IPCO to try to be a comprehensive national wholesaler and manufacturer again. And what does the experience of IPCO's Chlor-Alkali plant and WCFL's rock-phosphate operation show? Are there certain kinds of industries co-operatives should stay away from, or are there certain conditions to wait for before new ventures are taken on? The system's highly successful production and processing operations, such as the Canoe lumber mill and the nearby plywood plant, and the Co-op Refinery, are mainly operations that started small, when the technology was much less complex than today—the refinery in the 1930s, and the Canoe mill in the 1940s. Does this suggest there is some problem when co-operatives jump into full-scale production in complicated industries like the manufacture of chemical ingredients in the 1970s? Does it suggest that co-operatives should not enter into complex and expensive industries—or is it that they should do so only to meet an organized co-operative demand for the products?

The experience with inflation in the 1970s, and particularly with rising farm-input prices, raises some interesting points as well. Part of the tradition of retail co-operation is that co-operatives should sell at market prices; at one time this was even called a co-operative principle. Is this a principle that should still have been listened to in the 1970s, or still be followed today? What if market prices are seen to be unfair? When should a co-operative exercise price leadership and sell for less than the going rate? In gasoline, for instance, FCL and retail co-operatives currently earn relatively good savings—the margin on petroleum products is wider than on others, though, of course, the capital requirements and hence the need for reinvestment of savings are also higher. Perhaps it would be possible to reduce prices unilaterally . Would it be wise?

The bottom line is that even success entails its own dangers and its own questions. Conditions of rapid, almost desperate, growth entail the danger that expansion might be conducted too quickly or in the wrong way. Past successes in co-operative production may have encouraged co-operators to expand too optimistically. The 1970s illustrate the inherent challenges of massive growth, of expansion into new enterprises, and of unsettled economic conditions.

20

Planning, Integration, and Democracy, 1970–1982

The speed of economic change during the 1960s and 1970s, and the increasing integration of retail-sector businesses in general, made it critical that the Co-operative Retailing System (as it began to call itself in the 1970s, with capital letters) have some means of formulating collective plans that would be observed both by the wholesale and by most, if not all, of the retails. In competing organizations, where the central company owns the local units, local units can be instructed to follow plans. But in the CRS, the local units own the central, rather than vice-versa. Nothing can be imposed. In this kind of federated, democratic set-up, local units have to be *persuaded* to follow corporate plans. Finding means of persuading them, and of involving them in an effective planning process, was perhaps the most critical internal issue for FCL in the 1970s. This was new ground for co-operatives, territory uncharted by past experience. The answer that the system came up with was arrived at by trial and error, with the usual false starts that this method entails.

The Need for Planning

The need for planning became more acute in the 1970s largely because of the economic conditions co-operatives faced. During the inflationary and growth-oriented 1970s, it was important that costs and interest burdens be limited, that large projects be controlled, and that the capital tied up in inventories and accounts receivable be supervised. And because the activities of one part of the system affected the other, planning had to be co-ordinated.

On the one hand, FCL continued to depend on the retails. It was necessary for retails as a whole to handle a certain volume of some products in order to make them viable product lines for FCL. Programs for such products required planning by the system as a whole, retails and wholesale together. And at the same time, retails became more dependent on what FCL did. FCL developed merchandising and marketing programs that the retails needed to meet the competition, and returned patronage refunds that were increasingly important in keeping their local operations in the black. FCL also became involved in various forms of assistance to local retails, including taking care of any accumulated deficits in retails which were dissolving or amalgamating, and assistance to retails which were running temporary deficits (board policies Nos. 171 and 172). FCL's retail development and construction departments were involved in many co-op expansions and new facilities. In retail development, in production and distribution of feed and lumber, and in other areas, priorities had to be set between one region and another, between one retail and another—and those affected had to agree.[1]

The person who inherited and perceived the need for effective planning was Bill Bergen, FCL's chief executive officer 1970-79. In talking to Bergen, one gets the impression of a manager who is serious about professional management and who applies the management theory in which he was trained to the challenges he faces. Bergen was in a key position in the 1970s partly because, for a significant part of the decade, there was no equivalent leadership from the board side. "I worked with four different presidents in nine years. That's highly unusual in a co-op. And the changes weren't due to retirements—they were made for other reasons." As a result of this, claims Bergen, "there was a vacuum." The board was busy trying to resolve its own problems; "they had no time to work with management." And they were divided. Though in Bergen's opinion the structure was not bad (FCL had a full-time vice-president), "due to the individuals in place I was just spending twice as much time updating both [the president and the vice-president] . . . and listening to one talk about the other." It was in this context that the need for planning began to be addressed.

The FCL Mission Statement and Objectives

The first step in planning for FCL was to define the mission of the Co-operative Retailing System, and within that, the objectives of FCL. In 1972 the board produced a mission statement, similar to the one in use today, stating that the system's purpose was *"to improve the economic position of its members through co-ordinated procurement, manufacturing, and provision of services coincident with creating a sense of individual participation in, and belonging to, an organization whose aim is to work toward bringing about a better life."*[2] This statement was meant to sum up the economic, democratic, and social aims of retail co-operation more clearly and concisely than long-winded discussions of co-operative philosophy had done in the past, and in this way to provide a yardstick for assessing specific policies and operations—to determine what was and what was not relevant to the purposes of the system.

The evolution from this statement to today's provides an interesting comment on changes in co-operative philosophy. The above version of the mission statement suggests that the economic and participatory (or democratic) objectives of co-operatives are "coincident," a word that suggests objectives pursued simultaneously and equally. In the mid-1970s the mission was amended to say *"to foster social justice"* by improving the economic position of its members, "while" providing them with a sense of belonging and participation.[3] In other words, this version gave primacy to the social mission of co-operatives, and presented economic activity as the means to pursue the primary goal of "social justice." Democracy was still apparently an equal objective. But the 1981 (and current) version of the mission reverses this emphasis, saying that the goal is *"to improve the economic position of its member-owners . . . within a democratic structure."* Now the economic goal is paramount, social justice is no longer mentioned, and democracy is just a structure "within" which the economic goal is to be pursued. Since the introduction of a mission statement in 1972, the economic purpose of co-operation has come to dominate the others.

There was also an explicit attempt to break with the past. The 1972 annual report claimed that the members and officials involved in the system "generally possess an understanding of co-operatives, experience, knowledge and discernment, beyond that of pioneer founders of co-operatives in the West who often had little or no background of knowledge on which to rely." The 1974 annual report exhorted modern co-operative members to rely on their own understanding, not on the ideas of the past. "The process being followed," the report stated, concerning the development of the mission statement, " . . . is derived from modern concepts of advanced business management."[4] The attitude toward the system's past might be summed up by one of the management-personnel recruitment kits of the era: "history is dull, and Co-op has a lot of it."[5]

Following from the mission statement and objectives, annual reports proposed longer and longer lists of priorities to delegates, and the items on those lists got more specific and more insistent. In setting priorities for 1975, fourteen points were listed. Member retails were told that "all possible support should be given to merchandising and distribution programs arranged for the System by FCL." They were told that they should reduce their inventories and accounts receivable, and that "when renovating or refurbishing existing premises, completing new premises, or replacing existing signs, the new identification program should be followed." Further, "a feature in the 'President's Newsletter' [a circular to all retails], 'Action Time!', should be placed on the agenda for each board or council meeting to ensure that action is taken on matters outlined therein." Elected officers of retails were asked to make a "definite commitment" to attend seminars, and better representation from retails was requested at fall district conferences.[6] This was no longer a report to shareholders, but an attempt to plan for the system by spelling out operating and procedural tasks for the members to perform.

The attempt to use the annual meeting as a planning session, where policies were introduced for the first time and debated, seemed only to heighten tensions between the retails and FCL. Retails gave the impression that they felt policies were being forced upon them, and when forced to vote yes or no, many evidently felt they had no choice but to vote no and send a decision back to the drawing board. Tensions were apparent in the disputes over the Smith lumber mill and over feed mills, where delegates demonstrated that their support for system policies and decisions had not been earned in advance. But tensions with the members were nowhere more apparent than in the evolution of Westland Co-operatives.

Westland Co-operatives, 1972–77

When the regional amalgamation plan developed in 1965 did not meet its targets, discussion turned to the alternative already mentioned at that time: the creation of a single, centralized retailing co-operative to which individual persons throughout western Canada would belong (Chapter 16). Delegates requested in the late 1960s that the board study the idea, but the board dragged its feet somewhat. Quite likely the idea sounded too radical and too much of a break with co-operative traditions.[7] Finally, in the early 1970s, economic difficulties provided some urgency, and new management and new ideas produced a more favourable climate. The 1970 annual meeting approved in principle "the proposal that a centralized retail organization be created to provide for direct individual membership and service." K. A. Adie was appointed to head a study, and in 1971 a task force including FCL Vice-President Gordon Sinclair was appointed to assist him. Finally, in 1972, FCL, along with retail delegates, bit the bullet and went ahead with the incorporation of Westland Co-operatives.

Westland Co-operatives was a single separately incorporated co-operative which ran retail "units" in widely separated locations across western Canada. These units were formed when autonomous co-ops voted to merge with Westland, and were accepted under Westland's structure. The key to its integrated operations was that managers of Westland units were responsible to central managers, not to local boards as they had been when the co-ops were autonomous. Cost savings were expected from shared management and from centralized financial and operating policies.[8] Westland units still had members' advisory councils and sent delegates to Westland meetings, but in the implementation phase, FCL kept control of the new co-operative: the FCL board was the Westland board, and FCL delegates (including the Westland-unit delegates) constituted the Westland annual meeting. The decisions concerning Westland, therefore, were made by the existing system as a whole—autonomous retails, Westland units, and the FCL/Westland board and management.

The Westland proposal was controversial because it touched upon the fundamental structure of the system—the autonomy of local retail co-operatives. As Gordon Barker of Calgary Co-op says, "We'd been through it twice already—once in the UFA, once with Alberta Co-op Wholesale." He adds, "it would never work." In the past, centralized retailing had not worked, because centrals had difficulty managing local units, and because members lost (or feared they would lose) the pride of ownership, the sense of belonging and of control.

One of the delegate kits concerning the original Westland proposal, found in a box of old files, bears the handwritten notes of a troubled co-operator who saw "the essence of two choices" in the Westland debate. The first of these was "the slow disintegration of the co-operative movement as it is presently structured due to lack of change to meet the needs of a changing economy." The second choice (the Westland concept) was "the forerunner of a changed structure which while still retaining the co-operative name tends to diminish co-operative principles." The note-taker added one final jotting: the proposal was "taking away the independence of a co-op in that it becomes a 'Unit.'"[9]

Proponents of Westland rebutted these criticisms. Today, in 1988, the official policy of the system is area development (see below) rather than centralization, but one manager who supported the Westland concept in the 1970s told the author there is "nothing wrong with centralization as long as the lines of communication are looked after as well. . . . All that's centralized is the means of delivering the product or service." If a delegate system is not used well enough, "that's the retails' fault, not the central's." He adds, "some day, in my opinion, in order to compete in this world we're going to have to have a completely centralized operation. Just like the Wheat Pool." Others who share similar views—and even after the demise of Westland a number of them remain—hold out the prospect of co-operative development. As one retail president comments, local co-ops "don't have the equity to build or modernize facilities so people will want to shop there. And they don't have the management." He adds, "autonomy is great, but we can't afford it to the extent that every small co-op has its own operation." In his opinion, Westland was controversial because "the small independents fought it"; in the long run, according to this view, it will still become necessary.

Bill Bergen notes that Westland promised to solve several problems at one time: the problem of too many small co-ops with too much duplication of management and facilities; the problem of controlling and co-ordinating the system's expansion; and the problem of opening big new facilities to break into urban markets. Major chains, says Bergen, recognize that when new facilities open they must expect one or two years of losses. Only a large central co-op could carry locals that were in a deficit position. Without such a central, an autonomous local retail is a prisoner of the business cycle, lacking the cash to expand at the right time, unable to carry temporary losses.

Gordon Sinclair adds a similar concern. Retail co-operatives that failed in the 1970s and 1980s failed because of a lack of member loyalty. "The co-operative spirit was obviously dying. . . . There was a lack of co-operative leadership. . . . But if we had a centralized system we could have continued to operate those areas, even in a negative business sense, and helped develop that leadership." What was at stake, then, in the Westland debate, was not just whether a central should own locals, but also whether it should supervise their management, subsidize them when they suffered losses or needed expansion, nurse them when they were ailing. Westland was part of a larger debate about wholesale-retail relationships.

At first, the advocates of Westland prevailed in the annual meetings. Operations officially began on 1 January 1973 when Carrot River, Hudson Bay, Kelvington, and Kindersley co-ops merged with Westland. A fifth unit was a store at Mackenzie, B.C., which had been inherited by FCL at the time of the merger with BCCWS, and which was now re-organized as a Westland unit. This beginning already deviated from the Westland concept, for the plan had called for "block consolidation," whereby a number of existing co-ops in a small area would join together to form just a single Westland unit. These first five units, however, were widely scattered and few operating economies were possible. Moreover, in order to take in even this many units, the qualifications originally identified for entry into Westland had to be loosened. The original idea had been to impose strict guidelines for financing and viability. In 1972 it had been emphasized that "the organization must be built on sound foundations. . . . It must be built, not as a haven for the insecure, but as an aggressive force for new progress and benefits to the total system."[10] There were four original criteria, the first of which was that the retail show a net saving of 2 percent or a return of 8 percent on members' equity. When not enough retails could be found that were both willing to join Westland and could meet all four criteria, this prerequisite was altered, removing all reference to any net saving, and requiring only a 5 percent return on equity. This made it possible for retails with quite modest financial performances to be accepted.

Because Westland did not immediately achieve the operating economies forecast for the long term, it quickly became "necessary that the total System accept a fair proportion of the cost of Westland's administration and development," as delegates were told in 1973. "It does not seem fair that the five existing units plus those which join in the months ahead, should bear all the costs for a development to which the System is committed." FCL began subsidizing Westland's administrative costs.[11] Nor did this quickly change, for while they showed some operating improvements, the existing Westland units did not make above-average earnings, nor enough for the project to begin paying its own way. These were decisive developments, for Westland became identified as an FCL management project that was costing the system money and was, in the eyes of some, indeed serving as a haven for the inefficient.

At the annual meeting in February 1976 there was considerable discussion and detailed questioning of the report on Westland. One delegates' resolution, which was defeated, protested that "the board of Federated Co-operatives Limited are becoming preoccupied with the operations and politics of Westland Co-operatives." Other resolutions and discussion indicated criticism of how Westland Co-operatives was structured, and of the way that it received volume discounts and service-fee reductions from FCL. The matter of accepting thirteen new units into Westland (already defeated once in a mail ballot) was put to the vote at the annual meeting—and defeated again. The lowest approval rating was for the biggest of all applicants, Regina's Sherwood Co-op, indicating suspicion by the delegates that such big operations might receive favours or subsidies.

President Sinclair stated that as a result of the vote, "Westland Co-operatives is effectively stopped." By refusing to accept the new members, "the delegate body has made a decision." "We have had a demonstration of the fact that democracy is working in our co-operative organization."[12] The annual meeting the next year, 1977, voted that Westland be dissolved.

Why did the experiment not produce acceptable results? Pat Bell focusses on the dilution of the entrance standards. "It basically failed not because of the concept [but because of] the criteria we had for retails joining it. . . . I guess we got greedy and lowered the standards, and then we got into trouble. And when you get into operational trouble you get into political trouble. The good retails didn't want to join; only the poor ones did. And we let our guard down." Why did the delegates approve it when they obviously had so many reservations when it came to putting it into practice? Bell answers, "because they thought it was a logical concept—for the other guy. It was good for everybody but them."

Bill Bergen suggests there might have been some mistakes in the development of Westland—"perhaps a little bit too much democracy," meaning that membership was voluntary, and he suggests that possibly not enough time was devoted to it. He also notes that the aspects of local autonomy in the Westland plan, the procedures for involvement of local councillors, did not work very well. Mostly, however, Bergen thinks "it's one of those examples where you think you've done all your homework, but you haven't examined *culture* deeply enough." The culture of the Co-operative Retailing System was set against centralization. Like Bell, Bergen says delegates "went for it on the basis of saying yes, we will agree, but I'm reserving my vote as to whether it's right for us," for our own local co-op. The vote was "yes for someone else to do it."

The comments by Bell, Bergen, and other current managers, as well as by some directors and retail officers, indicate that the basic issues involved in Westland were never resolved. Many in the system still believe the idea was a good one and could have worked, that its failure was due to mistakes in implementation. Many others firmly believe that the idea is fundamentally flawed and unco-operative in nature. With its defeat, for a combination of reasons, the system simply agreed to forget the matter for the time being and get on with other pressing issues, which involved finding other solutions to the basic problems Westland had been intended to address.

Democracy and Member Relations: FCL and Its Members

In 1976–77, a new delegate and control structure came into force for FCL. In conjunction with this, the annual meeting in February 1977 was not given any list of priorities or tasks, not fourteen or twelve or even two as in previous years, but one single priority: "planning for the future of the Co-operative Retailing

System." Learning to work together was now the top priority. This represented a new approach to planning.

The same annual meeting that blocked Westland's development (1976) also saw the adoption of a new control structure based on a report by the structure committee of the FCL board. There were five key recommendations from this report. The first was that "more of the System's affairs be conducted on a Regional basis, with a Regional Conference to be held as an annual event in each of the six FCL Regions." Second, it was suggested that a new formula for representation at the annual meeting be devised "to reduce the number of delegates eligible to attend while retaining the concept of direct representation from FCL members." Third, the board of directors was to include a vice-president from each of the six regions. Fourth, the Executive Management Committee (EMC) was to be restructured "to enable retail managers in each Region to elect one member to the committee." In each region the regional vice-president, FCL region manager, EMC representative, and other FCL directors were to meet regularly to discuss operations in their area. The fifth recommendation concerned cost-sharing for conference travel and expenses. All five recommendations were carried after considerable discussion, though there was some dilution of the proposal for fewer delegates to annual meetings, and the intent of the original proposal was only achieved some years later.[13] These decisions created the control and planning process as it still exists in 1988.

The effect of these changes in structure was to remove much of the burden of discussion, co-ordination, and planning from the annual meeting, which, with nearly 500 delegates and a great deal of business packed into four days, did not seem to be serving the purpose. Instead, delegates now took their concerns first to conferences at the district level in June. These were discussed and dealt with again at regional conferences in the fall. Finally, at the annual meeting, policies that had already been thoroughly discussed at the grass-roots and regional level were voted on for decision. President Vern Leland observes that under this system, before delegates were asked to make a final decision, "there had already been a lot of dialogue and 'massaging' of programs. . . . That sure helped our system pull together."

A similar development has occurred with respect to the integration of co-operatives and the achievement of economies of operations, one of the original purposes of the Westland experiment. "Area development" has been a priority for the system since 1976 (since 1982 the system has had a formal area-development program) and, like the 'One-System' plan of the 1960s, one of the purposes is to promote and facilitate amalgamations among co-operatives within trading areas. There are a good dozen examples of co-operatives in the system that have been very successful in recent years with this kind of multiple-branch, area structure. Perhaps the leading example today, however, and the one mentioned most frequently by co-operators, is Pioneer Co-op in Swift Current, which has been a tremendous strength and success for the system. Its general manager, Gerry Doucet, has piloted the co-op through a quarter century of expansion and made a widely-recognized contribution to the system.[14]

However, area development also promotes consolidation among co-operatives that remain autonomous, so that they share costs or co-ordinate product lines and concentrations in order to reduce duplication. Both aspects of area development—amalgamation and co-ordination—have proceeded with some success, and continue to address the need for integration identified two decades ago and more. Centralized marketing and merchandising programs are also supported with fewer criticisms and complaints than they were in the early to mid-1970s. By more systematic organization of democracy—by meetings at many different levels, by dialogue, by regional structures—retail co-operatives and their wholesale are accomplishing much of what was once considered to be possible only if ownership were centralized.

Harold Empey, corporate secretary for FCL since 1979, says that the Westland concept is now "out of the question" for political reasons, but in any case "I don't see the need. . . . The system has become so strong and cohesive" that centralization is unnecessary. "I think we've got 'one system.' The only thing we still have is different balance sheets."

If these solutions helped improve member relations, democratic processes, and integration within the Co-operative Retailing System, there remained the broader and not unrelated question of relations with the individual members of the system, and their democratic control of their own local co-operatives.

Democracy and Member Relations: Retail Co-ops and Their Members

Proposals to centralize the system led to statements that centralization would have to be balanced by enhanced opportunities for individual co-operative members to become involved. Thus the 1972 annual meeting that reviewed the system's strengths and weaknesses, and proposed to create Westland, also saw the board of directors identify member relations and consumer interests as the first priorities in its list of tasks for 1973.[15] In 1973 a push for expanded member-relations activities became evident. An increased number of seminars were organized for local elected officials; retail co-operatives were urged to concentrate on analyzing their memberships and providing orientations for all new members; and consumer counselling, youth, and other general educational projects were expanded.[16] In 1974, however, a member relations committee report stated that the Co-operative Retailing System, while it had been effective in the economic parts of its mission, was not equally effective in "providing individual members with a sense of belonging to, and participation in, an organization of their own." Every retail was urged to form a member-relations committee.[17]

These suggestions to retails were repeated year after year, without the full, desired effect.

The system's fiftieth anniversary celebrations in 1978 provided an opportun-

*Kara Lee Comer, winner of the first Talent West show (1978). As part of the Co-operative
Retailing System's fiftieth anniversary celebrations in 1978, FCL started the Talent West
program, a ten-year series of competitions in which western Canadian young people
could show and be recognized for their talent.*

ity for a further stepping-up of member-relations activity. In 1977 the board
called for "the largest and most effective member relations program we have
ever undertaken" in commemoration of the system's birth. Late in 1978, FCL
created a Division of Member and Public Relations to concentrate these functions on an on-going basis. The establishment of this division, the directors said,
"is an assurance that due attention is, and will be, given to the social aspects
of the System's Mission and to its corporate and other responsibilities." The
mandate of its activity was extremely broad. Besides furthering understanding
of co-operation among members and employees of the system, and besides
increasing public awareness and appreciation of co-operatives (especially
among young people), it was also charged with the "social responsibilities" of
the system—efforts "to enhance the quality of life."[18] This was a diffuse and
far-reaching task to give to a single division.

The actual program of events in 1978 was far-ranging. Apart from ceremonies, seminars, and merchandising programs, innovative ideas included fes-
tivals for art, crafts, photography, stories and poems, and talent. The latter
was the origin of the very well-received Talent West, a ten-year program from
1978 to 1988 which gave western young people an opportunity to earn reward
and recognition in performing arts. As a way of contributing to the well-being
of members, an Operation Lifestyle campaign promoted farm and home safety,
nutrition, and fitness; and a tree-planting program was conducted so co-operatives could make a contribution to their communities in celebration of the

anniversary.[19] Members of the system look back on these social programs and many others like them as an important part of the system's contribution to western communities over the years.

As part of the 1978 celebrations, a play was commissioned entitled *A Generation and a Half*. Its theme was that the normal lifetime of a movement was only a generation and a half, unless it succeeded through education in drawing in a new generation of followers. The institutions and organizations might continue without this education, but the movement—the growth, the energy, the vitality that kept the organizations healthy—would not. The moral was that co-operatives needed to pay greater attention to their members. Following from this thought came the Growth from Within program, intended to be a permanent policy encouraging retails to educate, involve, take direction from, and earn the loyalty of their members.

Thinking on the subject of co-operative democracy was further reinforced by a Canada-wide project, the Co-operative Future Directions project, which involved many discussions among co-operative leaders between 1978–82. Also, in 1980, Alexander F. Laidlaw, a former general secretary of the Co-operative Union of Canada, prepared a paper entitled "Co-operatives in the Year 2000" for presentation to the Moscow congress of the International Co-operative Alliance. Laidlaw, then in his seventies, argued that co-operatives had entered an "ideological crisis" involving "gnawing doubts about the true purpose of co-

Scene from A Generation and a Half *by 25th Street Theatre, Saskatoon (1978), sponsored by FCL in conjunction with the co-operative system's fiftieth anniversary celebrations in 1978. Concerned with the origins and development of the co-operative movement, the play suggested that without continuing education the natural lifetime of a popular movement was "a generation and a half"—the lifetime of its founders, and little more.*

operatives and whether they are fulfilling a distinct role as a different kind of enterprise."[20] Laidlaw dealt with many aspects of change facing co-operatives, but among them he prominently posed several questions: "Do the democratic procedures that worked so well in small co-operatives in the past apply as well to very large co-operatives today? How can individuals participate in a meaningful way in a co-operative with tens of thousands of members? . . . What is the present state of education in the movement? . . . And finally, what is the end and purpose of it all? What is expected of co-operatives? How is success of co-operative enterprise to be measured?" Laidlaw died six weeks after presenting this paper, but the questions remain as one of his many legacies to the co-operative movement.

In the case of FCL, the measures taken in 1978 to re-establish a member-relations division, and the Growth from Within initiative, represented efforts to address these questions. A number of factors, however, limited the practical effect of these programs. Chief among them was that they were entirely dependent on the retails deciding to make member relations a priority.

A second limiting factor was the focus of the education that was already being provided by the system, which tended to consist mainly of technical training to help directors do their immediate jobs. Specialists in member relations were not being developed by the system.[21] Harold Chapman, who was in charge of some of these programs, recalls that "there was a lack of recognition of how complex the adult learning process is. I think it's unreal to think you can bring a group of directors together for a day and teach them how to conduct member relations."

Third, member relations became overshadowed in some respects by considerations of corporate image, which (though related) is quite a different matter. Member relations and co-operative education presume active participation by members who are personally developed by their experience. Mass-media advertising, including informational flyers, presumes passive readers who accept a specific, simple, and noncontroversial message. The attention given by the system to its image in some respects absorbed some of the attention that could have been devoted to member education and participation.

Finally, the development of a more bottom-line-oriented philosophy in the system seems to have led to concern mainly with short-term benefits of member-relations programs. While Growth from Within has been mentioned many times since 1978, it has frequently been in the context of persuading members to increase their average purchases, which is an extreme simplification of the original idea.[22] Similarly, a definition of the purposes of co-operative democracy, adopted in 1981, stated that democracy was to "generate . . . a sense of loyalty and commitment" among members, as well as to enable members "to provide information that will assist [board and management] to make decisions."[23] These are valuable objectives, but the language used implies that the concern is to *get* more out of members, not how to *offer* them more participation, understanding, or personal development. This does not begin to address the broader questions posed by Laidlaw.

In short, while member relations and democracy were much-discussed and efforts were made, the high objectives co-operatives have traditionally held for these areas were still not met. The system was much more successful, by the end of the 1970s and into the 1980s, in improving the relationships among the retails and FCL, than in improving its relations with its individual member-owners.

Conclusion and Questions

Rapid growth and unsettled industrial conditions caught up with the Co-operative Retailing System in the 1970s, and required the creation of new structures for democracy, control, and planning. This was accomplished in the end by compromise, with neither the existing set-up, nor the radically new idea of Westland Co-operatives, prevailing. Instead, the seeds of a partnership between the retails and the wholesale were sown, a partnership that has been tested and strengthened by the still more severe economic challenges of the 1980s. This is a positive achievement.

Like all compromises, this one leaves some of the fundamental issues unresolved. Could Westland Co-operatives have worked? Were the reasons for its failure economic, or political, or were they rooted in co-operative principles? Is the existing ownership, management, and control structure of the system a permanent solution? The comments gathered by the author in the course of writing this book imply that the system is fundamentally divided on these questions. Many, particularly officials of successful retails, defend the structure of autonomous retails as an essential basis for the system; while many others, especially managers in large organizations, predict on-going centralization in the future, perhaps even a Westland by another name.

Not only Westland, but several other projects in the 1970s illustrated a deliberate attempt to break with the traditions of the co-operative movement, traditions that were apparently seen as anachronisms and obstacles to growth and adaptation. But how outdated were the tenets of co-operative "philosophy"? Centralization had been tried before, and rejected on the grounds that success and autonomy went together for retail co-operatives. Did Westland disprove this assumption? The IPCO Chlor-Alkali plant in Saskatoon, and perhaps the WCFL rock-phosphate venture (Chapter 19), not to mention some retail expansions in the 1970s, contradicted the idea espoused by early co-operative leaders that growth must be gradual and always follow rather than lead or speculate upon the demand of members. Weren't the old co-operative thinkers right? Selling at market prices was once another co-operative principle; the attempts to fight inflation in the mid-1970s by selling below prevailing prices led to shortages, financial losses, and problems of allocation. Member relations have always been a priority for co-operators, but the scope and form of member-relations programs today are different. Is "co-operative education" in the old sense still necessary—people talking to people about co-operatives, asking what the problems of members and of the community are, examining how co-operatives of all kinds can help? It is true that co-operatives today tread new ground and require new solutions. But could it be that in some things, at least, the pioneers still have something to teach us?

21

Merger and Co-operative Development in B.C., 1970–1982

The amalgamation with British Columbia Co-operative Wholesale Society (BCCWS) in 1970 expanded FCL's activity westward to the Pacific coast. In terms of east-west expansion this meant FCL reached its full, present geographic extent, covering all four western provinces as well as eastward into Ontario to the Lakehead. Relative to the other provinces, B.C., lagged far behind in co-operative development. Though its population was larger than any of the other provinces, its co-operatives were far fewer and its co-operative wholesaling suffered from lack of purchasing volume.

From the day of the amalgamation, therefore, a second issue was raised: co-operative development, meaning the expansion of old co-operatives and, especially, the creation of new ones. In other parts of the system there had been little worry about creating new co-ops; since the mid-1960s the task had been to reduce, not increase, the number of co-operative associations on the prairies. Did the system still have what it took to generate new co-ops, new members, and new member support? B.C. was a test, and a test whose results were ultimately mixed. While, over-all, co-operative expansion occurred in B.C., consumer co-operation did not expand to levels comparable to the other provinces, and some notable collapses of co-operative associations in the 1980s marred the record.

Amalgamation of British Columbia

Amalgamation of the British Columbia Co-op Wholesale Society into the consumer system of the western provinces had been discussed since the time of the Alberta amalgamation in 1961. In 1965, FCL's directors reported that BCCWS had inquired about the subject. "An amalgamation at this time would not be appropriate," the directors concluded, because "current programs impose considerable burden on our manpower and other resources."[1]

B.C.'s concern was co-operative development, for the volume of the consumer co-ops in B.C. was too small, and their geographic dispersion too great, to permit the development of a strong co-operative system. This was also why FCL management and directors had justifiable doubts about an amalgamation, for it would mean taking on an immense and difficult geographic region containing few co-operatives. FCL would then have to rise to the expectation of providing the same level of service as in other regions.

In April 1967 BCCWS and the B.C. Management Advisory Committee released a preliminary study "on co-operative merger into one or more units in B.C."[2] In effect the study recommended "the One System concept" as the means for B.C. to improve financing, purchasing, personnel, education, and co-operative development. In B.C. there were to be seven regional co-operatives created by amalgamation of locals. Worried by the growth of big private competitors, President A. Swenson of BCCWS asked in 1968, "how can consumer co-operatives, continuing as separate and independent entities in their own communities, survive in the environment created by these corporate operations?"[3] A new Committee on Co-operative Restructuring was appointed at that time which included Lewie Lloyd, retired president of FCL.

Clearly, BCCWS was looking at bigness and integration as the answer to breaking into the provincial retail markets, and in the absence of amalgamation with FCL, it was seeking ways to do this on its own.

Nevertheless, in spite of these proposals, it proved exceedingly difficult for BCCWS to make headway. Bob Boyes had to attend the 1969 BCCWS annual meeting and ask "for the meeting's patience respecting the prospect of amalgamation." He also cautioned against undue haste and excessive centralization, warning of the danger that centralized new organizations might "become too far removed from our people" and lose sight of their purpose.[4] In spite of such warnings, and in spite of fears and concerns expressed by delegates, when Barney Johnsrude presented the interim report of the committe on restructuring, delegates confirmed the policy of restructuring and accepted the committee's report.

Because of the state of the economy, BCCWS never had the opportunity to implement the recommendations of the committee. The wholesale had been making good progress in sales during the 1960s, doubling sales from $7.3 million in 1964 to $15.3 million five years later. In 1957, BCCWS had 4.7 percent of FCL's sales; in 1969, 8.8 percent. The B.C. wholesale was gradually and steadily building up a respectable volume. Unfortunately, the nature of the economy meant that, as with FCL during the same years, increasing sales did not necessarily mean increasing savings. BCCWS had managed just $160,000 savings in 1967 (1.3 percent), and this fell in 1968 to a mere $40,827 (0.3 percent). BCCWS was worried, and appointed a task force which conducted studies, consulted with FCL and other co-operatives, and commissioned a special auditors' study. The auditors projected a "serious shortage of working capital" that would handcuff the wholesale, and BCCWS proved unable to reverse the trend. The record sales of 1969 left a net loss of $277,000 on the books, with losses and failures by local co-operatives, along with overdue accounts and excessive accounts receivable, contributing heavily to the crisis. The consumer movement in B.C. did not have the volume, the capital, or the basis of strong local societies to weather the stresses of the late sixties.[5]

The board of BCCWS came to the conclusion in January 1969 that the wholesale "could not survive in its present form. . . . It was decided therefore to place the affairs of the Society before Federated Co-operatives Limited."[6] At meetings in February 1970, representatives of FCL accepted the amalgamation proposal, in spite of FCL's own preoccupations. Even moreso than the amalgamation of 1961, this was an amalgamation conducted out of co-operative solidarity and long-term vision, and certainly not out of immediate financial advantage for FCL. FCL warned, however, that "since merger has come about sooner than expected, members of the B.C. Co-operative Wholesale Society will need to be patient with respect to new development."[7] The amalgamation became effective on 1 May 1970, and on that date, for the first time, consumer co-operatives from the Lakehead to the Pacific Ocean were united in a single network.

Co-operative Development in B.C.

As representatives of FCL noted in 1973, the merger with B.C. had come "at a most inconvenient time." Three years were to elapse "before FCL was able to devote energies and resources to assist in the expansion of consumer co-operatives in British Columbia."[8] While FCL was busy with other priorities, "extensive studies" were made of the situation in FCL's newest region. "An immediate and high priority was given to assisting retail co-operatives in B.C. that were threatened by financial or operational difficulty," said FCL, and $869,000 in loan guarantees were approved to help five B.C. associations. Finally, in 1972, the money began to flow. Two major expansions were funded that year, and twenty-one projects involving $4.237 million were planned for 1973.

One of the projects to which the FCL board gave approval was "the development of a major retail co-operative facility to serve the lower mainland of B.C." which would offer price discounts instead of patronage refunds, and which would offer high-volume, low-cost service with no advertising. Those familiar with the Superstores in western Canada might note a certain family resemblance, and it seems likely that this was the kind of competition the proposed store was intended to meet. The concept came from a key report on "Emerging Co-operatives and Growth" by J. Hargreaves, A. Baribeau, and A. Christmann. The report considered how co-operatives could break into urban markets, particularly into Vancouver, and how they could close what the authors saw as a "'consumer–institution' gap," a gap illustrated by the "mushrooming" of direct charge and other new co-operatives outside of the established system. "The energy of these people as well as their concerns need to be converted to meaningful action."[9] To do this the report chose as models the Swedish example of large-volume, low-cost "hypermarkets" in shopping centres, the Swiss "Migros" stores that offered discount prices instead of patronage rebates, and others, including direct-charge co-ops.

The report made two recommendations. First, it proposed that a "total service shopping centre" be developed in the Lower Mainland of B.C. "This centre would include groceries, bakery, cafeteria, hardware (with catalogue sales for major household [appliances]), dry goods, home improvement centre, and a discount pump operation, plus some other services." It would lease space to a credit union and to other services, have charge-card sales, and it would sell food at 5 percent below market price with no patronage refunds. FCL would underwrite the development, according to the proposal, and the unit would become part of Westland when the latter was ready. The second recommendation was to support the service-fee co-ops on Vancouver Island, about which more will be said below.

While Vancouver proved a very tough nut to crack, and remains essentially uncracked today, large co-operative development projects were pursued at other points in British Columbia. One of the earliest was Mackenzie, where FCL acquired through the amalgamation a store previously operated by BCCWS. FCL immediately put money in to double its size and set it up on a membership basis, and the Mackenzie store became the first Westland unit.

Another large project was the Mainline Co-op at Salmon Arm. Once again, this was to be a large co-op developed with wholesale leadership and support, opening its doors on the first day of business in sophisticated and spanking new facilities. A core of member support seemed guaranteed because of the close proximity of the Canoe lumber and plywood plants; as was noted on another occasion, "FCL is the largest employer in Salmon Arm."[10] One co-operator retired in B.C. notes this was "one of the finest stores in the interior" and had the benefit of "skilled operators"—but "the community didn't take fire." A current FCL manager adds, "sure, they had tremendous facilities. But they built too big for the community, and the facilities were in the wrong place, where no one could find them." Another senior manager observes simply: "over-sized for the community, over-built structurally, wrong location, lack of control on construction costs." The Mainline Co-op went wrong from the start and was eventually closed.

A third large project in the 1970s was the expansion of Surrey Co-op in Abbotsford and Cloverdale, which by the early 1980s was Canada's second-largest consumer co-operative. By 1982, with the onset of the recession, Surrey Co-op was in receivership, and the association was later dissolved. Though some co-operative retailing services remain in the local areas (such as Otter Co-op in Aldergrove near Abbotsford), the system now has no major retail affiliates in Vancouver, in Salmon Arm, or in Abbotsford.

Another effort in Kelowna was, according to some, slightly different. Here, organizational work was done to develop membership and leadership from the local community. The facility itself was not so grand as at Salmon Arm, but it still lost money when it opened, and the plug was pulled. "They must have spent a year developing people," observes one co-operator. "It takes time." He remains convinced the co-op had enough support and was about to take off, but was never given the chance. "It had lots of chances," retorts an FCL director, and management quotes statistics on inadequate sales volume and mounting losses.

These particular examples do not imply that co-operative development was a failure. From 1970 to 1982, retail co-operatives in B.C. grew from thirty-two thousand members to eighty-nine thousand, and from $43 million in purchases to $229 million—both of these are immense increases in little over a decade.[11] Clearly, amalgamation had brought benefits to B.C., as it had to the other provinces, and consumer co-operation had grown as a result. But the big co-operative development projects did encounter some very serious setbacks, setbacks that could raise questions about the way in which such large projects were undertaken.

Bill Bergen concedes that "the co-operative development didn't take place that we had assumed." In hindsight, he suggests, the system should have learned from lessons elsewhere. "We really discovered that you couldn't develop a co-op without the necessary leadership in the community. . . . Why didn't we realize that you couldn't super-impose co-ops in B.C.? . . . I don't have the answer." Another retired manager agrees: "You can't impose it and expect, after imposing it, that it will grow." He recalls Harry Fowler saying, "we can only be as big and as successful as the people in the community want us to be," and the implication is that the large co-operative development projects of the 1970s overlooked this dictum. They developed the stores and the inventory and the management, all with sufficient expertise, but they did not persuade or develop the members in the community.

New Trends and New Co-operatives

While the Co-operative Retailing System pursued big projects, other kinds of co-ops were emerging in British Columbia, particularly among younger urban people concerned with natural foods, low prices, and close involvement in their organizations. In 1973 a Victoria newspaper interviewed Liz Kenny, president of Fed-Up Co-operative Wholesale Association, a newly formed natural food supplier to thirty-six small B.C. co-operatives who "believe co-ops should not only be owned by their customers but should be physically operated by them with savings passed back to the customers directly in lower prices."[12] The co-ops preferred (according to the article) to be called "member-run co-operatives." As the story observed, these co-ops viewed FCL affiliates with "indifference or hostility," referring to them as "official" co-ops. "From my point of view," one of their members is quoted as saying, "there isn't much difference between them and other stores."[13]

The suspicion between Fed-Up and Federated was mutual. FCL's region manager was quoted as saying he preferred to call the new-wave co-ops "voluntary buying clubs" rather than co-operatives. "We don't organize voluntary buying clubs. Our experience has been that where these clubs have been successful it has been as a result of the effort of a very few members. Eventually they have wanted to have a store with staff." Ray Johnson credited them with representing a "new wave of social conscience and new consumer awareness," and stated, "I think they can do a job for the kind of customer who is prepared to put in the kind of effort that is necessary." But he also observed that individual co-op stores like Cloverdale or Terrace did "as much business in a week as the whole lot (member-run co-ops) do in a year."

Small though these member-run co-ops were, some co-operators in B.C. expressed concern in 1972 about the "division in [the] co-op movement," and argued that the Co-operative Retailing System should go some distance to helping the new co-ops in the interests of co-operative development. Suggestions were made for arrangements to enable local retails to work with local food producers (one of their key concerns) while FCL worked with those at the national levels.It was also suggested that a "cash-and-carry wholesale" operation be set up so that "small co-ops could pick up merchandise." District co-operators also pleaded that "we should not ignore these new food co-ops. Listen to them, work with them, convince them we are not part of [a] so-called corporate rip-off, look at supplying them with their 'natural' food requirements."[14] But little could be done to reconcile Federated and Fed-Up at that time. Ten years later, in 1984, Fed-Up Co-op Wholesale and two other new-wave co-ops finally joined FCL, but by that time the movement had lost momentum.[15] Fed-Up quickly went out of business, as did many of its member co-ops.

Co-operators in the system today like to contrast this economic failure with the success of some conventional co-ops in turning their misfortunes around during the 1980s. They refer to co-ops like Southwest Co-op in Maple Creek. "It was absolutely bankrupt" says one co-operator. "The banks, Federated, everyone told them they had no chance." But instead of shutting down, they appealed to their membership and raised about $100,000 in interest-free community subscription share capital. They improved their service, talked to their membership, and won increased support. The deficit was eliminated, $1.4 million in savings was accumulated over the next seven years, and member equity was increased from 4.8 percent to 50.8 percent.[16] "They have done something that many others have failed to accomplish," observes corporate Secretary Harold Empey. Similar success stories are recounted for co-ops like Carrot River, Otter (in Aldergrove, B.C.), and Ponoka. To co-operators in the established system, these examples demonstrate the strength and resilience of their co-ops, in contrast to what they see as the poor performance and failure of the new-wave co-ops.

Of course, the co-operatives that exhibited such turnarounds were located in the kinds of centres in which co-operatives were traditionally strong: mid-sized prairie cities or semiagricultural communities. None of them were located in the big urban centres of British Columbia, so the fading of the new-wave phenomenon still meant the near-elimination of consumer co-operation in these cities. There was, however, another alternative in B.C. during the 1970s that might have had the potential to organize the energy of the new-wave urban phenomenon into something more lasting. Co-ops like Nanaimo Mid-Island Consumer Services Co-operative (known locally as Hub Co-op) offered the possibility of a bridge between the established system and innovative urban co-operatives.

The Service-Fee Co-op Model: Hub Co-op in Nanaimo

The story of Nanaimo Mid-Island Co-op in the 1970s is one of the Co-operative Retailing System's success stories, but it is a success story with some different twists. It demonstrates that growth—not just sales, but growth into new com-munities—can come from on-the-spot innovation and adaptation to local cir-cumstances.

Hume Compton, one-time vice-president of Hub Co-op and director of FCL, recalls that the co-op got its start from the credit-union movement. This in itself is worthy of note, since in general the pattern has been the reverse: credit unions in western Canada, coming later than consumer co-operatives, were fre-quently founded and promoted by the established co-operative associations. At Nanaimo and in other communities in B.C., credit unions returned the favour—a fact which could suggest some patterns for possible ways of introduc-ing consumer co-operatives into more of B.C.'s urban communities. In Na-naimo's case, as in the case of new co-ops and credit unions in the 1930s and 1940s, co-operative development was a task to be pursued by co-operation among co-operatives.

In any case, it was in 1961 that the credit union in Nanaimo started a petro-leum co-operative under the leadership of Rod Glen. The key to the petroleum co-op was that it sold to members only, one of what Compton has called "three key policy decisions" that shaped the co-op from its earliest days.[17] A second innovation was that members were encouraged to prepay their purchases by buying coupons. This provided "float money" for the co-op, and also ensured that members had to make a firm advance commitment to the co-op and remain loyal once they bought their coupons. The third key policy was that shares were fixed at $40 per member; twenty years later this had been increased to $150—a great deal higher than the share requirements of most urban co-operative asso-ciations. This was to give members a meaningful stake in the co-op, and remove the need to borrow.

Hub Co-op board and management began to think of a food store after they studied the direct-charge co-op started in Ottawa in 1964 under the leadership of Ralph Staples of the CUC.[18] The idea of direct-charge was to sell only to members who paid a weekly fee, at wholesale prices plus a fixed mark-up to cover the co-op's expenses. Glen and Compton developed a variation of direct-charge that worked like this: as with the existing petroleum operation, the food store would sell to members only. These members would pay a weekly service fee to use the store, $2.50 per week for fifty weeks of the year. This service fee would cover the fixed costs of the co-op. The food would then be priced at wholesale levels, with the mark-up on the food being only enough to cover the operating costs. Finally, a 2 percent surcharge would be levied on purchases, and this would accumulate on members' behalf in $20 (later $40) loan certificates. The capital surcharge meant that the co-op borrowed from its members rather than from outside sources. In addition, each member would subscribe fifteen $10 shares, and a rule would be set that share capital should not fall below one-third of assets.[19]

Other features of the Nanaimo system included bare-bones facilities and services, and contractual obligations of members to the co-operative. Members did their own pricing, bagging, and carrying, and both hours and locations of service were restricted in order to hold costs down. The contract signed by members specified the duties expected of them, including payment of the service fee and capital surcharge. This was a co-operative that expected something of its members, that expected them to make some sacrifices in order to get some savings.

What is intriguing is that these ideas, though they appeared new and radical at the time, are really reformulations of many of the ideas that had guided consumer co-operatives in the 1930s. For example, Hub Co-op's much higher share-capital requirements are more like the original policies of the 1920s when ten- and twenty-five-dollar shares (a lot of money at that time) were required. Similarly, Hub Co-op's member-oriented policies are rather like what sustained the co-operative associations of the 1930s: a tight bond of membership, an expectation of loyalty, foregoing of advertising in favour of member communications. As in the associations of the 1930s, which were rudimentary in many ways, the focus is on the service provided to the member and not on the frills or the sophistication of the premises. The capital surcharge that accumulates in three-year certificates is Harry Fowler's revolving door reborn. And the service fee itself is intended to remove the risk from doing business, which is also the original purpose of the practice of selling at market prices and paying a patronage rebate at the end of the year.

Seen in the context of the co-operative movement's history and traditions, Hub Co-op's service-fee innovation looks not so much like a radical departure as it does like a clever and very carefully planned rearrangement of long-established co-operative procedures. It addresses what Compton calls weaknesses in the "outmoded system" of established retail co-ops (by which he seems to mean particularly urban, food-oriented co-ops), weaknesses that include shortages of internal capital; inability to accumulate capital when earnings are low; incurring debt to build in a speculative way rather than to serve existing membership needs; and aiming at nonmember business instead of relying on the loyalty and development of members. He bluntly criticizes "the idea that making it easy and painless for people to join and use a co-op will guarantee success."[20]

How did Nanaimo's system fare in practice? Hub Co-op opened its first store in 1971, and within six years had what Compton refers to as "one of the largest consumer co-operatives in North America." In 1983 its sales made it the third largest co-operative food retailer in Canada.[21] Its membership was not large for an urban co-op—eleven thousand people in 1982—but its average purchases per member—$3,500—were exceptional. Members lent the co-op an average of $245 each, and also held shares worth an average of $125 per member.[22]

On the other hand, even Nanaimo encountered problems in the 1980s, losing $413,000 in a single year as the recession hit in 1981–82, and struggling thereafter. Compton blames this on the severity of the recession in lumber, a main local industry; on a "vicious supermarket price war"; on "FCL's decision to close down its Vancouver distributing centre" in 1979, which increased costs (this is a controversial claim, as FCL put in a five-year assistance program to take care of such costs); and on a dilution of the original service-fee idea, through reluctance to increase the weekly fee in proportion to actual cost increases.[23] The price war mentioned by Compton involved competitors opening big new supermarkets whose capacities were far in excess of the volume of business they then held, in what looked like a deliberate attempt to take away Hub Co-op's members. In all likelihood, they ran up major losses in this aggressive effort, so that Hub Co-op's survival, not its earnings, should be the real indication of performance. But even if the losses are understandable, they still tarnish the lustre of the service-fee idea for the established system, which has become very bottom-line oriented.

The reaction of the co-operative system to this phenomenon was mixed at the best of times. There was definitely a certain disbelief. Compton recalls being at "loggerheads" with FCL. Hub Co-op's confident claims that it had the answer to the system's problems "didn't sit well with the advisors in the movement who figured they had everything worked out. . . . They kind of objected to us imposing ourselves on other people and giving our advice."[24] In the opinion of many, the key to Hub Co-op was President Rod Glen. The suspicion was that Glen's exceptional leadership and skill, not the inherent advantages of the service-fee system, were the reasons for Hub Co-op's success. The mixture of rules and procedures Glen worked out in partnership with his board of directors, though it worked in Nanaimo, seemed to prove difficult to adapt to circumstances elsewhere. Five co-ops in B.C. converted to a service-fee system in the 1970s, including Nanaimo, Campbell River, Duncan, Parksville, and Comox; some others like Prince Rupert also followed. Of these five, only the first two could be classed as commercial successes, though, of course, all achieved some success in service and in development of members.

There may be other explanations, however, for the failure of service-fee co-ops to spread more widely and successfully in B.C. Compton, along with Hub Co-op manager Stan Glydon and director Susan Vanlerberg, were quoted in 1983 to the effect that "the best thing that could happen" to service-fee co-ops in western Canada "would be a full-scale development commitment from Federated Co-operatives Limited."[25] They noted that in the Maritimes, where the regional co-op wholesale (Co-op Atlantic) had devoted staff and money to development of direct-charge co-ops, they had become very successful, providing an important part of the co-operative distribution network. FCL, however, did not make such development a priority; according to Bill Bergen, this was because FCL had other priorities in the 1970s, and because it already had established co-ops in most centres that would have been difficult to convert to a direct-charge system.

Now, Compton sees the service-fee idea "going backwards" under the pressure of the recession. Within five years he expects the pure service-fee system will be gone in the West. "It's a dead duck now. It's a waste of . . . time to even discuss a service-fee system," he suggests—because in his opinion no one in the established co-operatives will listen. "Another vehicle has to be found."

Conclusion and Questions

Why did the large co-operative projects not mobilize sufficient member support in B.C.? Was it lack of time? Will a large co-op project develop a viable community base if the wholesale is willing to keep it in operation long enough? Or is there some way that new co-ops can still start small and grow slowly on their own, like they did in the 1930s and 1940s?

The service-fee co-ops also raise two obvious questions: Why was Hub Co-op so successful for a decade, and, second, why did the idea prove difficult to maintain since that time or to imitate elsewhere? There is something about Nanaimo's decade of success that suggests features to be copied for successful urban co-operative development elsewhere—not the whole set of procedures, perhaps, but some of their underlying principles. Is lack of support from FCL, or from credit unions, one reason Nanaimo proved difficult to duplicate or sustain? What are the underlying principles of Nanaimo's success that could be applied or improved upon in other situations—Sales to members only? Economic incentives to stay loyal to the co-op? More meaningful commitment of capital by members? No-frills service and no advertising?

Nanaimo proves innovation and flexibility can bear fruit in adapting co-operative retailing to modern conditions. Where this innovation is based on profound thought about the principles involved and about the relationship with members, it can also gain the support of new generations and groups of consumers. Where co-operation succeeds as a people's movement, will such success *always* be temporary? Is the service-fee idea only one generation's answer to the question of co-operative development? The institutions they established, like the co-op in Nanaimo, will perhaps survive. But will new generations require new innovations, applying fundamental co-operative principles in still different forms?

PART EIGHT: REBIRTH, 1982–1988

Introduction to Part Eight

The recession of 1982 provided what was arguably the most severe economic test ever faced by the Co-operative Retailing System, comparable in its effects at least to the downturn of 1969–70, if not to the crash of 1929. What made the crash of 1982 so severe was that it caught a large, established system in the throes of barely controlled expansion. Co-operatives had a lot of money tied up and many were over-extended, vulnerable to the sharp recession with its lingering aftermath.

It is revealing that the tough times are those when co-operatives draw together and work best as a system. This was true in the 1930s, when it took the misery and deprivation of the Great Depression to drive home the lessons of co-operation, and lay the foundations for a movement of historic proportions. It is also true in the 1980s, which have produced the greatest degree of cohesion and harmony among retails and their wholesale that has existed since, probably, the 1950s when FCL was founded. If history is any example, hardship provides opportunities for forging unity among co-operatives, which in turn can lay a basis for decades of growth.

*   *   *

22

From Crisis
to Record Savings, 1982–1988

The recession of 1982 hit western Canada very hard. Income fell, unemployment rose, and retail markets sagged. As a regional co-operative unit, the Co-operative Retailing System could not escape or compensate for this region-wide trend. At the same time, specific industries in which the Co-operative Retailing System was heavily involved, notably agriculture, petroleum, and lumber, experienced especially sharp downturns, as demand and prices fell steeply. Almost every major commodity handled by the system fell at the same time, and this produced a crisis.

This crisis was most evident at the retail level, and although it was not without some advance warning, it was nevertheless a significant shock. Retail local savings fell across the system as a whole from $12.8 million in 1980—not in any case a high level—to a mere $1.2 million in 1981, amid high interest rates and forewarnings of recession. However, record FCL patronage refunds of $41.6 million greatly aided the retails, so that total savings remained high. The year 1982 was the real crunch. Local savings by retails were heavily negative, amounting to a loss of $18.1 million across the system, and meaning that some 116 retails remained in a net-loss position even after FCL's patronage refund. The recession had hit FCL as well, of course, so that FCL's returns to retails fell sharply. In 1982, FCL's net savings were a mere 0.1 percent of sales, barely in the black, and the lowest level since FCL, as such, was created in 1955.

In 1982, the whole system was, in the opinion of many of those who watched the crisis, teetering on the brink. Unless the trends were reversed, the system, or at least its key institutions, including FCL and many of the larger retails, might have gone over the edge.

"Stopping the Drain" 1982–84

During 1982, FCL board and managers observed the worsening trends, and decided that an "economic offensive" was necessary to realign the system. This offensive had two targets: first, FCL, and second, the retails.

Within FCL the action was swift and in some respects devastating. The Vancouver region office was closed; henceforth, B.C. co-ops were serviced out of

Edmonton and Calgary. The Retail Development Department was closed entirely. The staff complement was reduced by 250, or in excess of 20 percent, "through attrition, early retirement, layoffs, and severance."[1] Two production facilities, the sawmill at Revelstoke and the manufactured-homes plant at North Battleford, were kept or taken out of production to save costs. The *Co-operative Consumer,* published since 1939, was terminated. These actions were required, says Secretary Empey, "not only to make absolutely sure that the FCL situation remained very strong, but to set an example to the retails."

The home-office cuts were carried out between board meetings in the summer of 1982; the next step was a special board meeting in August to draw up an action plan for the retails. A review of retail operations found that thirty-six co-ops were in "serious financial difficulty." The FCL board approved a plan for each of these retails, intended to "prevent further deterioration of their position and the resulting financial risks to FCL and the System." These plans advised the retails in question to close nonviable departments, cut staff and salaries, increase working hours, and cut expenses and inventories. Wayne Thompson, treasurer in 1982, remembers, "we went out to the retail co-ops with very definitive action plans for each co-op. We didn't have the chance for the dialogue you'd like to have." The result was a difficult experience for those involved. It is important to remember that this economic offensive involved FCL representatives going out to present plans for major cutbacks to *autonomous* retail co-ops, co-ops that in fact were owners of FCL itself. President Leland remembers this was "a really traumatic thing." Closing down retails "just tears at the guts of an elected director." Pat Bell, chief executive officer at that time, uses almost exactly the same words. He had to go out and tell Red River to sell off its stores. "That churns your guts."

"It looked like we were going backwards," adds Bell, "and we were, to a degree. But you've got to find a new base, go back to a new start."

The "improvement of the viability of individual retail co-operatives" became FCL's first priority in 1982. Besides scrutinizing the most precarious operations and "cutting the drain" to save the system, FCL also tried to return the maximum possible amounts to retails, including through special assistance grants. In 1982, FCL provided $6.5 million in direct assistance, in addition to $13.3 million in patronage refunds, which barely sufficed to bring the retails as a whole above zero earnings. This, too, is usually a controversial action within a federation of co-operatives: it is rare that those that are successful will accept their wholesale society pumping direct assistance into those that are in trouble.

In 1987, a Minnesota economist noted that in the co-operatives of the American Midwest that used a federated structure, the recession was leading to severe stresses between the wholesale and its members. Frank J. Smith notes that until the recession the "cumbersome" machinery of autonomous retails federated together into a wholesale "clanked along serving [members'] needs in an acceptable fashion." But when the retails got in trouble the regional wholesale had to intervene, because the system as a whole needed to preserve enough volume and market presence to keep its operations viable. "What is the regional to do with a recalcitrant member co-op when the latter's performance not only puts its own existence in jeopardy, but jeopardizes the interests of the regional and, therefore, other locals[?]" The solutions, Smith suggests, are "management services" by the wholesale to the retail co-op; "selective local ownership" by the regional; or a "central" system.[2] In any of these cases, controversy is likely to arise as the cumbersome machinery goes to work.

In the case of FCL, there is little evidence that the machinery was cumbersome, nor was the controversy extreme. Harold Empey notes "retail co-ops that were successful had to take a reduction in earnings . . . from FCL in order to help those other retails get through a difficult time. They did that willingly. They understood the need and were prepared to support the whole system." One manager of a well-to-do retail co-op notes that, though there were a few isolated grumblings, he personally wanted to help the associations that were in trouble. "We need their volume. They're excellent assets for us to have in the system." And the associations that were in trouble, though presented with FCL's action plan in the worst possible way (without much warning or any substantial dialogue), recognized relatively quickly that there was no real alternative. Empey suggests that the fact retails accepted FCL guidance was a sign of their maturity. "*Plus,*" he emphasizes, "FCL was as careful as possible . . . to treat equal circumstances equally."

The action plan of 1982, even the controversy it entailed, turned out to be first steps in achieving a greater unity and cohesiveness in the system than had existed since well before Westland. Why was this so? It seems likely that a key part of the answer lies with the structural changes of 1976–77, which produced a planning process that began to build up trust between the retails and FCL; with changes in leadership and management, about which more will be said below; and with preparations prior to 1982 for the anticipated onset of a recession. Studies in 1981 helped identify where and how much help would be needed in the case of a recession, and began the emphasis on cost-cutting, control of expenses, and marketing which was the key to survival in 1982 and recovery thereafter. When swift action needed to be taken in 1982, it was, therefore, easier to take. "We were frightened by how fast the trend had come," says Thompson. "We knew immediately something had to be done."

The recession, as it turned out, lasted even longer than many had anticipated. In 1982 FCL's managers warned members that "a return to conditions regarded as 'normal' in the past can hardly be anticipated. Thus, recovery of the economy will spawn a new era to which the System will need to adapt." The nature of this adaptation was also laid out. "The experiences of 1982 have made us much more conscious of the importance of maximizing productivity, minimizing costs, and working closely together for marketing efficiency." In particular (the operating report for that year suggested), what was needed and merited was "confidence in our marketing abilities, principles, and services."[3]

The Era of Marketing

The new era of the 1980s may be characterized as the era of marketing, merchandising, and advertising. The concentration on aggressive marketing predates the 1982 recession—the position of marketing group manager was created as a new senior management position in 1979 and filled by K. A. Adie—but there is no doubt that the re-orientation of 1982 further reinforced this concentration. Harold Empey sees this as "a major change in thrust at the senior management level" to emphasize marketing and retail operations. "I found FCL in the mid-70s to be an organization that was not as aggressive in terms of marketing and merchandising as I thought it should be," says Empey. "We had talked about it [marketing], but we never really got going until the crunch came in '82." He suggests the 1980s have seen a "tremendous improvement in . . . image, in merchandising. . . . The retail co-ops of the Eighties will be known to have moved into first place in many of their communities."

Empey, along with Pat Bell and Bell's successor as chief executive officer, Wayne Thompson, all helped lead the management team in this new emphasis in the system. They were ably assisted by the board, the rest of senior management, the Executive Management Committee, and the Co-operative Managers' Association. Thompson gives great credit to all these groups and says the focus on marketing is "one of the biggest changes . . . that has taken place over the last number of years." Certain key phrases come out when current managers speak about these subjects. One of them (to quote Thompson again) is "more focus on services to the membership . . . less focus on expansion and growth for growth's sake." The idea, to quote another of the oft-repeated phrases, is that co-ops must cease "trying to be all things to all people," and must "concentrate on what they do best" in order to return the maximum "economic benefit" to the member. Instead of assuming they must grow, or that they must produce the products they sell, or that they must handle a comprehensive range of products, co-ops should instead concentrate on what can be done advantageously. Other lines should be abandoned; expansions and growth should be carefully scrutinized; and the bottom line should be respected.

Within FCL, these policies eventually bore fruit: 1986 was the first year since 1973 when every merchandising and production function of FCL earned a net saving. Every division in 1986 and 1987 contributed positively to the bottom line. Similarly for the retails, 1986 was the turning point. In that year only 16 of the system's more than 330 retails had a net loss after the FCL patronage refund, the lowest number since 1974. Retails' local savings were $20 million net, the highest since 1975. (See Appendices 5–8 for records of financial performance.) The message had certainly started to permeate the system.

One of the reasons that the performance of retails, as a group, turned around was that the new management group took a keen interest in retail operations. Thompson explains that the lessons of 1982 were made permanent by establishing a Retail Review Committee which reviews on a quarterly basis the per-

Three FCL chief executive officers (1988). Standing, left: W. E. (Bill) Bergen, CEO from 1970–79; standing, right: T. P. (Pat) Bell, CEO from 1979–83; seated: Wayne H. Thompson, CEO from 1983 until the present.

formance of retails that are running a local loss (that is, a loss on their own operations before receiving a patronage refund from FCL).

A growing "confidence" became evident in the system's slogans and advertising, another area of growth in the 1980s. In response to delegates' motions at annual meetings, the division started a campaign in 1979 to promote the co-operative "difference" through (mainly) institutional advertising. In 1980 a three-year program was launched on a shared-cost basis between FCL and the retails, which was to emphasize co-operative ownership, control, consumer rights, and CO-OP-label products. The slogan for the campaign was "The Spirit's Growing On."⁴ This was the first in a number of such campaigns, culminating in 1988's anniversary slogans: "Co-ops . . . Together . . . Serving the West!" and "Value . . . Service . . . Guaranteed!"

The revolution in thinking within the system is perhaps illustrated in one small anecdote. In 1963, the Saskatchewan Co-operative Women's Guild annual meeting approved the Rainbow Candle Lighting Ceremony, in which seven candles were lit in turn while the principles they represented for the movement were recited. These included Vision, Courage, Far Horizons, and Growth. They emphasized personal qualities and "the missionary or the educational aspects of the co-operative movement."⁵ At conferences in 1987–88, delegates could see modern versions of the same ceremony. Candles were lit and ceremonies performed, and this time the colours stood for operations like Advertising and Sales, Top-Notch Service, Image, and Target Marketing.

The emphasis is clearly on attention to the bottom line. A sentence repeated numerous times by managers and officials says that "if you have the bottom line, then member relations, communications, democracy, and all those other good things will follow."

Leadership and Stability

Alongside the decisive way the system responded to the 1982 recession, and alongside the new emphasis on marketing, the other key feature of the 1980s is the greatest stability in leadership that FCL has ever experienced.

From 1967–78, FCL had five presidents in eleven years. The fifth, Vern Leland, elected to that office in 1978, has remained ever since. This makes Leland the longest-serving president that FCL has ever had. FCL's First Vice-President, Ed Klassen, is similarly the longest-serving vice-president in FCL's history. (See Appendix 2). The stability in these two positions implies a further stability in the board and its policies, a stability that had been lacking in the 1970s.

When asked the secret of his long tenure, Leland prefers to direct the attention away from himself. "Maybe the board wanted to settle down" after the heated controversies of the 1970s, he suggests. Then, he adds, there is the effect of the increased attention to democratic and communication processes, and the revised structure based on regional vice-presidents and conferences. Leland claims these changes make for more harmonious relationships within the system, and less controversy. Also, he adds, "I'd be willing to bet we were the first co-operative organization of any size to start doing a formal appraisal of the president. Every year the board sits down and . . . we talk." This permits differences to be raised before they become a matter of confrontation or criticism.

Leland's own wide knowledge of the system and his commitment to talking to people should also be mentioned. Leland was a retail manager in the late 1950s, and a retail advisor for FCL in the 1960s, positions that enabled him to get to know how the system worked, and especially to understand the relationship between the retails and the wholesale. Only later did Leland become involved as an elected official and an FCL board member. When he became president, he says, "it really bothered me that we had all these divisions within the system. . . . I set a personal goal to be out of the office at least half the time, to talk to boards of directors, to try and understand the issues, to create a common bond."

Leland's name is mentioned with respect by co-operators, particularly elected officials, throughout the system, including by individuals who have otherwise been critical of FCL, its policies, and its past leaders. Wayne Thompson's name comes up equally often and with equal approval. One manager says Thompson "has taken the organization and turned it in a different direction than we have ever [gone] before in our lives—very market-oriented, very bottom-line-oriented, and convinced we have to be the best at what we do." Another retail manager of long experience in the system gives credit not just to Thompson but to Elmer Wiebe, Ken Hart, and their colleagues—"the new team at Saskatoon"—for being "extremely aggressive and very dedicated."

Thompson, like Leland, prefers to see it as a team approach. "I don't like taking glory which more rightly belongs to a total team . . . in this case the entire senior management and board of directors team." Working together in this way is, says Thompson, "the only way anything is ever accomplished."

Praise such as that quoted above does signify something, however. As the 1970s show, the Co-operative Retailing System can be critical of its leaders. If FCL's current board and managers have the respect of retail presidents and general managers, that is because they have paid attention to the retails and have done their share to earn such support. The positive comments and the team approach both reflect a much more harmonious and unified relationship than existed before 1982.

Pride and Celebration

In its anniversary year, the Co-operative Retailing System exudes a pride in its accomplishments and a determination to make them known and to continue them. In their sixtieth anniversary tour, FCL officials emphasized these themes, speaking of pride in the volume of goods and services which the system has delivered to its members over the years. In food, for example, FCL is a member of the United Grocers Wholesale Group, one of the largest buying groups in Canada. Through this kind of connection, FCL emphasizes that it can provide members with products, services, quality, and prices that are competitive with anyone else in the field. FCL is also an owner and the manager of Interprovincial Cooperative, holder of the CO-OP trademarks. IPCO is another guarantee of the quality and value of the system's products, conducting regular testing of CO-OP and other system brands. "Ours is one of the few companies that do that kind of extensive testing," observes Thompson.

This concern with quality on which the system prides itself also extends to its manufactured products. In May 1988 FCL's plywood plant at Canoe became the first plant in the world outside of Japan to receive the Japanese Agricultural Standard approved stamp. Before granting this standard, Japanese government representatives conducted on-site inspections, evaluated products and grading, and reviewed FCL quality-control measures. Leaders in the system point to this as another example of the kind of achievement which they celebrate in 1988.[6] Similarly in the area of animal feeds, FCL submits its products to intensive laboratory testing and presents them as among the best-balanced, most nutritional, and highest-quality feeds available. FCL is a member of Co-operative

The sawmill turns forty. Anniversary celebrations at the FCL-owned lumber mill at Canoe, British Columbia (1985).

Research Farms, the largest feed-research organization in North America. And the amazing story of the Co-op Refinery is part of every recounting of the system's accomplishments.

As it did for the fiftieth anniversary in 1978, the system attempted during 1988–89 to present these messages to members and to the public with advertising and merchandising campaigns, with special contests, and with a tremendous variety of local events, programs, and community projects.

"Many people," says Thompson, "don't realize the magnitude of our system, how we buy, the quality of our products." This is a message Thompson, President Leland, and their management team have been intent on driving home in 1988.

The Future

There is usually nothing surprising when the leaders of an organization predict growth for that organization, but in the case of FCL, its officers and managers predict growth with conviction, but also with a caution: they suggest growth will not be of the same kind as in the past, when it might have been too uncontrolled. Leland, for example, suggests the system is poised for "good solid growth in the next five to ten years," but also that as pressure for growth returns, the system will resist it.

One area where growth is evident is in the development of the Co-op Upgrader in Regina. The upgrader project, designed to produce a facility for upgrading heavy crude oil and feeding it to the refinery, has been years in the making, requiring careful negotiations with both federal and provincial governments. Harold Empey, who took over the central responsibility for the project in 1983, suggests "it's the largest project, I would guess, that any co-operative in North America has ever been involved in." He notes that the upgrader will be "very significant to our Refinery in that it supplies a guaranteed source of feed stock." It has been a concern of the refinery ever since 1934 that it has been dependent on outside suppliers for its crude oil, in a business where vertical integration is common. What is significant for the refinery is significant for the system, because the refinery has, over the years, been the largest and most reliable earner of savings for members. With the upgrader to support it, the savings on petroleum will not only be assured but increased.

But Empey gives the impression that the short-term economic benefits are the least of what can be expected from the upgrader. Over the long term, he believes it may lead to a "complete restructuring of FCL's balance sheet," providing capital for FCL that will enable the wholesale greatly to reduce its dependence on share equity, and therefore return a greater proportion of annual savings directly to the members in patronage refunds. "Perhaps eighty to ninety percent of the earnings of FCL could be returned to the members," suggests Empey, if upgrader earnings are put into reserves and permitted to replace share capital as a source of financing.

A ceremony to mark "oil in" at the Co-op Upgrader occurred on 9 November 1988. The first day of production was 24 November, when the upgrader processed twenty thousand barrels of crude. The grand opening of the Co-op

Starting a co-operative megaproject. This bulldozer was used in the sod-turning for the Co-op Upgrader (1986), a seven-hundred-million-dollar heavy oil upgrader on the site of the Co-op Refinery in Regina. The upgrader is designed to process Saskatchewan crude oil to an acceptable level for use in the refinery where it will be further processed into motor fuels and other commodities.

Upgrader will be on 24 June 1989, when thousands of people are expected to celebrate the inauguration of the most ambitious project ever undertaken by the Co-operative Retailing System.

In many ways the upgrader is a symbol for the system of what can be achieved by working together, and of what tremendous long-term benefits might be possible.

There are also other areas that have been the subject of attention in the 1980s, and which are likely to remain so in the 1990s. Two that come to mind are the concepts now known as Area Development and Growth from Within—in other words, the structure of local operations, and member relations and involvement. These are old ideas, often reaffirmed, never systematically realized. Is their time coming? For Growth from Within, one senior manager thinks so. "I think there's a better realization today of the need for co-operative education . . . than there was ten years ago," suggests Empey. "I think during the time we were on the fast road," experiencing rapid expansion, "too many of our managers believed all they had to do was to open their doors and let in customers." The 1980s have proved otherwise. "I expect we'll see more action on that [member education] in the next ten years than we've seen in the last twenty."

Conclusion and Questions

Comments about education raise important questions for the system's future, for it will be through education that new generations of co-operators will be motivated to maintain and build upon the strong institutional and economic base that the system has created and which it enjoys in 1988. These comments repeat what co-operators have said for decades, at least since Harry Fowler urged in 1955 that the system's "bigness" must be mitigated by expanded programs to educate members and new ways to involve them. But this raises two questions. First, why have so many retail co-ops done as little as they have to improve their member education programs in the intervening years?—what are the barriers to the kind of educational programs so long considered necessary? Are the barriers within the wholesale, in low priority given to educational programs when resources are allocated? Are they in the retails, in reluctance by local management to expend organizational energy and resources in educational programs? Or are they in the membership, in a lack of desire or need for understanding and involvement? And second, how will these barriers be removed to carry out the action needed in the coming years?

Chief Executive Officer Thompson replies, "better communications and education come with better bottom line results. Once you have the bottom line, the good things happen more frequently. In my opinion, more has happened and is happening today in our system than in any other period of history I'm familiar with." This suggests that the system's operating successes are generating and will continue to generate the kind of programs that will be needed.

Thompson cites the system's strong thrust on training and development as a direction consistent with the needs identified by FCL and retail boards and managers.

In both good times and bad, co-operators must ask themselves whether operating results lead to education and member involvement, or whether the reverse is true—education and member involvement leading to operating results. Perhaps both can be true—they reinforce each other.

The 1980s have produced what seems to be accepted by most of those active in the system as a winning formula—a focus on marketing, image, and efficiency—cutting back and focussing on what co-ops can do with excellence. The success of this formula in producing results on the bottom line, and in motivating member associations and their officers and staff, is evident. But how well have the lessons of the 1980s been learned? Top management personnel state their belief that the system, left to itself, is in danger of falling back into the expansionist errors of the 1970s. How real is that danger? How is it best headed off? If the winning formula has been thoroughly learned, the system's leaders at all levels should also be asking themselves: is today's focus permanent? If co-operatives are ever able to say that they have mastered their competitive circumstances, what will they concentrate upon next?

All of this, however, is raising questions for the future. The striking point about the system's experience in the 1980s is that it has produced an unprecedented degree of unity, goodwill, and pulling together in common causes, even or especially when the going has been tough. Leaders in the wholesale and in retails alike, among directors and among managers, express mutual respect and a uniform and sincere confidence about the system's prospects. Loyalty and optimism are strengths of the system in the late 1980s, and will be tools for whatever projects co-operatives may wish to accomplish in the future.

Celebrating the "oil in" ceremonies at the Co-op Upgrader in Regina on November 9, 1988, were four individuals closely involved with the project. Left to right: Art Postle, Treasurer; Harold Empey, Corporate Secretary; Vern Leland, President; and Bud Dahlstrom, Refinery Manager.

PART NINE: CONCLUSION

Reflections on Sixty Years

Sixty years are not even an average lifetime—the Co-operative Retailing System can hardly be considered old. There are many things that have proven too durable to change in so short a time. These include the basic objectives and organizational principles of the system: autonomous associations of co-operators, working together freely, making decisions democratically, providing service without profit as well as development for communities and for individuals. In many ways these things are now taken for granted, but they should not be, not when we look back to a time not so very long ago when they did not happen. Because co-operators have worked together in this particular way, wealth has been returned directly into communities across western Canada, wealth that in many cases would have flowed elsewhere to the detriment of those communities and of our regional culture and society. Because co-operators worked together in this way, tens of thousands of individuals have gained first-hand experience with democracy, with business, with collective solutions to local problems, and have become better fulfilled and more able individuals as a result.

Of all the constants over the years, perhaps the most stable and consistent theme is that of loyalty. In 1927–28 co-operatives were trying to demonstrate loyalty in banding together to found wholesales. On the one hand, the economic benefits of the co-operative system arise only to the extent that members are loyal. Loyalty provides the co-op with volume, volume earns greater savings, greater savings are returned to the member. That essential message applies to individual members of local retail co-operatives, to retail co-ops that are members of FCL, and to FCL in its dealings with IPCO and other third-tier co-operatives. The history of consumer co-operation is the history of people learning this lesson, and it is not yet complete. But on the other hand, this loyalty, once created, has tended to expand beyond the economic realm. Those who have been most deeply involved in co-operatives have often given evidence of a powerful organizational and philosophical commitment. For these people, co-operatives are not a service, a club, an employer, or an opportunity for personal development, but are more like an extended family, a culture. The Co-operative Retailing System is a regional culture, a kind of voluntary patriotism.

Though sixty years is a short time, it is long enough for tremendous change in the realm of ideas. It has seen a revolution in technology, perhaps more than one, and corresponding dramatic shifts in population and attitudes. At the height of consumer co-operative development, of the spread into new communities, consumer co-operatives made up a people's movement, and a people's movement is very sensitive to this kind of change.

The most obvious change is growth—for most of sixty years co-operatives knew nothing else. Starting, essentially, with nothing but volunteer labour, plus the power people wield by choosing where to spend and where not to spend the money they earn, co-operatives have built up vast physical assets, distribution networks, and productive enterprises. The few individuals who started this growth set an example that ultimately persuaded over three quarters of a million people, so far. But these are only the kinds of growth that are easily measurable. What of growth within people? Growth in quality of life? Perhaps that kind is too often overlooked.

With growth went education and participation. Consumer co-operation spread and became established through education, particularly during three key experiences: the farm movement, the Depression, and World War Two. The farm movement, including not only farm organizations but also other co-operatives, governments, and university departments, sponsored consumer co-operation and provided the basis for the new co-operative wholesale societies founded in 1928–29. These early wholesales struggled to establish the idea of

Dressed up for a party (1988). In commemoration of the Co-operative Retailing System's sixtieth anniversary in 1988, a number of FCL's eighteen-wheeler trucks were decorated with a new motif representative of the mountains and prairies of western Canada.

how a co-op wholesale worked and to get their operations up and running with very little capital and very large expectations (chapters 3–6). The farm movement, including existing agricultural co-ops, provided the fieldwork, the publicity, the study groups, and radio lectures that popularized the idea of consumer co-operation.

The Depression gave this educational activity focus and urgency, and taught people the hard way why co-operation was necessary. Undoubtedly the most important story of the Depression for co-operatives was the way farming communities banded together, epitomized by the zeal and dedication displayed by the farmers who bought shares and built the Co-op Refinery in 1934–35. The creation of the refinery may well be the most important and the most startling event in the history of the Co-operative Retailing System in western Canada. And the wartime experience, particularly the end of the war and the debate over what new order should come with peace and victory, contributed the confidence and the optimism that fuelled the co-operative movement. (See chapters 7–9.) All of these developments reinforced co-operative support, though the key remains that co-operative education was needed to organize this support and realize the potential of co-operation.

With the end of the war, the Co-operative Retailing System entered a new phase with a series of critical mergers. The refinery and the Saskatchewan wholesale united, forming a powerful union of production and distribution, and IPCO and other co-operatives broadened and diversified the co-operative movement. In this buoyant and optimistic environment, with the solid basis of organization and member loyalty provided by the experiences of 1929–45, consumer co-operation became a movement that permeated almost every part of rural western Canada (chapters 10–11).

Growth also meant more formalization of structures and, in a changing economic climate, consolidation. Staff and management became more professional, and co-operatives acquired a distinct organizational rather than philosophical identity. The merger between Manitoba and Saskatchewan in 1955 created FCL, and with it, a kind of co-operative patriotism higher than provincial loyalties, a precedent then extended to Alberta and which today unites the whole of western Canada in a single co-operative system. This "bigness" posed challenges in the areas of member education and communications, and many institutions—the Co-op College, the *Co-operative Consumer* newspaper, public relations federations, women's guilds—helped to meet these challenges and to keep co-operatives growing (chapters 12–15).

In growing, consumer co-operation also made the slow transition from a movement to a system. Gradually, the elements that supported the movement—the specially created educational agencies, the farm movement in the countryside, the urgency provided by the Depression and wartime experiences—dried up, and left co-operative institutions not only to perpetuate themselves by their own efforts but also to compete in a changing economy. But they were strong enough by now to assert themselves as a self-sufficient unit, which is what the "one-system" concept implies. Finding a substitute for the energy and innovation of the movement era perhaps proved more difficult. Co-operatives in some cases tried to work together with organized labour, and attempted to penetrate the major urban centres of western Canada, and they achieved successes in these efforts. By the end of the 1960s, consumer co-operation was no longer simply a farmers' movement specializing in farm products, but an expansive and modern movement aspiring to much more (chapters 16–18).

Some of the changes the movement and system experienced were cyclical. One of these was the recurring debate over centralization *versus* decentralization, a subject apparently decided in 1928, but second-guessed ever since. The essential decision was in favour of local autonomy, but repeatedly, co-operatives were attracted by the advantages of centralization for operational efficiency: the United Farmers' idea of a centralized co-operative, affiliates and associated stores, Alberta Co-op Wholesale stores, the "one-system" idea, and Westland. The history of the system has been more of an uneasy mix of the two principles than is usually admitted; there has never been a final decision as to which will predominate.

Other changes were slow, steady, and presented constant challenges. These included increasing competition, especially from chain stores, and urbanization. The growth of the cities and the decline in rural population faced co-operatives with the challenge of adjusting and consolidating in the country, and expanding in the cities by persuading new generations of urban consumers to participate in co-operatives. Both challenges continue today. The importance of urban co-operative development becomes obvious when a historical perspective is adopted. Compared with forty years ago (and compared with the regional population base) western Canadian cities are immense and still growing. Because of these demographic trends, the success of Calgary Co-op, particularly, has taken on a special magnitude and significance for the system as a whole.

The 1970s were possibly the most unsettled decade in the history of the system. Pressures posed by massive real growth in volume were compounded by unsettled and inflationary conditions. Expansions, especially in certain areas of co-operative production, strained the system's resources, as did the merger with British Columbia, the rescue and rebirth of IPCO, and other large and complex projects. At the same time, relations between retails and FCL were strained, particularly in the debates over Westland Co-operatives, and also more generally in the efforts taken to attain the degree of centralization and integration needed to compete in the marketplace. As an aside to these large events, co-operative development in B.C.—especially urban co-operative development—and service-fee co-operatives posed some as yet unanswered questions about consumer co-operative principles and techniques (chapters 19–21).

By the 1970s, another fundamental social change became apparent: the change from an economy of scarcity to an economy of abundance. In the beginning, in the economy of scarcity, co-operatives promised prosperity and pursued growth, not recklessly, but as soon as they could, horizontally, into every possible line of goods their members could require, and vertically, from retailing into wholesaling, from wholesaling into manufacturing. The goal was to have the co-op supply everything that was needed. In the economy of abundance, consumers have wide choice and competition is intense, sophisticated, and specialized, particularly in the cities. Members shop around, pick and choose, buy from the co-op only when the price is right. Managers, trying hard to compete, appeal not to members' convictions but to their shopping habits; some even become uncomfortable with the idea that members may be philosophically motivated. But then what becomes of the loyalty between the member and the co-operative? What becomes of the personal development of the member?

A couple of decades ago, co-operatives argued with vehemence that competitiveness led not to efficiency but to waste, duplication, frivolous gimmicks at consumers' expense, and costly advertising to manipulate consumers' ideas of their own needs. At that time they claimed that the co-op would be efficient, not because its members would come and go according to prices, but for exactly the opposite reason: they would stay and *tell* the co-op what to do, *control* its policies to ensure service and value. And in the process members would learn to exercise real power, not the apparent power of buying where a sale is on (which means average prices have to increase to pay for the specials), but the real power of ownership and control of the policies that shape the marketplace. Have consumers lost interest in this message?

If the 1970s involved a certain crisis of direction for consumer co-operatives, the 1980s solved that indecision the hard way. The crunch came in 1982 with devastating effect. But the system rose to the challenge and achieved a degree of unity, harmony, and aggressiveness that gives it a distinctive mood and appearance today. It did this by concentrating on working together, on improving retail performance, on aiding retails in difficulty. It did it by concentrating on marketing. Merchandising, advertising, image, and the "bottom line" came to the fore; price, value, and service for the member became heightened concerns. Co-ops concentrated on excellence and tried to "cease being all things to all people." This policy was rewarded with over-all financial success for the system, in spite of a persistent regional recession complicated by depression in key industries. To succeed commercially under such circumstances is a major accomplishment in itself. To forge at the same time a greater sense of unity and purpose is an even more positive achievement (Chapter 22).

How can this diverse history of change and adaptation be summarized? One way is by citing the system's economic contribution. Over sixty years the system has delivered the equivalent of over *thirty-two billion dollars* worth of wholesale goods at 1987 prices to its members (Appendix 5). This vast economic achievement was attained by western people working only with their own resources: the volunteer work of co-op officials, the capital raised from members, and the efforts of co-operative employees and managers. It represents only the wholesale volume of the system; local retails have delivered an even greater volume to their individual members, but there is no way to estimate how much that might be. And to estimate the actual contribution to the western economy, a multiplier effect would have to be applied to indicate the effect as a stimulant to other business. Even these statistics would fail to tell the whole story, because co-ops were also founded to provide *kinds* of services that would not otherwise have been available.

The savings realized by western consumers on the system's wholesaling activities amount to nearly *one billion dollars* over sixty years (Appendix 5). This is money that was kept in western Canada and in western communities when other, competing forms of business would have sent much of it elsewhere. This is money kept active in building and developing the communities in which co-op members live. It is their own money returned to them to be spent again for their own prosperity as well as that of their farms, towns, and cities.

Over its history the Co-operative Retailing System has contributed to western Canadian communities in countless other ways, through community projects and sponsorships, educational scholarships and events, youth camps, safety patrols, lifestyle campaigns, tree-planting, TalentWest and other contests, and many other good works.

In the end, it comes down to people. Three-quarters of a million people are now active in the system and benefiting from its services. Many benefit from the democratic and educational opportunities that co-operatives provide, and thousands are intimately involved as employees or as volunteers and elected officials. To all of these people, co-operatives mean personal fulfillment and development, and this, once again, enriches both members and their communities.

The Co-operative Retailing System will face many challenges in the future: on-going social and economic change, urbanization, changing consumer attitudes and values, the continuing need for integration and co-ordination. It must find new ways to educate consumers who will have new concerns—health, environmental protection, new kinds of convenience or new trends in preferences. There may be economic challenges from competitors. But it seems unlikely that future challenges will be any greater than those the system has already surmounted, in the 1930s, in the 1960s–70s, or in the 1980s. Consumer co-operatives have a proven record of successful adaptation to changing circumstances. In 1988, they have a solid financial and organizational base on which to build. And, most enduring of all, they have a philosophy which may be reformulated and reinterpreted by successive generations, but whose fundamental appeal is universal: the dream of a way of doing business that is ethical, that develops people and gives them power over the marketplace and over their own lives, that reinforces communities, and is fair.

*   *   *

NOTES

Following is a list of archives and their abbreviations used in the notes:
Federated Co-operatives Limited, Saskatoon (FCL)
Glenbow-Alberta Institute, Calgary (Glenbow)
Provincial Archives of Alberta, Edmonton (PAA)
Provincial Archives of British Columbia, Victoria (PABC)
Provincial Archives of Manitoba, Winnipeg (PAM)
Public Archives of Canada, Ottawa (PAC)
Saskatchewan Archives Board, Regina and Saskatoon (SAB)

All minutes, unless otherwise attributed, are from FCL's own archives.

Chapter One

1. "Co-ops Rate Among FinPost 500 for '87," CCA *News Service* 9,10 (31 May 1988), p. 2.

Chapter Two

1. On the British movement see Arnold Bonner, *British Co-operation: The History, Principles, and Organisation of the British Co-operative Movement* (Manchester: Co-operative Union Ltd., 1961).
2. "Report of I.C.A. Commission on Cooperative Principles," *Report of the Twenty-Third Congress at Vienna* (International Cooperative Alliance, 1967), pp. 154–215. The fourth principle was amended in 1969 to substitute the phrase "the economic results" at the start for the original "any surplus or savings." The amended 1969 version is given here. On the ICA see W. P. Watkins, *The International Co-operative Alliance* (London: ICA, 1970).
3. Ian MacPherson, *Each For All: A History of the Co-operative Movement in English Canada, 1900–1945* (Toronto: Macmillan, 1979), pp. 21–23 (quote p. 22).
4. Ibid., p. 24.

Chapter Three

1. See Louis Aubrey Wood, *A History of Farmers' Movements in Canada: The Origins and Development of Agrarian Protest, 1872–1924* (1924; reprint, Toronto: University of Toronto Press, 1975.)
2. MacPherson, *Each For All* (see chap.2, n.3), pp. 51–52.
3. Government of Saskatchewan, Dept. of Agriculture, *First Annual Report of the Co-operative Organization Branch* (Regina: 1915), p. 24.
4. "Interview between Mr. Orlikow and Mr. Shuttleworth," c. 1960, Provincial Archives of Manitoba (PAM), Oral History department, Tape No. 17 (in process of being catalogued). Shuttleworth is quoted here.
5. Interview by J. E. Cook and F. Johnson with Mrs. Nellie Peterson and E. Al Sherratt, Mayerthorpe, Alberta, 28 Feb. 1970, Provincial Archives of Alberta (PAA), 70.282. Peterson is quoted here.
6. F. J. Fitzpatrick, "Co-op History," *The Canadian Credit Institute Bulletin* No. 179 (April 1948), p. 3. Technically, Manitoba had passed a Co-operative Associations Act in 1887, but by a quirk of fate it had been forgotten. So far as can be determined, no association ever took advantage of it.
7. Ibid., pp. 3–4.
8. See Government of Saskatchewan, Dept. of Agriculture, *Thirtieth Annual Report of the Commissioner of Co-operation and Markets* (Regina: 1944), Table VI, p. 177.

264

9. Miss M. Mackintosh, Dept. of Labour, writing in the *Canada Year Book* for 1925, and the same for the following passages.

10. On Keen and the CUC, see Ian MacPherson, *Building and Protecting the Co-operative Movement: A Brief History of the Co-operative Union of Canada 1909–1984* (Ottawa: Co-operative Union of Canada, c. 1985).

11. Waldron to T. W. Mercer, 26 Jan. 1926, and M. to W., 13 Feb. 1926, Public Archives of Canada (PAC), CUC Papers, vol. 37 (General Correspondence 1926 C–D), file "Sask. Co-operation and Markets Branch, Dept. of Agriculture."

12. Wood to Keen, 8 Sept. 1923 and 3 Oct. 1923, CUC, 30 (G.C. 1923 A–H), f. "A."

13. K. to W., 29 Aug. 1923, 25 Sept. 1923, and 11 Oct. 1923, CUC 30 ibid.

14. K. to Waldron, 21 Sept. 1928 and 25 July 1923, CUC, 44 (G.C. 1928 C–E), f. "Co-operation and Markets Branch," and CUC, 30, f. "A" respectively. See also K. to W., 5 Jan. and 8 May 1928, CUC, 44, f. "Co-operation and Markets Branch"; K. to Wood, 29 Aug. 1923, and K. to G. L. Ingram, 21 Nov. 1923, CUC, 30, f. "A."

15. Wood to K. 22 Mar. 1929, CUC, 150 (Societies Correspondence 1929 A–L), f. "Armstrong."

16. K. to S. H. Hosken, 21 Aug. 1923, CUC, 140 (S.C. 1923 A–K), f. "Kamloops" and "Fernie Industrial."

17. *Working Together in W3!* (50th anniversary book for FCL region W3—Brandon—n.p., n.d.), pp. 30–31; "Moline—Pioneer Co-op on the Prairies," *Co-operative Consumer* 19/6/1964, p. 3.

18. *Working Together in W3!*, pp. 52–53.

19. *Co-op Consumer* 19/6/1964, p. 5.

20. Ibid., p. 16.

21. Ibid., p. 9.

22. Ibid., p. 7.

23. Ibid., p. 10, and the same for the following passages.

24. Ibid., p. 12.

25. Ibid., p. 13.

26. I.C.A., *Appendix to National Representatives*, 1927, CUC, 41 (G.C. 1927 E–K), f. "I."

27. See Manitoba Co-operative Wholesale *Annual Report* 1954, pp. 74–75, for a later argument by co-operators to this effect.

28. J. G. Mohl to Keen, 7 Sept. 1929, CUC, 150, f. "Edenwold Co-operative Association Limited."

29. K. to May, 5 May 1927, CUC, 41, f. "I."

30. See Waldron to Frank Scobey, Assiniboia UFC, 21 Mar. 1928, CUC, 44, f. "Co-operation and Markets Branch."

31. See Wood to Keen, 18 April 1929, and K. to W., 26 April 1929, CUC, 150, f. "Armstrong Co-operative Society."

32. K. to Waldron, 27 Sept. 1928, CUC, 44, f. "Co-operation and Markets Branch."

33. Wood to K., 2 Nov. 1929, CUC, 150, f. "Armstrong Co-operative Society."

34. W. to K., 5 Dec., 13 Dec., and 23 Dec. 1929, CUC, 150, ibid.; W. to K., 19 Dec. 1929, 10 Feb. 1930, and 23 Jan. 1930, and W. to Gordon Allen, 7 Sept. 1930, CUC, 152 (S.C. 1930 A–H), f. "Armstrong."

Chapter Four

1. Keen to J. T. Hull, 11 Sept. 1928, PAC, CUC Papers, 46 (G.C. 1928, L–P), f. "M"; quote from K. to Waldron, 4 Aug. 1928, CUC, 44, f. "Co-operation and Markets Branch."

2. "Historical Background of Manitoba Co-operative Wholesale Limited," c. 1948, PAM, MG 14 C 104 (Alexander D. Kennedy Papers), f. 14 ("Manitoba Co-operative Wholesale Limited Managers' School," 1948).

3. MCW *Annual Report* 1954, (see chap. 3, n. 27), pp. 80–81.

4. "Historical Background of MCW."

5. Roy W. Johnston, "Brandon, Jan. 13, 1926" (Original notes in author's possession).

6. Johnston's notes for meetings of purchasing committee, "Boissevain, Mar. 3 1926," and "Deloraine, Mar. 19, 1926," ibid.

7. Johnston's Entry for "Brandon. City Hall. July 29," ibid.

8. MCW *Annual Report* 1954, pp. 82–85. See also *Working Together in W3!* (see chap. 3, n. 17), p. 3.

9. Quote from "Historical Background of MCW"; membership statistics from MCW *Annual Report* 1954, pp. 85–87.

10. Johnston's 1929 memo and the *Tribune* both cited in MCW *Annual Report* 1954, pp. 88–89.

11. MCW *Annual Report* 1954, p. 90.

12. See J. T. Hull, Director of Education and Publicity for Man. Co-op. Wheat Producers, to Keen, 23 May 1928, and K. to H., 28 May 1928, CUC, 46, f. "M."

13. MCW *Annual Report* 1954, p. 93; "Historical Background of MCW."

14. See Keen, "The Birth of a Movement: Reminiscences of a Co-operator," (n.p., c. 1949), p. 33. Keen did analyze the printing plant decision in these terms shortly after it resulted in disaster, but this author did not find evidence that he opposed it in this way at the time the decision was made. Nevertheless, even if Keen's judgment may have been made with the benefit of hindsight, it is fully consistent with his co-operative philosophy and principles. He also wrote in September 1928 that he was unable to write an article on his itinerary in Manitoba because "to do so fully I would have . . . adversely to criticise many things I saw. . . . It does no good to discourage people, many of whom are doing their best." (Keen to Hull, 11 Sept. 1928, CUC, 46, f. "M.")

15. Magwood to Keen, 2 June 1928, CUC, 46, f. "M." Magwood was referring here to a proposal that Manitoba and Alberta progress quickly to set up an interprovincial buying committee. Saskatchewan was not yet organized.

16. MCW *Annual Report* 1954, pp. 92–93.

17. "Historical Background of MCW."

18. MacPherson, *Each For All*, (see chap. 2, n. 3), p. 124 (quote) and p. 161.

19. "Historical Background of MCW." See also *Working Together in W3!*, p. 4.

20. These and following figures from "Organization Report: For the year ending December 31st, 1930," PAM, MG 10 E6 (Manitoba Co-operative Conference. Miscellaneous Papers and Reports).

21. 1930 financial statement, MG 10 E6, ibid.

22. Ibid., p. 51.

Chapter Five

1. *Alberta Institute of Co-operation Proceedings 1928*, p. 44, PAA, 86.307 (Alberta Institute of Co-operation).

2. Ibid., 1929, pp. 162–168.

3. Ibid., 1930, pp. 123 (editor) and 128 (Moan).

4. Report of First Annual Meeting of ACWA, Swindlehurst to Keen, 23 April 1928, PAC, CUC Papers, 43 (G.C. 1928 A–C), f. "Alberta Co-op League and Alberta Coop. Wholesale Assn. Ltd."

5. S. to K., 6? Mar.? 1928, and 23 Aug. 1928, CUC, 43, ibid.

6. Minutes, ACWA executive, 23 Oct. 1928, CUC, 43, ibid. Swindlehurst, the secretary of ACWA, consistently referred to the Board of Directors of ACWA as its "executive," and that terminology is reproduced here since that is the way the documents are labelled.

7. Keen to Moan, 9 Nov. 1928, CUC, 43, ibid.

8. K. to Swindlehurst, 18 Oct. 1928, and S. to K., 12 Oct. 1928, CUC, 43, ibid.

9. Minutes, ACWA executive, 14 Jan. 1929.

10. Minutes, Meeting of ACWA executive with UFA, Calgary, 11 April 1929.

11. Minutes, Meeting of Managers, Edmonton, 13 May 1929.

12. Minutes, Second ACWA Annual Meeting, Olds Agricultural School, 27–28 June 1929.

13. Ibid.

14. Minutes, ACWA executive, 15–16 July 1929.

15. Minutes, ACWA 3rd Annual Meeting, Calgary, 20 Jan. 1930. On how the decisions were made in conjunction with meetings with government and UFA representatives, see ACWA executive, Members' Cloak Room, Parliament Buildings, 25 Sept. 1929, and next meeting, same place, n.d. (likely October or November).

16. Minutes, ACWA Board, 11 Mar. 1930, and Board, directors, and managers meeting, 12 Mar. 1930, both in Edmonton.

17. Minutes, ACWA Board, 13 Mar., 15 April, 21 May, and 20 June 1930.

18. Minutes, ACWA executive, 14 Aug., 15 Oct., 12 Nov., and 9 Dec. 1930.

19. Minutes, ACWA Annual Meeting, Strathcona, Edmonton, 14 Jan. 1931, and directors' report to same.

20. Minutes, ACWA Special General Meeting, Strathcona, 26 Feb. 1931, and statement by A. P. Moan for the meeting, dated 25 Feb. 1931.
21. Minutes, Special Meeting of CWS and UFA "called together by the Premier to discuss the question of collective buying," 25 May 1931.
22. Minutes, Joint CWS-UFA meeting in council chambers at the Parliament Buildings, 23 Jan. 1932, and ACWA exec., 25 Jan. 1932.
23. Minutes, ACWA Annual Meeting, 16 Jan. and 25 April 1934; Minutes of the Alberta Provincial Co-operative Union Convention, CUC-Alberta Branch, Edmonton, 25–26 June 1934; Minutes, ACWA General Meeting, Calgary, 16 Jan. 1935; Minutes, ACWA Board, 10 July 1935.

Chapter Six

1. Jim F. C. Wright, *Prairie Progress: Consumer Co-operation in Saskatchewan* (Saskatoon: Modern Press, 1956), pp. 60–64.
2. Circular to "The Secretary, Co-operative Association," n.d. [fall 1925], PAC, CUC Papers 37 (G.C. 1926 C–D), f. "Co-operative Markets Branch, Saskatchewan Department of Agriculture"; "Report of the Co-operative Wholesale Committee," SAB, B2 (SGGA Papers), VIII, f. 35 ("Co-operative Wholesale Society, 1925–1939").
3. "Cooperative Wholesale Society: History," SAB, ibid.
4. Report quoted in Waldron to Keen, 15 Feb. 1926, CUC, 37, f. "Co-operation and Markets Branch." In the following notes, W. always refers to Waldron and K. always refers to Keen.
5. Untitled verbatim minutes of managers' meeting at Regina legislature, 28 July 1926, CUC, 37, ibid.
6. CUC, 39 (G.C. 1926 N–W), f. "s."
7. W. to K., 19 Feb. 1926, in CUC, 37, f. "Co-operation and Markets Branch."
8. Minutes, Managers' meeting, Regina, 28 July 1926.
9. Keen to Waldron, 23 Feb. 1926, CUC, 37, f. "Co-operation and Markets Branch."
10. W. to Ketcheson and W. to Keen, 11 Aug. 1926, CUC, 37, ibid.
11. K. to Brown, 21 Jan. 1926, in SAB, B2, VIII, f. 35.
12. K. to Waldron, 17 Feb. 1927, CUC, 40 (G.C. 1927 A–D), f. "Agriculture Department, Saskatchewan Co-op & Market Branch W. W."; K. to May, 16 Mar. 1927, CUC, 41 (G.C. 1927 E–K), f. "I."
13. "Cooperative Wholesale Society: History."
14. Waldron to K., 9 Feb. 1928, CUC, 44, f. "Co-operation and Markets Branch, Saskatchewan Department of Agriculture."
15. K. to W. and W. to K., both 6 Mar. 1928, CUC, 44 ibid.
16. "Co-operative Chain of Stores Planned by United Farmers," stamped received 27 Feb., CUC, 44, ibid.
17. Waldron to K., 6 Mar. 1928, CUC, 44, ibid.
18. K. to W., 20 Mar. 1928, CUC, 44, ibid.
19. See K. to W., 12 Mar. 1928, on W.'s political problems; K. to W., 5 April 1928, on his western itinerary; W. to K., 11 April 1928, K. to W., 13 April 1928, and W. to C. G. Davidson, 26 April 1928, on the Lloydminster/Davidson question (also for K.'s second quote); and W. to K. 30 April 1928, on Lloydminster Association. All are in CUC, 44, ibid.
20. Minutes, First Annual Meeting of the Saskatchewan Co-operative Wholesale Society Limited, Saskatoon, 10 April 1929.
21. Waldron to K., 8 and 12 Dec. 1928, W. to Eliason, 20 Dec. 1928 (quote), and E. to W., 24 Dec. 1928, CUC, 44, f. "Co-operation and Markets Branch."
22. Minutes, SCWS Board, Regina, 9 Feb. 1929.
23. Barr, Stewart, and Cumming to UFC, SS, 15. Feb. 1930 (solicitors' report on fraud in the UFC Trading Dept.), SAB, B2, X, f. 69 ("Trading Department: Fraud, 1929–1930"); also K. to Waldron, 19 Feb. 1929, CUC, 48 (G.C. 1929 C), f. "Co-operation and Markets Branch."
24. V. J. Ferguson CA to G. H. Williams, 2 Nov. 1929, SAB, B2, X, f. 69.
25. K. to Waldron, 19 Feb. 1929, CUC, 48, f. "Co-operation and Markets Branch."
26. Ketcheson to K., 7 Mar. 1929, 16 Mar. 1929 (quote), and 27 Mar. 1929 (quote), CUC, 151 (S.C. 1929 M–W), f. "Saskatchewan Co-operative Wholesale Society, Limited."
27. Ketcheson to K., 20 April 1929, 17 May 1929, 28 May 1929, CUC, 151, ibid. The Board of SCWS passed a motion on 25 June 1929 asking the U.G.G. to withdraw from the CUC.

28. See K. to R. S. Law, Secretary of U.G.G., 26 Sept. 1929, CUC, 151, f. "United Grain Growers Limited."

29. Ketcheson to K., 24 Jan. 1930, 10 Mar. 1930, and 11 April 1930, CUC, 154 (S.C. 1930 S–Y), f. "Saskatchewan Co-operative Wholesale."

30. Ketcheson to K., 9 June 1930 (quote), 16 June 1930, 19 June 1930, 14 July 1930, 5 Sept. 1930, and 9 Nov. 1930, CUC, 154, ibid.

31. Minutes, SCWS Board, 25 Feb. 1930, 21 July 1930, and 24 Feb. 1930.

32. Wright, *Prairie Progress*, p. 70; see also Waldron to K., 13 Feb. 1923, and K. to W., 19 Feb. 1923, CUC, 30, f. "A."

Chapter Seven

1. Robert Meyers, *Spirit of the Post Road: A Story of Self-Help Communities* (Altona: Federation of Southern Manitoba Co-operatives, 1955), pp. 6–9 (quote, p. 9).

2. ACWA Board of Directors' Report, 1931.

3. McKay to Keen, 13 Feb. 1932, PAC, CUC Papers, 155 (S.C. 1932 A–D), f. "Saskatchewan Co-operative Wholesale Society Limited."

4. Figures from 1932 Report of the CUC Board, CUC, 2 (Series A Congresses 1915, 1929, 1930, 1932, 1933, 1936), f. "1932 Congress Regina."

5. Sask. Co-operation and Markets Branch, "Financial Results by Geographic Area," CUC, 58 (G.C. 1932 A–D), f. "Co-operation and Markets Branch."

6. A. H. Turner, *Co-operative Purchasing Associations in the Province of Saskatchewan*, Ag. Bulletin No. 95A (Regina: Govt. of Sask., c. 1942), Part II, p. 8, Table II; p. 24; p. 21, Figure 5.

7. Moan to Keen, 14 Mar. 1930, CUC, 152 (S.C. 1930 A–H), f. "Alberta Co-op. Wholesale Assn. Ltd."; Christensen, "Report of Supervisor at Meeting of Alberta Consumers Co-operative Organizations," Edmonton, 10 Nov. 1937, CUC, 87 (G.C. 1938 A–C), f. "C".

8. See 1936 MCW financial statement in PAM, Manitoba Co-op. Conference Papers.

9. As explained in McKay to Keen, 8 Feb. 1932, CUC, 157 (S.C. 1932 P–Y), f. "Saskatchewan Co-operative Wholesale Society Ltd." See also M. to K., 13 Feb. 1932, CUC, 157, ibid, enclosing a draft address to the UFC Convention explaining the scheme.

10. K. to Waldron, 19 Feb. 1932, CUC, 58, f. "Co-operation and Markets Branch"; McKay's draft address to the UFC Convention (see n. 9).

11. Arnason to K., 7 June 1935, CUC, 73 (G.C. 1935 C–I), f. "Co-operation and Markets Branch Saskatchewan Dept. of Sask. [sic]."

12. SFCL *Report to Shareholders* 1945.

13. Swindlehurst, "The Education of Co-operative Employees," 26 Oct. 1932, CUC, 156 (S.C. 1932 E–O), f. "Edgerton Co-operative Assn."

14. Moan to Keen, 3 Dec. 1930, CUC, 152, f. "Alberta Co-op. Wholesale Assn. Ltd."

15. "President's Report to Annual Meeting Winnipeg, Manitoba January 22, 1936," CUC, 169, f. "Manitoba Co-op. Wholesale Ltd."

16. Halsall to Keen, 26 Jan. 1935 and 8 April 1935, CUC, 161.

17. Statistics from "Financial Statement of the Alberta Co operative Wholesale Association Ltd. Year Ended December 31 1936" and "Alberta Co-operative Wholesale Association Ltd. 1936 Sales," CUC, 172 (S.C. 1937 A–C), f. "Alberta Co-operative Wholesale Assn Ltd."

18. "Manitoba Co-operative Wholesale Ltd. Financial Statements and Report: For the year ended 31st December 1936," CUC, 169.

19. Popple to 1937 MCW Annual Meeting, PAM, Manitoba Co-operative Conference B3; Keen to P., 16 Jan. 1937, CUC, 174 (S.C. 1937 H–M), f. "Manitoba Co-operative Wholesale Ltd."

20. See MacPherson, *Each for All*, (see chap. 2, n. 3), pp. 174–176.

21. See the documents in CUC 92.

Chapter Eight

1. "Consumers' Co-operative Refineries Limited: General Outline of Activities Prepared for Board of Directors, Co-operative Wholesale Society, Manchester, England," PAC, CUC Papers, 167 (S.C. 1936 A–C), f. "Cons. Co-op Refineries." Probably written by Harry Fowler. See also *Power to Live By: Commemorating 25 Years of Consumers' Co-operative Refineries Limited* (Regina: FCL, 1960), pp. 5–7.

2. "Co-op Refineries: General Outline of Activities" and Fowler to Keen, 13 June 1936, CUC, 167, ibid.
3. Minutes of meeting of 29 Mar. 1934.
4. Minutes, "An informal meeting of the following Co-Op Associations," 25 May 1934.
5. Minutes, Provisional Board, 3 July 1934.
6. Minutes, Provisional Board, 11 July 1934; on the Wilcox shares, Minutes, Provisional Board, 13 Nov. 1934.
7. Minutes, Provisional Board, 16 July 1934; 21 July 1934; 9 Aug. 1934.
8. Terry Phalen, *Co-operative Leadership: Harry L. Fowler* (Saskatoon: Co-operative College of Canada, 1977), p. 96.
9. Minutes, Executive, 31 Dec. 1934.
10. Phalen, *Co-op Leadership*, p. 96.
11. Ibid., p. 97.
12. Minutes, Board, 15 November 1934; Phalen, *Co-op Leadership*, p. 98.
13. Interview by author with Dorothy Fowler; Phalen, *Co-op Leadership*, pp. 86–88.
14. Phalen, *Co-op Leadership*, 63, 71–72.
15. Ibid., p. 72.
16. Minutes, Board, 18 June 1935; 4 Nov. 1935.
17. Phalen, *Co-op Leadership*, pp. 99–100.
18. Minutes, Board, 4 Nov. 1935, Schedule 8.
19. 1935 production statistics in CUC, 167, f. "Consumers Co-operative Refineries, Regina Sask.";
    Minutes, Board, 27 Dec. 1935.
20. Fowler to Keen, 13 June 1936, CUC, 167, f. "Cons. Co-op Refineries"; Minutes, Board, 17 Jan. 1936.
21. Minutes, Board, 6 July 1936; Fowler to Keen, 13 June 1936, as cited above.
22. Phalen, *Co-op Leadership*, p. 109.
23. Minutes, Board, 22 April 1936.
24. Fowler to Keen, 13 June 1936, and attached documentation and correspondence, CUC, 167.
25. Phalen, *Co-op Leadership*, pp. 113–115.
26. Minutes, Board, 6 July 1936.
27. *Power to Live By*, p. 9; and FCL *Annual Report*, 1959, p. 34.
28. Minutes, Board, 22 Dec. 1936.
29. *Power to Live By*, p. 9.

Chapter Nine

1. Popple's speech in PAC, CUC Papers, 169 (S.C. 1936 H–M).
2. Popple's remarks to MCW 1937 Annual Meeting, PAM, Manitoba Co-operative Conference B2.
3. Meyers, *Spirit of the Post Road*, (see chap. 7, n. 1), pp. 11–22 and 27.
4. Ibid., p. 48.
5. Ibid., pp. 39–46.
6. "Red River Consumer Co-operative Ltd. 1951–1975," and Christine White's comments quoted in booklet "Red River Co-op Fortieth Anniversary, 1937–1977," both in PAM, Longman Papers, f. 21.
7. Leif Osback, "The 'Fram Co-op'," in *Hoofprints and Homesteading: A History of Kinsella and Area*; Fram Co-operative Consumers Ltd., Memorandum of Association, 15 July 1937 (shown to the author by Leif Osback); and interview with Leif Osback by the author.
8. "The Co-operative Promotion Board. Broadcast No. 15, February 8 1937," in PAM, MG10 E6, "Manitoba Co-operative Conference. Minutes of Meetings, 1934–37."
9. Keen to Waldron, 27 July 1934, CUC, 71 (G.C. 1934 S–W), f. "W."
10. W. to K., 6 April 1932, CUC, 58 (G.C. 1932 A–C), f. "Co-operation and Markets Branch."
11. K. to Christensen, 15 Sept. 1937, CUC, 172 (S.C. 1937 A–C), f. "Alberta Section."
12. Dorothy Fowler, "A Tribute to the Pioneers of the World's First Co-op Refinery," Mar., 1984 (speech to annual meeting of FCL).
13 "Provincial Conference of Co-operative Trading Associations," minutes of meeting of 23–24 July 1935, in SAB, R261, f. XXXI.1.
14 Halsall to Keen, 29 Dec. 1936, CUC, 167 (S.C. 1936 A–C), f. "Alberta Section."

15. H. to K., 15 Feb. 1937, CUC, 172, f. "Alberta Section"; Christensen to H., 8 Sept. 1937, copy in ibid. See also C. to K., 25 June 1937, CUC, 81 (G.C. 1937 A–C), f. "Alberta—Supervisor of Co-operative Activities."
16. Minutes, Meeting of the Consumer Co-operatives in Southern Alberta, 27 Oct. 1938, CUC, 87 (G.C. 1938 A–C), f. "C."
17. See documents in CUC 87, ibid., and in CUC, 81 f. "Alberta—Supervisor of Co-operative Activities."
18. See "Programme for Short Course for Co-operators," CUC, 88 (G.C. 1938 C–H), f. "Co-operation and Markets Branch."
19. "School for Co-op Managers Proves a Real Success," *Co-op News*, 16,3 (Mar. 1942), p. 18.
20. "Terrace Co-op Celebrates 30th Anniversary," *Terrace Herald*, 17 Nov. 1976.
21. *Handbook of the Manitoba Federation of Agriculture*, pp. 7–13, PAM, Kennedy Papers, f. 15 "Manitoba Federation of Agriculture."
22. Ibid., p. 6.
23. Minutes, Board of Directors, Publications Co-operative Association Limited, 7 June 1940 and 17 Jan. 1941.
24. Minutes, Board, Publications Co-op. Assoc. Ltd., 21 Mar. 1941 and 20 Nov. 1941.
25. Keen to M. Llewelyn Davies, General Secretary of the Women's Co-operative Guild, London, 11 July 1921, CUC, 26 (G.C. 1921, A–J).
26. See K. to Arnason, 27 June 1932, CUC, 58.
27. Fowler, "A Tribute to the Pioneers."
28. *History of the Saskatchewan Co-operative Women's Guild: Jubilee Edition*, n.p., 1955, p. 9.
29. Ibid.
30. Ibid., p. 9.
31. Norman P. Priestley, "Co-operative Institutions: Clause Six of the C.C.F. Manifesto," CUC, 71, f. "W."
32. Keen to Halsall, 23 Aug. 1932, CUC, 156, f. "Killam."
33. Woodsworth to K., 15 May 1934, and Wood to K., 14 May and 3 Dec. 1934, CUC, 71, f. "W."
34. H. W. Wood, "Political Party System Formed on Competitive Basis Offers no Hope of Bringing Order out of the Present Confusion", article distributed to UFA speakers as reference notes, c. 1935, PAA, 83.115/141.
35. See PAA 74.353 on UFA Coronation Constituency Co-operative Association.
36. Halsall to Keen, 14 Sept. 1935, CUC, 161 (S.C. 1935 A–D), f. "Alberta CWS."

Chapter Ten

1. SCWS *Annual Report* 1941, pp. 5–7.
2. Ibid., p. 33; 1943, p. 4.
3. "Convenor's Address" appended to "Report of the Conference of B.C. Co-operatives on Collective Buying," PAC, CUC Papers, 92 (G.C. 1939 A–C), f. "Co-op. Wholesale of B.C."
4. "Co-operation Has Wide Basis, Deep Foundation," *Co-op Consumer* 6,18 (15 Jan. 1945), p.1.
5. See the comments by James Jackson, President of the Alberta Farmers' Union, ibid.
6. *Alberta Co-operative Leaders* (n.p.: Alberta Livestock Co-op, n.d.), p. 30, and the same for the following comments by Love.
7. For example, ibid., appendix, p. 54.
8. British Columbia Co-operative *News Service*, 1,7 (March 1944). See also "Outline of the History of the Co-operative Movement in British Columbia," PABC, BC Co-op. Union 13, f. 1.
9. Government of Saskatchewan, Dept. of Agriculture, *Thirtieth Annual Report of the Commissioner of Co-operation and Markets* (Regina, 1944), Table VI, p. 176.
10. SCWS *Annual Reports* 1938, 1939, 1940, 1941, 1942, 1943; SFCL *Report to Shareholders* for Special General Meeting, June 13–15, 1945 (including statistics on CCRL).
11. On the feed plants of the 1940s see Jack Trevena, *A Diary of Prairie Co-operation* (Saskatoon: Co-operative College of Canada, 1976, note 442, p. 171; note 473, p. 183; and note 480, p. 183.
12. See ibid., note 430, p. 168.
13. SCWS *Annual Report* 1941, p. 21.
14. SCWS and SFCL *Annual Reports* 1938–1945. On the origins of CCIL see MacPherson, *Each for All* (see chap. 2, n. 3), pp. 196–197.
15. "Revolving Door Plan Explained," *Co-op Consumer* 1,1 (15 Feb. 1939), p. 2.

16. "Wholesale Society Adopts the Revolving Door Plan," *Co-op Consumer* 1,6 (1 May 1939), p. 1.
17. SCWS *Annual Report* 1941, pp. 29–30.
18. Minutes, Conference of Co-op. Store Managers, Saskatoon, 26–27 Jan. 1938.
19. Minutes, Managers' Committee, 26 Sept. 1940; Minutes, Managers' Meeting, Saskatoon, 16 Oct. 1939.
20. Minutes, Saskatchewan Co-operative Wholesale Society, Saskatoon, 1 May 1939, CUC, 185 (S.C. 1939 M–S), f. "Saskatchewan Co-op Wholesale."
21. McKay to Keen, 7 and 30 Aug. 1939, CUC, 185, ibid.
22. SCWS *Annual Reports* 1940–1943.
23. Norman M. Macleod, "Prairies Afire with Enthusiasm for Co-operation," *The Toronto Daily Star*, cited in the *Canadian Co-operator* 35,11 (Nov. 1944), p. 18.
24. Minutes, SFCL Board of Directors, 20–22 Aug. 1946 (Manager's Report, appended).
25. Terry Phalen, "The Taxation Story," *Canadian Co-operative Digest* 14,4 (Winter 1971–72), pp. 4–25; here, p. 13.
26. See "Taxation of Co-operatives and Credit Unions" (Ottawa: CUC, 1978), p. 8.
27. Phalen, "Taxation Story," p. 9.
28. See for example, SFCL *Annual Report* 1947, p. 10.
29. Ibid.; also Phalen, "Taxation Story," pp. 9–10.
30. Phalen, "Taxation Story," p. 11.
31. Joe Dierker, "The Current Taxation Position of Co-operatives," *Canadian Co-operative Digest* 14,4 (Winter 1971–72), pp. 39–44; here p. 40.
32. Don Slimmon, *People and Progress: A Co-op Story*, (Brandon: self-published, n.d.)
33. *Working Together in W3!* (see chap. 3, n. 17), pp. 8–10.
34. Ibid., pp. 11–15.
35. Ibid., pp. 56–57.
36. Eric Hopkins, "The Place of the Co-op Store in the Community," *Co-op News* 29, 8 (Aug. 1955), pp. 1 and 6–7.
37. MCW *Annual Report* 1954, p. 68.

Chapter Eleven

1. Minutes, Joint Meeting of the Boards of C.C.R.L. and S.C.W.S., Regina, 13 Mar. 1944.
2. Minutes, Special Meeting of the Saskatchewan Co-operative Wholesale Society Limited and Consumers' Co-operative Refineries Limited, Saskatoon, 8 June 1944.
3. Ibid.
4. Interview by the author with Dorothy Fowler; see also Phalen, *Co-op Leadership* (see chap. 8, n. 8), pp. 155–156.
5. Articles of Association of SCWS, as amended to 1941, FCL Archives.
6. Minutes, SFCL Board, 20–22 Aug. 1946, pp. 6–7. See also minutes of 15–17 Oct. for Fowler's second quotation, a clarification to the 20–22 Aug. minutes.
7. Minutes, SFCL Board, 20–22 Aug. 1946, pp. 14–15.
8. Minutes, SFCL Board, 15–17 Oct. 1946, esp. McKay's "Report on Negotiations with Labour Unions" dated 16 Oct. 1947.
9. Minutes, SFCL Board, 23 Nov. 1946, p. 8.
10. Minutes, SFCL Board, 17–20 Dec. 1946, pp. 14–17, and 21–23 Jan. 1947, p. 14, where the appointments were confirmed.
11. MCW *Annual Report* 1954, p. 30.

Chapter Twelve

1. MCW *Annual Report* 1954, pp. 66–67.
2. Province of Saskatchewan, *Royal Commission on Agriculture and Rural Life*, Report #1, "The Scope and Character of the Investigation" (1955).
3. Ibid., "Mechanization and Farm Costs: A Summary," pp. 7 and 11.
4. "Alert, Interested, and Loyal Members Are the Guarantee of Steady Co-op Success," *Co-op News* 27,1 (Jan. 1953), p. 10.
5. MCW *Annual Report* 1954, chart on p. 31.

6. Government of Saskatchewan, Dept. of Co-operation and Co-operative Development, *Thirteenth Annual Report* 1957, Chart 1, p. 30.
7. "The Next Step Forward in Co-operative Retailing in British Columbia," in PABC, Co-op Union of B.C. Papers 9, f. 2, "BC Co-op Wholesale Society 1951."
8. MCW *Annual Report* 1954, pp. 69–71.
9. "A Challenge to Consolidate Issued to Co-ops by J. Russell Love," *Co-op News* 28,3 (Mar. 1954), p. 8. See also the February issue.
10. *Proceedings of the Fifth Annual Conference on Co-operative Education and Organization*, Univ. of Sask., 3–6 July 1956, p. 59.
11. MCW *Annual Report* 1954, p. 7.
12. "Financing and Control of Manitoba Co-operative Wholesale Limited," PAM, Kennedy Papers, f. 14.
13. MCW *Annual Report* 1954, p. 6; Urwin's speech in *Proceedings of the Fifth Annual Conference on Co-operative Education and Organization*, p. 58.
14. "Co-op Manager Says Merger Not Sell-Out," Winnipeg *Tribune,* 18 Dec. 1954.
15. "Co-op Delegates Vote for Merger," Winnipeg *Tribune* 6 Jan. 1955.
16. MCW *Annual Report* 1954, p. 8.
17. Ibid.
18. *Co-op Manager's Bulletin #5*, May 1956, p. 4.
19. "Report to the Special Meeting of Shareholders, Federated Co-operatives Limited. June 1955," in PAM, Kennedy Papers, f. 18 (Foreword by H. L. Fowler).
20. Halsall to Keen, 26 Jan. 1935, PAC, CUC Papers, 161 (S.C. 1935 A–D), f. "Alberta C.W.S.";
    Minutes, meeting on inter-provincial co-operative wholesaling, Saskatoon, 15 Nov. 1938.
21. *The Story of Interprovincial Co-operatives Limited* (Winnipeg?: n.p., 1949), pp. 7–8, 12, 18.
22. Ibid., p. 11.
23. Ibid., pp. 20–21, and "Plan and Policy of Inter-Provincial Co-operatives Limited," CUC, 200 (S.C. 1944 A–K), f. "Alberta Co-op. Whlse."
24. SFCL *Report to Shareholders* 1945, p. 23; Minutes, Board of Directors of Consumers' Co-operative Mills Limited, 16 Oct. 1946.

Chapter Thirteen

1. ACWA *Annual Report* 1951 (for year ending 31 Jan. 1952).
2. ACWA Financial Statements to 31 Jan. 1952, Glenbow, M2369, f. 132. The statements show a deficit account of $399,788.39 and a total net loss of $387,920.27. Later financial summaries, however, seem to treat this not as an operating loss but as a capital item offset by long-term liabilities, hence the positive earnings indicated in Appendix 3. Apparently, at the time of the financial statement, the long-term financing of the purchase of the UFA stores had not yet been worked out. ACWA financial statements, starting with 1951, include the sales and operating savings or losses of the former UFA retails.
3. ACWA *Annual Report* 1951.
4. Minutes, Meeting regarding refinancing A.C.W.A., Edmonton, 20 Dec. 1952, Glenbow, M2369, f. 132.
5. Ibid.
6. For this and the following passages see the pamphlets, speeches, and press releases concerning UFA history, in Glenbow, M1749, f. 41, "U.F.A. Co-operative Limited, 1957–65."
7. UFA Co-op *Annual Report* 1958 (to 12–14 Nov. 1958 Annual Meeting), pp. 7–13.
8. "Memo to the Board of Directors," n.d., Glenbow, M1749, f. 40, and the same source for the following passages.
9. J. R. Love, "Review of the Amalgamation Issue," pamphlet published by ACWA, n.d. (1958), in Glenbow, M1749, ibid., and the same for his following comments.
10. As published by the UFA Co-op in "Statement on Amalgamation Issue," in Glenbow, M1749, ibid., and the same for the following passages.
11. J. R. Love, "In Reply to Criticisms," pamphlet published by ACWA, n.d. (1958), in Glenbow, M1749, ibid.
12. "Report of the Committee to Obtain the Facts on a Proposed Amalgamation of the U.F.A. Co-op. and A.C.W.A.—1958 (Presented to FUA Convention by President A. Platt)," Glenbow, M1749, ibid.
13. Ibid, and the same for the following passages.

14. FCL *Annual Report* 1959, pp. 11–12.

15. Notes on Love's address taken by R. A. Findlay of Alberta Wheat Pool, Findlay to A. T. Baker, 3 Feb. 1960, Glenbow, M2369, f. 132, "Correspondence, reports, etc., 1951–1960 re Alberta Co-operative Wholesale Association."

16. FCL *Annual Report* 1960, pp. 17–20.

17. Ibid., pp. 20 and 28–29.

18. FCL Financial Statements, 1961 and 1962.

19. "A.C.W.A.—F.C.L. Merger Sanctioned," *Co-op News* 34,2 (Feb. 1960), p. 7.

Chapter Fourteen

1. J. R. Love, "Members' Capital in Co-operatives," *Co-op News* 28,12 (Dec. 1954), p. 21.

2. "Co-ops Faltering Says Economist," Winnipeg *Tribune,* 16 Jan. 1958.

3. "Relations with the General Membership" (1948 managers' course document), PAM, Kennedy Papers, f. 14, and the same for the following passages.

4. *Proceedings of the Fifth Annual School on Co-operative Education and Organization* (see chap. 12, n. 10), pp. 26–27, and p. 27 for the following passages.

5. "Co-operative Member in the '60s," *Co-op News* 34,5 (May 1960), p. 4.

6. H. E. Chapman, J. A. Fehr, and William Hlushko, "Western Co-operative College (Study of an Agency)," project study for Education 480, Univ. of Sask., 1963 (lent to the author by Chapman), p. 8.

7. "Manitoba Co-op Plans New School," Winnipeg *Tribune,* 20 Mar. 1953.

8. FCL *Annual Report* 1956, p. 35.

9. FCL *Annual Report* 1958, p. 37.

10. FCL *Annual Reports* 1959, p. 46, and 1960, pp. 12–13.

11. *Co-op Consumer* 19,7 (5 April 1957).

12. FCL *Annual Reports* 1958, p. 42; 1959, p. 43; 1960, p. 53; and 1964, p. 41.

13. FCL *Annual Report* 1958, p. 42.

14. FCL *Annual Report* 1956, p. 14.

15. FCL *Annual Report* 1957, pp. 12–13.

16. FCL *Annual Report* 1960, pp. 11–12.

17. FCL *Annual Report* 1961, p. 20.

18. FCL *Annual Report* 1958, p. 41.

19. FCL *Annual Report* 1959, p. 43.

Chapter Fifteen

1. See Chapter Nine on the origins and early development of the guilds.

2. FCL *Annual Report* 1958, p. 39.

3. Ibid., p. 8; FCL *Annual Reports* 1959, p. 9; 1964, pp. 42–43.

4. FCL *Annual Report* 1961, pp.17–18.

5. FCL *Annual Report* 1965, pp. 56–57.

6. FCL *Annual Report* 1964, p. 41.

7. "Challenge Facing Consumers Speaker Tells Winnipeg Meet," *Manitoba Co-operator* 11,42 (20 May 1954), p. 5.

8. Ibid., 28,12 (Dec. 1954), p. 29.

9. Fowler, "A Tribute to the Pioneers" (see chap. 9, n. 12).

10. *History of the Saskatchewan Co-operative Women's Guild* (see chap. 9, n. 28), p. 18; pp. 20–22. The name *Women's Co-operative Guild* was used until 1956, when incorporation under the Societies Act was granted, and the name changed to the form used in the present chapter.

11. Ibid., pp. 13–14.

12. Ibid., pp. 17–20.

13. Ibid., pp. 15–16.

14. Statement from "Saskatchewan Wheat Pool Flour Mill Division," 14 May 1958, PAM, P255, f. 6.

15. "Why Do We Need Co-op Labels?, n.d. [SFCL? 1953?], PAM, P255, f. 6, "Product Demonstration/ Information Manual."

16. FCL *Annual Report* 1958, p. 44.

17. "Co-op—Private Label Program," PABC, Add. MSS. 2460 (BC Co-op Union Papers), box 9 ("British Columbia Co-operative Wholesale Society"), f. 1, "BC Co-op Wholesale Society Introduction 1950." There is no date on this document; it dates from 1960 or later.
18. Ibid.
19. See memo from J. A. Slimmon dated 13 Mar. 1956 and other documents, in PAM, P255, f. 7, "Donna Rochdale 1955–1964."
20. FCL *Annual Report* 1960, p. 35.
21. MFAC *Annual Report* for year ended 31 May 1958, pp. 25–26.
22. Manitoba Women's Co-operative Guild *Mirror*, 1957, p. 3.
23. Ibid.
24. Ibid., p. 4.
25. Ibid.
26. Ibid., pp. 5 and 6.
27. Ibid., report on Alberta guild meeting, p. 9; minutes, Manitoba Women's Co-operative Guild Annual Meeting, 1957, in PAM Longman Papers, f. 20.
28. "Annual Report of Co-op Women's Guilds — Manitoba" (n.d., c. 1959), PAM, MWCG Papers, f. 2, "General and Executive Minutes 1951–1959."
29. See the MCWG *Mirror* 1967 and Lillian M. Russell to G. W. Leckie, 6 Dec. 1951, MCWG Papers, P254, f. 1, "Correspondence 1951–1965."
30. MCWG *Mirror* 1963, p. 6.
31. Swift Current Co-operative Women's Guild, *The Golden Curtain Rises: Poetry and Prose on Swift Current and District* (Swift Current: 1964).
32. See PAM, MWCG Papers, P254–257.
33. *History of Saskatchewan Co-operative Women's Guild*, p. 5.
34. MWCG *Mirror* 1958.
35. Memo "To Winnipeg Co-op Women's Guild and Rossmere Co-op Women's Guild," 27 Oct. 1965, PAM, MWCG Papers, f. 1.
36. MWCG Papers, pp. 40–41.

Chapter Sixteen

1. FCL *Annual Report* 1959, pp. 47–49.
2. FCL *Annual Report* 1964, p. 29.
3. Ibid., p. 30.
4. Ibid., pp. 44–45.
5. Ibid., p. 48.
6. Ibid., pp. 48–49.
7. Ibid., p. 51, and the same for the following passages.
8. Resolution No. 22, Minutes, FCL Annual Meeting, Saskatoon, 6–8 Feb. 1966.
9. "Regional Development Interest Grows," "West-Central Group Picks Control System," and "Co-ops in Southeast Not Agreed on Mergers," *Co-op Consumer* 30,2 (30 Jan. 1968), pp. 10–11.
10. "Independence Saps Strength, says Boyes," *Co-op Consumer* 30,3 (13 Feb. 1968), p. 1.
11. Government of Saskatchewan, Dept. of Co-operation and Co-operative Development, "Case Study of the Yorkton Co-operative Committee System of Member Representation," SAB, R110, f. 70a.
12. Government of Saskatchewan, Dept. of Co-operation and Co-operative Development, "Case Study of the Committee Structure, Function and Member Attitudes for the Pioneer Co-operative Association, Limited," SAB, R110, f. 70a.
13. See Susan Halliday Conly, *Co-operative Ventures and Visions: A History Honouring the 25th Anniversary of The Delta Co-operative Association Limited* (Saskatoon: FCL, c. 1987), pp. 1 and 52.
14. Rob and Nancy Millar, *A History of the Calgary Co-op* (Saskatoon: Modern Press, c. 1981), pp. 26–32.
15. Don Slimmon, "Co-ops: Heading Down the Wrong Road?," *Credit Union Way* c. 1983 (off-print supplied to author by Slimmon); Hume Compton, "Who's minding the store?," *The Co-op Member Bulletin* No. 9 (Nov. 1984), apparently a reprint from *The Atlantic Co-operator*, Aug. 1984; Ray Labossière, "Ray Labossière Has His Say," *The Co-op Member Bulletin* No. 2 (Nov. 1983). *The Co-op Member Bulletin* was published by Compton from Nanaimo.

16. See FCL *Annual Report* 1967, p. 27.
17. FCL *Annual Reports* 1968–71, pp. 46–47.
18. FCL *Annual Report* 1964, pp. 50–51.

Chapter Seventeen

1. Kurt W. Wetzel and Daniel G. Gallagher, "A Conceptual Analysis of Labour Relations in Cooperatives," *Economic and Industrial Democracy* 8 (1987), pp. 517–540; here, p. 517, and the same for the following passage.
2. "Labor Leader Urges Labor-Farm Co-operation," *Co-op News* 24,4 (April 1950), p. 19.
3. As reported in "Two Hands Are Better Than One," leaflet issued by B.C. Co-op. Union, n.d. (c. 1960), in PABC, B.C. Co-op. Union Papers, b. 13, f. 5.
4. FCL *Annual Report* 1956, pp. 9–10.
5. "Co-operatives and Labour Unions," pamphlet published by CLC and CUC, n.d.
6. Ibid.
7. FCL *Annual Report* 1957, p. 9.
8. "Employees Choose Union Under 'Hands-Off' Policy," Winnipeg *Tribune*, 24 June 1958.
9. "Three Week Holiday Set," Winnipeg *Tribune*, 24 June 1958.
10. B. Johnsrude, circular to B.C. co-op managers, 9 Oct. 1963, B.C. Co-op Union Papers, b. 13, f. 5.
11. "A presentation to the National Conference on Labour Relations in Co-ops — Toronto, Ontario, November 12, 1963," B.C. Co-op Union Papers, and the same for the following passages.
12. Ibid.
13. Wetzel and Gallagher, "Labour Relations in Co-operatives," pp. 532–533.
14. Ibid., pp. 536, 531, and 536 respectively for the three quotations.
15. "Surrey Co-op in Receivership," clipping from *The Province* in PABC clipping file.

Chapter Eighteen

1. MacPherson, *Each for All* (see chap. 2, n. 3), pp. 22–23, 63 and 80.
2. Ibid., pp. 80–81.
3. "City Co-ops Successful: City Co-ops in Regina and Saskatoon Do Over $6 Million in Business," *Co-op News* 28,4 (April 1954), p. 10; "Canada's Largest Department Store Opens in Regina," *Co-op News* 29,8 (Aug. 1955), p. 10. See also MCW *Annual Report* 1954, p. 9, holding the Saskatchewan cities up as an example for Manitoba.
4. "City Co-ops Successful."
5. *Proceedings of the Fifth Annual School on Co-operative Education and Organization* (see chap. 12, n. 10), p. 24.
6. Minutes, SFCL Board, 25–27 Nov. 1946, p. 16.
7. See materials for the Red River Co-op Special Membership Meeting (1960 or 1961) in PAM, Magnus Eliason Papers #352, and the same for the following information on Red River management contracts and expansions. See also "Red River Co-op Fortieth Anniversary, 1937–77," in PAM, Longman Papers, f. 21, "Red River Consumer Co-operative Limited 1951–1975," on the store closed in 1952 and the subsequent expansions.
8. FCL *Annual Report* 1958, p. 11.
9. "Opening of the New Winnipeg Co-op Super Market: Opening Address by J. R. Love," *Co-op News* 32,7 (July 1958), pp. 5 and 7.
10. See the documents concerning the Red River Co-op special membership meeting, 1960 or 1961, Magnus Eliason Papers #352.
11. FCL *Annual Report* 1958, pp. 10–11; "Federated Co-operatives To Make Largest Cash Repayment In Its History," *Co-op News* 34,1 (Jan. 1960), pp. 2–3.
12. "Red River Co-op Fortieth Anniversary, 1937–77," Longman Papers.
13. Manitoba Government *Report on Co-operatives* 1975, and the same for the following passages.
14. "Edmonton Co-operators Make Big Decision," *Co-op News* 34,7 (July 1960), p. 1; and "Edmonton Co-op Opening The Talk of The Town," ibid., 35,11 (Nov. 1961), p. 1.
15. Millar and Millar, *A History of the Calgary Co-op* (see chap. 16, n. 14), p. 11.
16. Ibid., pp. 10–12.
17. Ibid., pp. 19–20.
18. Ibid., pp. 19–25.

19. Quoted in Ibid., p. 25.
20. Ibid., pp. 19–38 and 9.
21. "Calgary Co-op Shows Another Growth Year," Canadian Co-operative Association *News Service* 9,1 (15 Jan. 1988), pp. 2–3 (comment from Calgary Co-op officials based on author's own interviews).
22. *Sixty Proud Years*, FCL insert to Mar. 1988 *Saskatchewan Report*, p. 7.
23. Millar and Millar, *Calgary Co-op*, p. 49.
24. Ibid., pp. 37–39.

Chapter Nineteen

1. Greg Yost, "Sleeping Giant Awakens in Saskatchewan: Co-op Sales Skyrocketing," Winnipeg *Tribune*, 28 June 1974.
2. FCL *Annual Report* 1967, p. 27 (FCL's investments detailed on p. 63).
3. FCL *Annual Reports* 1968, p. 39; 1969, p. 39; and 1970, p. 36.
4. FCL *Annual Report* 1970, pp. 10–11 and 36.
5. See Appendices. Painstaking readers will note that FCL's sales did not fall from 1969 to 1970; however, 1970 was the year of merger with B.C., and if the B.C. wholesale's volume is included in the 1969 total, then the 1970 volume does represent a decrease.
6. The figure of 138 percent real growth is from FCL's own calculations during the 1970s, based on the particular commodities it handled, and is derived from annual reports. The statistics in Appendix 5 are deflated with a general index which is less accurate, though using it enables comparisons over a longer period. This index somewhat underestimates the extent of inflation during the 1970s for the reasons noted in the appendix. According to the figures in Appendix 5, the real growth during the 1970s would have been 177 percent, which is an exaggeration.
7. FCL *Annual Report* 1979, p. 16, chart.
8. FCL and Westland Co-operatives *Annual Report* 1973, pp. 6–8.
9. Ibid., p. 17; "Labor Congress Has Tough Day at Food Inquiry," Winnipeg *Tribune*, 21 Mar. 1973.
10. "Federated Co-op To Double Capacity," Winnipeg *Tribune*, 13 June 1973, and the same for the following quotations.
11. FCL and Westland Co-ops *Annual Report* 1973, pp. 6 and 17.
12. FCL *Annual Report* 1972, pp. 10–11.
13. Ibid., p. 12, and ff. for the following information in the text.
14. FCL *Annual Report* 1978, pp. 21–22; see also 1977, p. 27.
15. FCL and Westland Co-ops *Annual Report* 1974, p. 80.
16. Ibid., p. 27.
17. FCL *Annual Reports* 1969, p. 17; 1970, p. 4.
18. FCL *Annual Report* 1972, pp. 13–14; FCL and Westland Co-ops *Annual Report* 1973, pp. 16–17. See also 1974, pp. 23–26; 1976, p. 13.
19. Minutes, FCL and Westland Co-ops Annual Meeting, 24–27 Feb. 1976, p. 8.
20. Minutes, FCL and Westland Co-ops Annual Meeting, 22–25 Feb. 1977, pp. 13–14 and 16.
21. Minutes, FCL and Westland Co-ops Annual Meeting, 25–28 Feb. 1975, p. 7.
22. FCL *Annual Report* 1979, p. 31, and the same for the following passages.

Chapter Twenty

1. See the remarks by Bill Bergen quoted at the start of Chapter 19.
2. FCL *Annual Report* 1972, p. 55, and 55 ff. for the following passages.
3. FCL and Westland Co-ops *Annual Report* 1976, as cited on the back cover.
4. FCL and Westland Co-ops *Annual Report* 1974, pp. 77–78.
5. "Consumer Co-ops" sheet, "Careers in Consumer Co-operatives" folder in PABC, B.C. Co-op Union Papers, b. 13, f. 2.
6. FCL and Westland Co-ops *Annual Report* 1974, p. 80.
7. See FCL *Annual Reports* 1967, p. 42; 1968, p. 58; 1969, pp. 9–11; 1970, p. 9.
8. FCL and Westland Co-ops *Annual Report* 1973, p. 62.
9. In PABC, B.C. Co-op Union Papers, b. 13, f. 3.
10. FCL and Westland Co-ops *Annual Report* 1972, p. 18, and the same for the following passages.
11. FCL and Westland Co-ops *Annual Report* 1973, p. 64.

12. Minutes, FCL Annual Meeting, 24–27 Feb. 1976, pp. 19–26 (Sinclair's comments, p. 26).
13. Ibid., pp. 13–14.
14. See also Chapter Sixteen on this subject.
15. FCL *Annual Report* 1972, p. 61.
16. FCL and Westland Co-ops *Annual Report* 1973, pp. 81 and 85.
17. FCL and Westland Co-ops *Annual Reports* 1974, p. 62; 1975, pp. 73ff.
18. FCL *Annual Report* 1978, pp. 13 and 32.
19. See "50th Anniversary Program of Events: Co-operative Retailing System 1928–1978," FCL, 1977.
20. A. F. Laidlaw, *Co-operatives in the Year 2000* (Ottawa: CUC, c. 1980), p. 9, and p. 8 for the following quote.
21. FCL *Annual Report* 1977, p. 8.
22. For example, FCL *Annual Report* 1981, p. 6, clearly links "Growth from Within" to persuading members to "increase their patronage and thereby assist their associations."
23. Ibid.

Chapter Twenty-one

1. FCL *Annual Report* 1965, p. 23.
2. PABC, Co-op. Union of B.C. Papers, b. 10, f. 5 "BC Co-op Wh. Soc. 1967," and the same for the following passages.
3. BCCWS *Annual Report* 1967, p. 5.
4. Minutes, BCCWS Annual Meeting, Burnaby, 17–18 April 1969.
5. BCCWS *Annual Report* 1969, pp. 1–4.
6. Ibid., p. 4.
7. Ibid.
8. FCL, "Submission to the Select Standing Committee on Agriculture, Province of British Columbia," April 1973, p. 9, and 9 ff. for the following, PABC, B.C. Co-op Union Papers, b. 13, f. 3.
9. "Report on Emerging Co-operatives and Growth," B.C. Co-op Union Papers, b. 13, f. 3, and the same for the following passages.
10. FCL *Annual Report* 1980, p. 32.
11. FCL *Annual Report* 1982, p. 3.
12. "Food Co-ops Adopt Dual Tracks," Victoria *Times*, 24 May 1973, p. 23, and the same for the following.
13. As well as the story quoted, see the documents in B.C. Co-op Union Papers, b. 13, f. 3 and f. 5.
14. Minutes, FCL, 1972 District Meeting, Electoral District E18, B.C. Co-op Union Papers, b. 13, f. 5.
15. See CUC *News Service*, Oct. 1984.
16. Statistics drawn from FCL President's Newsletter.
17. Hume Compton, *Time for Change: An Opportunity for Progress in Co-operative Retailing* (Nanaimo: self-published, 1982), p. 7.
18. See R. S. Staples, "The Direct Charge Consumer Co-operative," *Canadian Co-operative Digest* 13,1 (1970), pp. 8–13.
19. Ibid., pp. 8–9.
20. Ibid., pp. 1–9.
21. Hume Compton, *Canada's Unique Co-op Experiment: The "Direct Charge" System in Transition* (Nanaimo: self-published, 1984), inside front cover.
22. Compton, *Time for Change*, p. 9.
23. Compton, *Canada's Unique Co-op Experiment*, pp. 5ff.
24. Quotations from author's interview with Compton; see also Jim Duggleby, "Direct Charge Co-operatives," *Credit Union Way*, Oct. 1983, pp. 17–21.
25. Staples, "Direct Charge Co-operatives," p. 19, and the same for the following passages.

Chapter Twenty-two

1. FCL *Annual Report* 1982, pp. 4–5 and 26, and pp. 4–5 for the following passages.
2. Frank J. Smith, "Some Regional Co-op. Dilemmas," Staff Papers Series, Staff Paper P87-2,

Jan. 1987, Department of Agricultural and Applied Economics, University of Minnesota Institute of Agriculture, Forestry, and Home Economics, pp. 3–10.

3. FCL *Annual Report* 1982, p. 13.

4. FCL *Annual Report* 1979, p. 45.

5. *Saskatchewan Co-operative Women's Guild*, booklet (Regina: Co-operative Union of Saskatchewan, 1966); *History of the Saskatchewan Co-operative Women's Guild* (see chap. 9, n. 28), p. 12.

6. FCL President's Newsletter.

APPENDIX ONE

Glossary of Terms

Cross-references are italicized

accounts payable, accounts receivable   Accounts payable are bills owed to others; accounts receivable are bills to be collected from others.

ACWA   *Alberta Co-operative Wholesale Association Limited.*

affiliate plan   Plan developed by *SCWS* in 1933–34 to increase co-operative sales volume in *bulk farm commodities*. Under the plan, groups of farmers organized by the *UFCSS* or by Saskatchewan *Wheat Pool* agents and field men purchased from SCWS without incorporating as co-operatives. Since they did not need to incorporate or raise share capital, goods could be purchased co-operatively even where local capital and organization were insufficient to create a co-op. *Patronage refunds* were accumulated on their behalf in share capital accounts, however, so that they could eventually form an *autonomous retail co-operative.*

Alberta Co-operative Wholesale Association Limited (ACWA)   Wholesaling and feed manufacturing firm serving and owned by Alberta co-operative stores, 1928–1961 (merged with *FCL*). ACWA was reorganized in 1938 after business difficulties during the Depression. Notable figures include William Halsall, who preserved it through the Depression; Dave Smeaton, manager 1938–47; and J. Russell Love, president 1938–61. ACWA purchased a chain of stores from the *UFA* in 1951.

annual meeting   The official, legally required meeting each year at which the members of a co-operative (or, in *second-tier* and some other large co-operatives, the *delegates*) elect the *board of directors*, amend by-laws, receive reports and financial statements, etc. FCL's annual meeting is held in March.

assets   All things of economic value owned by a business; on a *balance sheet*, the assets of a co-operative are accounted for so as to balance the *liabilities* plus the *members' equity*. Assets usually consist of three types: fixed assets (land, buildings, and equipment); current assets (cash, *accounts receivable*, inventories); and other assets (investments, advances, etc.).

associated stores   Semi-autonomous co-op stores supervised and provided with accounting and/or management services by the larger co-op wholesale. Manager Robert McKay of *SCWS* proposed the first associated stores plan in 1939. During World War Two many private stores were bought and organized as co-op associated stores, with a view to making them eventually into *autonomous retail co-operatives*. This was to speed the development of store associations out of the existing *bulk commodity* associations, and increase the volume in *store goods* so SCWS could handle them economically. In 1951 *BCCWS* also adopted an associated stores plan, and this was also intended as a measure to speed up store development.

autonomous retail co-operative   The basic unit of membership in the *Co-operative Retailing System*; a local co-operative association joined by individual people, and which sells (*retails*) goods to them. Autonomous retail co-operatives own *FCL* in the same way that the individual members own the autonomous retail co-operative. Other kinds of organizations that have been part of the Co-operative Retailing System include: locals under the *affiliate plan* of the 1930s; *associated stores* in the 1940s and 1950s; stores owned by co-op wholesales (Alberta, 1951–61, and a few other cases in Manitoba and B.C.); and Westland Units in the 1970s (see Chapter 20).

balance sheet   A statement of the financial position of an organization. For a co-operative, it looks roughly like this:

current assets	current liabilities
+fixed assets	+long-term debt
+investments	=LIABILITIES
+other assets	
=TOTAL ASSETS	share capital
	+retained savings (reserves)
	=MEMBERS' EQUITY

The "balance" is: TOTAL ASSETS = LIABILITIES + MEMBERS' EQUITY.

BCCWS   *British Columbia Co-operative Wholesaling Society.*

board of directors   Part of the *management team* of a co-operative, elected by the members to appoint, supervise, and work with senior managers.

bonds   When an individual purchases a bond from a business (including a co-operative), he or she is lending that business money in exchange for a legally secured commitment that it will be repaid with interest. Many co-ops have raised the capital they needed for expansions by selling bonds to their members.

British Columbia Co-operative Wholesaling Society Limited (BCCWS)   Wholesaling firm owned by and serving co-operatives in B. C., 1939–70 (merged with FCL). The BCCWS was not able to grow quickly until after World War Two when economic restrictions were ended, but thereafter it grew steadily and without a setback until its merger with FCL. Its savings, however, and the difficulties of serving widely-spread co-operatives in B. C., led BCCWS by the 1960s to propose merger with FCL. Notable figures include S. F. Ricketts, Secretary (1939–45) and popularizer of co-operation, and president A. Swenson (1950–70), longest-serving wholesale president in the history of the system.

bulk commodities   Coal and heating fuel, petroleum products, and binder twine, the staple products handled by early co-operatives. Farmers needed these products in large quantities, so it was comparatively easy to organize group orders for full rail car loads. The rail cars were then, in the beginning, unloaded by volunteer labour, directly off the track and into the member's wagon. Buying clubs and co-ops based on bulk commodities therefore needed no paid staff, virtually no facilities, and little capital. Some of this changed in the 1930s when federal legislation was amended to require coal sheds and petroleum tanks; with this change many buying clubs converted to co-ops and raised share capital. Apples, flour, salt, fence posts, and other commodities were also purchased in bulk by local buying clubs.

Canadian Co-operative Association (CCA)   Educational and representative organization for Canadian co-operatives created in 1987 by the merger of the *Co-operative Union of Canada and the Co-operative College of Canada.*

Canadian Co-operative Implements Limited (CCIL)   A farmer-owned agricultural machinery co-operative organized in 1940, and which bought the Cockshutt farm machinery factory in Winnipeg in 1944. The *co-operative wholesale societies* of western Canada were instrumental in its creation and, in the early years, in selling its products. It has been reorganized several times and is now less than one-half co-operatively owned.

capital   The money at the disposal of a business, including a co-operative, with which to purchase or expand facilities, buy inventories, etc. Capital can come from a number of sources, including *share capital, bond* or debenture issues, bank loans, and accumulated *net savings* on operations.

CCIL   *Canadian Co-operative Implements Limited.*

CCRL   *Consumers' Co-operative Refineries Limited.*

consumer co-operative   A *co-operative* whose members are the people who purchase from it; opposite of a *producer co-operative*. A consumer co-operative could handle any kind of goods, hence the variety in the Co-operative Retailing System. When farmers form a co-op to obtain agricultural inputs for their farming operations, or when farmers or city people form a co-op to obtain food, both are consumer co-operatives.

Consumer, The (newspaper)   See *Co-operative Consumer, The.*

Consumers' Co-operative Refineries Limited (CCRL)   A co-operative petroleum company located in Regina which refines crude oil and markets the products. Founded in 1934, CCRL merged with *SFCL* in 1944 and has since that time been operated as a wholly-owned subsidiary of SFCL and then *FCL*. Notable figures from 1934–44 include Harry Fowler, secretary-manager, and O. B. Males, superintendent. See Chapter 8.

co-op, co-operative   A business organization adhering to all six of the co-operative principles adopted by the International Co-operative Alliance in 1966: open and voluntary membership, one vote per member, strictly limited interest on share capital, net savings returned as *patronage refunds* or used for collective purposes, co-operative education, co-operation with other co-operatives. See Chapter 2.

co-operative association   Another way to describe, mainly, *autonomous retail co-operatives.* Deriving from provincial legislation, the term also has applied to co-operatives operating community halls, marketing local livestock, and so forth.

Co-operative College of Canada (1955–59 known as the Co-operative Institute, 1959–73 as Western Co-operative College)   Educational institution funded by major co-operatives to provide training and *co-operative education* to their personnel and directors (1987 merged with the *Co-operative Union of Canada* to form the Canadian Co-operative Association).

Co-operative Consumer, The   Newspaper published by the Saskatchewan co-op wholesales (*SCWS* and *CCRL,* later *SFCL),* and then by *FCL,* from 1939 to 1982. Coming out every two weeks, the *Consumer* for most of its life provided about a dozen pages of news on co-operative, consumer, farm, home, and women's affairs, and also advertising of co-operation and of CO-OP products. Its circulation was about 70,000 in the late 1940s, reached 200,000 in the 1960s and 300,000 in the mid-1970s, then fell as some retails ceased subscribing on behalf of their members.

co-operative credit society   A federation of *credit unions,* intended to even out cash balances among different credit unions and otherwise facilitate their operations. The first co-operative credit society was the Saskatchewan Co-operative Credit Society incorporated in 1941, which was instrumental in co-operative development by lending its reserves to co-operative associations for their expansions.

co-operative education   Co-operative education is one of the official co-operative principles, but has not had a precise definition. In the beginning it included instruction of co-operative officers and employees in technical tasks related to their roles, but this would probably now be called "training," and it included some of what we would now call publicity and advertising. The essential element was education about co-operative history, philosophy, purposes, and ideals — the kind of education that motivates and builds understanding and commitment.

co-operative movement   Phrase used to refer to all members, leaders, and staff of *co-operatives* working together, including in different kinds of co-operative organizations, sectors of the economy, and countries. Use of the word "movement" indicates co-operators see themselves as a popular force organized for change — "change" historically conceived as the end of scarcity, of profit-taking, and of concentration of power in the hands of a few.

Co-operative Retailing System   Term that began to be used in the early 1970s to describe how *FCL* and the *autonomous retail co-operatives* that own it work together as an economic unit.

Co-operative Union of Canada (CUC)   Educational and lobbying organization representing co-operatives across Canada, 1909–88 (now merged with the *Co-operative College of Canada* to form the Canadian Co-operative Association). In its early years the CUC was primarily an association of *consumer co-operatives* and provided them with several of the services later provided by *wholesale* societies. Starting in the 1930s *producer co-operatives* systematically became members of the CUC. Provincial sections of the CUC were active between the late 1930s and the early 1970s.

co-operative wholesale, co-operative wholesale society   The model for co-operative *wholesaling* generally accepted by the *co-operative movement* is that of the Co-operative Wholesale Societies of England and Scotland, both formed in the 19th century. Following this model, *FCL* and the other co-op wholesales that preceded it are "co-operative" in two senses: first, their *own structure* is that of a *co-operative,* following co-operative principles. Second, they have generally *admitted only co-operative associations as members.* Profit businesses are generally excluded because, if the co-op wholesale admitted them, savings would be going to investors, not to consumers. With few exceptions co-operative wholesales have also not admitted individuals as members, because if they did they would be engaged in retailing. At various times it has been thought that this would stretch their capital and expertise too thin, invite charges of unfair competition from private merchants, and, most of all, undermine the local basis of co-operation that was thought to offer members personal involvement and control, and earn their loyalty in return.

Co-op Refinery   *Consumers' Co-operative Refineries Limited.*

Co-op Upgrader   A $700 million joint project involving FCL and the governments of Saskatchewan and Canada, to build a heavy oil upgrader adjacent to the site of *CCRL* in Regina. The Upgrader came on-stream in November 1988, and processes heavy crude to the point where the existing refinery can use it.

cost-plus pricing   A method of setting *retail* prices as *wholesale* costs plus a fixed amount to cover handling, which generally means they are significantly below the established market prices. *Profits* (in a profit business) or *net savings* (in a co-op) are not provided for, nor does the business build up capital and facilities in the same way as if market prices are charged.

credit union   A local financial *co-operative* providing individual members with loans, and receiving their savings deposits. Although legally distinct from banks, credit unions have taken on almost all the functions of banks (as far as transactions with their members are concerned). In western Canada few credit unions were founded before the 1940s. They have become popular since that time, in many places with the encouragement or sponsorship of consumer co-operatives.

CUC   *Co-operative Union of Canada.*

current assets, current liabilities   Fluid wealth and short-term debts. Current assets include cash, inventories, and accounts receivable. Current liabilities include loans and accounts payable. A ratio of 2:1 between current assets and current liabilities has traditionally been considered desirable for a business organization, including a co-operative, to have sound financing for its operations.

delegates   The locally-elected or chosen people who represent members in the affairs of a second-tier co-op like *FCL,* or in the affairs of a local retail that has adopted a district structure. One of the duties of delegates is to attend annual and general meetings of the co-operative and cast votes on behalf of members. In the case of FCL, the members, which are co-operative associations, choose the delegates who represent the association at the annual meeting. A formula whose nature has changed over the years determines how many delegates each member may send (based on a minimum of one delegate per member association, plus additional delegates reflecting sales volume).

Depression   The Great Depression of the 1930s. Started by the stock market crash of 1929 which inaugurated a decade of low demand, deflation (falling prices), unemployment, and poor or unsettled markets, in western Canada the Depression was made worse by drought and bad crops. Some recovery was evident by 1935, and particularly by 1938.

direct-charge co-operative   Original term (and name still used in central and eastern Canada) for *service-fee co-operative.*

earnings   See *profit, net saving.*

equity   See *members' equity.*

FCL   *Federated Co-operatives Limited.*

Federated Co-operatives Limited   A *co-operative wholesale society* whose owners are over 330 *autonomous retail co-operatives* in western Canada. FCL was formed in 1955 by merger of *Saskatchewan Federated Co-operatives* and *Manitoba Co-op Wholesale.* Mergers with the other provinces' co-op wholesales, *ACWA,* and *BCCWS,* came in 1961 and 1970 respectively. Sales volume in 1987 was $1.4 billion, with net savings of $63.6 million. Main commodities handled are (in order of sales) food and pharmaceuticals, petroleum products, lumber and building materials, hardware, agricultural and crop supplies, feeds, and family fashions. FCL is involved in production of oil, petroleum products, lumber, feed, and agricultural chemicals. Home office is in Saskatoon.

guild   See *Women's Co-operative Guild.*

horizontal integration   Having a single business handle a wide range of different commodities — "horizontal" because the business "spreads out" sideways into new lines of goods (opposite of specialized). Early co-ops and their wholesales specialized in bulk commodities, and from the 1940s to the 1960s spread out energetically into new fields to serve more of their members' total consumer needs. This horizontal integration paralleled some industry trends (chain stores, supermarkets, department stores). In the 1980s this concept is no longer as prevalent; co-ops talk instead about "doing what we do best and not being all things to all people." See also *vertical integration.*

ICA   *International Co-operative Alliance.*

International Co-operative Alliance (ICA)   An organization representing co-operatives around the world. (Consumer co-operatives in western Canada are represented through the *Canadian Co-operative Association.)* The ICA has formulated the official co-operative principles known as the "Rochdale Principles," which are recognized by co-operators as defining the essential features of all co-operative organizations. See Chapter 2.

Interprovincial Cooperative Limited (IPCO)   A "third-tier" co-op founded by the western Canadian co-op wholesales in 1940 to co-ordinate their purchasing, and which is now owned by all the regional co-op wholesales in Canada and by the three prairie *Wheat Pools.* IPCO is the holder of the CO-OP trademark. IPCO was originally intended also to extend co-operative control into manufacturing (*vertical integration),* but its production enterprises, especially a chemical plant in Saskatoon, encountered difficulties in the 1970s. It now operates mainly as a procurement agent and is managed by FCL under contract. Prior to its reorganization in 1971, the spelling of its name was Interprovincial Co-operatives.

liabilities   The debts of a business organization, including a co-operative. These consist of *current liabilities* (loans payable and *accounts payable,* plus other items such as bonds or share dividends due in the immediate future) and long-term debt (loans, etc., not yet payable). Liabilities together with *members' equity* balance the *assets* of a co-operative on the *balance sheet.*

management team   The *board of directors* of a co-operative plus the top *managers* hired by them. In general, in large co-operatives today, the directors set general policies, and the managers make specific operational decisions. Among consumer co-operatives in the West these roles were not clearly separated in this way, however, until the 1950s.

managers   Senior salaried personnel. The general manager or chief executive officer is hired by the *board of directors,* and in turn that person hires and supervises departmental managers who hire and supervise most other employees. The directors and the top managers work together as a *management team* to run the operations of a co-operative.

Manitoba Co-operative Wholesale Limited (MCW)   Wholesaler, manufacturer of feed, and packer of oils and greases for *autonomous retail co-operatives* in Manitoba, 1927–55 (merged with *Saskatchewan Federated Co-operatives Limited* to form *FCL).* MCW was the first functioning *co-operative wholesale society* in Canada, and was based mainly on *bulk commodities,* especially petroleum products. Notable figures include Walter Popple, manager and president in the 1930s; its other two general managers Ed Chown and C. B. "Bun" Fraser; and J. J. Siemens, director and promotor of co-operative education. With the 1955 amalgamation MCW contributed many education, publicity, and retail services personnel to FCL.

margin   The difference between the price at which goods are bought, and the price at which they are sold. A business, including a co-operative, pays its expenses out of the margins on the goods it handles, and anything left over after that is *profit* for a profit business or *savings* for a consumer co-operative.

marketing   Term for the various functions required in getting products from the manufacturer to the consumer. Colloquially "marketing" is used particularly to describe targeting specific products at specific groups, matching up products with buyers, advertising, etc.

market prices   It is a generally accepted rule among co-operatives that they buy and sell at prevailing market prices. Since they do not take profits, it would be possible for them to undercut market prices in many cases, but co-operators have discovered it is wiser to charge prevailing prices and return all or part of the excess (after the cost of the goods and expenses are paid) to members at the end of the year as a *patronage refund.*

MCW   *Manitoba Co-operative Wholesale Limited.*

members   Members of an *autonomous retail co-operative* are individuals who purchase one or more shares. Members of a *co-operative wholesale society* are co-operatives who purchase shares in the wholesale. These members control the co-operative by electing the *board of directors* and by making certain other kinds of decisions at annual and general meetings. In both cases the distinctive feature about membership in a co-operative is that *members benefit only by using* the co-operative, and benefit more the more they are *loyal to it in their purchasing.* A profit company rewards its shareholders according to how much money they already have, and have invested in the company; a consumer co-op rewards its shareholders according to how much they spend.

members' equity   Members' equity in a consumer co-operative consists of their *share capital* plus the "retained savings" of the co-operative: the portion of the *net savings* that has not been paid out to members, but instead has accumulated in reserves to give the co-op capital with which to undertake new projects. These two sums together represent how much the members "own" of their co-operative (as opposed to the portion to which banks or other lenders may lay claim). At one time it was a goal that this total should be at least 50% of total assets; 35% or about one-third is now more generally considered an appropriate level. If members' equity is too low a percentage of assets, the co-op may be too dependent on borrowed money, face high interest charges, and develop a poor credit rating.

merchandising   Putting merchandise on the shelves; receiving, storing, distributing, and displaying goods.

net savings   The money left at the end of the year after a consumer co-op has taken in all its receipts and paid all its bills (the equivalent of a profit firm's *profit).* The difference between net savings and profit is that the net savings belong to the people who contributed them, the *customers,* whereas "profit," even though also derived from the customers, belongs instead to *investors.* Perhaps the most important feature of a co-operative is that there are no "investors" at all in the usual sense — the customers are the only investors, and they are rewarded in proportion to their custom, not to their initial investment.

patronage refund   It is one of the official co-operative principles that if the *net savings* are to be distributed, they should be distributed to members in proportion to their patronage, not in proportion to their investment. Every member gets back exactly what he or she contributed through purchases to the co-operative's operating surplus. This is a *patronage refund.* There are two main reasons why consumer co-operatives decided on this procedure, instead of cutting prices and returning savings in that way. First, it provides security for the co-operative. A co-operative could try to sell at cost, but it would then have to know its costs exactly, in advance — one error could send the co-op into a deficit situation. When co-operatives tried price competition in the past, they also found that small merchants accused them of unfair competition, and large merchants willingly entered into price wars to try to "break" the co-operative. Second, the patronage refund helps the co-op build up capital. It is paid out only to members, so people join, buy a share, and contribute a few dollars to the co-op's capital. Also, the members and the directors they elect usually choose to hold part of the refund back as retained savings, to build up the co-operative's reserves and enable it to undertake new projects.

producer co-operative   A co-operative that transacts business with its members in their capacity as producers of a good or service. In other words, the co-operative does not sell to its members; it buys from them and markets for them (opposite of a *consumer co-operative*). Some co-operatives have mixed the two roles.

profit   The earnings beyond costs of a business that is owned by private investors, that is, a business whose purpose is to reward investors mainly in proportion to their investment. See *net savings* and *patronage refund* for an explanation of how co-operatives differ.

regional conferences   Part of the FCL democratic control structure instituted in 1976–77. Delegates of member associations within each of FCL's five operational regions (Winnipeg, Saskatoon, Regina, Edmonton, Calgary) meet in the fall to hear about and discuss programs and policies, and to pass resolutions which go on to the *annual meeting* held in March.

retail, retailing   Selling products to end users (mainly to individuals). A retail co-operative is one whose members are individual people. Retail prices are prices including all the costs of production, *wholesale* distribution, and retail store operation.

"revolving door"   A plan for capital accumulation in co-operatives, pioneered especially by the *Co-op Refinery* in the last half of the 1930s and then adopted by most co-operatives. Under the revolving door plan, *patronage refunds* were retained by the co-op for a specified period as "patronage loans," then paid out to members. In between, the co-op had the funds for use in financing operations and expansion. The revolving door was replaced in the late 1950s by other ways of accumulating *share capital*.

Saskatchewan Co-operative Wholesale Society Limited (SCWS)   A *co-operative wholesale society* founded to take over the assets of the *Trading Department* of the *UFCSS* in 1928 (merged with *Consumers' Co-operative Refineries* to form *Saskatchewan Federated Co-operatives Limited* in 1944). SCWS was the first to develop an *affiliate plan* to increase sales volume under the conditions of the *Depression*. SCWS became involved during 1938–44 in production of flour, feed, and coal, and acted as a centre of leadership and ideas for development of new kinds of co-operatives (*IPCO, CCIL,* financial co-operatives). Notable figures include Robert McKay, manager (1931–46).

Saskatchewan Federated Co-operatives Limited (SFCL)   Formed by the merger of *Saskatchewan Co-operative Wholesale Society* and *Consumers' Co-operative Refineries Limited,* SFCL was the first *co-operative wholesale society* to link a large manufacturing operation with a fairly comprehensive *wholesaling* operation. SFCL undertook co-operative store development, refinery expansion, crude oil exploration, and entered into lumber manufacturing. In 1955 it merged with *Manitoba Co-op Wholesale* to form *FCL*. Notable figures (all continuing on to FCL) include president George Urwin (1944–59), secretary Harry Fowler (1946–59), and treasurer/general manager/chief executive officer Dave Stewart (1951–70).

SCWS   *Saskatchewan Co-operative Wholesale Society Limited.*

second-tier co-operative   A central co-operative owned by local co-operatives, for example, a *co-operative wholesale society,* which is owned by *autonomous retail co-operatives.* The co-ops of which *individuals* are members, the autonomous retail co-ops, are considered "first-tier".

service-fee co-operative   A new kind of *consumer co-operative* developed in the 1960s which does away with *patronage refunds* and sells below *market prices* instead. Several modifications to the normal consumer co-operative structure are necessary to do this: sales are to members only, and members must pay a weekly service fee which covers the co-op's costs.

SFCL   *Saskatchewan Federated Co-operatives Limited.*

SGGA   *Saskatchewan Grain Growers' Association.* See *Trading Department, UFCSS.*

share capital   The equity held by members in their share accounts with their co-operative. Originally, these accounts consisted only of the money members put in to join the co-op; in those days this amount was much greater ($10 or $25 in 1920s currency, the equivalent of at least $70–175 in 1987 dollars) than it is today ($5). In the *Depression,* when money was scarce, share values were lowered, and it became more common for members to pay only a small down-payment on the shares, and pay off the rest gradually out of their accumulated *patronage refunds*. This was further modified in the late 1950s, when the *revolving door plan* of "patronage loans" was converted into equity capital. Since that time, it has become common for patronage refunds to be paid to members in shares. Each member builds up capital in proportion to his or her purchases, and this stays in the co-op as long as it is needed (unlike the "revolving door," which automatically distributed it at a later date). When the co-op members and directors decide to pay out cash, they do so by redeeming shares, which is exactly equivalent to a refund on patronage.

surplus, net surplus   See *net savings.*

third-tier co-operative   A co-operative whose owners are *second tier co-operatives,* that is, whose owners are federations of local co-operatives. Example: IPCO, owned by FCL along with other regional co-operatives and co-operative wholesales.

Trading Department (of the *SGGA* and *UFCSS*)   A *wholesaling* operation created by the *SGGA* in 1914 mainly to sell to local Grain Growers' lodges and buying clubs. The Trading Department, after a rocky road including heavy losses on binder twine inventories as prices fluctuated, and corruption, embezzlement, and incompetence by one of its managers, was taken over by *SCWS* in 1929. Its connections with local farmers' clubs and lodges, in particular, provided a valuable base for the new co-operative wholesale.

UFA   *United Farmers of Alberta.*

UFBC   *United Farmers of British Columbia.*

UFCSS   *United Farmers of Canada, Saskatchewan Section.*

UFM   *United Farmers of Manitoba.*

UGG   *United Grain Growers.*

United Farmers of Alberta (UFA)   Farmers' organization formed in 1909 by the union of the Alberta Farmers' Association and the Society of Equity. The UFA entered provincial politics and formed the government of Alberta, until it was defeated by Social Credit. The UFA retired from politics in 1935. In 1931–32 it started wholesaling activities, organizing purchases for UFA locals. In 1948 it left its educational functions to the new Farmers' Union of Alberta, and changed its name to UFA Co-op. It operated a chain of retail stores, sold to *ACWA* in 1951. The UFA has continued to operate in petroleum distribution and other bulk sales to farmers.

United Farmers of British Columbia (UFBC)   Provincial farmers' organization founded in 1917.

United Farmers of Manitoba (UFM)   Representative and educational organization for farmers, successor in 1920 to the Manitoba Grain Growers' Association of 1903. The UFM sponsored and promoted co-operative education, including supporting consumer co-operation.

United Farmers of Canada, Saskatchewan Section (UFCSS)   Formed in 1926 by the amalgamation of the older *SGGA* and the younger and more strident Farmers' Union of Canada. The mix of the two organizations seems to have been an uneasy one, particularly in 1927–28 when factions were divided about whether or not to call for compulsory "pooling" of grain. The UFCSS also inherited the *Trading Department* of the SGGA, and eventually turned the Trading Department over to control by consumer co-operatives in 1928 to provide the nucleus for *Saskatchewan Co-operative Wholesale Society.* UFC support was important to the wholesale, particularly in organizing locals for its *affiliate plan* of 1933–34.

United Grain Growers (UGG)   Farmer-owned grain handling company formed in 1917 by the union of the Grain Growers' Grain Company (1906) and the Alberta Co-operative Elevator Company (1913).

vertical integration   Having a single business both manufacture, distribute, and market a given commodity; "vertical" integration because the company extends control upward or downward through different phases of the processing and sale of a single product. Co-operatives, observing that many of their competitors were vertically integrated, strove for vertical integration themselves, expanding from retailing into wholesaling, from wholesaling into manufacturing. If consumers controlled the entire process, for example, of producing oil, refining it, distributing it to retails, and selling it, the savings they received would be the combined savings on every step of the process. Since the 1970s, particularly with the reorganization of *IPCO,* consumer co-operators have been much less eager to pursue vertical integration, with the exception of petroleum products.

WCFL   *Western Co-operative Fertilizers Limited.*

Western Co-operative Fertilizers Limited (WCFL)   Fertilizer company formed by FCL and the Alberta and Saskatchewan *Wheat Pools* in 1963 to produce fertilizer for western Canadian farmers (Manitoba Pool participated later). Although FCL was instrumental in forming WCFL, it ceased handling fertilizer in 1984 and has withdrawn from WCFL in 1988.

wheat pools (Alberta, Manitoba, Saskatchewan Wheat Pool)   Co-operative grain handling and farm supply organizations. The Wheat Pools were founded in 1923–24 to market grain, "pooling" the production of all member farmers to sell at the best possible time and divide the best possible price among them. This function was taken over by the federal Wheat Board when the pools encountered financial trouble early in the *Depression.* The proper names when the organizations were founded were Alberta, Saskatchewan, and Manitoba Co-operative Wheat Producers Ltd., but each has always been known as the "Wheat Pool."

wholesale, wholesaling   A wholesale procures goods, keeps them in inventory, and distributes them to local retails, who sell them in turn to individual customers. The wholesaler is a "middleman" between the manufacturer and the local store. Although the *co-operative wholesale societies* of western Canada are referred to as "wholesales" for short, the term is misleading in some ways. In the beginning, for example, they were not wholesales; they did not purchase goods and maintain inventories to any significant extent until the 1940s, they merely grouped the orders of member retails. Also, however, they are much more than wholesales, because they engage in manufacturing and processing, in training and development of retail staff, in co-ordinated *merchandising, marketing,* and advertising involving retails, and in audit, financial, management, and other services to retails.

Women's Co-operative Guild, Women's Guild   Voluntary women's organizations formed for purposes of *co-operative education,* and to support consumer co-operatives and develop participation in them by women. Guilds were mainly active in western Canada from the 1940s to the early 1970s. They were usually each associated with a local consumer co-operative, and federated together into provincial women's guilds. Their activities included study groups and courses for women, product testing and demonstration, ceremonies and presentations at co-op meetings, sponsoring and catering for local recreational events and meetings, recommendations on co-op policies (e.g., co-op memberships for women, "associate directorships" for women), and advocacy of policies concerning health, education, international peace, and other areas. The original name was Women's Co-operative Guild, but the Saskatchewan provincial guild changed its name to Co-operative Women's Guild when it was reorganized in 1956.

APPENDIX TWO

Top Officers and Management of FCL and its Predecessors

MANITOBA CO-OPERATIVE WHOLESALE LIMITED

FOUNDED 1927
MERGED 1955 WITH SASKATCHEWAN FEDERATED CO-OPERATIVES LIMITED
TO FORM FEDERATED CO-OPERATIVES LIMITED

President	E. D. Magwood	1927–29
	Walter F. Popple	1929–42
	D. J. Wallace	1942–45
	Wilfrid McSorley	1945–55
Vice-President	George Brown	1927–29
	Walter F. Popple	1929
	E. D. Magwood	1929–
	F. W. Ransom	–45
	J. J. Siemens	1945–52
	C. C. Hunt	1952–55
General Manager	E. D. Magwood	1927–29
	Walter F. Popple	1929–42
	E. B. "Ed" Chown	1942–50
	C. B. "Bun" Fraser	1950–55
Secretary	Roy W. Johnston	1927–
	D. J. Wallace	–42
	E. B. "Ed" Chown	1942–44
	Mary McGuire	1944–49
	J. J. Siemens	1949–55

ALBERTA CO-OPERATIVE WHOLESALE ASSOCIATION LIMITED

FOUNDED 1928
MERGED 1961 WITH FEDERATED CO-OPERATIVES LIMITED

President	Amos P. Moan	1928
	William Halsall	1928–30
	J. R. Hanning	1930–34

President	E. R. Rasmussen	1934–41
	J. Russell Love	1941–61
Vice-President	William Halsall	1928
	J. R. Hanning	1929–30
	E. R. Rasmussen	1930–34
	G. Gaudin	1934–37
	J. D. Manners	1937–39
	T. Trimble	1939–40
	J. Russell Love	1940–41
	William Hoar	1941–47
	Dan Gamache	1947–49
	George E. Church	1949–53
	P. H. Goettel	1953–61
General Manager	A. P. Moan	1929–32
	Carter Strather	1932–34
	William Halsall	1934–38
	"Dave" Smeaton	1938–47
	R. V. Davies	1947–51
GM and Treasurer	E. T. "Ted" Mowbrey	1951–61
Secretary-Treasurer	Thomas Swindlehurst	1929–34
	William Halsall	1934–38
	Edward Peterson	1938–52
Secretary	R. N. Gibb	1952–60
Secretary & Controller	E. J. d'Archangelo	1960–61

SASKATCHEWAN CO-OPERATIVE WHOLESALE SOCIETY LIMITED

FOUNDED 1928 AS SASKATCHEWAN WHOLESALE SOCIETY LIMITED
INCORPORATED 1929 AS A CO-OPERATIVE
MERGED 1944 WITH CONSUMERS' CO-OPERATIVE REFINERIES LIMITED
TO FORM SASKATCHEWAN FEDERATED CO-OPERATIVES LIMITED

President	W. H. Beesley	1928–29
	A. J. "Andy" Allison	1929–30
	C. G. "Scotty" Davidson	1930–39
	James McCaig	1939–44
	George Urwin	1944
Vice-President	William Laird	1928–29
	C. G. "Scotty" Davidson	1929–30
	Robert "Bob" McKay	1930–31
	A. J. "Andy" Allison	1931–
	Frank Jones	
	J. B. Clark	–40
	E. H. Lockwood	1940–42

Vice-President	George Urwin	1942–44
	James F. Gray	1944
Secretary-Manager	H. W. "Harry" Ketcheson	1928–31
	Robert "Bob" McKay	1931–44 (–1946)
Treasurer	H. L. Smith	–44

CONSUMERS' CO-OPERATIVE REFINERIES LIMITED

FOUNDED 1934
AS CONSUMERS' REFINERIES CO-OPERATIVE ASSOCIATION
RENAMED 1935, MERGED 1944 WITH SASKATCHEWAN
CO-OPERATIVE WHOLESALE SOCIETY LIMITED TO FORM
SASKATCHEWAN FEDERATED CO-OPERATIVES LIMITED

President	C. O. Smith	1934
	E. E. Frisk	1934–44
Vice-President	V. C. Thomas	
	D. V. Runkle	
	T. W. Barmby	
Secretary-Manager	H. L. "Harry" Fowler	1934–44
Treasurer	E. T. "Ted" Mowbrey	1934–44 (–1951)

SASKATCHEWAN FEDERATED CO-OPERATIVES LIMITED

FOUNDED 1944 BY MERGER
MERGED 1955 WITH MANITOBA CO-OPERATIVE WHOLESALE LIMITED
TO FORM FEDERATED CO-OPERATIVES LIMITED

President	George Urwin	1944–55 (–1959)
Vice-President	McDermid "Dan" Rankin	1944–47
	L. L. "Lewie" Lloyd	1947–55 (–1961)
General Manager	Robert McKay	(1931–) 1944–46
Management Committee (1)	Harold L. Benson	
	(Production Manager)	1946–51
	R. F. Stephenson	
	(Distribution Manager)	1946–49
	Ted Mowbrey (Treasurer)	1946–51
	Harry Fowler (Secretary)	1946–51
Management Committee (2)	George Urwin (President)	1951–55
	Harry Fowler (Secretary)	1951–55
	D. E. "Dave" Stewart	
	(Treasurer)	1951–55

Secretary	Harry Fowler	1946–55 (–1959)
Treasurer	Ted Mowbrey	1944–51
	Dave Stewart	1951–55

BRITISH COLUMBIA
CO-OPERATIVE WHOLESALE SOCIETY

FOUNDED 1939
MERGED 1970 WITH FEDERATED CO-OPERATIVES LIMITED

President	L. H. C. "Les" Phillips	1939–40
	D. G. MacDonald	1940–41
	W. A. Wilkinson	1941–47
	B. H. Creelman	1947–50
	A. Swenson	1950–70
Vice-President	J. White	1939–
	W. W. McMyn	–48
	D. G. MacDonald	1948–53
	B. G. Shepherd	1953–57
	K. F. Harding	1957–69
	H. A. Turner	1969–70
General Manager	L. H. C. "Les" Phillips	1939–52
	R. L. Simpson	1952–56, 1969–70
	Barney Johnsrude	1956–69
Secretary	S. F. Ricketts	1939–45
	G. M. Holtby	1945–46
	L. H. C. "Les" Phillips	1946–70

FEDERATED CO-OPERATIVES LIMITED

FOUNDED 1955 BY MERGER
FURTHER MERGERS 1961, 1970

President	George Urwin	(1944–) 1955–59
	H. L. "Harry" Fowler	1959–63
	L. L. "Lewie" Lloyd	1963–67
	R. H. "Bob" Boyes	1967–74
	Gordon M. Sinclair	1974–77
	L. J. "Leo" Hayes	1977–78
	V. J. "Vern" Leland	1978–
Vice-President*	Wilfrid J. McSorley*	1955–57
	Lewie Lloyd	(1947–) 1955–61
	C. N. Wells	1959–61, 1977–78
	C. E. Wood	1959–63

Vice-President*	Bob Boyes	1961–67
	Morris Jevne	1961–67, 1968
	Gordon Sinclair*	1963–74
	M. L. Brown	1967–72, 1974–75
	Gordon Barker*	1974–78
	E. "Ed" Klassen*	1974–
	H. E. Turner	1974
	E. W. Curry	1975–79
	L. K. Ferguson	1975–78, 1979–85
	Leo Hayes	1975–77, 1978–
	G. L. Tarr	1975–76
	Vern Leland	1977–78
	E. R. Adams	1977–79
	G. C. Kemp	1978–
	H. E. Wessner	1979–
	R. J. Barichello	1979–81
	C. King	1981–85
	C. W. Loov	1985–
	T. Smith	1985–87
	W. D. Keenleyside	1987–
General Manager**	D. E. "Dave" Stewart and C. B. "Bun" Fraser (joint managers)	1955
	Dave Stewart	1955–65
	Bun Fraser	1965–68
Chief Executive Officer**	Dave Stewart	1965–70
	W. E. "Bill" Bergen	1970–79
	T. P. "Pat" Bell	1979–83
	Wayne H. Thompson	1983–
Secretary**	Harry Fowler	1955–59
	Don Tullis (Secretary-Treasurer 1959–68)	1959–77
	Pat Bell	1977–79
	Harold L. Empey	1979–
Treasurer	Dave Stewart	1955
	Don Tullis (Secretary-Treasurer 1959–68)	1955–68
	Bill Bergen	1967–70
	Pat Bell	1970–79
	Wayne Thompson	1979–83
	A. L. "Al" Pasloske	1983–87
	A. R. "Art" Postle	1987–
Executive Assistant	Tony Dummer	1955–70
	C. W. Kennedy	1968–70

source: Annual Reports and board minutes.

note: Information concerning vice-presidents, secretaries, and treasurers is incomplete, as this information is not always contained in the early annual reports, and because some of the corporate documents for the 1920s-40s are unavailable.

Dates in parentheses show how long the person named served in the same position in a predecessor or successor organization.

*number of vice-presidents: 1955–57: two
1957–59: one
1959–73: three
1973–74: one
1974–76: four
1976–87: six (by region)
1987– five by region

In 1955–57, 1974–75, and 1984-, FCL had a First Vice-President, and in 1971–74 it had a full-time Vice-President (indicated by * beside name).

**position of CEO created 1965; position of GM discontinued 1968.

***from 1977 Corporate Secretary.

APPENDIX THREE

Chronology of Events

For names and abbreviations see Appendix 1

General	Manitoba	Saskatchewan	Alberta	B.C.
1901.		Territorial Grain Growers' Association (TGGA) formed at Indian Head to protest rail company shipping policies		
1902.			Society of Equity organized in Alberta	
1903.	Manitoba Grain Growers' Association (MGGA) formed			
1905. Alberta and Sask. became provinces; E. A. Partridge of Sintaluta went to Winnipeg to observe the Grain Exchange		TGGA gave way to Saskatchewan Grain Growers' Association (SGGA)	Alberta Farmers' Association formed as a provincial political and educational body	
1906. Formation of the Grain Growers' Grain Company (GGGC)				
1907.	Manitoba farmers became the first to demand government-owned elevators			

Year		Manitoba	Saskatchewan	Alberta
1908. Federal legislation for co-ops passed unopposed by House of Commons; defeated 19–18 in Senate after lobbying by Retail Merchants Association				
1909. Co-operative Union of Canada (CUC) formed				Society of Equity and Farmers' Association joined to form the United Farmers of Alberta (UFA)
1910.		The Manitoba government created a system of government-owned grain elevators	Saskatchewan Purchasing Co. incorporated as a joint-stock company, but intended to function as a co-operative for purchase of bulk supplies	
1911.			Rejecting government ownership, Premier Scott created Sask. Co-op. Elevator Co. (SCEC)	
1913. General legislation for co-op. associations passed by all three prairie provinces			Sask. government created a Co-operative Organizations Branch	Alberta Co-op Elevator Co. (ACEC) incorporated by act of the legislature; earliest true retail co-operatives in western Canada founded, July 1913
1914. Start of World War One; with wartime price inflation co-ops prospered; first surviving co-ops founded in all three prairie provinces			SGGA opened a Trading Department selling in bulk to Grain Growers' locals and co-ops	

General	Manitoba	Saskatchewan	Alberta	B.C.
1917. GGGC merged with ACEC to form United Grain Growers (UGG)				United Farmers of British Columbia (UFBC) formed
1920. Severe post-war recession hit retail co-ops; hereafter the number of associations fell steadily until 1928	MGGA became the United Farmers of Manitoba (UFM)			
1923.		Drive to form a Wheat Pool in Saskatchewan fell just short of target	Alberta Co-op. Wheat Producers (Alberta Pool) formed	
1924.	Manitoba Co-op Wheat Producers (Manitoba Pool) took over the government elevator system	Saskatchewan Co-op. Wheat Producers (Sask. Pool) formed, took over the SCEC elevators		
1925.		Retail co-ops proposed to take over the SGGA Trading Department as a co-op wholesale		
1926.	At the UFM convention in Brandon, farmers talked about forming a co-op wholesale; organization began	SGGA joined with the Farmers' Union of Canada to form United Farmers of Canada, Sask. Section (UFCSS)		
1927.	17 Nov.: Manitoba Co-op Wholesale Ltd. (MCW) incorporated to serve 8 co-ops			

1928.	MCW opened its first office at 460 Main, Winnipeg	Annual Meeting 29 Feb.–2 Mar.: UFCSS voted to separate and reorganize Trading Dept.; 30 July: Sask. Wholesale Society Ltd. incorporated as a preliminary organization	10 Mar.: Alberta Co-op. Wholesale Association Ltd. (ACWA) incorporated	Formation of a Co-op. Wholesale Society discussed by UFBC
1929. Tues. 29 Oct.: "Black Tuesday" (crash of New York stock market, start of Depression)	MCW opened a printing plant	2 Feb.: Sask. Co-op. Wholesale Society Ltd. (SCWS) incorporated by act of the legislature, took over UFCSS Trading Dept.	ACWA purchased inventories and signed a large contract to handle lumber	
1930. Wheat Pools caught with inadequate financing when grain prices fell below the level of initial payments— government intervention is required to save the Pools; MCW, SCWS, and ACWA agreed to work together in twine, oil, and other purchases	MCW operating with staff of 3 (316 McIntyre Bldg., Winnipeg); MCW printing plant closed; directors pledged personal property as security for MCW bank loans	Independent oil co-ops created near Moose Jaw, Regina, and Weyburn	ACWA in acute financial difficulty, mainly as a result of lumber contract	
1931. Oil co-ops developed in Saskatchewan and Manitoba		Agreement reached with Sask. Wheat Pool to sell SCWS coal, twine, etc.; staff at this time = 1 manager, 1 bookkeeper, 2 clerks		
1932.				Origins of UFA Co-op: a committee of UFA leaders began co-ordinating bulk purchasing by UFA locals

298

General	Manitoba	Saskatchewan	Alberta	B.C.
1933. Concentration of ownership in the oil refining industry increased as small oil refiners were bought up and disappeared		SCWS plan to assist retails in building coal sheds approved; distribution of farm supplies through UFCSS and Pool agents provided basis for Affiliate Plan of 1934	ACWA's lumber obligations finally discharged	
1934.		Co-op Refinery incorporated by 10 Regina-area oil co-ops; SCWS Affiliate Plan officially adopted	ACWA debts settled; for the next four years ACWA is largely dormant, run on the side by William Halsall out of Killam Co-op	
1935.		27 May: CCRL commenced operations	UFA government (in power since 1921) defeated by Social Credit	
1936. Oil price wars in areas of Manitoba and Saskatchewan served by co-ops		Sask. Section of CUC formed; B. Johnsrude hired as first provincial organizer for co-ops	Alta. Co-op Council formed, forerunner of Alta. Federation of Agriculture; A. H. Christensen became Supervisor of Co-operative Associations	
1937.		SCWS and CCRL began to work closely together through joint marketing of tires; 1st Co-operative School held at Univ. of Sask.	Alberta Section of CUC formed	

1938. An interprovincial bulk commodity purchasing committee was formed, formalizing relations among MCW, SCWS, and ACWA; significant sales increases for all wholesales start 30 years of uninterrupted expansion	SCWS opened a Regina branch, arranged to bring in CO-OP tractors from the U.S., adopted a life insurance plan for employees, and provided assistance to the Lethbridge Co-operative Coal Mine operated by unemployed miners. CCRL adopted 3-year revolving-door financing	ACWA completely reorganized with new head office in Edmonton, new manager (Dave Smeaton), and contractual obligations of member associations to purchase from the wholesale	May: a conference of 21 co-op associations discussed collective buying; 11 Oct.: BCCWS incorporated
1939. The first CO-OP tractor was imported from the U.S., beginning co-operative involvement in the farm machinery business	SCWS adopted revolving-door financing, purchased a flour mill at Outlook, and had its powers widened in its charter; CCRL started an Expansion Program; *Co-operative Consumer* newspaper began publication; Manager McKay of SCWS laid the groundwork for an Associated Stores expansion plan	ACWA began distribution of CO-OP Maid Feeds	BCCWS had 10 member associations who had contributed $428 equity; Sept.: BCCWS opened a Vancouver office at 555 Howe St.
1940. 17 Sept.: IPCO incorporated by federal charter; CCIL obtained a charter and opened an office in Regina	June: CCRL cracking plant came on-stream, increasing capacity to 1,500 barrels/day; CCRL operated its first 12-month year; CCRL started a crude oil exploration program; SCWS invested in Hy-Grade coal mine near Drumheller; SCWS superannuation scheme organized; Saskatchewan Women's Co-operative Guild organized		

General	Manitoba	Saskatchewan	Alberta	B.C.
1941.	MCW acquired a new office with a warehouse in the Aldous Building on Donald St.; staff now 8, total inventory $1,000	SCWS started grocery service from Regina; Sask. Co-op. Credit Society incorporated		BCCWS set up an Education dept. under C. D. Clarke
1942.	Annual Managers' Conventions started in Manitoba	New SCWS office opened on 23rd St. in Saskatoon; SCWS started feed manufacture in Saskatoon; CCRL increased capacity to 2,500 barrels/day		
1943. CUC restructured into provincial sections	Manitoba began producing CO-OP feeds; *Manitoba Co-operator* began publication with MCW involvement	SCWS purchased an office and warehouse on Rose St. in Regina; SCWS opened a feed plant in Regina; Co-op Fidelity and Guarantee Co. Ltd. incorporated; Sask. Co-op. Superannuation Society created		
1944. CCIL purchased Cockshutt factory in Winnipeg; McDougall Royal Commission on Co-operatives and Taxation appointed	MCW purchased property at Vine and Whyte, and built a feed plant on it; MCW purchased Penn Oil Companies Ltd. and organized it as an "Oil Division"; MCW moved into a new head office at 230 Princess St., Winnipeg	SCWS purchased Cushing feed plant on Duchess St. in Saskatoon; SCWS purchased the Empire Coal Mine near Drumheller; SCWS and CCRL merged to form SFCL; SFCL set up a dry goods dept.; the provincial government established a Dept. of Co-operation and Co-operative Development		

1945. Co-ordinated by the new provincial sections of the CUC, co-ops prepared briefs for the McDougall Commission; McDougall Commission reported—co-ops found its recommendations acceptable	MCW established a hardware department; MCW began to develop a wholesale grocery service	SFCL purchased the remainder of the Hy-Grade coal mine; SFCL purchased the Shuswap Lumber Co. at Canoe, B.C.; SFCL opened a grocery dept. in Saskatoon; Co-op Life Insurance Co. incorporated	ACWA acquired a warehouse in Edmonton	BCCWS set up an Associated Stores dept. and a Farm Supplies dept.
1946. The federal government introduced new legislation for income taxation of co-ops, much more restrictive than recommended by the 1944–45 Royal Commission; co-ops fought the new provisions, but a tax on 3% of capital employed was imposed; IPCO began handling hardware; CCIL began production	Co-op Vegetable Oil plant opened at Altona; MCW set up a pension plan; MCW built a new feed plant at Winnipeg; MCW Audit dept. now served 95 locals	SFCL purchased a new head office building on Ave. D in Saskatoon; Hy-grade mine, CCRL, and the Outlook flour mill reorganized as wholly-owned subsidiaries; SFCL adopted a 5-year expansion plan	ACWA entered into an agreement with the UFA on petroleum distribution	BCCWS created a Merchandising dept. and opened its first warehouse; warehouse facilities are leased at 1164 Homer St., Vancouver
1947.		SFCL opened a Lumber dept.; Sask. Pool opened a flax plant in Saskatoon; Federated Agencies Ltd. incorporated for insurance sales; Sask. Co-op. Superannuation Society took over the old SCWS and CCRL plans	ACWA began a warehouse in Grande Prairie to serve the Peace River area	

General	Manitoba	Saskatchewan	Alberta	B.C.
1948. Consumers' Exploration Co. Ltd. (set up by the three prairie co-op wholesales) struck oil near Princess, Alta.; CCIL reorganized as a centralized co-op (end of district structure)			ACWA expansion program started; Management Service and Audit depts. created; UFA withdrew from educational activities and changed its name to UFA Co-op	BCCWS admitted 15 new member associations for a total of 68
1949.	MCW opened Dry Goods, Construction, and Insurance depts.; Grocery Dept. began stocking inventories	Outlook flour mill closed; Sask. Wheat Pool flour mill in Saskatoon opened; SFCL management reorganized	ACWA bought a new feed plant in Edmonton; ACWA established a branch warehouse in Calgary	
1950.		Refinery Expansion Drive started; Managers' Advisory Committee active; Tisdale branch warehouse opened	21 stores purchased from the UFA	BCCWS reviewed its Associate Stores Plan
1951. IPCO opened a coffee and tea plant in South Burnaby, B.C. (peanut butter added later to the same plant); IPCO began handling major appliances under Viscount brand	MCW and the Federation of Southern Man. Co-ops sponsored an organizing committee for an "International Co-op Institute"; MCW discontinued Dry Goods; Personnel dept. opened	24 Aug. was declared "Co-operation Day" and saw celebrations at the Refinery of the new expansion to 6,500 barrels/day; SFCL established a branch warehouse at Swift Current; SFCL Training Program started	ACWA opened a new Edmonton warehouse	
1952. Co-op Fire and Casualty became active on a national scale; Co-op Trust created; IPCO opened a canning plant at Beamsville, Ont.		Yorkton branch warehouse established; Regina feed plant closed; Empire mine closed; CCRL began a new Expansion Program	ACWA experienced severe financial strain as a result of its expansion	BCCWS acquired new premises, a warehouse and offices in South Burnaby (the first facilities it owned)

1953. IPCO opened a chemical plant in Winnipeg formulating herbicides and pesticides from prepared ingredients; Canadian Co-op Credit Society incorporated under federal charter	MCW opened a Lumber dept.	SFCL opened a new Regina warehouse for lumber; Refinery Expansion Bonds were sold; construction began on a catalytic cracking unit for the Refinery	Grande Prairie warehouse closed	BCCWS received 14 new member associations for a total of 97; BCCWS completed a warehouse expansion
1954. The directors and managers of MCW and SFCL discussed a merger		A $7.5 million expansion increased CCRL's production to 12,000 barrels/day; 18 Aug. saw more Co-operation Day celebrations at the Refinery; SFCL opened new Regina branch offices and warehouse and replaced its Swift Current warehouse; SFCL leased a planer mill at Chase, B.C. (near Canoe)	ACWA annual meeting proposed merger with SFCL	
1955. MCW and SFCL merged to form Federated Co-operatives Ltd; IPCO began handling CO-OP "Indian Brand" fertilizers; the Co-op Institute conducted its first course	New Winnipeg grocery warehouse established			
1956. IPCO entered into automotive supplies by introducing CO-OP tires	First Co-operative Public Relations Federations organized for district-level promotion of co-operation and co-operative education; new emphasis on retail expansion adopted by FCL; Canoe lumber mill burned down		ACWA opened a new lumber dept. and started a petroleum expansion drive	Management reorganization in BCCWS; 3-year expansion drive announced

General	Manitoba	Saskatchewan	Alberta	B.C.
1957. New CO-OP insignia adopted by IPCO: the red "CO-OP" inside a green badge		New, more modern and more highly mechanized lumber mill opened at Canoe; FCL started a Co-op Identification Program to improve the attractiveness and recognition value of retail and wholesale facilities	ACWA opened a new farm supplies dept.	Warehouse on Telford Avenue, Vancouver expanded
1958.		Co-operative Union of Manitoba formed; new coke plant went into production at the Refinery	Farmers' Union of Alberta set up Goldeye Camp; Co-op Union of Alta. ceased activities	
1959. The Royal Commission on Price Spreads of Food Products in Canada reported, responding to public concerns about food pricing and commercial fairness		FCL and ACWA annual meetings approved merger effective 1962; Co-op Institute renamed Western Co-op College, land purchased for permanent facilities in Saskatoon	ACWA took steps to close out its direct-membership departments; Alta. Wheat Pool started a fertilizer service	Completion of 3-year expansion drive: 9 major new retail developments carried out, number of lines of merchandise handled by BCCWS doubled; now 125 member associations in BCCWS
1960. Amalgamation of FCL and ACWA speeded up to 1961		18 June: nearly 40,000 people attended the 25th anniversary celebrations at CCRL; new Saskatoon feed plant opened at Sutherland; Winnipeg feed plant enlarged; new Winnipeg offices and warehouse opened at King Edward and Notre Dame; Co-op Savings Bonds, Series "A" issued by FCL ($10 million authorized), to finance expansion; cost-plus pricing adopted for groceries	ACWA Dry Goods dept. closed	BCCWS changed over from expansion to a 3-year period of consolidation; BCCWS representatives negotiated with FCL about a possible merger
1961. 31 Oct.: ACWA-FCL merger effective; old CO-OP label program with Red, Blue, and Green labels replaced by modern CO-OP and Harmonie brands		New Saskatoon warehouse opened; Regina warehouse expanded; Tisdale warehouse closed; Canoe lumber mill expanded; CCRL Expansion Program launched to reach 22,500 barrels/day; fresh meats program started; Code of Ethics for Co-operatives adopted		BCCWS reorganized its wholesaling service and opened a new warehouse; finances became "strained" in the aftermath of expansion

1962. Wheat Pools decided to handle farm supplies; Carter Royal Commission on taxation heard briefs for and against harsher taxation of co-ops

Western Co-op College opened new facilities in Saskatoon; Hy-Grade mine closed

1963. IPCO accepted the Wheat Pools, which were now handling farm supplies, into membership

1964. FCL and the Sask. and Alta. Pools formed WCFL; official opening of new IPCO 2,4-D complex in Saskatoon; in response to continuing consumer concerns the federal government created an "Advisory Council of Consumers"

FCL established an Agricultural dept. to handle chemicals, fertilizers, and twine; P. S. Ross and Partners were engaged as management consultants to study the structure of FCL; Western Co-op College completed an expansion

1965. 9 Oct.: WCFL opened a new fertilizer plant at Calgary

Consultants' report received, FCL reorganized management and member relations to embody the new "One System" concept, and to adopt a new statement of objectives for FCL; new Calgary offices, warehouse, and feed plant acquired; lumber mill purchased at Smith, Alberta; FCL began supplying pharmaceutical products

1966. Co-operative Union of Sask. reorganized as the Co-operative Development Association

Plywood plant completed at Canoe; cutting rights obtained in area of Smith mill; expansion planned; regional amalgamation plan approved to reduce the number of retail co-ops from 500 to 100–140 by the end of 1969

Expansion of Burnaby warehouse begun; B.C. Managers Conference studied amalgamation into 5–6 regional co-ops in B.C.

General	Manitoba	Saskatchewan	Alberta	B.C.
1967. IPCO opened a new $300,000 chemical facility in Toronto, expanded its Winnipeg formulating plant by $250,000, and started a $5 million expansion of its Saskatoon complex			New Edmonton warehouse and office building opened; addition planned for Winnipeg facilities; plans for a new head office in Saskatoon finalized; a Director of Urban Retailing was appointed to encourage development in the major cities	Construction of an interior feed mill at Prince George begun; groceries, lubricants, building supplies, heavy hardware moved to a leased warehouse on Euclid Avenue, Vancouver, because of shortage of space
1968.		Further discussion of how to implement the "One System" concept — discussion of centralization of the whole system; member relations programs shifted more to the responsibility of the retails; FCL's role in central advertising programs increased; reorganization of FCL management announced; Managers' Advisory Committee plus regional M. A. C.'s and consultative committees on specific products and programs; new feed mill opened at Brandon; first major strike in 40-year history of system: Canoe mill and plywood plant shut down for 7 months		
1969. Sharp downturn in prairie farm economy, 1969–70, due to depressed export markets and inability to market grain surpluses; Sask. Pool entered into feed distribution		First fall in sales for the wholesale since 1937; FCL management reorganization resulted in a 25% reduction in management personnel; advanced computerization undertaken		
1970. FCL and BCCWS amalgamated effective 1 May; FCL took over management of IPCO, whose Saskatoon chemical complex had run into serious financial difficulties		FCL net savings fell to record low of 1.4%; FCL board approved policies for financial assistance to dissolving or amalgamating retail co-ops; crude oil exploration suspended indefinitely; new $4.5 million Saskatoon head office building opened; delegates at the FCL annual meeting approved in principle the idea of a centralized retailing co-operative		
1971. IPCO taken over by FCL as a wholly-owned subsidiary		FCL board approved a policy for financial assistance to retails running deficits; FCL annual meeting voted to incorporate a centralized retailing co-operative, and to start its development in the Saskatoon region		

1972. Western Co-op College decided to rename itself the Co-op College of Canada; Co-operative Union of B.C. closed; Sask. Co-op Development Assoc. ceased activities

17 April: Westland Co-operatives incorporated; feed plants purchased by FCL at Melfort, Moosomin, and Weyburn; FCL equity structure changed to pay more back to large retails; new Inventory Management System developed by FCL for use by retails to cut costs

1973. International "Energy Crisis" leads to high inflation, shortages, and a falling dollar; WCFL expanded its Calgary plant by $5.75 million and bought a plant in Medicine Hat

1. Jan.: Westland Co-ops began operations with merger between 4 Saskatchewan retail co-ops and Westland, joining one B.C. unit already in Westland; plywood plant and lumber mill at Canoe expanded; FCL fought inflation by holding down prices on many goods, especially farm supplies, leading to losses on some products and to shortages and rationing; increased focus on relations of retails with their members; the phrase, "The Co-operative Retailing System," became common in official documents to describe FCL and its member retails

1974.

New CCRL expansion begun, aimed nearly to double capacity from 28,500 barrels/day to 50,000; new Vancouver area distribution centre opened on Annacis Island; Calgary and Edmonton warehouses expanded; expansions planned for Saskatoon, Regina, and Winnipeg; feed mill purchased at Lethbridge; start of FCL policy of encouraging Home Improvement and Farm Centres; new identification program leads to an all-red CO-OP badge insignia; at delegates' insistence some green is retained in the surrounding colour scheme

1975. Major co-operatives set up a financial package to enable CCIL to continue operating; Northland Bank incorporated, with the intention that it become a co-operative bank

FCL purchased a plant at Lanigan for construction of manufactured (pre-fab) homes; Prince George feed mill closed; new Edmonton mill begun; "Country Morning" label introduced; peak circulation of the *Co-op Consumer* (310,000)

1976. WCFL subsidiary Canadian Fertilizers Ltd. opened two plants at Medicine Hat

FCL adopted a new democratic control structure which created a Vice-President, an Executive Management Committee representative, a committee, and a fall conference in each of the six operational regions; future of Westland Co-operatives debated; new Area Development program started; Otterburne, Manitoba feed plant purchased to replace outdated Winnipeg plant; "Tempo" program of gasoline distribution to private retailers started

General	Manitoba	Saskatchewan	Alberta	B.C.
1977. 3rd CFL plant opened in Medicine Hat	Westland Co-operatives was terminated and its 16 Units converted back to autonomous retail co-operatives; the Smith, Alberta lumber mill was sold for $4 million after $1 million annual losses; the Lethbridge feed mill was sold for $2.7 million; CCRL production increased to 32,500 barrels/day as a new Platformer unit came on-stream; FCL started a new energy conservation program — by 1987 savings of 22.6% were achieved at CCRL, 41.5% on buildings, and 21.0% on the plywood plant; Canadian Arctic Federation accepted as a member of FCL, serving 30 Far North co-ops			
1978.	50th anniversary celebrations for the system included a renewed emphasis on member relations; a Member and Public Relations Division of FCL was created; CCRL production reached 43,000 barrels/day as a result of new crude-vacuum units and the larger Platformer already installed in 1977; Lanigan manufactured homes plant closed; instead FCL bought 50% of Designex Buildings Ltd. of North Battleford			
1979. 1 Nov.: IPCO returned to its original members after 8 years under FCL — sales now $71.9 million, savings $1.4 million; Co-operative Future Directions Project inaugurated by Canadian co-operators	Winnipeg warehouse expanded; Saskatoon warehouse renovated; frozen food service started out of the Calgary warehouse; Vancouver distribution centre closed and sold for $5 million (a capital gain of nearly $2 million); hardware and crop supply inventories from Saskatoon consolidated in Regina (both measures taken to reduce inventories); sawmill purchased at Revelstoke and expansion of the mill started			
1980. High interest rates begin to be perceived as a limitation to growth	Final phase of 6-year, $30 million Refinery expansion completed; FCL study of energy resources, alternative energy sources, and conservation leads, among other energy projects considered, to negotiations with SaskOil and the petroleum industry concerning a proposed heavy oil upgrader; Otterburne feed plant sold; 4th consecutive production record set by Canoe sawmill; start of a 3-year institutional advertising program; new delegate formula led to fewer delegates at annual meetings; reorganization of the *Co-op Consumer*, whose circulation had declined to 160,000, to include more "information" and pictures; Women's Participation Committee formed to encourage greater participation by women in the system			
1981.	New 3-year Refinery expansion program begun to complete the increase of capacity to 50,000 barrels/day, and to permit processing of somewhat heavier crude oil; 17 Dec.: Co-enerco agreement signed with federal government, allowing the system to increase its participation in crude oil exploration and production; FCL began a program to enhance the economic viability of retails; "Baker's Nook" introduced as the name for in-store bakeries in the system; Revelstoke sawmill closed as depression set in for the lumber industry; FCL took over sole ownership of Designex Buildings, makers of pre-fabricated homes; another study of the *Co-op Consumer*; circulation now 132,000			

1982. Severe economic recession, especially in western Canada

"Economic offensive" launched by FCL board and senior management: Vancouver region office closed; *Co-op Consumer* discontinued; Designex Manufactured Homes shut down; 250 staff cut; action plans presented to 36 retails judged to be in difficulties, resulting in closures of departments and reductions in staff, inventories, and expenses; new Calgary distribution centre opened; non-food inventories in Alberta consolidated there; zone pricing and inventory control programs introduced for food and hardware to lower costs and increase efficiency, aided by FCL's central computers; Refinery expansion program saw completion of new coking plant for processing asphaltic residues, and 3 new storage tanks; construction begun on a new fuel gas desulphurizer and sulphur plant; June: Co-enerco incorporated and active, arranged its first acquisitions of oil and gas wells

1983.

Aug.: agreement-in-principle signed for a Heavy Oil Upgrader by representatives of FCL and the governments of Saskatchewan and Canada; FCL board decided FCL would withdraw from fertilizer distribution; completion of Refinery expansion to 50,000 barrels/day; FCL board and senior management began to turn the priority from assisting retails that were in trouble to emphasizing aggressive merchandising and marketing

1984.

PetroPower 50 — 50th anniversary celebrations for CCRL; further consolidations in distribution: the Regina distribution centre began supplying non-food items to Winnipeg Region retails; sensing greater competition, FCL adoted a greater emphasis on advertising, including the start of red-and-white "Cash Saver" promotions; new policy statement on Training, Education, and Development adopted by the FCL board

1985.

19 Oct.: sod turning for the Co-op Upgrader; first real rise in sales by FCL in 5 years; $1.7 million modernization of the plywood plant at Canoe increased the automation of the production process there; Revelstoke lumber mill closed; cedar mill at the Canoe site also closed; increased attention to the image of the Co-operative Retailing System became a leading corporate priority for the Marketing Group; "Pump 24" of card-activated 24-hour gas and diesel pumps started; first two "bake-offs" established (small bakeries producing goods from frozen dough), enabling more retails to have in-store bakeries; new CO-OP label products included decaffeinated coffee, dental floss, shampoo, frozen fish fillets, new carbonated drinks

1986.

Recovery continued — local retail net savings doubled; for the first time since 1973 all departments contributed positively to FCL's net savings; construction continued on the Co-op Upgrader; "Action year" in the Co-operative Retailing System image campaign saw repainting of facilities, cleanups, and improved merchandising; Area Development continued to be stressed as a priority for the system; CO-OP noodles, frozen perogies, salted peanuts, luxury cat food, lawn and garden bags, acetaminophen tablets, spaghetti sauce, and other products were introduced

General	Manitoba	Saskatchewan	Alberta	B.C.
1987. A federal Co-operatives Secretariat was formed; the CUC and the Co-op College united to form the Canadian Co-operative Association		A $4 million isomerization unit came on-stream at CCRL, improving the lighter gasoline blends by removing sulphur and enhancing octane levels without the use of lead; a petroleum distribution drive sought to increase gasoline volume by establishing new outlets in urban areas and on highways, including gas bars and including facilities directly owned by FCL; a commitment was made to begin a long-planned further modernization of the Canoe lumber mill; FCL proposed a 60th anniversary theme of "Co-ops . . . Together . . . Serving the West," and a marketing theme of "Value . . . Service . . . Guaranteed." A 60-week program of advertising and special offers was planned in conjunction with the anniversary, and the system adopted new uniforms for the occasion		
1988.		The new Co-op Upgrader came on-stream		

source: Annual reports, retrospective summaries published by the companies in question, government and newspaper reports, other published sources.

note: Dates given in various sources for some of these events vary, because of differences in financial years *vs.* calendar years, and because of differences between when a program or expansion is decided upon, when it is operational, and when its official opening is celebrated.

For greater detail on many of these events see Jack Trevena, *Prairie Co-operation — A Diary* (Saskatoon, Co-operative College of Canada: 1976).

APPENDIX FOUR

Summary of Sales and Savings of FCL and its Predecessors, 1928–87

note: Figures are approximate, because different accounting procedures were used at different times and by different wholesales, and the figures have been compiled from a wide variety of sources. See Appendix Five for total figures corrected for inflation.

SALES—TOP LINE in each year
NET SAVINGS—SECOND LINE in each year (losses in parentheses)

Year	Manitoba	Saskatchewan	CCRL	Alberta	B.C.
1928	130,000	—	—	—	—
	(loss)	—	—	—	—
1929	278,000	635,000	—	72,000	—
	(1,000)	6,000	—	—	—
1930	334,000	586,000	—	62,000	—
	7,000	7,000	—	(8,000)	—
1931	274,000	488,000	—	20,000	—
	1,000	6,000	—	—	—
1932	326,000	385,000	—	18,000	—
	4,000	8,000	—	(2,000)	—
1933	228,000	315,000	—	11,000	—
	2,000	5,000	—	1,000	—
1934	305,000	341,000	—	2,000	—
	4,000	8,000	—	—	—
1935	320,000	441,000	253,000	26,000	—
	8,000	7,000	30,000	—	—
1936	296,000	531,000	521,000	31,000	—
	15,000	20,000	25,000	—	—
1937	397,000	501,000	432,000	42,000	—
	20,000	9,000	12,000	—	—
1938	481,000	1,032,000[1]	653,000	50,000	—
	27,000	33,000	127,000	8,000	—
1939	615,000	1,498,000	1,051,000	59,000	—
	37,000	60,000	152,000	18,000	—
1940	778,000	2,226,000	1,632,000	80,000	—
	47,000	72,000	246,000	16,000	—

Year	Manitoba	Saskatchewan	CCRL	Alberta	B.C.
1941	990,000	2,889,000	1,921,000	164,000	10,000
	60,000	87,000	304,000	23,000	1,000
1942	1,354,000	3,752,000	2,295,000	129,000	18,000
	89,000	98,000	258,000	34,000	2,000
1943	1,544,000	4,456,000	2,395,000	219,000	36,000
	106,000	102,000	149,000	38,000	4,000
1944	2,068,000	4,007,000[2]	2,753,000[3]	312,000	33,000
	140,000	135,000	170,000	56,000	2,000
1945	2,244,000	7,136,000		400,000	49,000
	148,000	301,000		51,000	—
1946	2,952,000	9,381,000		505,000	85,000
	193,000	559,000		102,000	7,000
1947	3,694,000	11,320,000		603,000	226,000
	180,000	831,000		51,000	11,000
1948	4,478,000	13,289,000		769,000	218,000
	199,000	434,000		11,000	11,000
1949	4,872,000	14,804,000		1,368,000	336,000
	162,000	384,000		29,000	11,000
1950	5,095,000	17,047,000		1,922,000	544,000
	132,000	526,000		5,000	10,000
1951	5,710,000	19,226,000		2,732,000	659,000
	183,000	982,000		34,000[4]	11,000
1952	6,361,000	23,921,000		2,557,000	756,000
	191,000	1,786,000		93,000	(12,000)
1953	7,246,000	28,927,000		4,805,000	1,059,000
	239,000	1,882,000		67,000	19,000
1954	7,634,000	31,625,000		6,612,000	1,269,000
	292,000	1,023,000		—	16,000
1955		41,674,000		6,857,000	1,539,000
		1,535,000		50,000	24,000
1956		46,051,000		7,766,000	2,078,000
		2,058,000		56,000	27,000
1957		50,231,000		6,722,000[5]	2,340,194
		2,077,000		68,000	17,000
1958		54,054,000		7,589,000	3,190,000
		3,152,000		119,000	13,000
1959		61,558,000		8,291,000	4,104,000
		4,199,000		128,000	11,000
1960		67,310,000		9,146,000	4,560,000
		3,591,000		99,000	(6,000)
1961		71,941,000		11,428,000	5,261,000
		3,208,000		102,000	7,000
1962		94,826,000			5,619,000
		2,896,000			19,000
1963		103,360,000			6,920,000
		4,580,000			90,000
1964		110,988,000			7,295,000
		5,063,000			118,000
1965		132,568,000			8,333,000
		4,678,000			119,000

Year	Manitoba	Saskatchewan	CCRL	Alberta	B.C.
1966		150,628,000			10,149,000
		4,428,000			155,000
1967		169,621,000			11,779,000
		4,162,000			160,000
1968		176,387,000			13,448,000
		4,262,000			41,000
1969		173,989,000			15,304,000
		5,015,000			(277,000)
1970		183,388,000			
		2,628,000			
1971		232,441,000[6]			
		2,880,000			
1972		285,575,000			
		10,216,000			
1973		358,218,000			
		14,582,000			
1974		486,971,000			
		15,761,000			
1975		595,084,000			
		8,029,000			
1976		696,982,000			
		15,554,000			
1977		761,735,000			
		18,972,000			
1978		875,564,000			
		24,727,000			
1979		1,061,596,000			
		25,008,000			
1980		1,122,606,000[7]			
		31,013,000			
1981		1,327,037,000			
		50,091,000			
1982		1,371,808,000			
		11,525,000			
1983		1,374,486,000			
		27,415,000			
1984		1,359,372,000[8]			
		28,956,000			
1985		1,435,276,000			
		32,726,000			
1986		1,399,410,000			
		66,346,000			
1987		1,427,997,000			
		63,626,000			

source: Annual reports; financial statements; retrospective summaries by the organizations named.

1   15-month financial year.
2   7-month financial year.

3   11-month financial year.

4   Financial statements for ACWA in 1951 showed a loss of $387,920 because the purchase of the UFA stores that year had not yet been put on long-term financing. When the purchase was later re-financed, the operating deficit for that year was readjusted.

5   Sales appear to have fallen for ACWA as the stores purchased from the UFA in 1951 were sold or converted to autonomous retails. In 1956, for example, Calgary Co-op was created out of the former UFA/ACWA store in Calgary. For 1951–56 in particular, therefore, ACWA sales figures include some retail business as well as wholesale business.

6   Includes sales of IPCO and Northern Industrial Chemicals Ltd., taken over in 1971 as wholly-owned subsidiaries (sales $22 million in 1971, for a net loss of about $700,000).

7   No longer includes sales of IPCO ($71.9 million in 1979).

8   FCL withdrew from fertilizer distribution in 1984; sales by its crop supplies division fell by $20 million from 1983 levels.

APPENDIX FIVE

Total Sales and Savings of FCL and its Predecessors, 1928–87, Actual and Corrected for Inflation

Actual sales and savings are as recorded by FCL for its own and its predecessors' sales. These do not in every case correspond to the figures in Appendix 4, because of the variety of sources from which the figures in Appendix 4 are taken.

Sales and savings corrected for inflation are expressed in terms of 1987 dollars.[1] The growth in these figures represents, roughly, the growth in the actual volume of goods and services provided to members.

Losses are in parentheses.

| Year | ACTUAL | | CORRECTED FOR INFLATION | |
	Sales (dollars)	Net Savings (dollars)	Sales (1987 dollars)	Net Savings (1987 dollars)
1928	130,000	—	1,183,000	—
1929	913,000	9,000	8,192,000	88,000
1930	993,000	(1,000)	9,226,000	(9,000)
1931	782,000	6,000	7,702,000	59,000
1932	729,000	6,000	7,892,000	65,000
1933	554,000	5,000	6,150,000	55,000
1934	648,000	9,000	7,074,000	98,000
1935	1,192,000	46,000	12,905,000	498,000
1936	1,353,000	60,000	14,294,000	634,000
1937	1,351,000	41,000	13,827,000	420,000
1938	1,911,000	193,000	19,558,000	1,975,000
1939	2,711,000	266,000	27,964,000	2,744,000
1940	4,100,000	360,000	40,689,000	3,573,000
1941	5,149,000	474,000	47,169,000	4,343,000
1942	6,623,000	486,000	58,229,000	4,273,000
1943	7,806,000	420,000	65,973,000	3,550,000
1944	8,074,000	468,000	66,522,000	3,856,000
1945	9,879,000	535,000	79,396,000	4,300,000
1946	12,923,000	861,000	100,769,000	6,714,000
1947	15,841,000	1,073,000	113,397,000	7,681,000
1948	18,751,000	655,000	119,823,000	4,186,000

Year	ACTUAL Sales (dollars)	Net Savings (dollars)	CORRECTED FOR INFLATION Sales (1987 dollars)	Net Savings (1987 dollars)
1949	21,370,000	522,000	130,816,000	3,195,000
1950	24,593,000	599,000	147,109,000	3,583,000
1951	27,841,000	1,143,000	149,474,000	6,137,000
1952	33,305,000	1,939,000	171,096,000	9,961,000
1953	41,088,000	2,131,000	211,080,000	10,947,000
1954	45,955,000	1,339,000	232,436,000	6,773,000
1955	49,090,000	1,609,000	247,338,000	8,107,000
1956	55,895,000	2,141,000	271,194,000	10,388,000
1957	59,293,000	2,162,000	281,427,000	10,262,000
1958	64,833,000	3,284,000	304,413,000	15,419,000
1959	73,953,000	4,339,000	339,924,000	19,944,000
1960	81,016,000	3,684,000	367,235,000	16,699,000
1961	87,355,000	3,317,000	394,603,000	14,984,000
1962	99,905,000	2,915,000	445,155,000	12,989,000
1963	110,280,000	4,670,000	481,556,000	20,392,000
1964	118,283,000	5,181,000	504,726,000	22,107,000
1965	140,901,000	4,797,000	582,272,000	19,824,000
1966	160,777,000	4,583,000	636,307,000	18,138,000
1967	181,400,000	4,322,000	690,797,000	16,459,000
1968	189,837,000	4,303,000	700,525,000	15,879,000
1969	189,293,000	4,738,000	668,393,000	16,730,000
1970	183,388,000	2,628,000	619,171,000	8,873,000
1971	232,345,000	2,880,000	760,930,000	9,432,000
1972	285,475,000	10,216,000	890,410,000	31,864,000
1973	358,218,000	16,769,000	1,022,365,000	47,859,000
1974	486,971,000	15,761,000	1,210,497,000	39,178,000
1975	595,084,000	8,029,000	1,328,041,000	17,918,000
1976	696,982,000	15,554,000	1,422,191,000	31,738,000
1977	761,735,000	18,972,000	1,446,193,000	36,019,000
1978	875,564,000	24,727,000	1,558,409,000	44,011,000
1979	1,061,596,000	25,008,000	1,712,673,000	40,345,000
1980	1,122,606,000	31,013,000	1,626,785,000	44,941,000
1981	1,327,037,000	50,091,000	1,738,419,000	65,619,000
1982	1,371,808,000	11,525,000	1,653,237,000	13,889,000
1983	1,374,486,000	27,415,000	1,578,069,000	31,476,000
1984	1,359,372,000	28,956,000	1,509,133,000	32,146,000
1985	1,435,276,000	32,726,000	1,544,956,000	35,227,000
1986	1,399,410,000	66,346,000	1,463,070,000	69,364,000
1987	1,427,997,000	63,626,000	1,427,997,000	63,626,000
Cumulative Total (60 years)			$33,298,356,000	991,545,000

1   These are obtained by using the GNEIPD (Statistics Canada Cat. 11–210). The GNEIPD is based on a multiplier for 1981 prices of 1.000. Each year's sales were divided by the GNEIPD for that year to produce 1981-equivalent values, then multiplied by the GNEIPD for 1987 to produce 1987-equivalent values.

It should be noted that this is a crude measurement which does not take account of the specific inflation rates for the commodities handled by the system, in the regions where the system operates. For example, in the 1970s petroleum probably experienced greater price inflation than most commodities, and FCL probably handled more of it than most commodities. The full amount of inflation in FCL sales would then be greater than the correction, and the figures given here for the 1970s and 1980s would still be somewhat excessive relative to the earlier eras.

APPENDIX SIX

FCL Sales by Division, 1955–87

See Appendix Five for total FCL sales.
All figures are in *millions* **of dollars**
TOP LINE in each year is *sales,* **BOTTOM LINE is** *net savings*
Losses are in parentheses.

year	petroleum	lumber[1]	agro[2]	feed[3]	dry goods[4]	food[5]	hardware	other
1955	20.4	7.0	—	1.6	0.8	7.0	4.1	
	0.6	0.2		0.1	0.0	0.2	0.2	
1956	21.5	7.1	1.1	1.8	0.8	7.6	5.1	
	0.7	0.3		0.2	0.0	0.2	0.3	
1957	22.7	6.8	1.2	2.6	1.0	8.7	6.2	
	0.7	0.3		0.2	0.1	0.3	0.3	
1958	22.9	7.7	1.2	2.8	1.0	10.3	6.4	
	0.9	0.3		0.3	0.1	0.4	0.5	
1959	23.8	8.9	1.6	3.1	1.3	13.1	8.0	
	0.9	0.4		0.3	0.1	0.5	0.6	
1960	25.7	9.3	1.6	3.0	1.3	14.9	9.1	
	1.2	0.4		0.2	0.1	0.5	0.6	
1961	24.3	10.9	2.0	4.3	1.8	16.6	9.2	
	1.2	0.5		0.3	0.0	0.6	0.7	
1962[6]	27.6	11.6	3.9	6.2	2.8	27.2	13.0	
	1.4	0.5		0.3	0.1	0.6	0.7	
1963[6]	27.8	14.3	5.3	5.6	3.1	25.0	13.9	
	1.5	0.7		0.4	0.1	1.0	0.8	
1964[6]	28.4	16.8	3.3	6.0	3.9	28.2	15.3	
	1.6	0.8		0.2	0.1	1.0	0.9	
1965[6]	30.7	18.4	3.3	5.4	4.8	41.7	14.1	
	1.7	1.0	0.1	0.3	0.2	1.2	0.7	
1966[6]	34.3	21.7	8.1	6.4	5.4	56.1	15.0	
	1.7	1.0	0.2	0.3	0.2	1.1	0.6	
1967[6]	34.9	20.2	11.3	7.9	6.4	61.1	17.8	
	1.5	0.9	1.1	0.2	0.2	1.3	0.6	
1968[6]	35.1	18.9	14.3	8.0	6.3	67.3	18.4	
	1.5	1.0	1.1	0.4	0.1	1.3	0.4	
1969[6]	35.1	18.0	9.2	7.5	6.6	71.0	18.3	
	1.5	0.7	0.8	0.5	0.2	1.3	0.6	
1970	38.5	20.9	6.9	9.0	7.5	77.3	20.2	1.1[7]

year	petroleum	lumber	agro	feed	dry goods	food	hardware	other
	5.1	(0.9)	(0.7)	0.1	0.1	(0.3)	(0.5)	(0.1)
1971	45.1	25.5	10.0	10.0	8.5	83.0	23.9	24.2[8]
	5.9	(0.3)	(0.9)	(0.1)	0.1	(0.5)	(0.3)	(0.7)
1972	49.9	35.6	12.9	10.7	9.4	94.9	30.8	37.7[9]
	6.7	2.8	(0.5)	(0.2)	0.1	0.5	(0.1)	(0.2)
1973	60.6	46.8	17.9	18.7	10.1	115.9	38.1	45.0[10]
	9.5	5.4	0.3	0.3	0.1	0.5	0.5	0.1
1974	88.4	54.4	34.5	25.0	13.4	151.6	57.2	53.4[11]
	9.6	0.3	2.9	(0.9)	0.2	0.9	1.6	1.1
1975	123.0	60.9	398.8	22.5	14.4	191.5	65.5	65.3[12]
	10.4	(0.5)	(2.1)	(1.2)	0.0	(0.6)	0.4	1.1
1976	157.4	83.0	37.0	28.5	17.1	220.0	75.5	61.3[13]
	10.6	2.4	0.3	(0.9)	0.2	0.1	(0.4)	0.4
1977	179.3	94.3	33.7	26.7	16.3	249.8	78.8	62.0[14]
	9.4	4.2	(0.5)	(1.4)	0.2	3.3	(0.3)	3.3[15]
1978	205.9	100.7	52.5	24.2	18.5	293.8	86.1	93.7[16]
	10.0	8.4	(0.8)	(0.4)	0.3	4.9	0.3	2.0
1979	253.4	142.6	71.4	31.7	24.3	335.8	104.2	98.3[17]
	7.6	8.8	2.2	(0.5)	4.4	3.7	0.6	2.2
1980	327.9	129.0	78.3	39.2	28.3	388.2	107.1	24.6[18]
	24.8	(0.8)	1.3	0.7	0.4	3.8	0.4	0.5
1981	456.6	134.4	74.8	39.8	31.3	448.8	120.2	21.2[19]
	43.1	(3.3)	2.2	0.4	0.5	6.2	1.5	0.3
1982	503.0	113.6	74.5	41.2	26.7	484.8	120.0	9.0[20]
	20.7	(7.1)	(1.3)	1.3	0.3	4.8	(4.4)	(4.0)[21]
1983	518.4	130.6	71.8	39.0	20.4	481.7	110.0	2.6[22]
	22.3	(0.2)	0.4	1.3	0.3	7.2	(1.7)	(0.1)
1984	515.6	116.6	51.0	43.5	19.8	496.4	116.3	0.2[23]
	22.8	(4.8)	1.6	1.8	0.3	8.6	(1.4)	(0.0)
1985	559.7	122.3	51.3	44.9	18.9	523.0	115.0	0.1[24]
	24.6	(5.1)	1.9	2.4	0.3	9.0	0.6	(1.5)[25]
1986	507.2	123.1	55.7	38.7	19.5	537.8	117.6	—
	48.3	3.6	1.2	1.2	0.3	10.7	0.9	—
1987	507.5	134.8	49.9	38.4	18.9	555.8	122.6	—
	40.7	9.7	1.0	1.7	0.3	13.2	2.9	(5.8)[26]

Source: FCL Annual Reports.

---

1 Later known as Building Materials, Forest Products; 1955–61 includes coal and wood fuel.
2 Fertilizer 1956–65; Crop Supplies later.
3 Includes flour, 1955–64; savings include fertilizer savings.
4 Now Family Fashions.
5 Includes fresh meat products since 1963, pharmacy products since 1965.
6 Savings figures for 1962–69 refer to merchandising operations only.
7 B.C. retail stores acquired through amalgamation with BCCWS in 1970.
8 B.C. retails: 2.3 sales, (0.0) slight loss
Northern Industrial Chemicals Ltd.: 1.8 sales, (0.8) loss
IPCO: 20.0 sales, 0.1 net savings.
9 B.C. retails: 3.2 sales, 0.0 slight net savings
Northern Industrial Chemicals Ltd.: 2.3 sales, (0.8) loss
IPCO: 32.2 sales, 0.6 net savings.

10	Retail outlets:	3.5 sales, 0.0 slight net savings
	Northern Industrial Chemicals Ltd.:	1.4 sales, (0.6) loss
	IPCO:	40.1 sales, 0.6 net savings.
11	Retail outlets:	3.4 sales, 0.0 slight net savings
	IPCO:	50.1 sales, 1.1 net savings.
12	Retail outlets:	3.3 sales, (0.2) loss
	IPCO:	61.9 sales, 1.2 net savings.
13	Retail outlets:	3.3 sales, 0.0 no appreciable savings or loss
	IPCO:	58.0 sales, 0.4 net savings.
14	Retail outlets:	3.2 sales, (0.0) slight loss
	IPCO:	58.8 sales, 0.6 net savings.
15	Includes besides IPCO also 2.7 extraordinary gain.	
16	Retail outlets:	3.6 sales, (0.1) loss
	IPCO:	67.8 sales, 1.3 net savings
	Retail development:	22.4 sales, 0.8 net savings.
17	IPCO:	71.9 sales, 1.4 net savings
	Retail development:	26.4 sales, 0.7 net savings.
18	Retail development.	
19	Retail development.	
20	Retail development.	
21	Extraordinary loss (also slight loss on retail development).	
22	Retail development.	
23	Retail development.	
24	Retail development.	
25	Extraordinary loss (also slight loss on retail development).	
26	Extraordinary loss.	

APPENDIX SEVEN

Statistics on FCL Performance, 1955–87

notes:

Net savings as % of sales reflect the difference between selling price and all costs. Out of these savings must come all cash refunds to members as well as capital for operations and expansion (in share and reserve accounts). Net savings vary widely among the products handled by FCL, from 1–2% on food to 5–10% on petroleum products.

Net savings as % of members' equity are a measurement for co-operatives equivalent to measuring return on investment for profit companies.

Members' equity as % of total assets shows, in effect, how much of the co-op is owned and financed by members. The greater the proportion of members' equity, the more the co-op is financed from internal sources, the lower its interest burden, and the better its credit rating. In the late 1940s it was considered desirable that this percentage be 50%; later, 35% became a target.

Current assets/current liabilities is a ratio showing how well financed the co op's operations are. A ratio of 2:1 (or 2.0 as shown here) is considered a sign of a sufficiently well-financed business.

year	net savings as % of sales	net savings as % of members' equity	members' equity as % of total assets	current assets/ current liabilities	operating and administration costs as % of sales
1955	3.7	15.0	44.5	3.3	—
1956	4.5	16.4	47.2	3.3	12.2
1957	4.1	15.2	49.5	3.5	14.2
1958	5.8	20.5	51.7	3.8	13.8
1959	6.8	24.6	52.9	3.9	13.7
1960	5.3	19.2	49.3	2.2	13.5
1961	4.5	16.3	45.3	2.7	13.3
1962	3.1	13.9	43.1	2.2	11.1
1963	4.4	19.4	46.2	2.9	9.8
1964	4.6	19.5	49.0	3.2	9.6
1965	3.8	16.8	43.0	2.3	10.4
1966	2.9	15.0	39.8	2.1	9.6
1967	2.5	13.2	38.8	2.2	9.8
1968	2.4	12.8	37.2	2.1	9.2
1969	2.9	14.1	38.8	2.0	10.4
1970	1.4	7.3	35.9	1.7	10.8
1971	1.2	8.7	31.3	2.1	10.8
1972	3.6	23.7	38.4	3.0	9.4
1973	4.7	31.0	43.0	2.6	8.5
1974	3.2	25.6	36.5	1.7	7.4

year	net savings as % of sales	net savings as % of members' equity	members' equity as % of total assets	current assets/ current liabilities	operating and administration costs as % of sales
1975	1.3	12.9	31.0	1.6	7.5
1976	2.2	20.8	32.7	1.7	7.6
1977	2.5	21.1	36.4	1.9	7.8
1978	2.8	22.8	40.8	2.0	7.0
1979	2.4	20.0	39.8	1.5	7.0
1980	2.8	21.0	44.7	1.9	7.5
1981	3.8	26.9	47.5	1.8	7.0
1982	0.1	6.5	44.7	1.7	8.8
1983	2.0	14.6	47.7	2.4	8.0
1984	2.1	14.1	50.6	2.2	8.2
1985	2.3	14.4	52.9	2.3	8.2
1986	4.7	23.8	58.8	2.8	8.1
1987	4.5	20.4	58.8	2.5	7.8

source: FCL annual reports and financial statements.

APPENDIX EIGHT

Statistics on Retail Performance, 1970–87

year	sales (millions)	NET SAVINGS total (millions)			as % of equity	members' equity as % of total assets	retails with net loss after FCL refund	active members[1]	average sales[2]
		local	from FCL[3]	total					
1970	317.8	2.2	2.4	4.6	5.6	44.8	108	492,000	636
1971	348.8	6.0	2.6	8.6	10.0	44.9	65	493,000	696
1972	401.5	9.5	7.2	16.7	17.5	46.0	33	520,000	823
1973	503.2	14.9	14.2	29.1	25.5	46.8	13	562,000	956
1974	663.0	22.1	13.0	35.1	26.0	44.7	12	624,000	1,061
1975	825.3	20.7	7.7	28.4	19.8	39.1	36	718,000	1,149
1976	956.0	10.9	13.2	24.1	15.3	37.1	61	770,000	1,242
1977	1,050.0	6.4	14.6	21.0	12.5	35.9	74	745,000	1,409
1978	1,206.4	14.0	19.7	33.6	17.8	35.1	53	761,000	1,585
1979	1,395.6	18.7	20.0	38.7	18.4	33.7	40	862,000	1,619
1980	1,604.3	12.8	25.9	38.8	16.8	32.4	49	939,000	1,709
1981	1,931.7	1.2	41.6	42.8	16.9	32.2	40	961,000	2,010
1982	1,989.8	(18.1)	19.8[4]	1.7	0.7	31.7	116	972,000	2,048
1983	1,895.7	14.2	29.0[5]	43.2	17.3	36.9	39	935,000	2,028
1984	1,813.0	(0.1)	32.0[6]	31.9	12.2	38.4	53	919,000	1,973
1985	1,980.3	9.6	35.7[7]	45.3	15.3	40.8	35	962,000	2,058
1986	1,894.4	20.0	63.5[8]	85.5	24.1	48.8	16	886,000	2,139
1987	1,982.9	22.7	67.1[9]	89.8	22.0	52.8	9	899,000	2,205

source: Annual reports.

1   FCL officials estimate that 750,000 individuals are active members in 1988. This is because of the existence of members with multiple memberships in different retail co-ops.
2   Per active member.
3   FCL patronage refund to retails, plus 1982–87 FCL direct assistance to retails.
4   $13.3 million refund, $6.5 million assistance.
5   $20.2 million refund, $8.8 million assistance.
6   $23.3 million refund, $8.7 million assistance.
7   $29.1 million refund, $6.6 million assistance.
8   $53.0 million refund, $10.5 million assistance.
9   $58.6 million refund, $8.5 million assistance.

INDEX

Numbers in bold indicate a page where a photograph appears.

About the Author

Brett Fairbairn was born in Winnipeg but spent most of his formative years in Saskatoon. He was educated at the University of Saskatchewan and at Oxford University in England where he went as a Rhodes Scholar in 1981, and received his D.Phil. in 1988.

Brett has been the recipient of numerous academic awards and fellowships and is the author of several forthcoming articles in his special research areas which include German social and political history, co-operatives, and the history of democratic politics. He is an assistant professor in the Department of History at the University of Saskatchewan, as well as an associate member of the Centre for the Study of Co-operatives on the same campus. In addition, he is the editor of the *Canadian Journal of History* and a member of the editorial board of *NeWest Review,* a journal of culture and current affairs in western Canada.

With his academic background and his lifelong belief in the power of co-operatives to institute a just and equitable system of meeting human needs, Brett Fairbairn was ideally suited to writing this history of the Co-operative Retailing System. *Building a Dream* is his first major publication.

Brett lives in Saskatoon with his wife, Norma, and their two young daughters, Catherine and Elena.